PEOPLES OF
THE NORTHWEST COAST
Their Archaeology and Prehistory

KENNETH M. AMES · HERBERT D.G. MASCHNER

PEOPLES OF THE NORTHWEST COAST

Their Archaeology and Prehistory

With 173 illustrations

Thames and Hudson

for
Jane M. Ames and Joanna M.M. Ames
for
Katherine L. Reedy-Maschner

*Frontispiece: Haida house frame on the Queen
Charlotte Islands, with a door pole in front and
carved roof supports visible through entry.
The entryway is the mouth of the lowermost
figure on the pole.*

© 1999 Thames and Hudson Ltd, London

First published in hardcover in the United States
of America in 1999 by Thames and Hudson Inc.,
500 Fifth Avenue, New York, New York 10110

First paperback edition 2000

Library of Congress Catalog Card Number
98-60253
ISBN 0-500-28110-6

Printed and bound in Slovenia

Contents

Acknowledgments

This book began when Maschner called Ames one evening in 1992 with an idea for a book on Northwest Coast archaeology that was thematic rather than lineal, focused on variability rather than similarity and continuity, and written for a worldwide audience. Ames took little convincing and we agreed he would take the role of senior author. In the division of labor, detailed outlines and long discussions were held to plan the chapters. Ames developed the preliminary drafts of all chapters except the one on warfare. Maschner reworked them, adding sections on the archaeology of southeast Alaska, his own theoretical views and interpretation, and data on topics he was investigating. Maschner went on to write substantial sections of several chapters in the process of reworking Ames' original compositions. Maschner did all the maps and he and Ames collected and organized other illustrations.

We have many people to thank and will probably miss some. For this we apologize in advance. Many colleagues provided us with information, unpublished manuscripts, suggestions, arguments and the occasional pointed but necessary critique. We thank Virginia Butler, David Huelsbeck, Gary Wessen, Tom Connelly, Rick Minor, Kathy Toepel, Roy Carlson, Pat Lambert, R.G. Matson, Gary Coupland, Doug Reger, Dave McMahan, Bill Workman, Mike Jochim, Al McMillan, Al Marshall, Max Pavesic, Jerry Cybulski, Pat Sutherland, Bjorn Simonsen, Knut Fladmark, Don Mitchell, Leland Donald, Gay Calvert, Jim Haggerty, Brian Hayden, Terry Fifield, David Archer, George MacDonald, Randall Schalk, Greg Burtchard, Mary Ricks, Robert Boyd, Yvonne Hajda, R. Lee Lyman, Madonna Moss, Jon Erlandson, Mark McCallum, Steve Langdon, Napoleon Chagnon, and Brian Billman. Colleagues who went out of their way to help with illustrations include Roy Carlson, Margaret Holm, Hilary Stewart, R.G. Matson, David Hurst Thomas and Lisa Stock, and the entire staff of the Stark Museum of Art. We owe a particular debt to Roy Carlson. Both Ames and Maschner would like to thank the numerous undergraduate and graduate students at Portland State University and the University of Wisconsin-Madison who listened to these ideas first and provided useful, if sometimes withering, critiques.

We would like to thank Aldona Jonaitas for reading an earlier draft of the chapter on Northwest Coast art and Brian Ferguson for reading and commenting on a paper that eventually became the chapter on warfare. Wayne Suttles gave Ames the benefit of his profound knowledge and understanding of the Northwest Coast and its cultures. George MacDonald encouraged Ames to work on the coast and provided the resources and opportunities. Brian Fagan provided useful advice in the initial planning of this book and his assistance will always be appreciated. David Huelsbeck and Wayne Suttles critically read the final draft, taking considerable time and pains over it. We very much appreciate their help. Of course, none of these people are responsible for any of the errors in what follows.

Ames was shown the joys of scholarship by his father, Kenneth L. Ames, who did not live to see the finished book, dying in April 1994 at the age of 84. It was he who taught Ames to be most skeptical of one's own favorite ideas.

Maschner would like to thank his parents, Herbert Maschner and Jane Schermerhorn, for instilling in him the notion that even if you don't know where you are going in life, at least act like you do. He would also like to thank both of his grandmothers, Geneva Parker and Bess McIntire.

Preface

Except when it is raining, summer days are very long in Prince Rupert Harbor, on British Columbia's extreme northern coast. For Ames, this book has its roots in those long twilights. In the summer of 1969, he was a crew chief on the National Museums of Canada's North Coast Prehistory Project's excavations at the Board-walk site, a large village site spanning the last 5,000 years that was across the harbor from the town of Prince Rupert. The crew was big, and the pace hectic. On clear evenings, he sometimes took a cup of coffee down to the site, a deeply stratified shell midden, and sat at the bottom of the large excavation units, studying the stratigra-phy. It was often the only chance he had to think and try to puzzle out what these complex piles of sea shells and dirt meant in terms of human history. That fall, he worked up his ideas in a seminar paper for Lewis Binford at the University of New Mexico, and has not stopped trying to grapple with the coast's history ever since.

Growing up in Alaska, Maschner seldom considered that he would ever conduct archaeology there. After an undergraduate career that included research projects in Honduras, France and the High Plains of Wyoming and South Dakota, he was con-vinced that his career would be elsewhere. Thus, he was quite surprised to find himself in the Master's program at the University of Alaska learning arctic archae-ology and ethnography. His interests in complex hunters and gatherers grew during the mid-1980s and were realized in 1987 when he entered the University of Califor-nia-Santa Barbara with the goal of investigating the later prehistory of southeast Alaska. One year later he found himself on a beach in the Tebenkof Bay Wilderness Area with two students, 3000 lbs. of gear, a boat and motor, 100 gallons of fuel, a beautiful sunset, an incoming tide, and no idea exactly where he was. This began a long-term research effort that has, over the last 10 years, included a number of complex, maritime-adapted societies across the North Pacific.

Without doubt, part of the coast's fascination is its beauty. It is one of the most beautiful places on earth in which to live and work. Another part are the challenges its archaeology presents. Sites are complex, and often rich (and equally often barren of the data one has worked hard to obtain), and hard to interpret. The climate, the sea, and the land all present the archaeologist with difficulties to test skill, strength, and intelligence. But most Northwest Coast archaeologists don't live on the coast, nor do they spend most of their time braving a driving rain while running a small boat across an inlet, or trying to drive a gear-laden truck across soggy ground. Most spend their time quietly in their offices.

The real challenge and source of fascination is the history of the coast's peoples, as revealed by archaeology. This history is rich and long, and has much to teach. It is also miserably incomplete. For anthropology, the Northwest Coast has often played a central but paradoxical role in attempts to understand human culture. On the one hand, evidence about the coast's peoples has often been used to address fundamental questions about human nature and culture: Why does social inequality exist? How do peoples use and adapt to their environments? What does the structure of myths tell us about how people see their world and act in it? How do non-Western peoples think and what meaning does their art have to them? And so on.

On the other hand, the coast's cultures contradict many notions held by anthropologists and by the public at large. The coast's peoples hunted, fished, and gathered wild foods, yet they lived in large communities, produced one of the world's great art styles and were ruled by an aristocracy. One often reads introductory anthropology and archaeology textbooks where some sweeping generalization about human cultures is made, and it almost invariably ends: "...of course, the cultures of the Northwest Coast are an exception to that." The author of the text would then go on to ignore the coast. Our fascination with the coast is also due to that exceptionality.

This book has several goals. One is simply to convey our fascination with the coast, and perhaps win some converts. We also wish to attack a stereotype about the histories of non-Western peoples, particularly of hunter-gatherers. We address this issue in more detail in Chapter One, but we want to show that they are not "people without history," whose pasts were timeless and unchanging. We also wish to show that they are not primitive remnants of some remote ancient condition that all humans once shared, but which industrial societies have long since left. All human societies have histories of the same length and their cultures are the product of those histories of identical length. They do not represent some previous stage of human development.

This book has several audiences. The primary one is the public. We have tried to write a book that any educated person with an interest in the region can read with pleasure. Archaeologists are beginning to recognize that one of the field's urgent needs is the widespread dissemination of its results. There is far too little popular archaeology written about North America by professional archaeologists. This audience has been the most difficult for us to write for. We have tried to follow the dictum of physics, a field which produces a lot of good works aimed at the public: if you can't explain it clearly and simply, you probably don't understand it and should leave it out. The reader can judge whether we are successful.

A second audience includes university undergraduates and graduate students, for whom the book can serve as an introduction to the archaeology of the coast, to pressing research questions about that archaeology, and as a resource. A third related audience is our professional archaeological colleagues, both regional specialists and others. For non-specialists, the book is an introduction to the coast's archaeology. For Northwest Coast and hunter-gatherer specialists, many of the ideas and approaches here are new.

Native Peoples, First Nation Peoples, are our fourth, and perhaps most important audience. At a time when many Native peoples either have doubts about archaeology, or find it altogether useless, we hope to demonstrate some of its value. The coast's peoples have preserved their histories through their oral traditions. Archaeology is another route to learning and supplementing that history.

When we began working on the text, Colin Ridler, our editor at Thames and Hudson, insisted that we present our views of things, rather than trying to balance and evaluate all competing ideas. We have tried to do that. Therefore, what follows is what we think happened and why, and what we think to be important. For issues which are not yet settled, and there are many, we either discuss them in the endnotes, or provide enough citations that the interested reader can pursue the issue.

A Note on Dates

All dates used in this work are calendar ages, unless they are specifically indicated as radiocarbon dates. Until recently archaeologists seldom converted, or calibrated, radiocarbon dates to calendar dates. However, calibration is currently simplified by the availability of high speed personal computers and computer programs that will calibrate radiocarbon dates into the Gregorian calendar. Recent advances have also extended far into the past the age at which radiocarbon dates can be calibrated. We have calibrated all radiocarbon dates younger than 15,000 radiocarbon years ago, which date produces a calendrical age of 15,500 BC. Calibrations were carried out on IBM-compatible PCs, using two programs, CALIB© v. 3.0.3c. (the Radiocarbon Calibration Program, developed at the Quaternary Research Laboratory, University of Washington, Seattle) and OXCAL© version 2.01 (Radiocarbon and Statistical Analysis Program, Research Lab for Archaeology, Oxford). The reader is referred to Pearson and Stuiver 1986, Stuiver and Pearson 1986, Stuiver and Reamer 1986, and Stuiver and Reamer 1993. We include a radiocarbon date calibration table.

Radiocarbon date calibration table

Date in radiocarbon years BP (before the present)	Approximate calibrated calendar date
500 BP	AD 1450
1000 BP	AD 1000
1500 BP	AD 600
2000 BP	AD 1
2500 BP	600 BC
3000 BP	1250 BC
3500 BP	1850 BC
4000 BP	2500 BC
4500 BP	3300 BC
5000 BP	3850 BC
5500 BP	4300 BC
6000 BP	4850 BC
6500 BP	5400 BC
7000 BP	5700 BC
7500 BP	5950 BC
8000 BP	6450 BC
8500 BP	7100 BC
9000 BP	7650 BC
9500 BP	8200 BC
10,000 BP	8950 BC
10,500 BP	9800 BC
11,000 BP	10,600 BC
11,500 BP	11,100 BC
12,000 BP	11,600 BC
12,500 BP	12,200 BC
13,000 BP	12,900 BC
13,500 BP	13,700 BC
14,000 BP	14,300 BC
14,500 BP	15,000 BC
15,000 BP	15,000 BC

Prelude

At dawn on 7 February 1777, the crews of Captain James Cook's two vessels, the *Resolution* and the *Discovery*, saw the coast of what is now Oregon.[1] Cook, using Sir Francis Drake's name for North America, called the land New Albion. According to Cook: "The land appeared to be of a moderate height, diversified with hill and Valley and almost every where covered with wood. There is nothing remarkable about it, except one hill, whose elevated summit was flat; it bore from us east at noon. At the northern extreme the land formed a point, which I called Cape Foul Weather from the very bad weather we soon after met." They met the bad weather at four the next morning, and were buffeted on and off for three weeks. The mountain Cook observed is Mary's Peak, in the Oregon coast range; Cape Foul Weather is still Cape Foulweather.

At first Cook headed south along the coast, but was forced out to sea, where he turned north. The Oregon coast, beautiful though it is, is also a nasty lee shore. Cook tacked back and forth, sometimes getting within sight of land, but missing the mouth of the Columbia River and later, the Strait of Juan de Fuca, which he doubted existed. All early explorations along the west coast of the continent looked for the fabled straits of Anian which supposedly would allow passage through the continent. It was not until 29 March that Cook was able again to stand in toward the shore, and to begin to look for water. His two ships entered what is now called Nootka Sound, on the west side of Vancouver Island. The Nuu -chah-nulth people who live on Nootka Sound preserve traditions of this momentous event; it was Cook's voyage and logs that formed a basis for British claims to much of the west coast of North America.[2] The Nuu-chah-nulth were themselves formerly called Nootka. According to their traditions, the name Nootka derives from their attempts to get Cook to move his ships. They were telling him "nu.tka.ʔicim, nu.tka.ʔicim," which means, "Go around the harbor!" – in other words "Move your boats!" – but the English thought they were saying that Nootka was their name. When the ships first arrived, according to Nuu-chah-nulth traditions recorded in 1974, the major chief, Maquinna, sent some warriors out in a couple of canoes to investigate. Upon seeing the white men, the warriors decided that the English were fish who were appearing in Nootka harbor as humans.

Cook was not the first foreigner on the Northwest Coast. George Quimby has suggested that among the flotsam and jetsam along the coast were the remnants of hundreds if not thousands of ships that had drifted in from the shores of Asia over the last 1,700 years or so. There is a tradition among the Clatsop and Tillamook on the Oregon coast of a shipwreck, thought by some to preserve an account of the wreck of a Spanish galleon in the 15th or 16th centuries.[3] The galleon is believed to have been carrying a cargo of beeswax, a material which has frequently turned up in the sands at the mouth of the Nehalem River on the Oregon coast. But these early haphazard contacts did not have much effect on the course of history on the coast.

The Spanish conquest of Mexico and then of Peru in the early 16th century changed all that. In 1513, six years before Cortés began his campaign against the Aztecs, Vasco Nunez de Balboa was officially the first European to see the Pacific Ocean. In November 1521, the ships of Ferdinand Magellan entered the Pacific Ocean – the same year that Cortés and his native allies vanquished the Aztecs, destroying Tenochtitlan, their capital city, and founding Mexico City on the ruins. By 1565, Spanish ships were crossing the Pacific in both directions. There is no record, beyond the Clatsop narrative, of any of this activity as yet directly affecting the Northwest Coast. Significant indirect effects may have included smallpox.

In 1577, Francis Drake entered the Pacific on his circumnavigation of the globe. During his voyage he beached and careened his ship, the *Golden Hind*, somewhere along the North American coast, leaving behind a metal plaque. The San Francisco Bay area of the California coast is usually thought to have been the place, but a few people believe that Drake reached as far north as the Oregon coast.

In 1773, Antonio Bucareli, the Viceroy of New Spain in Mexico City, caused the organization of an expedition north along the coast. Spanish sailors had already entered San Diego and Monterey Bays. Juan Perez sailed north in the *Santiago*, first to Monterey and then north, encountering bad weather. On 19 July 1774, the ship reached the Queen Charlotte Islands. The next day, 21 canoe-loads of natives approached the ship wanting to trade, preferably for sharp-edged iron objects. These people were certainly the Haida. Perez then turned south, arriving somewhere near Nootka Sound on 8 August, although he does not appear to have entered it. Again, the Spanish traded with the natives. Perez headed south again, arriving off San Francisco by 26 August.

A series of Spanish voyages followed, reaching as far north as Cape St Elias on the Pacific coast of Alaska in 1779. This expedition would be the last by the Spanish along the coast until 1789 when they established a fort at Yuquot, in Nootka Sound. This action was spurred by Cook's expedition, and the increasing number of American and British fur-trading vessels along the coast. Establishment of the fort was accompanied by a renewal of Spanish voyages along the coast, but by 1795 the effort was spent, and the fort was torn down. They left behind many place names, some detailed explorer's journals as well as hard feelings among their Nuu-chah-nulth hosts at Yuquot, but they had little long-term direct effect on the Northwest Coast. The English, Americans, and Russians provided that.

The Russians were probably the first Europeans to voyage to the northern Northwest Coast; they were certainly the first to leave written accounts. In July 1741, Vitus Bering, a Dane in the service of Russia, sighted Mt St Elias, the 5,500 m (18,000 ft) peak that stands near where Alaska, British Columbia, and the Yukon boundaries meet. Bering anchored for a day at Kayak Island, a little south of the mouth of the Copper River in Prince William Sound, before turning west and beginning his homeward trip to the Russian Pacific coast. That trip took a year of sometimes terrible hardships; but when the Russians regained their home port of Petropavlovsk, they brought with them hundreds of sea-otter pelts that they had collected. The sea-otter pelts, not imperial ambitions, initially fueled the growing European presence on the Northwest Coast.

For the next two decades, the focus of the Russian trade for sea otters was in the Aleutian Island chain, but as the otters' numbers began to decline, the Russians began to look further east and south. The Russian government, under Catherine the

Great, dispatched naval expeditions across the Arctic Ocean, and along the Alaskan coast. The Arctic expeditions were twice turned back by pack ice, but the North Pacific expeditions produced charts of the Aleutians and the Alaska Peninsula. It was these expeditions that pushed the British into dispatching Cook to the Pacific. Continued Russian naval activity in the North Pacific in the 1780s led Spain to lay aside its short-lived claims to Nootka Bay.

Despite the naval activity, it was Russian merchants who firmly established their countrymen in Alaska. Grigorii Shelikov founded the first Russian settlement in North America on Kodiak Island in 1783, in a brutal conquest of the island. His successor, Alexsandr Baranov, founded a settlement at Sitka, in southeast Alaska. That settlement was destroyed by the Tlingit in 1802, but reestablished at a new location, the site of the present city of Sitka, Alaska, in 1804. In 1812, Baranov founded Fort Ross on the California coast – the most southerly extent of Russian expansion in North America.

In 1784, Captain Cook's journals were published, and his accounts of the Northwest Coast's potential wealth in furs became well known, although people in Europe and in the newly formed United States had not been ignorant of the Russian trade in furs to China. In 1785, James Hanna, sailing the appropriately named *Sea Otter*, sailed from Canton, China to Nootka Sound and back, selling 560 pelts for 20,400 Spanish dollars. In 1787, the first American ships bound for the Northwest Coast, the *Columbia Rediviva* and the *Lady Washington*, sailed from Boston, arrived at Nootka a year later, and found three English ships already there, noting that two others had recently left. In the next 10 years, dozens of ships cruised along the coast in quest of furs. They traded metal, beads, guns, cloth, and other European products for the precious hides.

The fur trade continued until the early 1840s when near extinction of the sea otter, the decimation of other sea mammals along the coast, and changing fashions in Europe and China, caused its end. The maritime fur trades were replaced by fur trading companies, including the Hudson's Bay Company, which for a time, ruled a commercial empire in the Northwest. By the 1840s settlers and missionaries were beginning to enter the Northwest, particularly Oregon's Willamette Valley, which was the original destination of the Oregon trail. Settlers had a far greater impact on Native culture than did the fur traders, who sought not to displace Native people, but to buy furs from them. Settlers displaced people, leading to significant disruption of Native societies and cultural mores.

CHAPTER ONE

Introduction

The early voyagers along the coast encountered people who contradicted many of the basic assumptions that Europeans held about human societies, particularly the ones that linked cultural complexity with agriculture. As the science of anthropology developed, the Northwest Coast continued to be an exception to all the rules; it could not be fitted into most of the classifications anthropologists devised for cultures and societies. Northwest Coast peoples were hunter-gatherers, not farmers, yet they had elites. They had a significant art style. Why? What was special about the coast? Part of the answer has to do with the coast itself, as we shall see. But another part of the answer is that anthropologists and archaeologists really did not know as much as they thought about hunter-gatherers.

The Northwest Coast

The stereotype of hunter-gatherers has them all living in small, mobile groups, with few possessions, and dependent on foods in season. As a consequence they have little or no property, and no fixed and permanent differences in social power and prestige, in other words, they have an egalitarian social structure. This stereotype exists because many hunter-gatherers worldwide do exhibit these characteristics, though not necessarily closely or comfortably. The societies of the Northwest Coast differed markedly from this common stereotype of hunter-gatherers. They were the most socially complex hunting and gathering societies known on earth and had social and   Pl. 1
cultural features, such as social stratification, that are usually assumed to be attributes of farming peoples. Beyond social stratification, Northwest Coast culture traits include living in large permanent villages and towns (i.e. being sedentary), full-time specialists, an elaborate and complex material culture, ownership and control of property, and monumental architecture. Their human population densities were among the highest in pre-modern North America, irrespective of economy. Their towns and villages ranged in size from a few score to more than a thousand individuals. Some of these towns stood for several hundred years, requiring enormous effort and skill to maintain. These societies confound ideas about the development of social complexity during human history and many of the traits expressed on the Northwest Coast are exactly those traits widely viewed as the basis for the development of civilization. It has always been assumed by historians, anthropologists, archaeologists, and others that farming is necessary for these traits to evolve. The non-farming hunter-gatherer societies of the Northwest Coast possessed all those

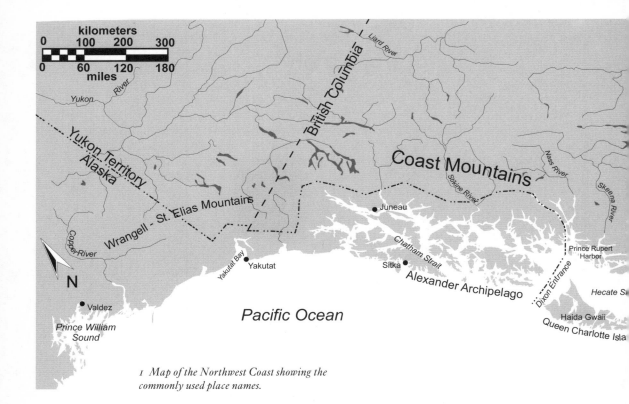

1 Map of the Northwest Coast showing the commonly used place names.

traits, and did so for at least the last 2,500 years if not longer. More recently, archaeologists have found that other such "complex" hunter-gatherers existed in the past in many parts of the world.

The discovery of complex hunter-gatherers – also known as as "affluent foragers" – is one of the century's more important archaeological breakthroughs, though perhaps one of its more obscure ones as well. When people think of major archaeological discoveries they immediately think of tombs, individuals frozen in glaciers or cities lost beneath jungles. These are single, spectacular finds, but the discovery of complex hunter-gatherers is the discovery of an entire form of society, once thought to be unique to the Northwest Coast, and represents a significant expansion of our knowledge and awareness of the range of human cultural and social behavior. It also has enormous implications for our understanding of how human cultures change and evolve. Brian Hayden, an archaeologist at Simon Fraser University, argues forcefully, for example, that the first steps leading to the domestication of plants and animals about 10,000 years ago could only have been taken by affluent foragers; farming, of course, is the most significant change in human subsistence in the last million years. Without the Northwest Coast, and its extensive ethnographic and archaeological literature, we doubt the concept of "complex hunter-gatherers" could have been possible, and understanding them very difficult.

Another stereotype of hunter-gatherers is one that Eric Wolf, a cultural anthropologist, has labeled "people without history" – people whose societies and cultures are treated as timeless and unchanging, whose lifeways when the first European

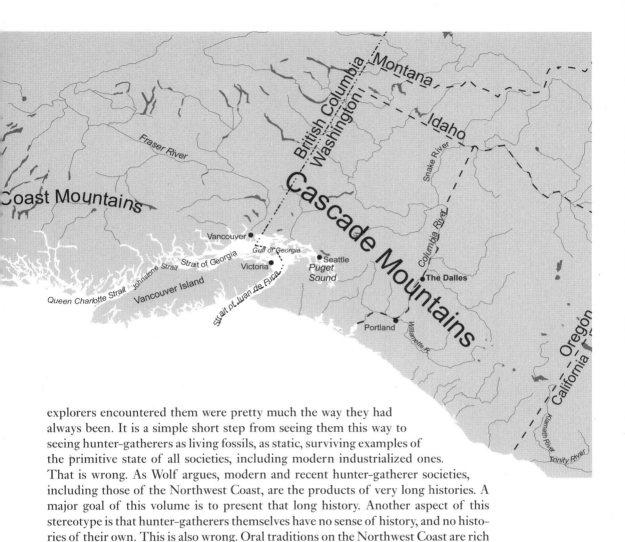

explorers encountered them were pretty much the way they had
always been. It is a simple short step from seeing them this way to
seeing hunter-gatherers as living fossils, as static, surviving examples of
the primitive state of all societies, including modern industrialized ones.
That is wrong. As Wolf argues, modern and recent hunter-gatherer societies,
including those of the Northwest Coast, are the products of very long histories. A
major goal of this volume is to present that long history. Another aspect of this
stereotype is that hunter-gatherers themselves have no sense of history, and no histories of their own. This is also wrong. Oral traditions on the Northwest Coast are rich
in historical information central to their societies and their definition of humanness:

> A group that could not tell their traditions would be ridiculed with the
> remark, "what is your 'history'?" And if you could not give it, you were
> laughed at. "What is your grandfather's name? And where is your crest? How
> do you know your past, where have you lived? You have no Grandfather. You
> cannot speak to me, because I have one. You have no ancestral home. You are
> like a wild animal, you have no abode.[1]

Northwest societies produced one of the world's most famous art styles. The art
made power, obligation, and history tangible and visible. Great artists, some of them
titleholders (high-status individuals), carved and painted house fronts, masks,
boxes, funerary posts, and totem poles, on a commission basis, like the painters and
sculptors of Renaissance Italy, although the artists of the coast may have been held
in higher esteem and enjoyed broader support. Some of them may also have been
more dangerous because of their spirit powers.

Pl. 57
Pl. 28

Pl. 33

The social and economic relationships, art, history, spirituality, and world view of Northwest Coast people were expressed in many ways, but none were so famous as the potlatch - a feast, a theatrical performance, a giving away of wealth and a confirmation of status that has fascinated Westerners since first contact in the late 18th century. As a ceremony, the potlatch has probably received more attention from anthropologists and other social scientists than any other single ceremony in the human repertoire, and has played a central role in the growth of anthropology and of social theory generally. Almost every social theory devised in the last hundred years, from French structuralism to Marxism, has had to grapple with the potlatch. In November 1894 Franz Boas, the principal founder of anthropology in North America, observed and marvelously described a series of potlatches and other ceremonies among the Kwakwaka'wakw (formerly Kwakiutl) of Fort Rupert, at the northern end of Vancouver Island. Although other potlatches have been described, Boas' descriptions remain at the heart of the non-Native understanding of the institution. The timing of Boas' work, given its importance, is ironic. The Canadian government banned the potlatch in 1885 because missionaries and Indian agents believed the institution was pernicious. In their view it encouraged idleness, licentiousness, and thriftlessness, leading the Natives to give away their great wealth which Westerners thought should be invested in economically productive ways, and slowing their progress to civilization. This effort at forced culture change failed, the law was finally dropped in 1951, and legal potlatching resumed.

The research of Boas and many others, including Native people such as George Hunt and William Benyon, which began in the late 19th century and continues today; the detailed observations of earlier travelers on the coast, such as Captain Cook, and the Lewis and Clark expedition, to name only two of the most famous; and innumerable other sources have produced one of the largest and richest ethnographic literatures that exists for any comparable portion of the globe. This literature has attracted many students of humanity who have the seen the cultures of the Northwest Coast as a fertile source of insights into human nature and human culture. Archaeologists depend heavily on it as a source of information and analogies about other, less well-known peoples. One of the central goals of Boas' research was to explain the societies he studied through their histories, which he reconstructed using the cultures he described, their oral traditions, and their languages. But he made little or no use of archaeology, since little was then known about the archaeology of the coast at that time.

Part of the fascination of the coast derives from its great beauty and environmental richness. When we look at a map of the Northwest Coast, we tend to see the land masses as the shapes, and the water as voids between the land. Viewed this way, the Northwest Coast is the fringe of the North American continent, arcing in a great curve first south by southeast from Yakutat Bay on Alaska's south coast to the western entrance of the Strait of Juan de Fuca, through which has been drawn the border between the United States and Canada. Here the coast begins its slow bend back westward by tending south by southwest. The Northwest Coast finally feathers out at Cape Mendocino, in northern California.

In this perspective, there are two Northwest Coasts, one north of the international boundary, and one south. For once, arbitrary national boundaries actually reflect changes in topography and geology – though not in culture. The coast north of the 49th parallel is ragged, marked by islands great and small, deep fjords, twist-

ing sea passages, and broad expanses of shallow water and pockets of great deeps. Pl. 3
South of the border, the land's end is knife sharp, notched here and there by bays Pl. 2
and estuaries, and serrated by high headlands. The continent's very edge glitters
with long white beaches.

But there is another way to look at our map of the Northwest Coast. We can see
the ocean as the substance, and the land as the void, as in a good navigational chart.
Now the Northwest Coast is the northeast edge of the vast North Pacific Ocean,
part of a coastline that stretches in an enormous crescent from Cape Mendocino
around to the southernmost tip of Kyushu in the Japanese Archipelago and the
mouth of the Yangtze River on China's east coast.

Taking this second perspective makes good sense at the beginning of a book on
the archaeology and history of the Native people of the Northwest Coast. In their
art, frequently it is the form of the voids defined by carved shapes that actually have
substance, and in their oral traditions heroes must frequently go on journeys to the
ocean floor, to negotiate with the chiefs of the sea creatures – salmon, sea mammals,
and others – upon which they depended for food.

The northeast edge of the North Pacific begins in the Gulf of Alaska, and runs
southward, lapping around the myriad islands of the Alaskan and British Columbia
coasts, touching their shores in thousands of kilometers of rich intertidal habitats,
fingering far into the continent in deep fjords and broad bays. South of the Strait of
Juan de Fuca, the waters meet the land straight on, except where small bays and
estuaries create rich pockets of littoral and estuarine habitats. The sea is anchored in
the south at Cape Mendocino in California. Both land and sea are roped together by
the great rivers, such as the Stikine, the Skeena, the Fraser, the Columbia and the
Klamath, that drain the continent and up which the ocean – or the keepers of the
game – sent billions of salmon on their regular upstream journey to reproduce and
die – and feed the people.

The Northwest Coast culture area is some 2,000 km (1300 to 1400 miles) long, in
straight-line distance from north to south. It is actually much longer, since the coastline is so intricate, but we will use the 2,000 km figure. How long is that? It is roughly
the distance between New York and Cuba, between London and Istanbul, or Canton
in South China and Tokyo. However, there are other kinds of distances. If one
travels in a straight line from London to Istanbul, all of the languages spoken along
the trip, except Turkish, are members of the Indo-European language family, while
Turkish is a member of the Ural-Altaic language family. The Northwest Coast was
the second most diverse linguistic area in North America after California. A 19th-
century traveler along the coast passed through the areas of 11 language families
encompassing 39 different languages. Today, some of these languages are extinct,
while others have surviving speakers. Many Native groups have developed language
programs for the preservation of their spoken tongue. It is harder to enumerate the
different cultural groups or tribes along the coast than it is to count their languages.
The Northwest Coast volume of the Handbook of North American Indians has
chapters covering 29 socio-linguistic groups; these are groupings that share a
common language or language family and are closely linked culturally and socially.
However, these were not single political entities, nor were they single societies. The
Tlingit, who occupied southern Alaska, for example, were an ethnic group with
three major regional tribal groupings. These tribal groupings comprised 16 smaller
local groups, each local group divided into villages and households. Similarly, the

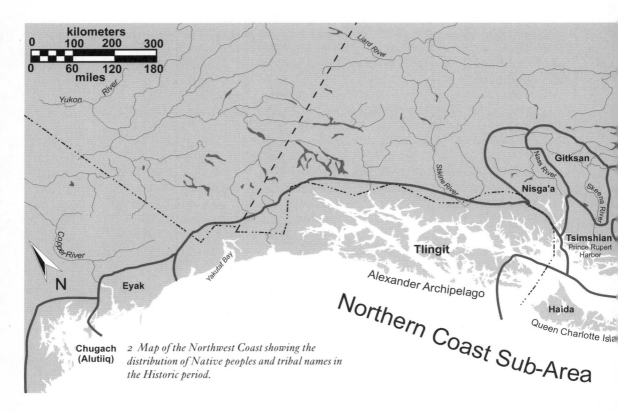

2 *Map of the Northwest Coast showing the distribution of Native peoples and tribal names in the Historic period.*

Nuu-chah-nulth on the west coast of Vancouver Island are actually over 20 named local groups, and the Coast Salish, the largest linguistic group on the coast, have scores of local groups. The local groups differed among themselves in their traditions, practices, histories, and so on. Within local groups, the village or town was the political unit, and the household the economic unit. As a result, while Northwest Coast societies share many common cultural features, there is also a significant and interesting amount of cultural and social variation.

Despite this variation, or perhaps because of it, students of the coast's people have come to recognize three general cultural regions or subareas within the Northwest Coast, a northern, a central, and a southern subarea. However, anthropologists have had considerable problems in drawing the boundaries between the subareas. There has been little difficulty in recognizing the northern area, which always includes the Tsimshian, Haida and Tlingit. But, as anthropologist Wayne Suttles has noted, "there has been...less agreement about a Wakashan [central] area, and great disagreement about anything south of Vancouver Island."[1] The central subarea always includes the Nuu-chal-nulth groups along Vancouver Island's west coast, and the Kwakwaka'wakw of northern Vancouver Island and adjacent portions of the British Columbia mainland. Other mainland groups are the Heiltsuk (formerly Bella Bella), Haisla, and Nuxalk (formerly Bella Coola). The southern area always includes the Coast Salish speakers of southern British Columbia and northwest Washington, but the placement of other groups causes problems. The international boundary between the USA and Canada also creates some confusion, since in Canada the southern coast usually refers to the southern British Columbia

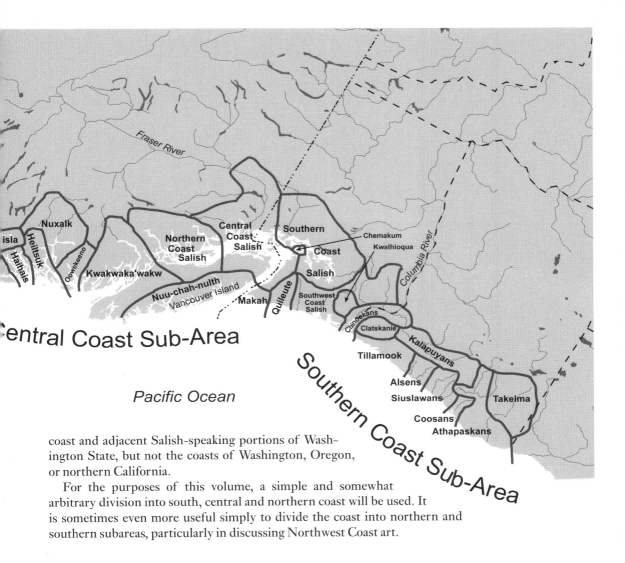

coast and adjacent Salish-speaking portions of Washington State, but not the coasts of Washington, Oregon, or northern California.

For the purposes of this volume, a simple and somewhat arbitrary division into south, central and northern coast will be used. It is sometimes even more useful simply to divide the coast into northern and southern subareas, particularly in discussing Northwest Coast art.

Historical sources

There are three lines of evidence that we will use in developing our account of Northwest Coast Native history during the past 11,000 years: written descriptions of Northwest Coast Native cultures that span the last 250 years; Native oral traditions; and archaeology.

Written sources

The earliest recorded accounts of Northwest Coast peoples were made by European explorers during the 18th and early 19th centuries. Some of their accounts are short, but others, including those by the British sea captains James Cook and George Vancouver, Spaniards such as Malaspina and Moziña, and Americans such as Lewis and Clark, are lengthy and reliable accounts of the peoples they met, including the economic and social practices to the extent that they saw them. The explorers were quickly followed by fur traders, drawn by the coast's numerous sea otters, whose dense lustrous pelt was in high demand in China. Initially, the fur traders stayed on their ships, making few forays to the coast, but many of the ships' captains and first officers left accounts similar to those of the explorers. As the fur trade expanded and terrestrial mammals, particularly the beaver, became increasingly important, fur trading companies established permanent land posts, which drew Native settlers beginning in 1812. The factors of these posts, as well as other individuals, left valuable accounts in their diaries, letters, and journals.

The fur traders were followed by missionaries and settlers. The first European farm on the Northwest Coast may have been that of Alexander MacKay, established in the vicinity of Portland, Oregon in 1828. The fertile Willamette Valley of western Oregon was the destination of the Oregon trail, drawing thousands of settlers beginning in the late 1840s. Unlike the fur traders, these people came to stay. The fur traders did not usually try to settle, take land or force the Natives into living like Europeans. The nature of the fur trade itself, in which the fur traders depended entirely on the Native people for furs, Native people's skill at trade, and their military prowess coupled with the sheer size of many of the Native groups, ensured that the fur traders treated Native peoples more or less as equals even when they saw them as inferiors. The traders did not interfere in Native life beyond the fur trade. The effects of the fur trade were not minor, but were as nothing compared to what would follow.

Many of the newcomers wished either to significantly alter Native ways, or to displace indigenous peoples completely. Relations between Europeans and Native people became increasingly hostile during the 1840s, and open conflict between Natives and Europeans much more common. The US government began its policy of removing Native people to reservations in the 1850s, and the campaign in British Columbia to ban the potlatch began at about the same time. Many individuals did, however, produce useful accounts of Native life and society. The Reverend Myron Eels, a missionary on the Skokomish Reservation in western Washington, wrote an important monograph about Coast Salish groups. James Swan is a more famous instance. He spent three somewhat disreputable years living as an oyster farmer on Washington's Willapa Bay, but producing the 19th century's best-known popular work on the region – *The Northwest Coast, or Three Years' Residence in Washington Territory* – in 1857. For several years, he was a school teacher on the Makah Reservation on the extreme northwestern corner of Washington State, writing a monograph on the Makah based on that experience, which was published in 1870. A century later, the American novelist, Ivan Doig, drew on Swan's published works and notebooks for Doig's meditation on modern life on the Northwest Coast entitled *Winter Brothers*.

However, it is to Franz Boas that credit must be given for the vast majority of ethnographic accounts and descriptions of Northwest Coast cultures. The German-born Boas was trained as a physicist and geographer at the University of Berlin, the apogee of a continental research training in the late 19th century. His doctoral dissertation was on the color of water, a major problem in optics at the time. After completing his dissertation, Boas conducted geographic and ethnographic fieldwork among the Inuit, who live in north-central arctic Canada, producing a monograph in 1884. Desiring a change from the arctic, and already interested in the

Northwest Coast, Boas made a three-month trip to the coast in 1886. The trip was extraordinarily hectic, and his letters home are filled with his worries about having enough time and finding Native people who would talk to him. Boas would make 13 more trips to the coast between 1888 and 1931, working with people from virtually every major group in the region, producing an unparalleled series of publications dealing with peoples from Oregon to Alaska, but his primary research throughout his career was with the Kwakwaka'wakw at Fort Rupert, British Columbia. Starting in 1896, Boas taught anthropology at Columbia University and many of his graduate students conducted fieldwork along the Northwest Coast, as have many of their graduate students after them. In 1897 Boas organized the Jesup North Pacific Expedition to conduct research on the North Pacific Rim. This expedition, financed by Morris K. Jesup, president of the American Museum of Natural History, was an ambitious program of research into the ethnology, archaeology, physical anthropology, and linguistics of northeast Asia and northwestern North America. It was not a single expedition, but a series of field trips by individuals into the region between 1897 and 1903. The expedition involved work by a great many people and produced a prodigious amount of data. Many of the expedition members, such as John Swanton, continued to conduct research and publish on the Northwest Coast after the expedition ended. Boas' impact on Northwest Coast studies in part reflects his own research, but also what must have been extraordinary energy, hard work, and an ability to inspire others.

Field research by Boas and other ethnographers in North America at this time was undertaken with a strong sense of urgency. Europeans widely believed that Native people would soon be extinct, either culturally (biological descendants of Native people would survive, but they would have become culturally European), or physically extinct – they would disappear completely. The ethnographic fieldwork was done to create a record of these supposedly dying cultures for posterity.

This view of the impending disappearance of Native peoples made sense within the context of late 19th-century North America. Native populations had declined catastrophically during the century, with some groups, such as the Mandan of the north-central Plains, becoming almost biologically extinct. Government policies, on both sides of the US/Canadian border, actively and passively focused on turning Native peoples into Europeans as quickly as possible. Ethnographers concentrated on collecting information on Native life before the advent of Europeans; the concern was not with their current circumstances, but their past. This is dramatically illustrated by Edward Curtis' famous photographs of Native people taken during the early years of the 20th century. They were not of life at the time they were taken, but represent reconstructions of what Curtis thought life had been like in the past. The costumes in his Northwest Coast photographs were made explicitly for the photographs, for example. Because ethnographers and others wanted information about life before Europeans, they focused on what is now called memory culture. They interviewed elderly people who either remembered the time before contact, or who remembered their parents' accounts of earlier days. Researchers like Boas also collected narratives of myths and histories of the period before contact.

Important assumptions underlying this effort were that Native peoples had only lived in North America a few centuries, perhaps 2,000 years, and that their cultures had changed little or not at all either during the preceding centuries or during the period after Europeans first entered the region in the mid to late 18th century. They also assumed that contact with Europeans had initially had little effect on Native lifeways; the extent of culture change and disruption during the 19th century is currently a controversial issue (see Chapter Two).

Ethnographic research continues on the coast. During the past 40 years it has shifted away from memory culture to a concern with Native peoples in their modern context, though attempts to reconstruct Native life at the time of first contact continue.

Oral traditions

Collecting oral narratives was a central part of the research methods of Boas and other early anthropologists on the coast. As a result, there is an enormous literature, published and unpublished, of Native narratives. There is a bias in Western scholarship against oral traditions as evidence, and while anthropologists have made extensive use of recorded oral traditions to investigate Native world views as well as their social and cultural practices, archaeologists have made little use of the narratives as historical data. This bias extends beyond archaeology. In a recent land claims case in British Columbia, the judge disallowed the oral traditions of the two Native groups, the Gitksan and the Wet'suwet'en, on the grounds that because they were oral they did not constitute historical evidence. This is ironic, because Native people were active in collecting and recording their oral traditions and supplying these materials to anthropologists from the 1880s on.

Boas did not live on the Northwest Coast for any extended period, as he did among the Inuit. He relied heavily on local individuals who collected materials and artifacts for him. Many of these people were Natives, and the practice was not limited to Boas. George Hunt was Boas' principal associate in his work among the Kwakwaka'wakw. Hunt was born of Tlingit-English parentage but had grown up at Fort Rupert and spoke Kwakwala.[2] Boas' work with Tsimshian materials relied on two Tsimshians: Henry Tate, who collected narratives, and Archie Dundas, who assisted Boas in transcribing the stories. William Benyon, whose mother was Tsimshian, collected a great many narratives, sending them to several ethnologists. Louis Shotridge was a high-status Tlingit who supplied materials to researchers at the University of Pennsylvania Museum as well as publishing himself. These Native researchers contributed a significant amount of the data, materials, and interpretations used by Boas and others in the late 19th and 20th centuries.

Nineteenth-century assumptions about the rapid disappearance of Native peoples were wrong, and Native cultures on the Northwest Coast have persisted and undergone a renaissance over the last 20 to 30 years. They have maintained their oral traditions and have initiated projects to collect their own oral traditions, and to publish them if appropriate.

Archaeology

As in many other parts of North America, archaeology on the Northwest Coast grew rapidly after World War II, though archaeological research had been conducted on the coast as early as the 1870s. Most of the early workers on the coast were avocational archaeologists. Charles Hill-Tout is the best known of these individuals. He explored sites along the lower Fraser River in the 1890s, publishing widely on his results in Canada, Britain, and the USA. Harlan I. Smith, who was hired for the Jesup North Pacific Expedition by Boas to conduct archaeological research as part of the expedition's program, may have been the first professional archaeologist to pursue fieldwork on the coast, which he did in British Columbia and Washington. The US Department of Agriculture Forest Service conducted excavations at the old Russian Fort in Sitka in 1934 and 1935. They recorded prehistoric materials but no analysis was undertaken. In 1938, Philip Drucker conducted a rapid survey of parts of the British Columbia and southeast Alaska coasts, but significant professional excavations were a post-war phenomenon. In the late 1940s Carl Borden, of the University of British Columbia, began his excavation program at a number of sites within the metropolitan area of Vancouver, British Columbia. Many of these sites were located in city parks along the shoreline. At the same time, Arden King of the University of Washington conducted excavations at the Cattle Point site on San Juan Island of Washington. In the late 1940s and early 1950s Frederica de Laguna was excavating in the Yakutat and Angoon areas of southeast Alaska. In her excavations she was finding little time depth in her search for prehistoric Tlingit materials.

At the beginning of the 20th century, the general view among scholars was that Native peoples had lived in North America for perhaps 2,000 years. This view had to be abandoned in the late 1920s when tools were found in the ribcage of a bison at a site near Folsom, New Mexico. The bison had been a member of a species, *Bison antiquus*, that was larger than the modern bison, and which had become extinct at the end of the last Ice Age, an event dated in the late 1920s to about 10,000 years ago. Despite this, archaeologists working in the Northwest continued to think that 2,000 years was about the maximum age for Native occupation of the coast and interior Northwest.

One of the most important results of archaeological work in the 1950s was the clear demonstration of human antiquity in the Northwest. Archaeologists began using radiocarbon dating, the now standard technique for dating organic matter that had recently been developed by Willard Libby. The Lind Coulee site, located in the dry interior part of Washington State, was excavated by Richard Daugherty in the early 1950s. Daugherty recovered modern bison (*Bison bison*), and charcoal samples dating almost 8,700 years ago firmly establishing human antiquity in the Northwest just after the ice age. However, the Five Mile Rapids site, near The Dalles, Oregon, proved the clincher.

The site is located at the upstream end of the Long Narrows, where the Columbia River abruptly narrowed, flowing for several miles through a narrow rocky channel before it was dammed. The Long Narrows was the major Native salmon fishery in North America, now beneath the reservoir of The Dalles Dam. The construction of the dam meant that not only would the Long Narrows be inundated but so would any associated archaeological sites. Archaeological salvage projects began within the soon-to-be-flooded reservoir. Luther Cressman, of the University of Oregon, and a number of graduate students began excavations at the Five Mile Rapids site in 1952, eventually exposing a deeply stratified archaeological site. At the bottom of the exposure, the archaeologists recovered some 150,000 to 200,000 salmon vertebrae, indicating the antiquity of salmon fishing in the Long Narrows, and collected charcoal dating to some 9800 years ago, thus clearly placing humans on the Columbia River and within 320 km (200 miles) of the coast by 10,000 years ago.

Archaeological research has continued to expand on the coast since 1950, though not uniformly. Many parts of the coast remain poorly known to archaeologists, as a result of arduous logistics, sometimes difficult weather, dense vegetation, and the usual shortage of funds. The archaeologically best known region is the Gulf of Georgia, an area that includes the metropolitan areas of Vancouver, British Columbia; Victoria, the capital of British Columbia; and Seattle, Washington. The region has the highest population density on the coast north of San Francisco, the most universities, the most development, and the most archaeologists. This is the area where Borden conducted his pioneering research and where many of his students still work. As we shall see in Chapters Three and Four, all of this has important implications for our understanding of the archaeology of the Northwest in general. At this point, it is enough to say that the Gulf of Georgia sequence for the past 10,000 years is the most fully developed for any comparable region of the Northwest Coast.

Complex hunter-gatherers

The coast's Native societies and economies are the world's best examples of complex hunter-gatherers, or affluent foragers. The terms "forager" and "hunter-gatherer" are used interchangeably here, and refer to peoples whose subsistence economy is derived almost exclusively from wild rather than domesticated plants and animals. Since the late 1970s, archaeologists have come to realize that many hunter-gatherer societies in the past did not fit the stereotype of what such societies were like. These ancient foragers were similar in important ways to the 19th-century societies along the Northwest Coast. These people are called affluent foragers or complex hunter-gatherers. The former term stresses their productive subsistence economy and general material well-being, while the latter term focuses on their social and political organization.

To understand complex hunter-gatherers, it is first necessary to know something about what are called "generalized hunter-gatherers," or more simply, foragers. Richard B. Lee and Irven DeVore, in their famous edited book *Man the Hunter*, provide the classic definition of foragers: "We make two assumptions about hunter-gatherers: (1) they live in small groups, and (2) they move around a lot."[3] As we noted above, such hunter-gatherers do exist; and their study has been a major focus of anthropological and archaeological research since the publication of the Man the Hunter volume.

One of the reasons for this focused and intensive research is that it is quite likely that hunting and gathering as a way of life will disappear within the next few decades. Although there is controversy over details, some form of foraging has been the basic hominid method of adapting and adjusting to the environment for at least two million years. Put another way, foraging was the ecological niche of ourselves and our ancestors until the widespread adoption of agriculture less than 10,000 years ago. Generalized foraging was the ecological framework within which many of the decisive developments in our evolution occurred, including the dramatic expansion of our brain, our complete dependence on technology, and our acquisition of language, the crucial development for the existence of culture as we know it. Some anthropologists, and even doctors, have argued that many of the illnesses of modern life are due to our trying to fit hunter-gatherer biology into a sedentary, agricultural or urban way of life. Cancers of the stomach and bowels are unknown among modern hunter-gatherers, as is heart disease and breast cancer, and the suggestion is that their coarse, varied and unprocessed diets along with their more regular exercise, may be the reason. A recent assessment of hunter-gatherer health by David Cohen[4] indicates that hunter-gatherers were and are at least as healthy, if not healthier, than most third-world farmers, and even healthier than the ancient farmers who replaced them in many parts of the world. Another reason, then, for intensively studying hunter-gatherers is that they may hold some answers to fundamental questions about human nature that are unanswerable without understanding them.

Complex hunter-gatherers differ from Lee and DeVore's definition. They generally have these important characteristics:

1. They do not move around as much as foragers. They are semi- to fully sedentary. Sedentary people live in one place for most of the year, but usually for much longer periods, such as a generation or more. Semi-sedentary peoples spend one or two seasons (usually at least winter) in the same settlement year-after-year, but may be mobile for the rest of the annual cycle. Sedentism, from the Latin verb *sedere*, "to sit," represents a major change in human life with far-reaching consequences. In essence, sedentary peoples own and control property; they inherit it; they have rules about it; their social organizations are profoundly affected by property. Foragers may have property, but not much, and most of that is small and easily moved.

Because they are not mobile, sedentary people tend to make heavy investments in the places where they live. Mobile foragers, who move many times during a year, simply cannot build substantial houses, walls, dig wells, and the like. Sedentary people do, which strongly ties them to the places where they live. They accumulate more objects. Mobile foragers must keep their possessions to a minimum, since they walk everywhere and move often.

2. Complex hunter-gatherer economies were based on producing large amounts of processed and stored foods. Some anthropologists and archaeologists argue that food storage was the crucial development leading to social complexity and farming, not sedentism. We argue that minimally both sedentism and storage are required. Food can be stored in two ways. One way is to process and set aside some amount of it for the winter. Another form of storage is through social relations that give one access to food resources in other areas. Often marriages occur between forager groups that permit members of each group access to the other's territory and resources. While the peoples of the Northwest Coast actively arranged such ties, they depended heavily on large amounts of stored foods. Stores are a form of surplus, and therefore another form of property, which must be owned, controlled and distributed. Ordinary foragers do not usually put up stores, but consume their food as they harvest it.

3. Complex hunter-gatherer economies were household based. One of the key archaeological indicators of the presence of affluent foragers in the archaeological record is evidence for substantial houses. This is also evidence of sedentism. On the Northwest Coast, households varied in size from 30 to well over 100 people. They might all live in one house or in several, but they were a single social group, and it was this group that controlled access to resources and all forms of property.

4. Foragers harvest what is available to them in their environment, when and where it is available. They tend to exploit those resources that provide the greatest return for the least effort, not because they are lazy but because that is the most economical course open to them for supporting their small populations. In contrast, the subsistence economies of complex hunter-gatherers tend to focus on

relatively few but very productive resources, yet intensively and simultaneously exploit a wide range of those resources. On the Northwest Coast, for example, subsistence economies concentrated on salmon, halibut, herring, sea mammals, and elk or deer. However, literally scores of other food resources were exploited at the same time. These so-called secondary resources provided back-up in case a major resource, such as salmon, failed (as they invariably would), and also provided important nutrients and variety in the diet. It is likely that Northwest Coast people could not have taken the risk of focusing on salmon, for example, if they had not also been able to exploit many other foods. Also, complex hunter-gatherers exploited resources that required considerable effort and work by many people to harvest and process. Salmon on the Northwest Coast is an example of such a resource. Processing salmon for storage had to been done quite rapidly, preferably within about 72 hours of the fish being caught, otherwise they rotted. A group could catch a large number of the fish, but if no one was available to simultaneously fillet and prepare the fish for drying, the effort in catching them was wasted.

5. Another stereotype of hunter-gatherers is that they live passively in their environment, having little or no effect on it. This is not particularly true of any hunter-gatherers, but not at all true for affluent ones. While they did not domesticate particular species of plants and animals (most did have dogs), they manipulated their environments to increase productivity. In western North America, burning was the major technique for this, and people from California to at least northern British Columbia periodically burned their surrounding areas. Burning encouraged grasslands at the expense of forests and improved harvests from berry bushes, oaks and other plants. Burned areas were also more attractive to game animals than mature rainforest.

6. The technologies of affluent foragers were complex. Part of this may have been the result of sedentism. Mobile hunter-gatherers must carry their tools with them, and so their technologies tend to be light, portable, and often expedient. Sedentary people need not carry their worldly possessions everywhere, and so invest more in their technology. Also, affluent foragers have specialized tackle and gear to efficiently harvest the resources they are heavily dependent upon. On the Northwest Coast, this tackle ranged from a wide array of nets to an equally wide array of boats, designed for particular purposes and circumstances. Specialized equipment also develops as a consequence of craft specialization as well, such as the carving tools used by Northwest Coast artisans. Susan Kent, an archaeologist interested in sedentism and material culture, regards this elaboration and growth of material culture as an inevitable outcome of prolonged living in one place. Many of us can see this in our own lives. When young, everything we own may fit in the back of a small car, but buy a house, have children and the possessions proliferate.

7. Complex hunter-gatherers had larger populations and higher population densities than foragers. In North America, the largest regional populations lived in California and in the Northwest Coast, both areas occupied by complex hunter-gatherers. Agricultural areas, such as the Southwest, Midwest and East, had lower densities. This runs counter to what most people would expect. Community sizes on the Northwest Coast ranged from less than 100 to almost 2000 people. To put that in perspective, the largest town anywhere in Native North America was Cahokia, a very large settlement east of St Louis, Missouri. At its peak (c. AD 800 to 1200) Cahokia may have been home to 30,000 people. In the Southwest, Pueblo Bonito, a

large Anasazi settlement in northeastern Arizona, may have housed 5,000 people (several thousand more probably lived in the vicinity) around AD 1100. These places are remarkable for their size. But in general, most agricultural communities on the continent were no bigger, and many were smaller, than hunter-gatherer communities on the coast.

8. Finally, complex hunter-gatherers had social hierarchies, with permanent leadership positions with high status, prestige, and even power. Mobile foragers live in small groups where individuals may exert power over their fellows by virtue of their personality or skills. But these lack permanent leaders, and they can completely ignore the temporary leaders they have. Among complex hunter-gatherers, there appear to have been inherited leadership positions. These positions may or may not have had power (essentially the ability to make other people do what they do not want to do), but they did have high prestige, dignity, and authority, receiving respect and honor from other members of the society – though people could also ignore them. On the Northwest Coast, there were two social classes, free and slave. Within the class of free people, there were two to three basic ranks. In the top rank were chiefs and their immediate families who formed a regional elite or oligarchy. Chiefs held many titles, rights, and privileges. Below chiefs was a sort of middle class, whose members individually owned few titles. Below these people were "commoners," free people who held no titles. Outside this social hierarchy were slaves. As slaves, they did not exist socially, did not even possess gender (a social role, as opposed to sex, which is biological), and could be disposed of as their owner chose. The elite depended on slave labor. Slaves were ultimately war captives. Most Northwest Coast societies had rules that the offspring of a free person and a slave was a slave. We will discuss social complexity in more detail in Chapter Six.

Another aspect of complexity is occupational specialization. Many Northwest Coast individuals were full- and part-time specialists in a wide variety of crafts and pursuits. Common specializations included woodcarving, carpentry, basket making, shamanism, harpooner, blanket making, and so on. Specialization leads to a greater range of skills being available to perform crucial tasks, particularly those that needed to be done all at the same time. Both women and men could be specialists, and the work of both was important to the household economy. There is also some evidence for community-level craft specialization. Boas reports that Tsimshian villages brought different presents for a major potlatch:

> Then the young chief sent word to a man of the tribe of Gitlan of the
> Tsimshian, who knew how to make carved wooden dishes; and he sent word
> to the Gispaxlats to make carved wooden spoons; and he sent word to the
> Ginaxangik to make carved wooden boxes; and he gave order to the
> Gidwulgadz to make deep wooden dishes with carving; and he gave word to
> the Gitdzis to make carved wooden spoons; and he gave orders to the
> Ginadaxs to make much mountain-goat meat and tallow; and he gave order to
> the Giludzar to pick cranberries and crab-apples, and he gave orders to the...[2]

And the list continued.

There is also evidence from the Northwest Coast, the Eastern United States and elsewhere, that complex hunter-gatherers participated in far-flung trading networks and what archaeologists call "interaction spheres." These are regions across which people maintain close social and economic ties. These links can be based on trade, but marriage and kinship ties are crucial.

Ancient affluent foragers have been found in many parts of the world, and in many time periods, although most commonly within the last 12,000 years. The best-known examples include the Jomon of Japan, which lasted from 12,000 to 2,000 years ago over much of Japan, and which may have been the first culture in the world to use pottery containers. Another important example are the Natufian peoples of the Middle East, who between 14,000 and 12,000 years ago were the first people to domesticate plants. Other affluent foragers may include many of the Upper Paleolithic cultures of Europe who created the famous cave art. The Natufian serve as a good example for some of the traits listed above for complex hunter-gatherers: 1) They lived in small villages, in houses which may have been relatively permanent – Natufian houses appear to have had stone foundations, implying some investment of effort and some form of sedentism; 2) Natufian folk depended heavily on stored foods, particularly grains such as wheat, but they also intensively exploited other resources, including antelope herds. They may have managed these herds by selectively culling animals;[5] 3) Differences in grave goods among excavated Natufian burials suggest that some form of social or economic inequality may have existed in Natufian society; 4) Natufian material culture was richer than that of more mobile contemporary hunter-gatherers.

Affluent foragers were "discovered" as the result of the global, post-World War II explosion in the pace of archaeological research. By the late 1970s, it was clear that some of the ancient foraging cultures being discovered could not easily be reconciled with ideas about hunter-gatherer behavior based on modern generalized hunter-gatherers, or modern agriculturalists. After the war, archaeologists became increasingly interested in two broad research projects: the origins of agriculture and the emergence of complex societies. At first, these were seen as related questions, since agriculture had to come before social complexity. The research on agriculture initially seemed straightforward, because it also assumed that given the first opportunity, foragers would happily and even gratefully adopt agriculture, since hunting and gathering was thought to be hard and chancy.

The accumulating information on hunter-gatherers made it clear that some of them, even in marginal environments, may not need to work very hard to feed themselves reasonably well. Richard B. Lee did a time and motion study among some San in the Kalahari Desert over several weeks, and discovered that they spent only a few hours a week in searching for food. James Woodburn made similar observations among the Hadza of East Africa. Studies such as these led Marshall Sahlins, an anthropologist, to describe generalized hunter-gatherers as the world's first "affluent societies." By affluence, Sahlins meant not the kind of material affluence we mean in this book when we describe affluent foragers, but a zen-like lifestyle in which people had what they wanted, and they did not want very much. Some of these data on forager work effort have been challenged, and Sahlins' notion of zen foragers has been sharply criticized, but the study by Mark Cohen of ancient hunter-gatherer health indicates that foraging was not the grim, dispiriting food quest imagined by early anthropologists and archaeologists, and it is clear that generalized foragers do not work as hard as people in industrial societies do.

It has also been learned that some hunter-gatherers have lived near, or among agriculturalists for millennia, and have steadfastly not become farmers. The Native people of southern California lived close to the ancient farmers of southern Arizona for nearly 2,000 years. While they traded for agricultural products, they never adopted farming. Agriculture only seems like the logical thing to do from the standpoint of people who have been farmers for a few millennia. It may seem quite illogical from the standpoint of a forager. So the questions in the minds of archaeologists began to shift to what were the conditions that forced hunter-gatherers into becoming farmers?

The other major archaeological research problem of the post-war period has been the origins and development of complex societies. At first archaeologists investigated the world's earliest, pristine civilizations, such as those in Mesopotamia, China, Mesoamerica, and the Andes. Research emphasized the causal processes that would bring people to live for the first time in societies marked by strong degrees of social inequality. Archaeologists working with hunter-gatherers began to recognize that many of these same processes and results occurred among the ancient societies they were studying.

As researchers came increasingly to understand that they were dealing with hunter-gatherers in the past whose political, social and economic organizations were unlike those of modern and ancient generalized hunter-gatherers, they turned more and more to the ethnographic literature of the Northwest Coast to gain an understanding of what affluent foragers were like. Almost all interpretations of complexity among hunter-gatherers are dependent on that literature. Most of the complex hunter-gatherers who have been ethnographically described lived on the Northwest Coast. Most of the rest lived in California. But, ironically, almost all the archaeologists using the literature relied almost exclusively on the ethnographic materials, without recourse to what was known about the archaeology. It must be admitted that one reason for this is that it has not been easy to learn about Northwest archaeology, since the pace of publication on the region has not kept up with the pace of research. The effect of this has been to treat the peoples of the Northwest Coast as peoples without history.

This brings us to a fundamental idea underlying this book: hunter-gatherers have dynamic, unpredictable histories, yet histories that can inform us about crucial aspects in the evolution of human cultures and societies. Social theorists have long held that there are some developmental thresholds in the course of human history that once crossed, can never be recrossed. The great archaeologist, V. Gordon Childe, described these thresholds as revolutions. He believed there were two such revolutions during the last 10,000 years that rivaled the industrial revolution: the transition to farming, and the transition from small villages to cities. Peter Wilson, another archaeologist, has argued that the shift to settled, sedentary life has been an even more important change for humans than agriculture, cities or industrialism. But, the point here is that these transitions are usually seen as permanent – once sedentary, sedentary forever. Having crossed these points of no return, societies are inevitably and irreversibly drawn into major economic, social, and political changes. Work on foragers suggests that some hunter-gatherer groups have skipped back and forth across these thresholds several times, without apparently ever getting caught up in major social changes, while others have indeed been sucked firmly, even rapidly into new directions of change. One of these directions is towards increasing social complexity and inequality.

Basic themes

Three basic themes run through this volume. The first is that hunter-gatherers have long and rich histories; the second is our answer to the question of how and why cultures change, or evolve, through time; and third, is the issue of regional similarity and local variation, or, in its environmental version, regional richness and local variability. These three themes taken together provide the framework for our answer to the questions of how and why complex hunter-gatherers evolved on the Northwest Coast, and why that is important. We have already introduced the first theme of hunter-gatherer history. In this section we discuss cultural evolution, and regional similarity and variability.

There are a great many theories about the causes of culture change, and it would require at least another book to fully present and defend our views, so we can only summarize them here. Cultural evolution, to our minds, is the product of the decisions people make and the behavioral consequences of those decisions. The essence of cultural evolution is not grand, remote processes, but what individual humans do every day: their intentions; the decisions they make and the actions they take on those intentions; their evaluation of those decisions based on the consequences of their acts, and how people alter their ideas and behaviors in the light of those consequences. We do not mean here just decisions like that of Napoleon to invade Russia; we mean decisions such as whether to have coffee or tea in the morning, whether to drive to work in one's car, or to take the bus. Equally as important is what gets passed on to the next generation: what children learn, and what of that they use as they become adults.[6] Cultural evolution is the outcome of daily life, not the result of a grand plan.

What is the basis for making decisions and for evaluating them? Decisions are made and their consequences evaluated on the basis of our intentions and values. We usually have reasons for deciding to do things, to have that cup of coffee or tea. We are not suggesting that humans always make decisions on the basis of some rational calculation based on complete or even accurate knowledge. We all know that many decisions are often made on the most tenuous grounds. However, whatever the basis, we choose among options available to us (though there may be only one), and we evaluate their consequences: the cup of coffee gave a better wake-up jolt, but the car trip was snarled in traffic and took too long. Wake-up jolt and a fast commute were among the criteria for evaluating this morning's choices. On the other hand, the car trip may have had nothing to do with commuting efficiency: perhaps we had just bought a very expensive, prestigious car, and thoroughly enjoyed showing it off, revelling in the new, higher social prestige we thought we displayed – so being stuck in traffic was a good outcome for that purpose.

We also don't make all the decisions that affect our lives; others do, and their choices, and evaluations of consequences are in terms of their values and intentions, not ours. They have power to shape the contexts within which we make our decisions, and we may have as much influence over them as we have over the weather. In that sense, they are as much a part of our environment as the weather.

What are the sources of these intentions and values? One is culture,[7] the shared ideas, beliefs, values, mores, world views, practices, and information in the minds of human beings. Culture is socially shared with others in the same cultural group and with the next generation. It is prescriptive, telling us what is good or bad behavior, wise or foolish behavior. Cultural information profoundly affects how we under-stand the world around us and structures the way we relate to other people as well as to the rest of our environment. It is a system of knowledge about the world and how it works. And it is passed on from one generation to the next through social learn-ing.[8] Culture then has a social history. Any culture today consists of the surviving forms of all the ideas and practices ever introduced into that cultural tradition through time and transmitted from one generation to the next.[9] Not all the ideas or practices, just those that were transmitted from one generation to the next. Thus, culture is profoundly historical.

Though culture is shared, it is not uniform. We have each learned a version of our culture, which is not exactly the same as the versions others have learned. Addition-ally, cultures may contain more than one form of an idea or practice, as the history of religion clearly shows. Even in the most rigid religion, variations of thought and interpretation inevitably develop, some of which may even become religions in their own right, while others wither away, and disappear. There may be some parts of life where a wide range of ideas and behaviors can flourish and others where only a very few will work. There is, for example, great variability in the world in concepts about the supernatural, but very limited variety in the form of fish hooks. Shamanism, Hinduism, Buddhism, Catholicism, etc., may all "work" more or less equally, but there are only a few ways to actually catch fish.

Another source of our goals and values is our biology. While this topic is enor-mously controversial it seems inevitable that aspects of our behavior have some kind of genetic basis. Recent theories of cognition, for example, assert that we carry in our brains what might be termed "hardwired modules" or potentials for certain kinds of behavior. Steven Mithen,[10] for example, has recently argued that we have several such modules, including one for accurately learning some natural history information, another for tool making, and yet another for operating effectively in socially complex situations. In an earlier work, he suggested that we also carry, hard-wired in our brains, "rules of thumb," for making rapid decisions, decisions that we may not be conscious of making.[11] These are what we term "hunches" or intuition. But beyond that, we may also have innate propensities for certain kinds of behaviors. We are, for example, terrestrial primates, closely related to chimps, gorillas, and bonobos (formerly called pygmy chimps). While these cousins of ours display a wide range of behaviors, chimps and gorillas organize themselves into dominance hierarchies, and the presence of social inequality in many human societies may simply be an expression of the same propensities. The various ways we organize our dominance hierarchies may indicate how flexible we can be in expressing these innate "propensities."[12]

The effects of biology may be even simpler, reflecting how biological evolution works. We may be geared, as a result of millions of years of evolution, towards eval-uating our decisions on the basis of how their consequences affect our reproductive potential, in other words, we tend to do those things that will maximize our genetic contribution to the next generation. These evaluations may be on the basis of those rules of thumb of which we are only dimly aware, if at all.

Whatever their source, the different ideas, practices, and behaviors are sorted and winnowed according to their consequences. As a result, some cultural variants persist, perhaps becoming more common, while others disappear. Automobiles replaced the horse and buggy; Christianity survived; Mithraism did not.[13] These examples indicate that this approach to cultural evolution applies equally to technology and beliefs.

The consequences of some decisions and actions are visible to us in a very short time, while for others, the consequences can take scores or even hundreds of years to appear, and sometimes the short-term and long-term outcomes are contradictory. Smoking a cigarette may be immediately gratifying, yet can lead, after 20 or 30 years, to lung cancer. The acceptance of the automobile quickly solved one pollution problem – city streets littered with the droppings of thousands of horses – yet set in motion a train of effects that continues to cascade and grow, and that has structured much of the modern world. So, while we speak of human decision making as the basic cause of cultural evolution, the consequences of our decisions can take on lives of their own, and even become part of the environment (both natural and cultural) within which we, as individuals, make our own, subsequent, decisions.

Differences in the environments, technology, and the scale of the societies and economies involved affect how long such consequences may take. For example, continual irrigation of agricultural fields can lead to the accumulation of salts (salinization), and the complete loss of their fertility. In the modern American Southwest, intensive irrigation of fields began in the 1920s, and salinization is already a problem, while several thousand years ago in Mesopotamia (modern Iraq), salinization sometimes took a millennium or more to be felt. Of course, people cannot know that today's decisions will have such consequences in a millennium, or even a few decades.[14] Thus, culture change is in part driven by these unforeseen outcomes.

What does all this mean for understanding cultural change? In Chapter Five, we will discuss changing subsistence and economic patterns, and the importance of local and regional variability in the environment for understanding those changes. These phrases are jargon, a shorthand, for: Over the last 11,000 years on the Northwest Coast, as everywhere else, people made decisions each day about what to do, based on the season of the year; the tools, techniques, and knowledge they possessed; and their situation (were there small children in the household, or elderly parents? were stored foods running short, or was there several weeks supply left? were the seas unexpectedly calm, making a trip out of the bay to fish for cod suddenly seem like a good idea? or were there storm clouds lying low in the direction they had planned to fish?). Under some circumstances, they chose (or were forced) to increase the amount of food they produced, not for just one season, but over many years. In other cases, they had to change which fish they caught, and perhaps even learn new techniques, because of changes in their local environment.

This may seem quite obvious, but, while it is easy, and even necessary, to discuss these matters in terms like "intensification" (increasing production per capita – i.e. someone producing more food) or "environmental variability affected the evolution of the economy," the human decision making that is the basis for evolutionary change should not get lost.

The third, central theme of this book is that of local variability and regional similarity, and its environmental equivalent, regional richness and local variability. Earlier in this chapter, we described the linguistic and social variability along the coast, and how that variability seems to cluster into regions, and how anthropologists have struggled with it. This local/regional pattern is fundamental to understanding the coast.

1 Four Clackamas Indians. Painting by Paul Kane in 1848. The Clackamas were Chinookan speaking peoples who lived in what is now the metropolitan area of Portland, Oregon. These four display some characteristics of high status individuals, including cranial deformation and the nasal ornament.

2 (above) Cape Blanco, Oregon, showing the long, straight, exposed coastline typical of much of the Oregon Coast.

3 (below)The north end of Pacific Rim Park, looking toward Clayoquot Sound. The scene shows the variety of landforms and coastlines common to the coast of British Columbia and southeast Alaska.

4 (*above*) *Small estuaries, such as that of the Khutze River of northern British Columbia were very localized, but highly productive habitats for human use.*

5 (*right*) *Rainforest on Vancouver Island, dominated by tall evergreens and ferns on the forest floor.*

Environment and Ecology

6 (*below*) *The estuary of the Stikine River, southeast Alaska.*

7 (*below*) *Meadows and high ridges in Manning Provincial Park, British Columbia. Coastal peoples hunted mountain goat and mountain sheep in high elevation areas such as these.*

8 (*left*) *Khutze River, British Columbia showing elevation contrasts typical of northern and central coasts.*

9 (*above*) *Deep midden at Namu. The photograph is of the River Front trench, and is illustrative of the deep, massive shell middens found on the central and northern coasts.*

Shell Middens

10 (*left*) *Fish trap at Annette Island, southeast Alaska, 1910. The photograph shows the kind of place often used on the coast for fish traps – rapid, turbulent water. The catwalk also illustrates the kind of structure used for dip netting along the entire length of the coast.*

12 (*right*) *Fishing for salmon with a plunge net on the Klamath River, California.*

Fishing and Storage

11 (*below*) *Fish drying on racks at the Tlingit Village of Tuxshecan, 1891. Racks such as these probably stood along the beaches in front of most coastal villages and towns. The women in the foreground appear to be tending a fire beneath the near rack, while a puppy waits hopefully. The house in the middle back ground combines a European style log cabin with a traditional roof.*

Canoes

13 (top) Columbia River canoes and paddles, sketched by Paul Kane. Columbia River peoples used many sizes and styles of canoes, each designed for a particular purpose. (bottom) Northern Canoes sketched by Paul Kane. Note his skill in duplicating Northwest Coast designs on the canoe.

The Northwest Coast is a culture area marked by many similarities in culture and social organization, and yet also by strong local and even regional differences. The Northwest Coast art style, or idiom (Chapter Nine), is a case in point. Works of art from many parts of the coast share recognizable common features, but there are also important regional differences. The art from the Lower Columbia River is quite different from that to the north; art from the west coast of Vancouver Island differs from that in Alaska, though they all have common underlying principles and themes.

A common approach to regional similarity and local variability on the coast has been to try and present a picture of the "typical Northwest Coast group," which is sometimes based on one region, or even one tribe. For example, the Kwakwaka'wakw often play that role because they are the group that Boas studied the most, and for whom there is the most literature. Similarly, the better-known archaeological sequences, those from the Gulf of Georgia in the south and Prince Rupert Harbor in the north, set the standard for what is typical, because they are the best known. The danger is that by relying on "average" or "typical" conditions, we may be basing our ideas on cultures or circumstances that either never existed, or which are not really relevant to what we want to understand. But more importantly, by obscuring variation, we lose the very stuff of evolution, of change, of life itself. Variability in the environment, and variability in the decisions people make, and in the consequences of those decisions makes culture change possible. In a book of this kind, then, we must consider variability to understand what happened in the past.

On the other hand, the similarities are also real; different regions of the coast share important likenesses. If we focus only on variability, we literally miss the forests for the trees. How does regional similarity arise out of local variation? Is it simply the result of broad environmental similarities? In part yes, but that answer needs to be rephrased: regional cultural similarities exist because all the local places that make up a region are enough alike for a common set of solutions to work, or for a common set of goals to be achievable. Salmon runs are sufficiently predictable and rich in just enough places on the coast for stored salmon to have often been basic to the coast's economy, though not everywhere, and probably not all the time anywhere.

The other part of the answer lies in the phrase "a common set of goals." Northwest Coast peoples dealt with local variability by participating in large-scale social and exchange networks, through which they established connections with other people and other resources over sometimes vast regions. They thus developed regional social networks that came to share common cultural features with practices that persisted over long periods of time. This is culture history.

The book that follows, then, is structured around three ideas or themes: hunter-gatherers have dynamic, interesting, and important histories; these histories (cultural evolution) are the result of the everyday decisions of individuals; and both local differences and regional similarities are the fundamental stuff of culture change. These themes provide the framework within which we can explain the evolution of complex hunter-gatherers on the Northwest Coast.

This volume

In the next nine chapters we will describe the archaeology and history of the complex hunters and gatherers of the Northwest Coast. The chapters are organized thematically rather than chronologically. We chose this style because we believe that through a discussion of themes and important concepts, we can better place the Northwest Coast in an anthropological context. Thus, topics such as the subsistence economy, status and rank, warfare, and art, are distinct chapters with temporal and spatial components.

In Chapter Two we describe the spatial and temporal variability in the Northwest Coast landscape and climate. We show the major regional differences between the coast and the mountains, and the variability from north to south. We go on to describe the climatic and landscape changes that have occurred in the last 12,000 years and the effects of these changes on the distributions of food resources.

The next two chapters present a chronological outline of what is known of the archaeological history of the Northwest Coast. Chapter Three deals with the period between c. 11,000 and 4400 BC, Chapter Four with the period 4400 BC to AD 1775. In Chapter Five we demonstrate the considerable variability in how people subsisted over the last 13,000 years. We show that for the most part, the entire region has been founded on a marine subsistence strategy yet with many regional variations. Some areas follow the ethnographic pattern by subsisting primarily on salmon. Others have had diets dominated by a wider variety of species, including whales, halibut, cod, herring, or seals. We find that diets also change through time, with some areas becoming more reliant on salmon in the last thousand years.

Chapter Six discusses several topics, including the development of households on the coast, specialization and regional interaction. It is in this chapter that we pull together some of the issues of scale that we discuss in earlier parts of the book. We also address the relationships among the household economy, elite formation and gender on the coast. Regional interaction was crucial in the development of Northwest Coast societies because trade and social ties extended over vast distances.

The focus of Chapter Seven is how people on the Northwest Coast expressed rank and status, and how we identify it archaeologically. The three main areas of research that Northwest Coast scholars use to identify status and rank are burials, house size, and the trade in exotic items and materials. All three are seen to varying degrees on the Northwest Coast and, it is argued, may all have different meanings for the study of hunter and gatherer complexity.

Warfare was an important institution on the Northwest Coast and is the focus of Chapter Eight. Here we describe the history of violent contact in the region and how archaeologists identify warfare in the archaeological record. We show that warfare is widespread in southeast Alaska and occurs to varying degrees over the last 5,000 years. Two research projects oriented toward describing and explaining Northwest Coast warfare are described. The first is MacDonald's excavations at Kitwanga and the second is Maschner's study of prehistoric Tlingit warfare in southeast Alaska.

Perhaps the most enduring characteristic of Northwest Coast culture is its carvings and sculpture. No other institution in the region has attracted the world's attention like its art. Chapter Nine is an overview of Northwest Coast art. It is discussed from a number of perspectives and is seen as integral to the development of Northwest Coast culture. We trace its origins and discuss its changes through time from simple carvings and geometric designs 5,000 years ago to the specialized crafts and craftsmen of the modern era.

The final chapter is reserved for what we, as the authors, think is really going on in Northwest Coast prehistory. We do not agree on every issue, but we have come to a reasonable consensus on most. Chapter Ten is our arena for pulling together the threads of the past that make up the Northwest Coast. It will provide our view of one of the most fabulous histories and cultural landscapes in world prehistory.

CHAPTER TWO
Ecology: Environments and Demography

On the night of 28 March 1806, the Lewis and Clark expedition camped near what is now Portland, Oregon, on their homeward trip. They complained bitterly in their notes that the number of birds was so great and so noisy that the expedition could not sleep for the din.[1] Others were not so bothered by the coast's richness. The maritime fur trade was fueled by the accounts of vast numbers of sea otters in the journals of Captain Cook and others. People came along the Oregon trail on the strength of stories about the fertility of the Willamette Valley, and even now, the coast is legendary for the one-time profusion of its salmon runs.

This seemingly lavish environment led early anthropologists to believe that the ecology and subsistence economies of the Native people were not relevant to understanding their culture. This view was challenged by Wayne Suttles,[2] who showed that the coast's environment was not everywhere abundant, nor abundant all the time. There were occasions when the salmon runs failed and places where the salmon did not run at all. The crucial notion here is that the coast's environment is rich and complex, and the interaction between Native people and this complexity played a vital role in their demography, economies, societies, and histories.

When the fur trade began in 1792, the Northwest Coast was the second most populous region in aboriginal North America north of Mexico. California was the most populous. It is of interest that both these regions were occupied by hunter-gatherers, rather than agriculturalists. While it is obvious that these high populations were the product of the coast's rich environment, that observation is an oversimplification, and tells us nothing about how those high populations came to be, how they were sustained, and what crucial relationships there may have been among the coast's population, environmental and social histories.

The richness and complexity of the coastal environment is the result of the interplay between the coast's topography and climate and between land and sea. Ecology is not static, nor has the coastal environment ever been stable – in fact, that instability is a key part of its complexity – so we must also review the history of environments along the coast. In this chapter, then, we discuss the coast's landforms and climate, since it is the interplay between these that create the biotic environment; we then review the coast's terrestrial and marine environments. The last section summarizes what is known about the coast's demography over the past several thousand years.

Though this book is about the Northwest Coast, the largest region we mention is one known to geographers and geologists as *Cascadia*. Cascadia includes all of Washington State, most of the province of British Columbia, as well as southeastern Alaska, northern and western Oregon, northern California, northern and central Idaho, and western Montana. Put another way, Cascadia includes all of two culture areas: the Northwest Coast and the Intermontane Plateau, as well as portions of the Subarctic and Great Basin. To some extent this is arbitrary, and the region could be extended to include more of Pacific Alaska, and perhaps even the rest of California. However, it does include the heart of the Pacific coast's salmon region and major salmon rivers (excluding only the Sacramento and San Joquin Rivers of California). This vast region provides crucial context and background for several critical developments in Northwest Coast history, including the development of status differentials and the history of the art style.

Landforms

The coast's major topographic features are best seen from the west, from a vantage point somewhere out over the North Pacific. The major topographic features (mountains, valleys, and lowlands) run north–south. The region's great rivers run from east to west, and the weather moves from west to east. The region can be thought of as a giant blue and green tartan.

Pls. 2–8   Moving from west to east, the major north–south tending topographic features are: the continental shelf, the Outer Mountains, the coastal lowland, and the Inner Mountains. The continental shelf is a drowned coastal plain between the Outer Mountains and the abyssal depths of the North Pacific. The shelf's shallow, nutrient-rich waters attract and support a wide array of fish, sea mammals, and sea birds. Upwelling waters from cold ocean currents (the Alaskan and California Currents) support the plankton necessary for abundant marine resources.

In a few places, such as the outer coasts of Washington State and Oregon, the continental shelf is higher than the ocean, forming a true coastal plain. In other spots, including the outer islands of the Alexander Archipelago of southeastern Alaska and the west coast of Vancouver Island, there are small stretches of coastal plain. During the last glacial period, the coastal plain was exposed and, in British Columbia and Alaska, partially glaciated. It may have played an important role in the peopling of the Americas, and in the early occupation of the Northwest Coast (discussed in Chapter Three).

Immediately east of the shelf are the Outer Mountains[3] that include the Coast Ranges of northern California, Oregon, the Willapa Hills and Olympic Mountains of Washington, the mountains of Vancouver Island and the Queen Charlotte Islands of British Columbia, and the high, coastal mountains of southeast Alaska's Alexander Archipelago. The Outer Mountains end with the St Elias Range where British Columbia, the Yukon Territory, and Alaska meet. They vary from low hills to high, alpine peaks and are everywhere rugged and heavily vegetated. In places where the continental shelf is drowned, they rise directly from the sea, creating a precipitous and dangerous coastline. From Washington's Olympics northward, the Outer Mountains were glaciated during the last glacial advance; to the south, they were not.

The coastal lowland, or trough, may be the Northwest Coast's least-known, but perhaps most important environmental feature. It is now the route of the so-called "Inside Passage," plied by freighters, ferries, and luxury tour liners from Vancouver Island through southeast Alaska. The trough is a lowland between the Outer and Inner mountain ranges. North of Seattle, it is drowned; south of Seattle, it emerges from the waters to form the Puget-Willamette Lowland running south 800 km (500 miles) to Cottage Grove, Oregon. Both drowned and dry portions were important to Native subsistence economies. As we will see below, the drowned portions of the coastal trough contained some of the coast's most extensive and important shallow-water habitats. The Puget-Willamette Lowland was a distinctive environment that supported dense human populations, and in some areas, rather distinctive economies.

Climate[4]

The Northwest Coast has a maritime climate; summers are cool, winters are wet and mild. Growing seasons are long, and, on the southern coasts, winters can pass with no frost at all. Along the Pacific shoreline, winter and summer temperatures may vary little, and the two seasons are distinguished by the amount of rain, summers being dry. For example, despite its reputation, Seattle receives far less summer rain (often none) than New York City. Even quite wet places, such as Prince Rupert, British Columbia, will have several weeks during the summer when rainfall is sparse. Usually October and November are the wettest months. Mean annual temperatures become cooler from south to the north, but the entire coast is mild. Temperatures also become cooler as one goes inland from the coast (annual variation also increases). Rainfall comes primarily from fall and winter storms moving in off the North Pacific. As the storms strike the coast, they rise as they encounter the Outer Mountains, so that the coast's heaviest rainfall falls on the middle slopes and upper slopes, where annual precipitation in excess of 3,000 mm (120 in) is not uncommon. But there are extremes. Sequim, Washington, in the rainshadow of the Olympic Mountains, receives about the same rainfall as San Diego, California, while Conception Island, in southeast Alaska, is pummeled by over 10,000 mm (400 in) of rain annually. Away from the coast (and at higher elevations) precipitation may fall as snow, particularly on the northern coast.

The Outer Mountains, where they are high enough, create rainshadows on their eastern slopes and adjacent lowlands. It is these areas, just east of the Outer Mountains, where the lowest rainfall is found. The San Juan Islands of Washington State and the adjacent tip of the Olympic Peninsula are in the rainshadow of the Olympic Mountains and receive much less than 760 mm (30 in), and enjoy some of the sunniest weather anywhere in the region. The mainland coast of British Columbia, in the rainshadow of the higher peaks on Vancouver Island, is known locally as the Sunshine Coast. The maritime air masses rise again as they encounter the Cascades in the USA and the Coast Range in Canada, and rainfall again increases. East of the Inner Mountains, in central Washington and British Columbia, the rainfall effect is quite strong, and these areas are very dry, with continental climates.

Terrestrial environments[5]

Except for portions of the Puget-Willamette Lowland, the Northwest Coast is dominated by its vast temperate zone rainforests. The coastal forests are dominated by three tree species, western hemlock (*Tsuga heterophylla*), Sitka spruce (*Picea sitchensis*), and Douglas fir (*Pseudotsuga menziesii*). A fourth tree, western red cedar (*Thuja plicata*) is found in the coastal forests in less abundance, but played a major role in the region's technologies. Red cedar was the major source of the wood used in building large wooden houses, canoes, storage boxes, and in the famous art.

Pl. 5

Despite their appearance, these forests are not monolithically uniform, since they contain multiple ecosystems and small communities that provided diverse resources for the coast's people. The tree species present in any given place vary according to local differences in temperature, rainfall, proximity to the ocean, elevation, and latitude. Native peoples also affected the structure of the forest. They acted to increase the forests' productivity and to maintain preferred environments (usually grasslands or good berry grounds) by regular burning.[6]

Forests predominantly of western hemlock, western red cedar and Pacific silver fir (*Abies amabilis*) occur in wet, mild places. In cooler and/or wetter places, particularly north of the international boundary, Sitka spruce, with mountain hemlock (*Tsuga mertensiana*) and yellow cedar (*Chamaecyparis nootkatensis*), dominate the forests. Douglas fir and western hemlock predominate in the drier regions (less than 1800 mm [70 in]), particularly south of the boundary. Redwoods (*Sequoia sempervirens*) are important rainforest members in southern Oregon and northern California. Mountain hemlock, several species of fir *(Abies)*, Englemann spruce (*Picea englemanni*) and whitebark pine (*Pinus albicaulis*) are the most common trees in the region's middle and higher elevation forests from northern British Columbia south.

The drier portions of the coastal lowland in Washington and Oregon had a more open vegetation, in some places open grasslands or prairies. Oregon's Willamette Valley had an open oak savanna, with groves of Garry oak (*Quercus garryana*) standing among a broad grassland. Smaller prairies also occurred as far north as southern Vancouver Island. These were all maintained by deliberate burning. Many prairies are disappearing with fire repression, and the cycle of farm expansion followed by farm abandonment. The Willamette Valley, for example, now has extensive woodlands as a result.

Native peoples collected a wide array of plant materials from these forests for food, technology, healing, and other purposes. It is important to stress that the significance of plant foods in the diet declined going north along the coast, reflecting an overall decline in the productivity of terrestrial environments from south to north. Rhizomes (or ferns), roots and corms (or bulbs) of scores of plants were collected, and many were stored. Berries were an important source of sugars, and of taste, in diets heavily reliant on dried or smoked stored foods. In many areas, berries grow in disturbed habitats, and so berry grounds were sometimes burned to prevent their reverting to forest. Acorns and hazelnuts were exploited in drier portions of the southern coast.

Wapiti, or elk (*Cervus elaphus*) and two species of deer (*Odocoileous* sp.) were the most important large mammals, though black bears (*Ursus americanus*), two species of mountain sheep (*Ovis* sp.), mountain goats (*Oreamnus americanus*), beaver (*Castor*), and a wide variety of carnivores and even rodents were hunted and utilized for a range of purposes.

Freshwater fish were not as important as were ocean and anadromous fish (anadromous fish spend part of their lives in fresh water and part in salt water). Of the former, perhaps the two species of sturgeon (white sturgeon [*Acipenser transmontanus*] and green sturgeon [*A. medirostris*]) were the most important. Minnows (*Cyprinidae*) were also locally significant. The major anadromous fish were the six species of salmon and steelhead trout (*Onchorynchus* sp.), several species of smelt, including eulachon (sometimes called candlefish (*Thaleichthys pacificus*), since it is so oily, one can stick a wick in it, and light the wick). Fish oil was an important and treasured dietary supplement, particularly in the winter, to offset the physiological effects of prolonged consumption of dried foods.

Marine environments

Two marine environmental zones, the *neritic* and the *pelagic* or Oceanic, are important to Northwest economics.[7] The neritic zone includes waters from the high tide line to the edge of the continental shelf (about 200 m or 650 ft below high water), and is commonly subdivided into a littoral (or intertidal zone) spanning the area from high to low tide, and the sublittoral zone from the low tide line to the edge of the continental shelf. These waters include some of the most productive habitats available to humans: estuaries, intertidal flats, tidal marshes, rocky foreshores, and banks (broad shallows located off islands or some distance from the land that are productive, attracting a wide variety of plants, animals, fish, and birds). The drowned portions of the coastal trough have the coast's greatest expanse of these fertile neritic waters. The Washington and Oregon coast has the region's smallest body of neritic waters, since the continental shelf is quite narrow there.

Neritic fauna include a great diversity of fish (as a result of the tremendous range of fish habitats in these shallow waters). Of these, bottom fish, such as halibut and other flat fish, cod, and herring were the most important, although it is not unusual for archaeologists to recover more than 20 species of fish in an archaeological site. Birds are present in large numbers, the coast being along a major flyway. Ducks, geese, and swans were by far the most important. They were exploited for meat,

Pls. 2, 3, 6

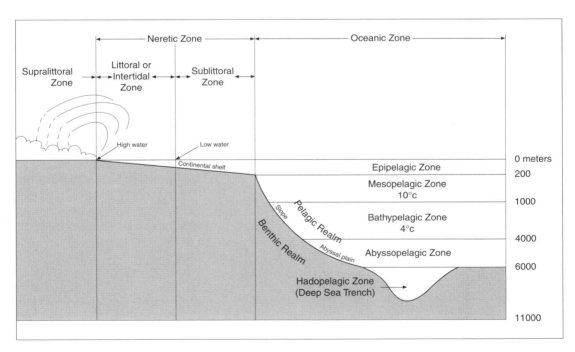

3 Zonation of the marine environments on the continental shelf.

feathers, and their hollow bones. Sea mammals were especially important, probably second only to fish as resources. Sea otters (*Enhydra lutris*), harbor seals (*Phoca vitulina*), and Northern sea lions (*Eumetopias jubata*) were the most significant sea mammals along the coast. But the California sea lion (*Zalophus californicus*), several species of porpoise, and grey whales (*Eschrichtius glaucus*) were also hunted. Whaling was important for the peoples on the west coast of Vancouver Island and the northwest tip of the Olympic peninsula.

The pelagic zone includes deep waters beyond the continental shelf. While this vast pelagic environment was not directly exploited, it is critical because it is where salmon grow to adulthood. Any changes in the conditions of the pelagic zone could have profound effects on the coast's peoples.[8] For example, El Niño, a warming of the waters of the eastern Pacific from Peru northward, can have catastrophic effects on the productivity of pelagic environments by decimating plankton and the fish, animal, and bird populations that depend on them. Warmer water can push more southerly forms north and disrupt the life patterns of cold-water-adapted species. Prolonged El Niños can cause severe terrestrial drought conditions. A decrease in ocean temperatures, on the other hand, can push more northerly species such as Steller's sea lion and the southern limit of salmon spawning southward, extending the range of species and increasing productivity in some areas. The pelagic zone is a significant part of the Northwest Coast's environment, even if it was not directly exploited.

Past environments

The environment of the Northwest Coast has changed in important ways during the past 11,000 and more years.[9] Knowing the nature of these changes is important for our understanding of cultural change along the coast, although it is not always easy to tie changes in climate and vegetation directly to human history. However, at the long temporal scales at which archaeologists work, it is frequently possible to see changes in human economy and society that occur at more or less the same time as climatic and other environmental shifts. Contemporaneity – happening at the same time – is not proof of a connection, but suggests possible causal linkages that need investigation. Our view is that climate or the environment do not cause anything. Rather, they set the parameters and rules under which people make decisions. If the rules change, so do the decisions, but not in any inevitable direction.

We will briefly discuss the environmental effects of glaciation, changing sea levels, vegetation changes, and changes in temperature and rainfall.

Glaciation

During the last ice age the northern and central coasts were heavily glaciated. However, the Pacific coasts of Washington, Oregon, and northern California were not. The last major glacial period in North America, the Wisconsin glaciation, began perhaps 100,000 years ago. During such a glacial period, the ice does not merely grow, advance covering vast areas, and then just sit for 100,000 years. The glaciers grow, shrink, disappear and come back again within a few thousands and tens of thousands of years. During interglacials – the long periods between glacial periods – the ice disappears altogether. Geologists debate over whether we are presently in an interglacial, or still in a glacial period, and whether we can anticipate another major glacial advance within the (geologically) near future.

The last major episode of Wisconsin glaciation, known in Cascadia as the Fraser advance, began more than 20,000 years ago and reached its peak some 16,000 to 18,000 years ago. In North America, two major glacial systems formed: the Laurentide ice sheet and the Cordilleran ice sheet. The Laurentide sheet developed over north-central Canada, and eventually covered virtually all of Canada east of the Canadian Rockies, and extended south over much of north-central and northeastern United States, scouring out the Great Lakes in the process. The Cordilleran ice sheet was much smaller, centered over the Canadian Coast Range, but included ice in the Alaskan Coast range. It eventually grew so that it formed one or more ice domes over British Columbia, burying most of the province. Lesser glacial lobes extended south into northern Washington State, including well down through Puget Sound, and out through the Strait of Juan de Fuca.

Deglaciation began by 14,000 years ago in some places, and was well advanced a millennium later. By 12,000 years ago most of the coastline itself had been de-glaciated, and by 9,500 years ago the ice had retreated into the coast range itself, where it gradually disappeared over the next two or three thousand years.

During the past 10,000 years, there have been at least two and perhaps three periods in the Northwest during which alpine glaciers formed and advanced. These episodes suggest declines in mean annual temperatures or a significant increase in snowfall. Glaciers form when snows do not melt over many summers. The first of these Holocene glacial events occurred sometime before 7000 years ago, and is poorly known because subsequent alpine glacial advances have obliterated the evidence. The second – usually termed the Neoglacial – occurred between 4,500 and 2,000 years ago. This is a period generally marked by cooler/wetter conditions than exist today. The last is commonly called the "Little Ice Age," and began about 500 years ago, and ended in the early years of the 20th century. Most of the world's alpine glaciers – as opposed to the ice sheets of Greenland and Antarctica – either formed during the Little Ice Age or grew considerably during that time. There has been a general major retreat of mountain glaciers in the world since the late 1940s.

Until recently, geologists thought that the Fraser glaciers essentially buried the entire coastline, presenting a solid ice wall to the sea. This certainly was the case along some portions of the coast, where the glaciers flowed out onto the continental shelf into sea water. It is possible though that some stretches of the outer coast were either never glaciated, or only briefly. The most likely candidates for such an ice-free pocket – or refugium as biologists call it – are the northern Queen Charlotte Islands and Prince of Wales Island. Soundings off Hecate Strait, between the Queen Charlottes and the mainland, indicate the presence of sea cliffs, suggesting that the strait was once water-free, and certainly ice-free. Botanists have discovered plant pollen and even fragments of plants in sediments off the northern tip of the island dating 16,000 years ago. Bear bones have been found in caves on Prince of Wales Island belonging to the height of the Fraser advance, perhaps around 18,000 years ago. The chance that such ice-free spots existed along the continental shelf during the last glaciation is important when we discuss the initial peopling of the coast in the next chapter. For the moment, we must leave the tantalizing prospect of these refugia for a discussion of the effects of glaciation and deglaciation.

Changes in relative sea levels are among the most important effects of glaciation on any coastal region. Of three major causes of changing sea levels, one is the result of continental drift and two result from glaciation. When glaciers form, they tie up increasing amounts of the earth's water, which ultimately comes from the oceans, causing lower sea levels. As the oceans become smaller – with a smaller volume of water in them – they become lower relative to the adjacent land masses. Changes in sea level due to changes in the volume of water in the oceans are *eustatic* sea level changes. At the height of the last glaciation, the world's oceans were 100 to 150 m (320 to 500 ft) lower than at present. Much of this lowering was the result of eustatic sea level changes. This discussion is actually quite relevant to the world over the next century. One of the possible outcomes of global warming produced by the so-called "Greenhouse effect," is the eustatic raising of the ocean as the result of increased melting of the Greenlandic and Antarctic ice caps. Even a meter or two increase would flood many of the world's major cities and drown significant portions of many coastal plains with their dense human populations.

The second glacial cause of sea-level changes are called *isostatic* changes: they result from the land going up and down. As glacial ice builds, it depresses – forces downward – the land beneath it and immediately adjacent to it. It also forces land some distance from the glacier up because the earth's crust slowly flows away from glacial fronts. For example, as ice built up in northern British Columbia, the mainland coast was forced down, while the Queen Charlotte Islands and southeast Alaska may have been lifted up by a bulge of earth forced out and up by the glacier. When the glacier melts, the processes reverse and the land in front of the glacier falls while the land under the glacier rises. Apparently these glacial bulges may move out from the front of a glacier like ripples in a pond and take centuries and millennia to flow away and dissipate.

In some places along the coast, the land beneath the glaciers sagged lower than sea levels fell, so those portions of the coastline remained under water, despite the eustatic fall in sea levels. In other places, the eustatic fall exceeded the isostatic fall, and areas now submerged were exposed. This history is only generally known for the Northwest Coast.

Another short-term effect of eustatic and isostatic sea level changes occurs early during deglaciation. As glaciers melt, the seas rise more rapidly than the land rebounds, so areas that are not now under water, and that were not under water at the glacial peak, were flooded by quickly rising seas. In the area of Vancouver, British Columbia, this immediately post-glacial marine transgression[10] briefly reached heights of 100 m (320 ft) and more above modern sea levels, flooding large areas. These events are usually short lived. Isostatic rebound catches up with eustatic sea rises, and sometimes lifts the land higher than the elevation of the modern land surfaces. After a time, the land surface may settle back down to its more-or-less modern position. Eustatic and isostatic sea level changes produce a complex, and locally variable, record of sea level changes.

Finally, as eustatic and isostatic changes occur, the continents grind along their appointed routes in continental drift, causing the land either to gradually rise, as along the outer coast of Vancouver Island, or fall, as on Vancouver Island's inner coast, the British Columbia mainland, and the Seattle area, or to catastrophically rise or fall. In Puget Sound, there is an extensive geological record of land surfaces abruptly rising above and falling below sea level by several meters during huge subduction earthquakes. Changes in relative sea levels caused by such tectonic shifts are termed *diastrophic* changes in sea levels (see box on tectonics and archaeology, Chapter Three).

Sea level changes are archaeologically important for a variety of reasons. First, early occupation sites on the coast may now be either under water, or far above the modern shoreline. Our knowledge of the early archaeology of the coast is partially determined by sea level changes since several thousand years of antiquity may be inaccessible to us. Second, even quite minor fluctuations in sea levels can significantly affect the ecological productivity of a small bay, or even a large portion of the coast. A slight lowering of sea levels could change a productive estuary into a dry dune field, for example. The effects on sea levels of Holocene glacial episodes is not known, but the volume of ice was probably too small to have had much effect on global sea levels.

The available sea level curves suggest somewhat disparate sea level histories for different parts of the coast. The story is simplest along the coasts of northern California, Oregon, and the southern Pacific coast of Washington State. Sea levels have risen steadily since *c.* 10,000 years ago when they stood some 60 m (200 ft) below their modern level. The most rapid rise occurred between 10,000 and 7,000 years ago, after which they rose much more slowly. Modern sea levels appear to have been achieved within the last 2,000 years or so, with water levels within 1–2 m (3–6 ft) of their present position within the last 4,000 years. This picture is complicated by gradual tectonic uplifting of at least portions of the Washington coastline, and probably Oregon's as well.

The picture is much more complex along the British Columbia and southeast Alaskan coasts, which were extensively glaciated. Evidence for the outer coastline (along the edges of the Outer Mountains) suggests that sea levels were at -100 to -150 m (-330 to -500 ft) perhaps 13,000 years ago. They rose rapidly, and by 8,000 to 6,000 years ago were higher, by perhaps 10 to 15 m (30–50 ft), than presently. Sea levels have subsequently fallen to their modern positions. Along the inner coast of the coastal trough, the patterns of sea level changes have been the mirror image of those along the outer coast. Because the trough was generally heavily glaciated and the land depressed, deglaciation caused a major marine transgression, and at *c.* 12,000 to 10,000 years ago, sea levels in some places stood 100 to 140 m (330–460 ft) *above* their present position. They then fell rapidly (as the land rebounded), so that by 8,000 to 6,000 years ago, sea levels were somewhat below their present levels. Sea levels achieved their approximate modern elevation about 5,000 years ago, though in some places they have continued to rise. It is likely that minor marine transgressions have occurred here and there along the coast within the last 5,000 years.

Vegetation changes[11]

Changes in the composition of the region's vegetation over the past 11,000 years are in part the result of the advance and retreat of glaciers and of the climatic shifts that cause glaciers to come and go. Long-term vegetation changes can be studied through the analysis of plant pollen that has accumulated in places where the pollen will be well preserved, and which are sediment traps – places where sediments will accumulate but not be lost through erosion. Bogs are the best for both reasons. The contents of many Northwest Coast bogs have been studied by palynologists (pollen specialists) who have developed a fairly detailed history of vegetation changes during the past 30,000 years or so. Many plants, in fact, either do not produce pollen, or do not pollinate in a way that will cause their pollen to end up in a bog, so the pollen record is incomplete. Sometimes plant macrofossils can supplement the pollen record. Macrofossils are plant (or animal) remains that are visible with the naked eye. Occasionally *vegetation mats* are found, and they contain needles, twigs, bark, stems, leaves and so on, giving us a glimpse of plant life not seen in the pollen record.

There is little evidence for extensive forests north of central Oregon during the height of the last glaciation at 17,000 to 15,000 years ago. Grasslands, tundras, and parklands were widespread. Parklands are grasslands with scattered trees and groves. Parkland trees included mountain hemlock, lodgepole pine, spruce and fir, depending on where one was. The climate of the southern coast (south of the ice margin) may have been more continental than at present, with stronger annual temperature extremes. The climate was also drier, as the Cordilleran ice sheet forced the Jet Stream south.

The forests expanded with the beginning of deglaciation about 14,000 years ago. The earliest forests appear to have been dominated by lodgepole pine, with willows and soapberries. Within 2,000 years or so, these forests were replaced along the central and southern coasts by denser, more diverse forests of Douglas fir, lodgepole pine, western hemlocks, mountain hemlocks, and perhaps Sitka spruce.

The period between 10,000–9,000 years ago and 7,000 years ago was marked by rapidly warming temperatures (an increase of perhaps 8° C mean annual temperature), accompanied by declining rainfall, particularly during the summers. Grasslands expanded[12] and the oak-savanna of the Willamette Valley extended its range into southern British Columbia, reaching its maximum extent around 7,000 to 8,000 years ago. Southern forests were dominated by Douglas fir and red alder. There is evidence for greater frequency of forest fires during this period. Northern forests (Vancouver Island to southern Alaska) were predominantly Sitka spruce and alder.

Temperatures declined and rainfall increased after 7,000 years ago. The period between 7,000 and 4,000 years ago was probably warmer that at present, but at least as moist. Forests changed in their composition to more moisture-loving (or tolerant) species. The forests, however, did not approximate their modern composition until between 5,000 and 3,000 years ago. Red and yellow cedar did not reach their modern distribution until that time. Even then, given red cedar's growth rates, it would have taken several hundred years after red cedar appeared in a region for there to be trees large enough to make the large canoes, house planks, posts and the like typical of Northwest Coast material culture. As two palynologists, Richard Hebda and Rolfe Mathewes, noted in the early 1980s, the first maturation of cedar forests corresponds to a proliferation of heavy woodworking tools in the region's archaeological record.

As the late Holocene glacial record shows, the region's climate has not remained stable over the last 4,000 years. There have been at least two colder/wetter episodes, the Neoglacial and the Little Ice Age, and the distribution of plants has shifted accordingly, though all vegetation changes cannot be explained by broad climatic shifts. This is seen clearly in the distribution of oak woodlands which, between 3,000 and 2,000 years ago, declined in southern British Columbia while the outer coasts show no measurable change.

Remarks

As a result of major climatic changes over the last 20,000 years and more, the Northwest Coast has undergone major environmental changes. Some of these, such as sea level fluctuations, have a direct effect on the archaeological record. All of them presented the coast's ancient and not so ancient peoples with problems to solve. Some changes may have been so rapid as to be seen in an individual's lifetime, while others spanned millennia, and would have been invisible to any given generation. Some changes may have had profound regional effects, while others, such as the abrupt drowning of a marsh as the result of an earthquake, may have been only of local effect, though still as profound to the people so affected. The Northwest Coast was not a uniform environment, either in time or space.

Significant though all the environmental changes we have described were, perhaps even more important were the arrival of Europeans and the introduction of Old World epidemic diseases in the 18th century, as we shall now see. The population decline caused by those diseases across the Americas was one of the greatest demographic disasters in human history. Likewise, though poorly understood, there were earlier demographic changes over the millennia that affected the course of history on the coast.

Demography

There are two major demographic issues. First, what were the effects of European colonization on Northwest Coast populations? Second, what were the causal connections among the productivity of the coast's environment (and patterns of change and variation in that productivity), population distribution and growth, and economic and social changes? Both of those questions depend on accurate population estimates for the immediately pre-conquest period. The estimates are difficult to build, since most censuses of Northwest Coast groups were first done after they had already suffered from epidemics of smallpox and other introduced diseases. The quality of the censuses can also be a problem. As a result, virtually all such estimates are controversial.

Despite these and other problems, Robert Boyd, a cultural anthropologist, has constructed late 18th- and early 19th-century population estimates for Northwest North America and written a definitive disease history from contact through the end of the 19th century. He conservatively estimates the coast's immediate pre-contact population at some 188,000 people, based on an estimated 33 percent loss from what he considers the region's first smallpox epidemic in *c*. 1775.[13]

Henry Dobyns, an historical demographer looking at all of North America, estimates far higher death rates from initial smallpox epidemics (so-called "virgin ground" epidemics, in which a population has its first experience of a disease, and so is likely to have little or no immunity to it). Dobyns suggests death rates as high as 90 percent. If he is correct, then the coast's population before 1775 could have been as high as a million people or more.[14] Boyd regards his own estimates as conservative, but hazards no guess as to how conservative. While we like Dobyns' estimates (they are closer to our own intuitions about the sizes of Northwest Coast populations), we will use Boyd's estimates since they are the more conservative.

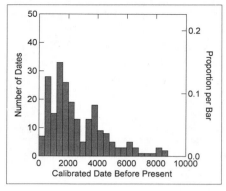

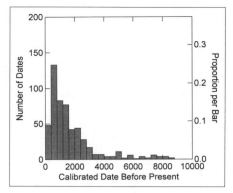

a

b

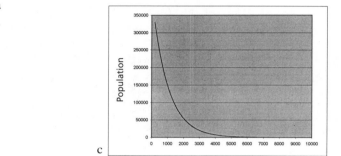

c

4 (a) Radiocarbon dates from the northern Northwest Coast as a proxy measure of population growth; (b) Radiocarbon dates from the southern Northwest Coast as a proxy measure of population growth; (c) Population growth simulation developed by Dale Croes and Steven Hackenburger (1988) based on a growth rate of 0.1 percent per year.

The first smallpox epidemic(s) may have been earlier than 1775. Dobyns believes there was a hemispheric smallpox pandemic in the 1520s, ultimately caused by the introduction of smallpox by the Spanish into Tenochtitlan, the Aztec capital (now Mexico City) in 1519–1520. Anne Ramenofsky[15] has studied the archaeological evidence for early epidemics in North America, and finds some archaeological support for Dobyns' early pandemic. Sarah Campbell, of Western Washington State University, applied Ramenofsky's techniques to archaeological data from central Washington State, and thinks she sees evidence that the postulated 1520 pandemic penetrated to the Columbia Plateau (immediately east of the southern Northwest Coast).[16] This remains tantalizing but unproven.

Smallpox, measles, malaria, whooping cough, typhus, typhoid, and influenza were all introduced to the Northwest Coast (and the rest of North America) by Europeans. Of these, smallpox was the most deadly, though locally other diseases were as serious. There were well-documented smallpox epidemics on the coast around 1775, and then again in 1801, 1836–1838, 1853 and 1862. Not all of these epidemics affected the entire coast. However, the cumulative effect was, for all of the Western Hemisphere as well as the Northwest Coast, the greatest demographic catastrophe in human history. Over the centuries of contact, Native populations dwindled by as much as 90 per cent and more, until, as noted in Chapter One, it was thought that they might become culturally and biologically extinct by the beginning of the 20th century.

There are only three limited studies of Northwest Coast population growth spanning a significant portion of the entire prehistoric period. Knut Fladmark, of Simon Fraser University, built a curve for the entire coast by adding up the total number of radiocarbon dates per 200-year period for the past 8,000 years. Following Fladmark's method, Maschner and Ames have presented similar radiocarbon date-based curves for the southern and northern Northwest Coasts respectively, but based on much larger samples than Fladmark's. Our curves suggest 1) somewhat differing patterns of population growth for the two regions, and 2) that peak populations may have occurred several hundred years (AD 1000–1100) prior to contact, with some subsequent decline. Populations at contact, then, would have been lower than their peak. The northern curve begins rising at 4000 BC, stabilizing between 2500 and 1200 BC when it rises again, reaching its apogee at AD 1000 after which it declines. The southern curve begins rising sharply between 2500 and 1200 BC (during the Neoglacial), peaks at AD 1000, and then declines. It is possible that these differing patterns reflect the different effects of the Neoglacial, on the productivity of the northern and southern coasts. The period of apparent stability on the Northern Coast between 2500 and 1200 BC corresponds to the Neoglacial, with population growth occurring before and after that cool/moist period, while on the southern coast, populations appear to start growing most rapidly during the Neoglacial. Such correspondences need to viewed with care, but the correlations are intriguing. The use of radiocarbon dates in this way is also a matter of controversy, so even the curves themselves should be interpreted with caution.

A different approach to prehistoric population dynamics is to construct models or computer simulations of how ancient populations might grow based on our knowledge of modern hunter-gatherers. Dale Croes and Steven Hackenberger, as part of Croes' long-term project at Hoko River on the Olympic Peninsula, generated a curve suggesting steady population growth over the past 8,000 years. They assumed that populations on the Olympic Peninsula grew exponentially during the past 8,000 years, using an annual growth rate of 0.1 percent. They predict population growth in the region would have entered a phase of exponential growth between 2500 and 1800 BC, a prediction supported by Maschner and Ames' southern coast curve. Archaeologists have also estimated general patterns of population growth from increasing rates of shell-midden accumulation and site numbers. Based on surveys along the west coast of Vancouver Island, for example, archaeologists Jim Haggerty and Richard Inglis conclude that Nuu-chah-nulth population levels were much higher in the late prehistoric period than during the Early Modern period[17].

Demographic data, including information on disease, diet, health, activities and life span, can be gleaned from the analysis of human skeletons, though skeletons provide only a general picture.[18] All this information can be combined to develop a general picture of the ecology of the early people on the coast for the past 5,500 years, the period for which we have skeletal samples. Both tuberculosis and non-venereal syphilis were present on the coast before the beginning of the modern era. Of course, since all evidence for diseases is restricted to skeletal remains, it is impossible to know the full range of health problems that may have afflicted the coast's peoples. People also suffered from iron deficiency anemia, though in varying frequencies along the coast. This can be caused by a variety of factors, making it hard to pinpoint a single cause, but some form of diarrheal disease is often implicated.[19] Stature, which is generally sensitive to diet and health, remained quite stable for both men and women over the past 5,000 years, suggesting no drastic changes in nutrition and health during that time, at least at the timescales we can measure with archaeological data. This fact is actually quite important, given that major economic changes are sometimes accompanied by changes in height. For example, the introduction of agriculture in regions of the world caused a decline in health, reflected in shorter stature.[20] Some kinds of analyses, which might indicate food stress and food shortages, have not yet been undertaken, and so there is a gap in our data.

People suffered from rheumatoid arthritis, as well as arthritis caused by wear and tear on the body. The Northwest Coast is damp, and so aches and pains were probably common. With a diet composed to a large extent of sea life, they also probably suffered from a variety of internal parasites. People generally lived into their 30s, though some lived well into advanced middle age and beyond. It is likely that death rates were high in the first year of life. Females are generally underrepresented in burial populations so it is difficult to determine if there were significant differences in death rates for the sexes. As we will see in Chapter Eight, there is considerable evidence for violence.

In general, people on the coast appear to have been as healthy as most pre-modern humans, and healthier than some. Populations appear to have grown during the Holocene, though the population histories of the northern and southern coasts appear to have been different.

CHAPTER THREE

The First Inhabitants of the Northwest Coast

The peopling of the New World

One of the most important areas of research in Northwest Coast archaeology, and one with the greatest controversy, is the timing and route of the first human colonization of the New World. To address this problem we must travel north to Alaska and Siberia, the initial homelands of all Native American peoples. There is little doubt that all Native Americans are descendants of northeast Asian ancestors. This reasoning rests on two quite independent lines of evidence. The first is biological, the second logistical. It has been recognized for many years that modern Native peoples of both North and South America are biologically most similar to indigenous peoples of northeast Asia. These similarities include characteristics of their teeth, physiology, blood types, skin color, hair form, and many other traits. This points strongly to an ultimate origin of America's Native peoples in northeast Asia. The second is proximity. If one looks at a map of the world, the only place where the Americas and Eurasia are close together is the Bering Strait, where Alaska and Siberia are less than 80 km (50 miles) apart. Modern Inupiag and Siberian Yupik peoples were known to boat across the Bering Strait or cross the winter ice pack on foot or dogsled. In the absence of large, ocean-going vessels, there is basically only one feasible route for entering North America.

During the peak of the last ice age northeast Asia and Alaska were connected by a broad land mass called the Bering Land Bridge.[1] This land bridge existed because so much of the earth's water was frozen in the great ice sheets that sea levels were over 100 m lower than they are today. Between 25,000 and 10,000 years ago, northeast Asia, the Bering Land Bridge, and Alaska shared many environmental characteristics. These included a common mammalian fauna of large mammals, a common flora composed of broad grasslands, wind-swept dunes, and tundra, and a common climate with cold, dry winters and somewhat warmer summers.[2] The recognition that many aspects of the modern flora and fauna were present on both sides of the Bering Sea as a remnant of the ice-age landscape led Hultein to name this region Beringia.[3]

Beringia extends from approximately the Lena River Valley in Siberia to the Yukon Territory in Canada.[4] It is through Beringia that small groups of large mammal hunters, slowly expanding their hunting territories, eventually colonized North and South America. On this archaeologists generally agree, but this is where the agreement stops. There are three broad areas of disagreement in explaining the peopling of the New World. The first is actually the domain of paleoecologists but is critical to understanding human history: what was Beringia like? The second and third are archaeological: when did the first humans colonize Beringia and ultimately North and South America, and in turn, by what route was this accomplished?

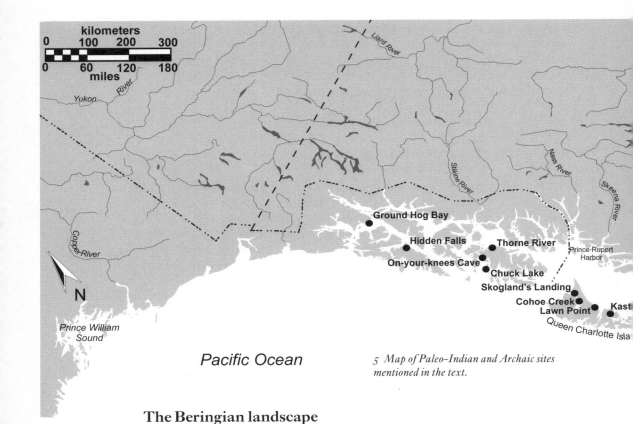

5 *Map of Paleo-Indian and Archaic sites mentioned in the text.*

The Beringian landscape

The Beringian landscape was very different from what it is today. Broad, windswept valleys, glaciated mountains, sparse vegetation, and less moisture, created a rather forbidding landmass. This landmass supported herds of now-extinct species of mammoth, bison, and horse, and more modern versions of caribou, musk ox, elk, and saiga antelope. These grazers supported in turn a number of formidable carnivores including the giant short-faced bear, the saber-tooth cat, and a large species of lion.

The presence of mammal species that require grassland vegetation has led Dale Guthrie to argue that, while cold and dry, there must have been broad areas of dense vegetation to support herds of mammoth, horse, and bison.[5] Further, nearly all of the ice-age fauna have teeth that indicate an adaptation to grasses and sedges; they could not have been supported by a modern flora of mosses and lichens. Guthrie has also demonstrated that the landscape must have been subject to intense and continuous winds, especially in winter. He makes this argument based on the anatomy of horse and bison, which do not have the ability to forage through deep snow cover. They need landscapes with strong winds that remove the winter snows, exposing the dry grasses beneath. Guthrie applied the term "mammoth steppe" to characterize this landscape.

In contrast, Paul Colinvaux has offered a counter-argument based on the analysis of pollen in lake sediments dating to the last ice age. He found that the amount of pollen recovered in these sediments is so low that the Beringian landscape during the

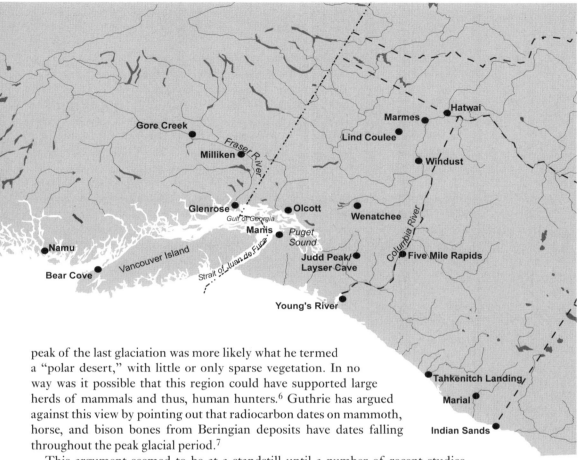

peak of the last glaciation was more likely what he termed
a "polar desert," with little or only sparse vegetation. In no
way was it possible that this region could have supported large
herds of mammals and thus, human hunters.[6] Guthrie has argued
against this view by pointing out that radiocarbon dates on mammoth,
horse, and bison bones from Beringian deposits have dates falling
throughout the peak glacial period.[7]

This argument seemed to be at a standstill until a number of recent studies
resulted in a spectacular suite of new finds. The first was the discovery of a 1,000 sq.
km preserved patch of Beringian vegetation dating to just over 17,000 years ago – the
peak of the last ice age. The plants were preserved under a thick ash fall from a volcanic eruption.[8] Investigations of the plants found grasses, sedges, mosses, and many
other varieties in a nearly continuous cover, as was predicted by Guthrie. But this
vegetation had a thin root mat with no soil formation, demonstrating that there was
little long-term stability in plant cover, a finding supporting some of the arguments
of Colinvaux. This mixture of continuous but thin vegetation supporting herds of
large mammals is one that seems plausible and realistic with the available data.

Perhaps the most surprising findings of recent research are in the nature of the
end of the ice age. Scott Elias has studied beetle remains from sediment cores drilled
in the Bering Sea dating to Beringian times. These sediments would have been part
of the land bridge before the large ice sheets melted. He has found that the beetles,
which are very sensitive to changes in climate, demonstrate that by 12,900 BC the
Beringian climate was rapidly changing. Through the study of beetles as well as vegetation, it appears that Beringia after 12,900 BC was much warmer than it is today. It
is estimated that the temperature was perhaps 5° C warmer by 11,600 BC and nearly
6–10° C warmer by 9000 BC. These same cores have also shown that the Bering Land

Bridge was present until nearly 9000 BC, much later than anyone had argued previously,[9] extending the possible timing of later migrations to the New World into the Holocene.

In contrast to arguments over the land bridge's environment, Powers, Hoffecker, and Goebel[10] have recently argued that the ultimate limiting factor to the colonization of Beringia is firewood for heat. From 25,000 to approximately 15,000 years ago, a period termed by paleoecologists as the "herb zone," grasses, sage, and sedges dominated the vegetation of Beringia. When the climate began to warm after 15,000 years ago, trees, primarily dwarf birch, began to colonize Beringia. It is at this time that we have the first convincing evidence of humans in Alaska – the first time when there would have been wood for fires for warmth and cooking.

Thus, the landscape into which early Native Americans first migrated was very different from what it is today. Prior to 12,900 BC it was much colder, windswept, and dry. Herds of large ice-age mammals moved between patches of thin vegetation. After that date the climate was rapidly warming and grasslands became more extensive, causing soils to form throughout Beringia. It appears that it was at this time, after approximately 15,000 years ago, that the first humans entered onto the Bering Land Bridge.

Of course, to people the Americas, it was not enough just to cross the land bridge; one had to get south of the ice sheets. Under full glacial conditions, North America supported two large glacial systems as we saw in Chapter Two: the Laurentide, and the Cordilleran. Between 19,000 and 15,000 years ago, the Laurentide and Cordilleran ice sheets may have met along a glacial front running east of the Canadian Rockies, roughly south from what is now Edmonton to Calgary, Alberta. As the glaciers began to retreat, an ice-free corridor was created, opening a passage between interior Alaska and the rest of North America. It is through this corridor that most scholars believe the remainder of North America was colonized.

Again, there is debate over the nature of this corridor, how wide it usually was, and what it was like. It seems quite unlikely that the first hunter-gatherers camping near the northern terminus of the corridor knew that a thousand miles to the south was a vast continent, empty of humans, but rich in everything else. Knut Fladmark has recently painted a quite depressing picture of the corridor, arguing that it was a wasteland of bogs, ice, and rock with little or no vegetation or mammals and thousands of feet of ice on either side.[11] But it has recently been shown that the corridor was probably quite wide by 14,300 BC. Interestingly, Yesner and Holmes have found large numbers of swan bones at the Broken Mammoth site in the eastern interior of Alaska dating to 11,200 BC.[12] If swans were migrating up the ice-free corridor, it must have had large marshes and grasslands by that time.

Fladmark offers an alternative route.[13] He argues that people entered the Americas by moving down along the west coast. The west coast was never completely glaciated, in fact some rather large areas, such as the northern portions of Graham Island in the Queen Charlotte Islands and some of the Alexander Archipelago, may never have been glaciated or were only briefly covered in ice. He suggests that people living along the southern edge of Beringia, along what are now the Aleutian Islands, could have moved gradually south, occupying the coasts of Alaska and British Columbia. Eventually, as they spread south, they would have moved south of the main glacial mass along the coast of Washington State. The Columbia River would have provided the first feasible route into the continent.

More support for Fladmark's route has recently come to light. One of the criticisms of Fladmark's theory has been that it was thought that the entire Gulf of Alaska was a shoreline of solid ice – how could humans travel and survive thousands of miles over the open North Pacific with nowhere to land? But new data indicate that portions of the Gulf of Alaska were deglaciated by 14,000 years ago[14] and most of it before 12,000 years ago.[15] Importantly, the North Pacific shoreline would probably have had deposits of driftwood that floated northward from the more temperate latitudes, providing firewood. In reality, both theories are feasible but neither are directly supported by the archaeological data.

The earliest known site in the Americas is Monte Verde, in southern Chile. The site dates to about 12,000–12,500 BC. There are other sites, in both North and South America, which may be older, but only Monte Verde is widely accepted by archaeologists as a site of this age. People must have crossed Beringia early enough to have been present at the southern end of South America by then.

The archaeology of Beringia

The story of the human colonization of Beringia and the New World ultimately begins in Siberia. Archaeology in Siberia has received a considerable amount of attention and is reasonably well known.

Two different artifact-manufacturing techniques provide the most important baseline for understanding the archaeology of eastern Siberia and far northeast Asia, and will in turn provide an organizing principle for North America. These techniques are simply divided into one based on the production of bifacial projectiles with no production of microblades (tiny blades most likely inset into the sides of bone or antler projectile points), the other based on the production of microblades and occasional bifacial knives. To archaeologists these are radically different means for producing stone tools.

Along the banks of the Lena and Aldan Rivers, and in many other areas of southern and interior eastern Siberia, Yuri Mochanov and his colleagues have documented dozens of late Wisconsin archaeological sites. While a few may date as early as 30,000 years ago,[16] the reliably dated sites are after 18,000 years ago.[17] These sites have tool assemblages composed of microblades, wedge-shaped microblade cores, burins, a small number of bifacial knives, and many flake tools. This complex of tools is what Mochanov has termed the Dyuktai Complex, based on his initial findings at Dyuktai Cave. The Dyuktai Complex has grown to include all the microblade sites in this part of the world. These artifacts have a very "Upper Paleolithic" character and seem to be the eastern extension of the classic Late Pleistocene adaptations of Europe and Central Asia.

At sites such as Ust' Mil and Ikhine 2, quantities of mammoth, horse, and bison are associated with dates perhaps as old as 25,000 to 30,000 years. More substantial and better-dated occupations occur after 18,000 years ago at Verkhne Troitskaya and a number of other sites along the Aldan River and on adjacent river systems.[18] All these sites appear to be hunting camps of peoples subsisting on large, ice-age fauna. The landscape at this time, although west of Beringia, may have been much like the "mammoth steppe" proposed by Guthrie. There are no known archeological sites anywhere near the Bering Land Bridge at this time.

By 13,700 BC there were two different artifact traditions in northeast Asia. The large river valleys of central Siberia continued to be occupied by peoples we associate with the Dyuktai Complex, while further east, along and near the western side of the Bering Land Bridge, a scatter of archaeological sites present a rather different picture.

At a number of sites along the shores of Ushki Lake on the east side of the Kamchatka Peninsula, Nikolai Dikov has found artifact assemblages consisting of small, stemmed projectiles, bifacial knives, stone and ivory beads, and substantial house floors dating to over 13,000 BC.[19] These projectiles have no known source and are only similar to artifacts of the Columbia River and southern Plateau region a few thousand years later (see below). The early Ushki Lake house floors are covered with burned salmon remains and there is evidence of large mammal hunting and domestic dogs.

Further north and on the Chuckchi Peninsula, a number of other sites with similar artifact assemblages, including items of adornment as at Ushki Lake, have been found that seem to be similar to the early Ushki materials. Since the interior of eastern Siberia is dominated by the Dyuktai Complex at this same time, it is possible that the Ushki Complex had its origins further south along the shores of eastern Asia.

By 9800 BC, the Ushki Complex in far northeast Asia had been replaced by the Dyuktai Complex. This transition is never more clear than at Ushki Lake where there are a number of Dyuktai Complex house floors stratigraphically above the Ushki Complex houses. This transition appears to have occurred throughout the region and is seen as a migration of peoples eastward out of the interior and onto the Bering Land Bridge.

While the Siberian data are still open to much discussion and the story is less than clear, the early archaeology of Alaska and greater eastern Beringia is even more confusing. The earliest archaeological sites in Alaska are generally associated with the Nenana Complex. Based on a number of sites in the Nenana River Valley on the north side of the Alaska Range, the Nenana Complex is composed of small bifacial projectiles, bifacial knives and scrapers, retouched flakes, and a number of other artifact categories.[20] Missing is any demonstrated use of microblades. At sites such as Dry Creek Component I and Walker Road, dates of around 11,400 BC have been obtained from thin habitation surfaces and small hearths. Because of the poor preservation, little is known of subsistence in the Nenana Valley at this time but at the Mead and Broken Mammoth sites 200 km (125 miles) to the east, there is evidence of elk, bison, caribou, swan, and "salmonoids." Both of these sites have similar assemblages to the Nenana Complex and date to the same time period.[21] Until recently, it was thought that there were no microblade assemblages in Alaska at this time, but a re-evaluation of the lower levels at Bluefish Cave in the Yukon Territory,[22] and the finding of microblades dating to 11,100 BC at the Swan Point Site in eastern Alaska,[23] have muddied this view.

In general, microblade assemblages do not become the dominant technology in Alaska until after 9800 BC. Termed the Denali Complex by Frederick West,[24] these materials are virtually identical to the Dyuktai Complex. Denali Complex artifacts are found throughout the interior stratigraphically above Nenana Complex deposits, along the shores of the North Pacific, on salmon-producing streams of the southern Bering Sea, and north to the arctic. Little is known of Denali Complex subsistence or behavior, although nearly every site appears to be a rather short-term-use hunting camp.

Contemporaneous with the Denali Complex are a few archaeological sites that appear to have a more Paleoindian-looking assemblage. This is seen primarily in the form of the projectiles, which are either long lanceolates as found by Robert Ackerman in the Kuskoquim Hills[25] or in the form of short and wide dart points found at the Mesa Site in the Brooks Range,[26] which look more like projectiles from the American Plains than from Alaska.

Migration

These findings allow an interesting story to be told about the initial colonization of Beringia and the New World, one that is based as much on conjecture as on actual data. But the argument is becoming more complete every year. We see three different migrations for the peopling of the New World.

We might argue for an early coastal migration from three lines of evidence. The first is that it now appears that a good portion of the North Pacific shoreline was deglaciated by 15,000 to 16,000 years ago. If this is the case, then these shorelines would have been the only source of firewood in Beringia prior to the expansion of dwarf birch into the region. Since heat was truly the only limiting factor, this was the first time humans would have at least been presented with the opportunity to cross the land bridge.

The second line of evidence is the presence of archaeological sites such as Ushki Lake on the western side of Beringia at this time. There are also numerous similar sites somewhat further south in northern Japan, Korea, and the Russian Far East. This may have been the source for both Ushki and any early migrants onto the Bering Land Bridge.

The last line of evidence is based on Monte Verde (see above). We have already argued that late ice-age shorelines are now long flooded by rising sea levels and thus, any evidence of an early coastal migration will be difficult to find. But the rockshelters and caves of southeast Alaska, the Columbia River basin, and elsewhere along the Northwest Coast, may eventually have evidence of such a migration. On high terraces of the southern California coast there may be sites dating to this age but stratigraphy is poor in this region. We would expect that since this early expansion out of Beringia is visible in South America but not, as yet, in North America, the early inhabitants of the New World stayed near the ice-age coast, leaving little impact on the rest of North America and contributing little to its archaeology.

A second migration out of Beringia is perhaps better documented and requires less discussion. The Nenana Complex is present in interior Alaska, quite near the entrance to the ice-free corridor, between 11,300 BC and 10,900 BC. The Clovis culture appears at the far end of the ice-free corridor by 10,800 BC. With the transition from bison and elk hunting to mammoth and bison hunting, we see a transition from small projectiles to Clovis points. Goebel has argued that there are few differences between Clovis artifact assemblages and those of the Nenana Complex except for the projectiles, and we basically agree with this assertion.[27] There is substantial paleoecological evidence that the corridor was wide and vegetated at this time. The presence of numerous swan bones at the Broken Mammoth site indicates that there was a vegetated terrestrial flyway between Alaska and more southerly regions.

Hoffecker, Powers, and Goebel have made a clear argument for a transition from the Nenana Complex to Clovis. They have also demonstrated that firewood must have played a significant role in the colonization of Beringia as a limiting factor. It is only after about 14,000 to 15,000 years ago that dwarf birch began to colonize the major Beringian river valleys, making an interior adaptation possible.

A third movement of peoples into Beringia seems to have occurred in the final centuries before the Bering Land Bridge was flooded. This is seen in the expansion of the Dyuktai Complex out of Siberia into Alaska after 9800 BC. This complex replaced the early Ushki technology in Kamchatka and the Nenana Complex in the Alaskan interior, where it is termed the Denali Complex. It then spread throughout eastern Beringia, ultimately being found everywhere in Alaska by 7650 BC, including the northern Northwest Coast. While there are a number of other artifact complexes in Alaska between 13,000 and 11,000 years ago (such as the later Paleoindian-like artifacts at the Mesa Site), none have the impact or regional distribution of the microblade sites of the Denali Complex. This complex does not spread further south through the interior, stretching into the Yukon Territory at its greatest extent.

For the Northwest Coast then, we have three possible sources of both archaeological finds and the people who produced them. The first is from an early and seemingly ephemeral movement of peoples down the coast after 16,000 years ago. The second, most likely related to the Clovis complex, would come from the east through the interior from the Great Plains and through the Plateau. The third would again be from the north, a late movement of peoples onto the Northwest Coast after 9800 BC.

The earliest inhabitants

There are two sites in Cascadia that may be older than 12,500 BC: Wilson Butte Cave and Fort Rock Cave. However, both are open to serious doubt. Wilson Butte is in south-central Idaho, near Shoshone, Idaho. Excavated in the early 1960s by Ruth Gruhn, now of the University of Alberta,[28] it produced a radiocarbon date of 15,000 BC from its basal deposits. The artifacts associated with the date are nondescript and not characteristic of any particular time period. The possibility exists that the lower deposits at the rockshelter were mixed. It is also not clear that the dated charcoal was cultural in origin. Fort Rock Cave lies in south-central Oregon and was dug in the early 1950s by Luther Cressman.[29] Early radiocarbon dates predate 12,500 BC but the questions about Wilson Butte Cave can be asked of Fort Rock Cave. Thus, neither is considered tenable evidence of a migration into Cascadia before 12,500 BC.

In the early 1970s the late Carl Borden of the University of British Columbia argued that a complex of cobble tools that had been recovered on late-Pleistocene terraces of the Fraser River above Vancouver B.C. represented a pre-Clovis culture, which he dubbed the "Pasika Complex." However, cobble tools are widespread in Cascadia, and were used throughout the region's prehistory. Cobbles are often handy and can be quickly turned into a range of general purpose tools. None of Borden's Pasika Complex materials were recovered sealed in an indisputable late-Pleistocene context. Thus, there are no sites in Cascadia that are indisputably dated before about 11,000 BC.

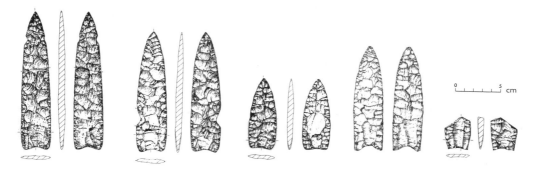

6 Typical Clovis points from southern Idaho.

Clovis: the second migration

The Clovis culture dates between 10,800 and 10,500 BC. Clovis represents the earliest widespread, non-controversial evidence of human occupation in North America south of Alaska. Clovis culture (so-named for Clovis, New Mexico, where the first materials assigned to Clovis were discovered and recognized) is characterized by large, exquisite bifaces and an extensive bone technology. Some of the bifaces are fluted. Most of the fluted objects were probably spear points and the flute was the means by which the points were hafted or attached to a shaft. Clovis stoneworking skills were among the finest in world history, and some of the bifaces are so thin that they would shatter on impact, indicating that they were clearly not intended for utilitarian activities.

Clovis materials are found throughout North America south of the glacial front. They are particularly common on the North American Plains, Midwest, and Eastern Woodlands, as well as southern Ontario, Canada. Clovis materials are rare in the Northwest, particularly west of the Coast-Cascade Range, but isolated Clovis points have been collected in the Puget Sound area and on the Oregon coast, as well as east of the Cascades. There is only one Clovis site in the entire region covered by this book.

The Richey-Roberts Clovis cache was discovered by a laborer installing buried irrigation pipes in an apple orchard near Wenatchee, Washington. The site was initially excavated by a volunteer crew of professional archaeologists from all over the Northwest and then subsequently by Robert Gramely, then of the Buffalo Museum of Buffalo, New York. The site appears to be a cache rather than an occupation site. A cache is a locality where objects were stored, hidden, or offered. In this case, the objects were probably in a pit. The bifaces are among the largest Clovis bifaces ever recovered; they are thin in cross-section, and occurred in pairs. The stone tools were accompanied by several bone shafts, probably foreshafts for darts. A similar cache of Clovis bifaces was recovered at the Anzic site in southern Montana, although there the materials were associated with a child's burial. There are no indications of a burial at Richey-Roberts.

Not directly in the area of study, the Dietz site is the only other Clovis site even near the Northwest Coast. Located in south-central Oregon, the site centers on a

(years)	General Northwest Coast Chronology	Southeast Alaska	Prince Rupert Harbor	Queen Charlotte Islands	Namu	Gulf of Georgia	Columbia Estuary
1800 / 1500 / 1000	Late Pacific	Late Phase	Prince Rupert I		Namu 6	Gulf of Georgia	Ilwaco 2
500 / 0				Graham Tradition			Ilwaco 1
500 / 1000	Middle Pacific	Middle Phase	Prince Rupert II		Namu 5	Marpole / Locarno Beach	
1500 / 2000 / 2500 / 3000	Early Pacific	Early Phase	Prince Rupert III	Transitional Complex	Namu 4	St. Mungo	Sea Island Phase
3500		Transitional Phase			Namu 3		
4000 / 4500 / 5000	Archaic			Moresby Tradition	Namu 2	Old Cordilleran Olcott	Youngs River Complex
5500 / 6000					Namu 1		
6500 / 7000 / 7500 / 8000		Paleoarctic		Intertidal Assemblages?			
8500 / 9000 / 9500 / 10000							
10500 / 11000 / 11500 / 12000	Paleoindian						
12500 / 13000 / 13500 / 14000							

7 *The chronology used in this book and other chronologies commonly used for regions of the Northwest Coast.*

dried lake bed or *playa*. The Clovis material was scattered along old beach lines associated with the ancient lake, which reached its maximum size at the end of the last glacial period.

Thus, the Northwest appears to have been lightly populated by Clovis peoples, in contrast to areas to the east, where the majority of Clovis sites are concentrated. The few scattered occurrences of Clovis points indicate that there was significant mobility over extremely long distances at this time but that the Northwest was either already occupied or the area did not have resources suitable to Clovis subsistence.

Finally, there is one locality on the coast that may be contemporaneous with Clovis. The Manis site is located south of Sequim (pronounced Squim), Washington on the Olympic Peninsula. The locality contains the bones of a mastodon dating to 10,800 BC, just before mastodons, mammoths, horses, camels, and a variety of other large mammals in North America became extinct. The mastodon remains lie along the edge of a kame terrace, a terrace formed along the flank of the glacier that extended some way out in the Strait of Juan de Fuca between the Olympic Peninsula and Vancouver Island. The locality was carefully excavated in the mid-1970s under the direction of Carl Gustafsen of Washington State University, but no indisputable artifacts were recovered in association with the elephant. However, Gustafsen and his co-workers found a small piece of bone protruding from one of the animal's ribs. When X-rayed they observed what they concluded to be a bone point which had partially penetrated the rib, which had then healed around the point. If the piece of bone is a bone point, and that remains to be confirmed, then Manis is the earliest, albeit indirect evidence for human occupation of the coast.

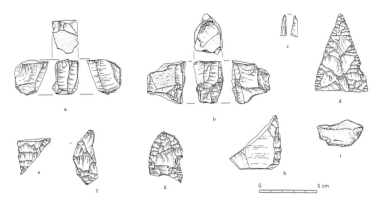

8 Artifacts from the Ground Hog Bay II site in southeast Alaska: (a, b) microblade cores; (c) angle burin on an obsidian microblade; (d) tip of knife or projectile; (e) fragments of obsidian bifaces; (g) chert biface; (h) retouched flake; (i) side-scraper.

The Archaic period (10,500 BC to 4400 BC)

This period on the Northwest Coast is not at all well known. It has been variously termed the "Early Boreal," "Paleo-Arctic," "Palaeomarine," "Microblade Tradition," and "Early Coast Microblade Complex." We choose to use the term Archaic as it comfortably represents the time period between the late Pleistocene and the rise of more permanent settlement, resource intensification, and changes in social organization.

Excavated Archaic sites are few and far between. This is in part due to fluctuating or rising sea levels all along the coast as well as subsequent vegetation changes. Many areas that were dry coastal lowlands at some point during this period are now under water. Other areas where sea levels may have been higher than at present (so sites are well above modern sea levels) are covered in dense rainforest vegetation, making site discovery virtually impossible.

Northern Northwest Coast

The earliest indisputable site on the northern coast, indeed anywhere on the coast, is Ground Hog Bay 2, which is located on the southern end of the Chilkat Peninsula, overlooking Icy Strait in southeast Alaska.[30] The site is on a marine terrace some

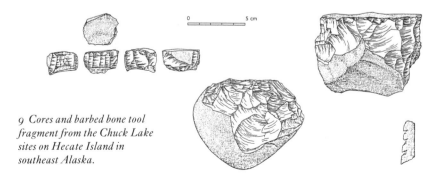

9 Cores and barbed bone tool fragment from the Chuck Lake sites on Hecate Island in southeast Alaska.

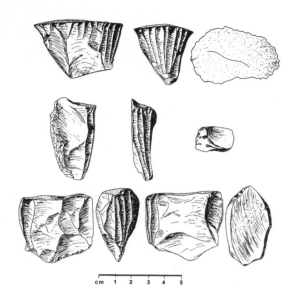

10 Microblade cores from the Queen Charlotte Islands.

10 to 15 m (33–50 ft) above present sea levels. Ackerman recovered two assemblages (Ground Hog Bay II and III) of artifacts mixed with beach gravels resting on glacial till. Two radiocarbon dates spanning the period between 9000 BC and 7800 BC are thought to date Ground Hog Bay III, the lower assemblage. This assemblage contains few artifacts but includes two obsidian biface fragments. Ground Hog Bay II dates between 7500 and 3500 BC based on an array of radiocarbon dates. This assemblage contains microblades, microblade cores, and blade cores as well as a variety of other stone tools including two additional biface fragments. The presence of microblades is a distinctive attribute of Archaic period assemblages on the northern Northwest Coast (see discussion below).

Hidden Falls is another major Archaic period site in southeast Alaska. The site lies on the eastern coast of Baranof Island, overlooking Chatham Strait. Component I at Hidden Falls was recovered from a buried soil, and is dated by its excavator Stanley Davis to about 6000 BC. Hidden Falls I contains microblades and microblade cores, as well as cobble tools and other, unifacial worked stone tools.[31] It lacks bifaces.

Thorne River dates to approximately 7000 BC and produced a number of microblades and microblade cores in the same styles as those found at Ground Hog Bay and Hidden Falls. The site is located on the banks of the Thorne River on the east side of Prince of Wales Island. Here Chuck Holmes, Dave McMahan, and Joan Dale found hundreds of microblades, many of obsidian.[32] No faunal remains were preserved.

Chuck Lake is the fourth major early Holocene site in southeast Alaska. It too is a microblade site, and dates to about 6500 BC. Robert Ackerman quickly recognized the importance of the site. Because it is located on a limestone formation, which results in better organic preservation, its deposits contain faunal remains. The shells of intertidal mollusca such as *Saxidomus giganteus* (Smooth Washington clam), *Protothaca stamina* (Pacific little neck clam) and *Mytilus edilus* (edible, blue or bay mussel) dominate the molluscans present, while both salmonid and non-salmonid fish such as halibut are present in the faunal assemblage. The identifiable mammalian fauna include rabbit, beaver, deer (caribou?), sea lion and seal. Except for the rabbit, these are represented only by teeth, though sea mammal longbone shafts were collected, as were longbone shafts of "medium" and "large" mammals.[32]

11 (right) Illustration of the manufacture and use of microblades. The core is held between the individual's knees in an anvil and struck off using a stone hammer and a bone or antler punch. Examples of hafted microblades are included at the bottom of the drawing.

The major early sites in northern British Columbia are on the Queen Charlotte Islands, but the data are sketchy. Philip Hobler collected pebble tools from the intertidal zone on the eastern side of Moresby Island, and believes that they eroded from sites occupied when the sea was lower than at present around the Queen Charlotte Islands, i.e before 7000 BC.[34] However these tools, mainly cobble tools and large flakes, could have been dropped in the intertidal zone much more recently, when sea levels assumed their modern elevation.[35]

12 (below) Experimentally hafted microblades based on forms found at the Namu site.

Centimetres

Knut Fladmark has investigated a number of Queen Charlotte Island sites on beach lines 10 to 15 m (33–50 ft) above their present positions.[36] These sites include Kasta and Lawn Point and date between *c.* 6500 and 3300 BC, when sea levels in the area began to fall. These sites produced microblades and unifacially flaked tools. No bifaces have been recovered. The tools are associated with small hearths on now buried beaches. Gessler has reported a radiocarbon date of 9000 BC from deposits below Kiusta, an historic Haida town on Moresby Island. However, no additional data have been forthcoming.

There are no recognized early Holocene sites on the northern British Columbia mainland. There may, nevertheless, be some that have not been recognized as such. Several sites in Prince Rupert Harbor have deposits that extend as much as a meter below modern seal levels, suggesting that occupation began when sea levels were below their modern levels, which occurred in this area between *c.* 6500 and 4000 BC. Gary Coupland reports a small microblade component at the Paul Mason site in Kitselas Canyon. This is the only such component currently known for the northern British Columbia mainland. Coupland assigns this material to his Bornite Phase, which actually dates to *c.* 3850 to 3000 BC, falling into the Pacific period. In addition to the microblades, cobble tools are a major member of the Bornite assemblage at the Paul Mason site in Kitselas Canyon.[37]

Microblade technology, coupled with an almost complete lack of bifaces, is the defining trait of the early Holocene on the northern Northwest Coast. As their name implies, microblades are small. The largest ones from Kasta and Lawn Point are under 35 mm (1 ²/₅ in) long. As discussed above, microblade technology is widespread at this time in northwest North America, particularly in Alaska. Microblade

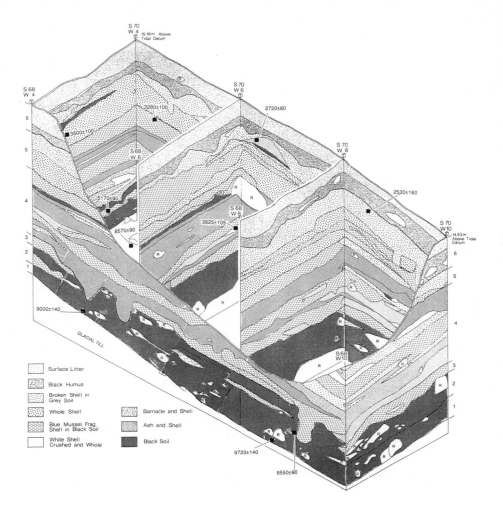

13 Three-dimensional view of the Rivermouth trench at Namu. The drawing shows the stratigraphy in all four walls of three excavation units. It also shows the differences between shell deposits in Archaic and Pacific period sites (note the small, discontinuous shell lenses in the "black soil" at the bottom of the profile, in contrast with the massive shell deposits above).

technology disappears from the coast after *c*. 4000 BC, at least it disappears as the dominant method of producing stone-cutting tools.

But there are exceptions. For example, on the Queen Charlotte Islands a stone-working technique called bi-polar reduction resulted in microblade-like artifacts lasting for another 3,000 years. This same technique was used in northwest Oregon and elsewhere until contact with Europeans. On the mainland coast of central southeast Alaska a number of sites have recently been described by Mark McCallum and Peter Bowers. These sites date between 1250 BC and AD 1 and have a strong technological emphasis on microblades and microblade cores.[38] As yet, the relationship between these late microblade assemblages and those of the earlier Archaic are not known. These sites will be discussed in the next chapter.

Fladmark argues that the microblades on the Queen Charlotte Islands were hafted into bone and antler handles and used as cutting and piercing tools, while it is clear from the Beringian data that they were mounted as side-blades on bone and ivory projectiles.[39] Both are quite likely. Microblade technology basically is a set of related methods to produce the maximum number of cutting edges from small pieces of raw material, such as small cobbles or pebbles. It is also a method of producing sharp-edged flakes that can easily be hafted (and removed when dulled) or mounted on organic (wood, bone, antler) tools. However, the microblades themselves tell us almost nothing about other aspects of life at this time.

Central coast

The major early Holocene site on the central coast is Namu, located on the British Columbia mainland, on Fitzhugh Sound at the mouth of the Namu River.[40] The earlier Holocene at Namu is split into Periods 1 (9000–5000 BC), and 2 (5000–3000 BC). According to Carlson, most Period 1 artifacts are debris from working cobbles, but some finished tools are present. Microblade technology appears at the site about halfway through the period, or around 7000 BC. Bone tools are present in Period 2 deposits (as a result of changed preservation conditions). The stone tools present in Period 1 persist through Period 2, including the microblades. Period 2 deposits contain "isolated lenses of shellfish" in the lowest levels. They also contain a wide array of fish, mammals, and birds. Cannon suggests that the range of fish present is "evidence of a well-developed early fishing technology."[41] The fish species are dominated by salmon, though herring, dogfish, and rockfish are also present in relatively significant numbers. Deer and harbor seals are the dominant mammals in the assemblage while porpoises and mustelids are present in important numbers. Namu is the most southerly of the early coastal microblade sites, though as we will see below, there are microblade sites contemporary with Namu at the base of Mt St Helens, in southern Washington State.

Bear Cove, on the northeast corner of Vancouver Island, is the other major Archaic period site on the central coast. Catherine Carlson[42] excavated the site in the late 1970s. Component 1 at Bear Cove is dated by a single radiocarbon date of 6500 BC near the base of the deposits. The Component 1 deposits are overlaid with a shell midden. Two dates from the base of that midden span a period *c*. 3340–2550 BC. Artifacts are primarily flakes and tools made from beach cobbles. One complete leaf-shaped biface was found, along with several fragments. The component also produced faunal remains, including rockfish, salmon, and a variety of other species of fish. Of the mammal bones, 78 percent are sea mammals, and 80 percent of the sea-mammal bones are those of dolphins and porpoises. Put another way, about two-thirds of all recovered mammal bones are those of dolphins and porpoises. These faunal materials were recovered from the top 36 cm (14 in) of the deposits containing the component. Therefore they may significantly post-date 6500 BC.

Bear Cove and Namu differ in that Namu contains microblades, but they have in common use of pebbles and cobbles for making other types of stone tools. This practice is also present in the Archaic period sites on the Queen Charlotte Islands.

South coast.

Glenrose Cannery is the major early site on the southern British Columbia coast. Glenrose is located on the Fraser River just south of the modern city of Vancouver,

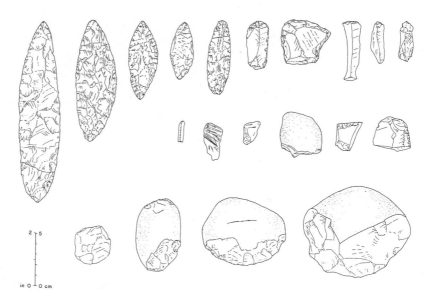

14 Early Archaic chipped stone artifacts from the Milliken site on the Fraser River. These cobble and leaf-shaped bifacial tools are common to assemblages on the southern Northwest Coast.

British Columbia. The site's excavator, R.G. Matson, calls the early component at Glenrose the "Old Cordilleran" component[43] (see discussion at the end of this chapter). This component is dated by a series of dates spanning a period between 6600 and 1600 BC. This latter date is clearly too young, and the 6600 BC date was derived from charcoal recovered a meter above the base of the deposits. Matson therefore dates this component between 7000 and 4300 BC. Artifacts are similar to those recovered at Bear Cove, and include large leaf-shaped bifaces, a variety of cobble and cobble-flake tools, and several antler wedges. The component lacks microblades. Faunal remains from the Old Cordilleran component include elk, deer, seal, salmon, sturgeon, flounder, eulachon, squawfish, and sticklebacks. There was also some collecting of edible mussels.

The canyon of the Fraser River is some 130 km (80 miles) above its mouth. During the early 1950s Carl Borden of the University of British Columbia excavated several sites in the vicinity of Yale, British Columbia in the Fraser River Canyon.[44] One of these is the Milliken site, which has an occupation contemporary with and quite similar to Glenrose Cannery, though it lacks organic remains. Borden inferred that it was a major, early fishing site because the locality was an historic Indian fishery.

There are far fewer known Archaic sites south of the international border, and virtually none on the present coastline. This may in part be due to sea level changes. On the Pacific coasts of Washington and Oregon, sea levels have risen over the past 12,000 years, so presumably most early sites are under water on the continental shelf. Some archaeologists, however, such as R. Lee Lyman, argue that the absence of early sites may reflect the ways in archaeologists have investigated the coast – they have focused on shell middens, virtually all of which post-date 2500 BC on this stretch of coastline.[45] The Washington-Oregon coast has also undergone significant

14 (*above*) *Four men of Masset, 1881.*
MacDonald (1983) identifies the man second
from the left as K!oda'i (translates as Beak) or
"Dr. Kude, as he was known to Europeans."
He was the most famous shaman of Masset of
this period. The man on the right is chief named
Xa'na, who was chief of Grizzly Bear house
(MacDonald 1983). The dance clappers on
their kilts are puffin beaks.

People

15 (*right*) *Elderly Haida woman with labret,*
or lip plug in 1881. Labrets were worn by
during the Early Modern period on the
northern Northwest Coast by free women, the
larger the labret the higher the her status. None
of the young women in Plate 33 (in 1904) are
wearing labrets, or show evidence of ever
having worn them.

16 (above) Chilkat Blanket, Tlingit, late 19th century. Chilkat blankets were woven by Chilkat Tlingit, and were highly prized along the entire length of the Northwest Coast as part of the regalia of high status individuals.

17 (below) Haida box, 1864. This is an elaborately carved example of the storage boxes that played fundamental roles in Northwest Coast life.

Arts and Crafts

18 (above) Cowichan (Coast Salish) spindle whorl, 19th century. Goat and dog hair were spun and woven in blankets and robes.

19 (above) *Mountain Goat spoon, Tlingit, c. 1840 . Spoons like this were used the full length of the coast during feasts. Some of the very earliest examples of Northwest Coast art are spoons such as this.*

20 (left) *Mountain sheep horn bowl, Haida, 1882. Mountain sheep horn had to be acquired in the alpine areas of the Coast Range. This bowl is an excellent example of the northern style of Northwest Coast art in the late 1800s.*

21 *Tlingit spruce-root hat dating to c. 1850, seen from the top. The designs making up the animal's body are distributed around the brim, with the claws visible on the reader's left.*

22 *Steatite pipe bowl in the form of a bird.*

23 *Tlingit basket, before 1860. It illustrates the kinds of geometric designs commonly found on baskets.*

24 (below) *Woman making tule mat, near Stanwood, Washington 1878. Tule mats were used for a wide variety of purposes, including as floor coverings and room dividers.*

25 (left) Cheslake's village, Bella Bella (Nuxalk), illustrating linear village layout common to Northwest Coast villages. The houses are aligned in rows up the slope of the hill.

26 (right) Haida village of Yan, on the Queen Charlotte Islands, 1881. The house frames in the near foreground illustrate the traditional northern two-beam structure, while farther along the house row, there are European-style houses with ship lap cladding and square windows and doors. In front of those structures, fish traps are visible. The house in the near foreground is Killer whale house, owned by "Property-moving." The house frame has raven carvings on the front house posts. The crests on the pole in front of the house are from top down: a grizzly bear with four potlatch cylinders on its head, Bear mother holding a cub, grizzly bear eating a frog, and grizzly bear with protruding tongue (MacDonald 1983).

27 (above) Village at Nootka sound, illustrating shed roof house style of the central coast, as well as the common appearance of the front of central coast villages. Drawing by John Webber of the Cook expedition, 1778.

Villages and Towns

28 (right) The Haida town of Skidegate, showing its central and southeastern portions in 1881. Northwest coast villages either faced the beach, or paralleled it in a linear array of houses.

House Interiors

29 (*above*) *Interior of a house at Nootka Sound. This drawing shows many features common to the interiors of Northwest Coast houses all along the coast, with dried fish hanging from racks in the rafters, the storage boxes stacked against the walls, along with baskets and other items. Activities in the house focus around the hearth in the floor. The two large carvings at the back are probably house posts*

30 (*left*) *Clatsop house interior, in the 1830s. This structure has two levels of sleeping platforms along its interior walls, the upper one with decorated screens. Trade goods, including muskets, a powder horn and a metal kettle are present. The are no visible storage boxes. Chinookan houses commonly had cellars to house stores. The painting is a somewhat romantic portrayal of the house; note the drapery in the upper right hand corner.*

31 *This painting is of the interior of a Chinookan lodge by Paul Kane in 1848, when the*
Chinook had been in contact with Europeans since 1792. It gives a good sense of the
interior of one of these houses, based on Ames' excavations of three of them. The painting
seems to portray the household early in the day, before people are stirring. The decoration
and the carvings provide a glimpse of the Columbia River version of Northwest Coast
art. The carved face in the roof-support timber has been duplicated archaeologically in
the rear of two these structures. This painting shows the back of the dwelling, probably its
high status end. Chinookan society, like all Northwest Coast native societies, was
stratified, and these sleepers are probably the chiefly family of this house.

32 *Photograph of the interior of Monster House, Chief Wiah's house, in Masset on the Queen Charlotte Islands. The house was built in the early 1840s, and torn down around 1900. It was one of the largest houses known on the northern coast. Note how the volume and impressiveness of the house is increased by the excavated interior – ground level is the third level up. The hearth is the traditional central hearth of a northern house, and it is surrounded by European-style furniture. The square window in the rear center of the photograph was one of two European-style glazed windows in the front of the house. The overall architecture is Haida, including the planked flooring.*

tectonic movements (see box). On the western Olympic Peninsula, for example, Gary Wessen, an archaeologist working for the Makah tribe, found a shell midden dating between *c*. 2500 and 200 BC about 12–15 m (40–50 ft) above current sea levels, on a marine terrace. This indicates significant uplift. It is possible then that some early sites may exist on this coastline on tectonically raised terraces. Additionally, people did not live only on the coast. Archaic sites should exist in areas now close to the modern coastline, but which 11,000 or 9,000 years ago were some distance inland. Such sites however are probably under heavy vegetation.

ARCHAEOLOGY AND TECTONICS ON THE NORTHWEST COAST[1]

ORAL TRADITIONS all along the Northwest Coast contain accounts of catastrophes, including massive earthquakes and tsunamis (tidal waves). One Nuu-chah-nulth tradition describes the human cost of such an event: "They had practically no way or time to try and save themselves. I think it was at nighttime that the land shook ... I think a big wave smashed into the beach. The Pachena Bay people were lost ... But they ... who lived at Ma:lts'a:s , "House-Up-Against-The-Hill," the wave did not reach them because they were on high ground ... Because of that they came out alive. They did not drift out to sea with the others." Despite these accounts, it has only been within the last 15 years or so that archaeologists have begun to recognize the possibly profound effects that earthquakes may have had on the peoples of the coast and on its archaeological record.

In the late 1980s, Brian Atwater, a geologist with the United States Geological Survey, documented a series of what seismologists call "great" earthquakes (magnitudes greater than 8 on the Richter earthquake scale – the famous and destructive San Francisco earthquake of 1906 was 7.8) on the west coast. He had discovered six buried marsh soils in Willapa Bay on the Washington Coast. These soils represented land surfaces which had sunk, or subsided, below modern sea level during great earthquakes over the past 3000 years. Atwater and other researchers have since found evidence of both subsidence and uplift (the land rises) along many portions of the coast. Some of these events appear to have affected much of the Northwest Coast. The most recent occurred about 300 years ago, and has left evidence from Cape Mendecino, California, to Vancouver Island. This earthquake may also have caused a 2 to 3-meter-high tsunami that reached Japan (Japanese records document a tsunami striking their Pacific coast on January 27, 1700). There is also evidence for smaller and more local earthquakes. Puget Sound was struck by an earthquake between AD 950 and AD 1000 which caused the land to drop as much as a meter in some places, and to rise as much as 7 meters in others. The earthquake also caused a tsunami within Puget Sound.

One can easily imagine the horror of being sucked out to sea by a tsunami that had swept in without warning, shattering houses and throwing around canoes. But the effects of these great earthquakes extend well beyond the tragedies of individuals and even entire villages. Ian Hutchinson (a geologist) and Alan McMillan (an archaeologist) have shown that the six great earthquakes originally documented by Atwater caused villages to be repeatedly abandoned along the coast from the Olympic Peninsula to the northern coast of Vancouver Island. Their evidence also illustrates how the earthquakes reshaped the landscapes humans used. Some villages, such as Yuquot, were regularly reoccupied. Others, like Hoko Rover, may have been abandoned permanently after an earthquake , and some, including several in Hesquiat Harbor, were first occupied after an earthquake (and then sometimes permanently abandoned after the next). The earthquakes reshaped the intertidal zones, moved bays, blocked estuaries, destroyed marshes, and drowned suitable village locations. They have also significantly shaped the archaeological record.

Most archaeological sites along the Oregon coast date to within the last 2000 to 1500 years. Many archaeologists have thought this to be the result of post-glacial sea level rises over the past 12,000 years drowning the sites. However, as Rick Monor and Wendy Grant (an archaeologist and geologist respectively) point out, sea levels along the Oregon Coast were close to their modern level by 4000 years ago. Why then the gap in dates of sites between 4000 and 1500 years ago? They suggest it may be the result of local subsidence along the coast caused by these great earthquakes.

How often do the earthquakes occur? About once ever 400 years on average, though they have no clear pattern of when they occur. It has been about 300 years since the last one.

1 The information in this box derives from Atwater 1987, Atwater and Moore 1992, Atwater et al. 1995, Buchnam et al. 1992, Connolly 1995, Darienzo and Peterson 1995, Hutchinson and McMillan 1997, Minor and Grant 1996.

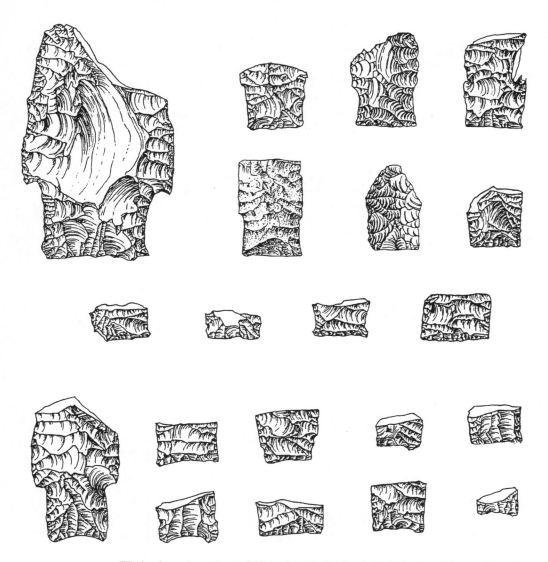

15 Windust lanceolate points and bifaces from the Paulina Lake site in central Oregon. These forms are widespread in western North America between 10350 BC and 7000 BC and mark the earliest Archaic technologies in eastern Cascadia.

The Cedar River Outlet Channel site in the foothills of the Cascades of western Washington illustrates some of the problems of such sites. The site (45K125) is located at the outlet of the Chester Morris Lake, and it and several sites were investigated as part of a flood control project in the mid-1980s. All sites are surface sites; there are no buried deposits. Time-sensitive projectile points appear to span the last 10,000 to 11,000 years. There are no faunal remains. Occupation of the area may have been particularly intense during the early part of the Archaic period, but it is impossible to confirm that assessment. Sites like 45K125 are found throughout the Puget Sound-southwest Washington area; they are always surface sites and thus

16 Cascade points from the Hatwai site in central Idaho. Cascade points are among the artifacts that identify the "Old Cordilleran Tradition" as first proposed by BR Butler. They are widespread in eastern Cascadia between 7000 BC and 3500 BC.

only limited information can be drawn from them.[46]

There are some relevant sites from the Lower Columbia River and adjacent uplands. Artifacts collected along the Young's River at the mouth of the Columbia by Rick Minor are similar to the large bifacial, leaf-shaped artifacts found elsewhere during this period. The Burnett Site, in the Portland Oregon metropolitan area, also has similar artifacts. It contains fragments of large stemmed points of the kind found east of the Cascades dating between 10,600 and 7650 BC. Two sites on the southern slopes of Mt St Helens also contain evidence of the Archaic period. Layser Cave and Judd Caves have assemblages dating between *c.* 5700 BC and 3850 BC. Both possess microblades and microblade cores as well as leaf-shaped bifaces and notched projectile points. Both sites contain salmon as well as deer and other terrestrial mammals. Cascadia Cave is located in the northern Cascade Mountains of northern Oregon, on the southern flank of Mt Hood. It has dates extending back to 6500 BC and contains a large number of leaf-shaped bifaces.[47]

But the crucial site for this period on or near the Columbia River is Five Mile Rapids located at the upstream end of the "Long Narrows" of the Columbia River, at the east end of the Columbia Gorge. The site was excavated in the mid-1950s by Luther Cressman of the University of Oregon. Before describing the site, it is important to provide a sense of its location.[48] The long narrows was a 65 km (40 mile) long gut through which the Columbia River passed (the narrows are now beneath the reservoir of the Dalles Dam). The narrowing of the river at this point made this the best place for a salmon fishery on the Columbia River. The Five Mile Rapids site overlooks the first big eddy above the narrows – the first good place for salmon to rest after leaving the narrows.

The deposits at Five Mile Rapids are quite thick. In the basal 2 m (6.5 ft), Cressman and his assistant recovered some 150,000 to 200,000 salmon vertebrae. The artifacts recovered are similar to those at sites downstream and upstream in the Columbia Plateau. Remarkably, despite the fish remains, the early occupation at Five Mile Rapids contains no specialized fishing equipment. These deposits are dated to *c.* 8000 to 7000 BC by radiocarbon dates from Cressman's project and by radiocarbon dates on the same deposits from a recent project which tested the base of Cressman's excavations. This project was directed by Virginia Butler of Portland State University.[49]

Only three sites on the Oregon coast, Neptune, Tahkenitch Landing and Indian Sands, have dates spanning the period from *c.* 7400 to 4000 BC. The artifacts recovered from these sites are not time sensitive (i.e. do not help us in dating the sites), or informative about economics. The exposures at all three are extremely limited. Tahkenitch Landing produced a small faunal assemblage discussed in Chapter Five.

Overview

People have been on the coast for at least 11,000 years. Further back in time, the historical record is cloudy, partially as a result of sea level changes, but also because of vegetation coverage and archaeological coverage. Lyman argues for the Oregon coast that archaeologists have not sought out and sampled geological deposits and landforms of the right age to locate early sites. One direction of future research on the coast urged by many workers is to do exactly that.

This chapter has stressed stone tools. That is in part because stone artifacts are usually all that are recovered from more remote periods of time. It is also because archaeologists use stylistic and technological differences in stone tools to date their deposits and to attempt to reconstruct the cultural boundaries and affiliations of ancient groups. Microblades and leaf-shaped bifaces have played particularly strong roles in this effort. In the late 1950s and early 1960s B. Robert Butler proposed that the geographic distribution of laurel-leaf-shaped bifaces, particularly a projectile point he dubbed the "Cascade Point" along the western mountains of North America, and down into northern South America, marked the geographic extent of a cultural tradition he called the "Old Cordilleran Culture."[50] His proposal was strongly criticized at the time, but was revived, on a more limited basis, as applying to the Northwest, by Frank Leonhardy and David Rice, researchers on the Columbia Plateau on the east side of the Cascades, who saw similarities between what they were finding along the Snake River in eastern Washington and the Old Cordilleran sites Butler studied along the Columbia in central Washington. The term "Old Cordilleran" was later adapted by Matson for the early occupation at Glenrose Cannery.[51]

Perhaps the most ambitious attempt to link archaeological stone tool styles to long-persisting cultural traditions and modern Native peoples on the coast is that by Roy Carlson of Simon Fraser University.[52] Carlson sees four cultural traditions in the material we have reviewed here: a microblade tradition in the north, and a pebble tool tradition, a stemmed point tradition, and the fluted point tradition to the south. He suggests that the pebble tool tradition represents the ancestors of the Coast Salish peoples of southern British Columbia, while the stemmed point tradition peoples were the ancestors of the present-day speakers of Sahaptin and Chinookan languages in the Columbia River drainage basin. Like many others, Carlson is unable to find any historical linkages between Clovis and later technological traditions in the region. He speculates that the appearance and spread of microblade technology may mark the migration into North America and subsequent spread of speakers of Na-Dene languages, a large phylum of languages that includes several language families. Among these are Athapascan or Na-Dene languages which occupy much of western Canada and interior Alaska. There is a general correspondence between the geographic distribution of microblades and Na-Dene languages in northwestern North America which has led many archaeologists to argue that the appearance of microblades marks the appearance of Na-Dene speakers. On the coast, while Tlingit is southeastern Alaska may be a Na-Dene language, Haida (spoken on the Queen Charlotte Islands) is probably not.

However, it is difficult, if not actually impossible, to link ancient material culture remains – archaeological data – to modern languages and their speakers. The on-going controversies over the origins – both when and where – and subsequent spread of Indo-European languages in Eurasia are excellent examples of the problems. Indo-European languages include virtually all the modern languages in Europe and many languages in a vast arc from southern Europe to India, and have been studied since the late 19th century. The archaeology of Europe is far better known than that of the Northwest Coast, yet there is no consensus on which archaeological cultures represent the first Indo-European speakers to enter Europe and there is no consensus whether that can even be established using archaeological data.

Much of this difficulty lies in a deeper difficulty for archaeologists, that is understanding the causes in variation in the forms or shapes of artifacts. This difficulty can be illustrated using microblades. Microblades are made from microblades cores, which are generally quite small. Microblades themselves can be mounted or hafted in a variety of ways to create cutting edges, cutting, slicing or piercing points or even shredding surfaces. For example, several microblades can be set end-to-end on the side of an antler handle to create a knife blade. When one microblade breaks or dulls it can be replaced, not the entire knife or even all of the stone blades. On the other hand, large blades can serve as well as can knife blades chipped from a single flake and hafted. Why use microblades? Microblade technology is an effective way to produce cutting edges where the raw material for stone tools is mainly small nodules or pebbles, is rare, or has to be transported long distances. It is also an effective way to make cutting edges and points when organic materials (bone, antler, and wood) are the primary raw materials in a technology. So the choice of using microblades may be the result of the size and distribution of nodules of stone suitable for making tools. In this sense, microblades indicate a particular utilitarian strategy which, under other circumstances, people might not use. If raw materials for stone tools were common, or large enough, people might decide not to make microblades. This discussion implies that ancient peoples knew a variety of stone toolmaking techniques and elected to use a particular one depending purely on practical circumstances.

On the other hand, people might have made use of microblade technology because that was their culturally preferred way of making stone tools. Again, they might know a variety of toolmaking techniques, but all things being equal, they would rather make microblades. A blade technology is radically different from one based on bifaces. When a biface is produced, material is removed until the final shape of the tool is reached, it is a *reductive* approach. This strategy reduces the amount of cutting edge present in the original raw material. Microblade technology is *additive*, as more blades are removed from the core, the amount of usable edge increases. These are very different ways to make stone tools.

For these reasons, we do not think connections can be made between specific modern groups and these very ancient technologies. We are also not at all convinced, for example, that what Carlson sees as four technological traditions are separate technological traditions. Except for its microblades, for example, Namu is very similar to non-microblade assemblage sites to the south. In another example, the

Paulina Lake site, in central Oregon, combines artifacts representing Carlson's stemmed point and cobble tool traditions in a single assemblage.[53] However, we agree with Carlson and others that the archaeological record of the Northwest Coast indicates long-term continuity in the coast's material culture from the earliest (post-Clovis) times onward, and that there is no archaeological evidence to indicate large-scale displacement and movements of peoples. A major question about this period concerns the degree to which these people depended upon marine and riverine resources, particularly salmon. We postpone this question until Chapter Five, where we focus on subsistence economy. However, it is unlikely, given the environmental difference between the southern and northern coasts around 6500 BC, that there is a single coast-wide answer. But the origins of maritime subsistence economies is important in the coast's archaeology and is often debated.

A.L. Kroeber, the great American anthropologist of the early 20th century, suggested that Northwest Coast cultures originated as peoples from the interior moved down the region's rivers, adapting first to riverine environments, then upon their arrival on the coast, to the coast's littoral habitats (shallow, near-shore and inter-tidal zone environments). Eventually, as people acquired the necessary skills and knowledge, they began to exploit the offshore and deep-water environments of the coast, i.e. they became maritime. Another equally old view is that maritime-adapted peoples, perhaps related to the ancestors of the Inuit, moved down the outer coast, bringing their maritime skills with them. A more recent version of this idea is that the earliest people along the coast, the migrants making use of the Fladmark route, had to have a maritime adaptation simply to survive. Most recently, Carlson has suggested that the historic maritime adaptation on the coast is as old as the first occupation of the coast, and it was coastal people who moved upstream, bringing their maritime skills with them, adjusting first to estuarine and riverine environments, and then making the shift to terrestrial hunting and gathering.

The evidence that we will review in Chapter Five suggests to us that the region's first people possessed a flexible technology and a set of skills that allowed them to exploit a wide range of environments, but particularly wet environments from lakes to sea shores. By the time the archaeological record opens and we can get a glimpse of the entire region of Cascadia, it is occupied by hunter-gatherers sharing the same food-getting equipment, at least in the south. We see no evidence of upstream or downstream movements. We suspect that the region's wet environments formed a continuum for its first occupants, who made use of intertidal zones, near-shore environments, and pothole lakes.

How can we characterize these early people along the coast? The reader should first remember that this lengthy period is marked by the post-glacial environmental changes. Sea levels, particularly before 6500 BC were changing, sometimes swiftly; the post-glacial warming and drying trend that peaked at 6500 BC was under way. Plant distributions were changing as a result of deglaciation, sea level changes and climatic changes. The coastline these early people knew is not the coast we know today.

CHAPTER FOUR

The Pacific and Modern Periods

Introduction

The Pacific period spans nearly 6,200 years, from 4400 BC to AD 1775, the approximate time of the coast's first smallpox epidemic. The period shows both great changes and profound continuities. It is during this period that the coast's peoples became complex hunter-gatherers, settled into large villages, became socially stratified, and developed their famous art style. These changes involved important innovations in technology, economy, and social organization; but they were also the results of people reworking and reorganizing ancient practices. Old tools were used in new ways; old resources exploited with new intensities; old design motifs presented in new forms and combinations. Some changes were swift, and probably clearly visible to the people of the time; other changes were much slower and likely invisible to the people they affected.

The period's continuities extend beyond material culture. All available archaeological, linguistic, and biological evidence indicates that there were no major influxes of people onto the coast over the past several millennia. For example, the body builds of people living on the coast have changed little, if at all, over the past 3,000 to 4,000 years,[1] and while Early and Middle Pacific populations on the northern coast did differ slightly in head form from historic Haida and Coast Tsimshian, these differences do not inevitably mean population changes since similar changes in head form have occurred worldwide. Linguistic data suggest some shifting of peoples along the coast, and expanding and contracting territories, but no major migrations during at least the last 3,000 years, with one or two exceptions, chief of which are indicated by the presence of Athapascan languages in northern California and Oregon.[2]

Archaeological evidence for the beginning of the Pacific period is seen in the region's subsistence economy and residential patterns. These changes are marked by the appearance of large shell middens and in the interior by the contemporary appearance of semi-subterranean pithouses in the interior of Cascadia.

Archaeologists use a variety of names for this period. We call it the Pacific period for several reasons. Developments on the coast during this period parallel similar ones elsewhere in Cascadia and farther south in parts of central and coastal California where the term Pacific for this time period was first used.[3] Our use of this term stresses our view that ultimately much of what we describe below reflects processes that affected large portions of western North America and the eastern North Pacific basin, far beyond the region defined as the Northwest Coast. The actual time periods discussed in this chapter reflect our views of the timing of crucial events and trends coast-wide. The succeeding chapters will examine those events and trends, as well as sites and localities that do not fit these apparent trends at all. Overall, these variations reflect the complexity of economic, social, and political change on the Northwest Coast.

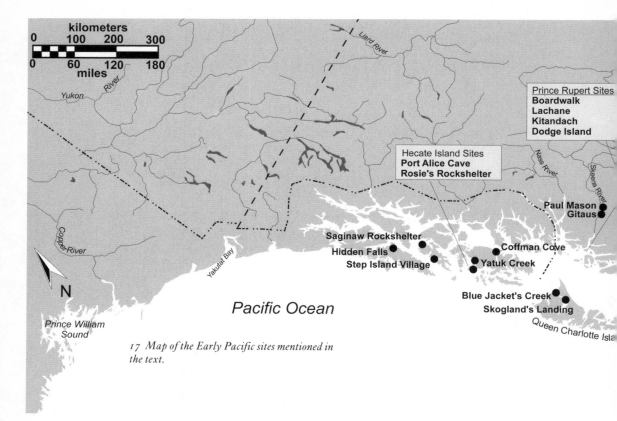

17 Map of the Early Pacific sites mentioned in the text.

Since most of the remainder of this book deals directly with the Pacific period, our purpose here is to outline the period's culture history, introduce the reader to key regions and sites, and to elucidate a number of important cultural developments.

Early Pacific period (4400 to 1800 BC)

About 5000 BC, the climate, which had been warmer and drier, became cooler and moister, summers in particular. Along much of the coast, sea levels were within 1 to 2 m (3–6 ft) of their modern positions by 4400 BC, and achieved their current positions by 3000 BC. Exceptions include the west coast of Vancouver Island, where sea levels were at their current position at the beginning of the period, rose several meters by 3000 BC, stabilized there for a time and then fell slowly over the next 2,000 to 3,000 years. Stabilizing sea levels permitted the development of productive littoral environments in most places. The lower courses of rivers draining into the ocean also stabilized as a consequence, encouraging the growth of ecologically productive estuarine and deltaic environments. It was also during this 3,000-year span that the coastal rainforest began to develop[4] (see Chapter Two).

Changes in climate and sea level helped usher in important changes in human subsistence and settlement patterns, including an expanded use of intertidal resources, such as marine mollusks, and a less mobile way of life. As people collected and ate shellfish, they dumped the shell debris in heaps or piles known as middens –

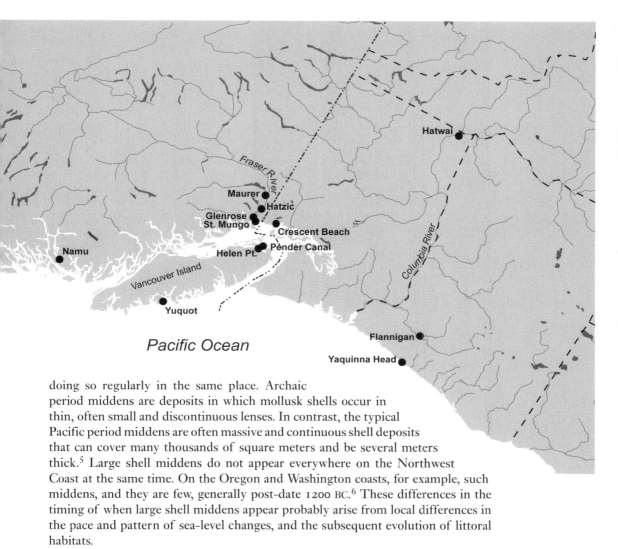

doing so regularly in the same place. Archaic
period middens are deposits in which mollusk shells occur in
thin, often small and discontinuous lenses. In contrast, the typical
Pacific period middens are often massive and continuous shell deposits
that can cover many thousands of square meters and be several meters
thick.[5] Large shell middens do not appear everywhere on the Northwest
Coast at the same time. On the Oregon and Washington coasts, for example, such
middens, and they are few, generally post-date 1200 BC.[6] These differences in the
timing of when large shell middens appear probably arise from local differences in
the pace and pattern of sea-level changes, and the subsequent evolution of littoral
habitats.

Increasing shellfish use was part of an overall expansion in the region's subsistence economy that we will discuss in Chapter Five. It is no coincidence that large
shell middens appear on the coast at the same time that pithouses are present in the
archaeological record elsewhere in Cascadia. This development is discussed in more
detail in Chapter Six, but we think it possible that many of these early middens were
first produced by pithouse settlements along the coast. Beyond these developments,
shell middens also have important implications for the nature of the coast's archaeological record during the Pacific period.

Pl. 9

Shell middens are alkaline in their chemistry because of the presence of thousands if not millions of mollusk shells. As a result, they are excellent environments
for the long-term preservation of bone and antler. Archaeologists thus have excellent data on some subsistence practices during the entire Pacific period that are
lacking for many Archaic sites. On the other hand, middens are not always good
environments for the preservation of plant materials, important not only in the diet

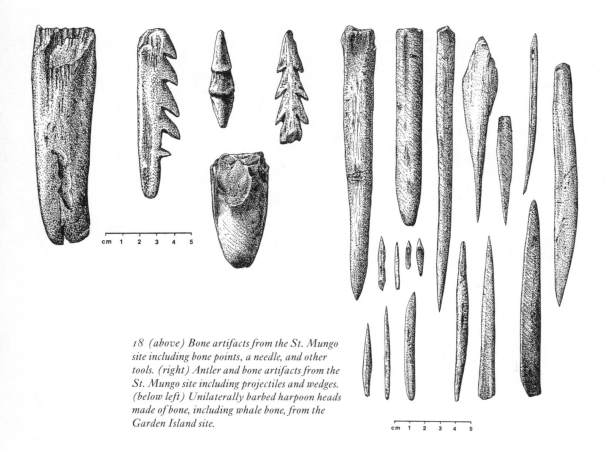

18 (above) Bone artifacts from the St. Mungo site including bone points, a needle, and other tools. (right) Antler and bone artifacts from the St. Mungo site including projectiles and wedges. (below left) Unilaterally barbed harpoon heads made of bone, including whale bone, from the Garden Island site.

of the region's people, but also as the foundation of their technology. As we have already commented, the coast's peoples were among the world's premier carpenters and wood carvers, yet wood rarely survives in middens. Wet sites – waterlogged sites in which decay is slowed or even almost stopped – help fill that gap. Wet sites are found all along the coast and are an increasingly important focus of archaeological research.

The presence of human burials in the middens is another significant event marking the beginning of the Early Pacific. Among the earliest burials are several multiple inhumations from Namu dating around 3400 BC. The appearance of these inhumations may reflect a new burial practice that developed simultaneously with the formation of shell middens, but it may also be the simple result of better preservation (the alkalinity of shell middens) thus allowing us to see an ancient burial practice in the archaeological record for the first time. There are cemeteries clearly present by 2500 BC if not by 3400 BC. The presence of cemeteries is likely to indicate some degree of sedentism, group territories, or both. These issues will be addressed in Chapter Six.

Generally, the basic framework of the coast's economy for the entire Pacific period develops during the Early Pacific, if not during the latter portions of the Archaic period. Overall, this appears to be a time of diversification in the food-getting economy. The major focus was on resources from the neritic zones, although

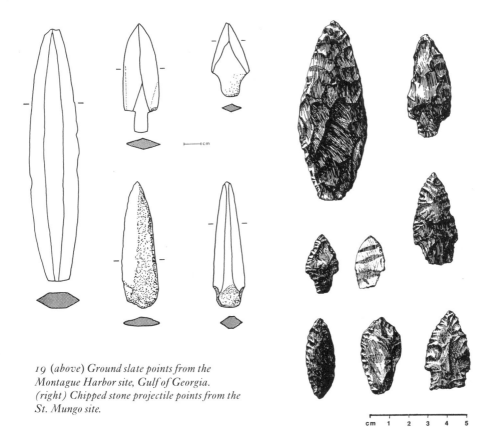

19 (above) Ground slate points from the Montague Harbor site, Gulf of Georgia. (right) Chipped stone projectile points from the St. Mungo site.

terrestrial and riverine habitats were also important. There is a significant debate, which we will discuss in Chapter Five, over whether food storage was a crucial part of the region's economy during Early Pacific period. In our view, it was not.

There were important technological changes during the Early Pacific, including the virtual disappearance of microblades from the northern coast, the introduction of a variety of bone and antler tools, and the widespread appearance of ground- or polished-stone tools. Despite the disappearance of microblades, chipped-stone tool technology continued in most parts of the coast.

Bone tools, of course, were in use throughout the Archaic period, but by the Early Pacific they begin to dominate coastal archaeological assemblages. In part, this is the result of the improved preservation conditions of shell middens, but many bone and antler tool types appear for the first time.[7] The proliferation of tool forms also includes some that were present in Archaic assemblages in small numbers, but which are far more common and varied during the Early Pacific. Among these are unilaterally and bilaterally barbed harpoon heads. Harpoons are essential for harvesting marine mammals and large fish in open water. Harpoon heads are attached to a foreshaft so that when a sea mammal is struck, the harpoon detaches and stays in the animal's body, hence the barbs. Harpoon heads are made with some means to attach a line, the other end of which is in the hands of the harpooner. The line prevents the harpooned animal from escaping, or, if it dies, from sinking. Harpoons are

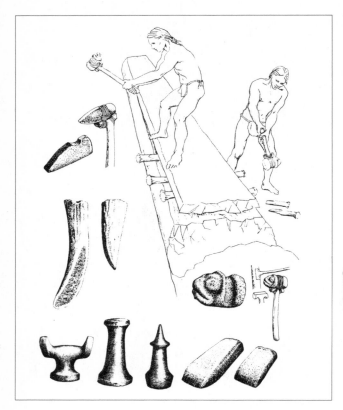

20 Drawing showing how planks were split from logs, and illustrating an array of woodworking tools, including, (clockwise from man on log) hafted mauls, hafted maul heads, celts or adz blades, nipple maul, flat-topped maul, stirrup maul, antler splitting wedges, and large celt or adz blade.

21 Three views of a typical ground-stone celt.

usually not fatal; like fish hooks their function is to attach the hunter to the prey. Harpooned animals are killed with clubs or lances. Once dead, floats are attached to them to keep the carcass from sinking.

The appearance of ground stone in Early Pacific sites complements the diversification in bone and antler tools. Lance and spear points of ground slate are among the first ground-stone implements. These points probably armed the lances used to kill harpooned sea mammals. The points could also arm spears, or be hafted as daggers or knives. Ground stone, including ground slate, appears across the world during the Holocene[8] and is commonly associated with full and partial sedentism and maritime hunting and fishing, replacing, or supplementing, chipped stone. The reasons for this are not altogether clear, since slate is brittle, and will break if dropped on a firm surface; it can, however, be ground to a hard, sharp point ideal for piercing the thick, blubber-padded hides of sea mammals. Other important ground-stone tools include celts.

Celts were used ethnographically as the blades of adzes – woodworking tools. Celts range in size from quite large ones that were mounted in handles for chopping down trees to very small ones used in a variety of handles for carving and working wood. Celts were also made of marine shell, and the earliest of these are Early Pacific in age. The celts present in Early Pacific sites are all small, but are indirect evidence of some forms of carpentry. Bone and antler wedges were used to split wood and are present during the Archaic; but the adzes indicate woodworking beyond simply splitting the wood. In addition to celts, mauls (ground-stone hammers) appear in the record at this time. These were used to drive wedges and adzes. These changes reflect increased use of the emerging rainforest.

Ground-stone tools are quite durable, but require greater initial effort in their manufacture than the typical chipped-stone tool. Thus, their presence indicates increased investment in time and labor in some kinds of tools and therefore increased importance of the tasks performed with those tools.

Middle Pacific period (1800 BC to AD 200/500)

By 1800 BC sea levels were stable and in their modern positions, permitting the evolution of rich neritic habitats in most areas. Tectonic uplift along the outer coasts of Vancouver Island and the Queen Charlottes, however, caused slowly lowering sea levels, which did not achieve their current levels until around AD 1. It is not until after that date that we see extensive settlement in these areas.[9] Though modern climatic patterns prevailed, there was at least one cool and moister interval that caused minor glacial advances in some mountain areas. The coastal forests probably assumed their modern form during the Middle Pacific, as particular species such as western red and yellow cedar achieved their modern distributions.[10]

This period is marked by some of the most dramatic developments in the coast's lengthy history. We now see evidence for plank houses and plank-house villages (indicating that people now lived in one spot for all or most of the year). We also see the first evidence for permanent social inequality in some areas. There is a new emphasis on a storage-based economy, accompanied by a significant intensification of salmon fishing in many regions. There is evidence for interpersonal conflict and warfare. And we see the development of the coast's art style into something approximating its modern form. The timing of these events is a matter of considerable controversy. There are essentially two competing chronologies: a long one that would put these developments much farther back, perhaps to the beginnings of the Pacific period, and a short one, used here, that places these developments at around 1800 BC, but perhaps as early as 2000 BC. We will review the evidence in the following chapters and return to the issue in Chapter Ten.

Pls. 25–31

Among the technological additions is still more variety of bone and antler tools, including the widespread presence of composite toggling harpoon heads. Composite harpoons differ from barbed harpoons. Barbed harpoons are cut or carved from single pieces of antler or bone, while composite harpoons are made of three pieces bound together. Two harpoon valves are carved of antler or bone. Each has a socket at one end to form a female haft, and either a socket or slot at the other to receive a point. The points could be ground-slate or shell blades, or small bone bipoints. Small composite harpoons were used against salmon, sea otters, and seals, for example, while large ones were used on whales. The basic principle was the same as with barbed harpoons, except that toggling harpoons attach themselves to the prey by twisting sideways in the animal's body.

Toggling harpoons represent a major technological improvement. They could be made from smaller pieces of raw material and used against a wider variety of prey. The bone bipoints could be used to arm harpoons, but also as fish-hook barbs, teeth in fish rakes and so on. The widespread use of these tools marks the presence of an

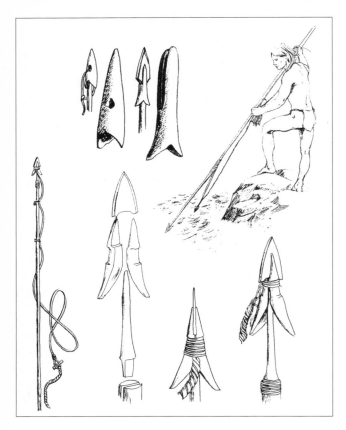

22 *Diagram of a simple toggling harpoon (top) and a composite toggling harpoon (lower).*

increasingly flexible technology made from modular parts. Composite harpoons do not usually replace barbed harpoons; they are an addition to that technology. They probably indicate increased exploitation of a wide variety of neritic resources and perhaps of habitats.

Plank houses and wooden boxes were in use by the beginning of this period. Houses are present in a number of sites dating from the early Middle Pacific. Boxes are present by the end of the Early Pacific.[11] There is indirect evidence for canoes as well. Celts became much more common on the coast, and there was a greater diversity of mauls. In many parts of the coast, celts were now made of nephrite, a particularly hard stone. Nephrite is found in only a few places and so had to be widely traded. On the west coast of Vancouver Island, stone celts are quite rare, shell being used instead, suggesting that access to nephrite and other suitable stone was difficult.

Among the ground-stone tools that appeared during this period were girdled and drilled netsinkers. Their presence suggests an expansion of fishing. In the expanding context of fishing, wooden fish weirs began to be constructed at the start of the Middle Pacific if not earlier.

There is a great deal of poorly understood variability along the coast during the Middle Pacific, particularly in the frequencies and kinds of chipped-stone and ground-stone tools in different sites. In some ways, this variation makes it difficult to establish local and regional patterns. Microblades, for example, are present in sites in the Gulf of Georgia, absent in many sites to the north, and then present again in a number of sites around the mouth of the Stikine River. Other sites on the northern coast lack both microblades and bipolar technology at this time.

Late Pacific period (AD 200/500 to *c*. AD 1775)

The Late Pacific environment was basically the modern form by AD 1. Fluctuations are seen in a warmer and drier interval between AD 1150 and 1300, and the cooler and wetter Little Ice Age after AD 1350.

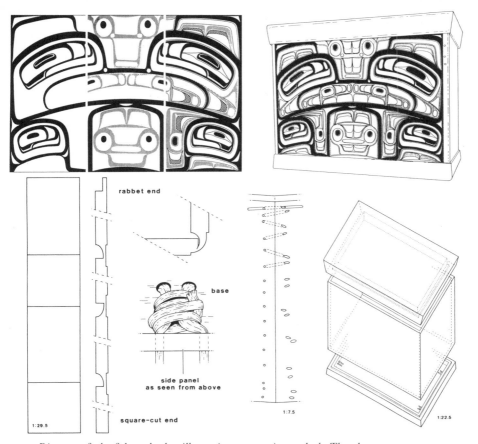

23 *Diagram of a kerfed wooden box illustrating construction methods. These boxes were made from single planks that were soaked, notched as shown, and then bent into a square and lashed together. The bases were sewn to the sides and all joints sealed with pitch to make them water tight. During the Early Modern period such boxes were often elaborately decorated.*

Most archaeologists working on the coast feel that the cultures of the Late Pacific differed little, if at all, from those observed and recorded by the first European visitors to the coast. In this view, the people of the Late Pacific are both the direct biological and cultural ancestors to the coast's modern Native peoples. As we have seen, there is reasonably strong evidence for cultural continuity on the coast overall for at least the last 3,000 years, if not longer. However, the evidence for continuity leads some archaeologists to treat the Late Pacific as a period of stasis, a period of complete cultural stability. This to our minds is like arguing that because there has been cultural continuity in China for the last 3,000 years, nothing important or interesting has happened there. On the Northwest Coast, with the overwhelming evidence for cultural continuity, there is also evidence for considerable dynamism. The evidence shows that this was a turbulent period.

The major, coast-wide events marking the beginnings of the Late Pacific include a major shift in mortuary ritual, a general decline in the use of chipped stone in those areas, such as the Gulf of Georgia, where chipped stone had previously been important, shifts in settlement, changes in subsistence in some areas, a coast-wide escalation in warfare, and some rather dramatic shifts in demography. Available evidence suggests that populations on the coast may have peaked around AD 1000–1100, and then declined.

Midden burials had been an important part of Northwest Coast funerary ritual from the beginning of the Pacific period. Between about AD 500 and AD 1000, the practice ceases (with occasional exceptions). Ethnographic funerary rituals were diverse, including interment, cremation and exposure, but usually the dead were removed from the residential site. It is most likely that this pattern developed and spread at the beginning of the Late Pacific. This shift in mortuary practices was one of the coast's major cultural changes of the last 5,000 years.

Artifacts present in sites up and down the coast closely resemble the tools present at European contact. Some heavy-duty woodworking tools appear for the first time during the Late Pacific. These tools include heavy pile drivers and extremely large adzes. It is also at this time that we have evidence for extremely large houses.

Regional variability
Northern coast
Early Pacific period

Artifact assemblages from this period contain ground-stone tools, including ground-slate points, small adzes, abraders, slate saws and debris created as a byprod-uct of making ground-stone tools. Ground-stone artifacts at Hidden Falls also include beads, pendants, and labrets that will be significant to our discussion of social changes in Chapter Seven. The widespread disappearance of microblades from the northern coast during this period is the most visible technological change in this region during the Early Pacific. However, in some places microblade technol-ogy may have simply been replaced by bipolar technology, another, and technically less demanding method of producing small flakes and blades. Half of the 737 stone artifacts in the Early Pacific assemblage at Hidden Falls were produced in this manner.[12] Bipolar cores are also present in sites on the Queen Charlotte Islands. Microblades themselves are present at the beginning of the period at the Paul Mason site, on the Skeena River, 160 km (90 miles) from the coast,[13] and at the Irish Creek site, in southeast Alaska,[14] but are not present later. Sites in other parts of the northern coast have virtually no chipped stone of any kind except for the ubiquitous cobble and cobble spall tools (the former are made from the river cobble itself, the latter from flakes and spalls removed from cobbles). For example, there are virtually

no chipped-stone tools in a midden on Hecate Island, in sites on Kuiu Island, or in Prince Rupert Harbor.[15] The geo-graphic variation in relative use of chipped-stone tools and in bipolar

24 Antler point or leister barb, Garden Island site, Prince Rupert Harbor. Points such as this could be hafted in pairs and used as a fish spear (liester).

technology is difficult to explain at present. It may reflect local differences in the availability of suitable stone or strong, materially-based social boundaries.

An increased variety of bone and antler tools are present throughout the north coast, including unilaterally and bilaterally barbed bone points and harpoons, as well as barbs, awls and punches, and antler wedges. Bone fish hooks and fish-hook shanks occur on the Queen Charlottes, but are absent on the British Columbia mainland and in southeast Alaska. This clearly must reflect differences in fishing techniques, which in turn must point to differences either in the fish being taken or the environments where fishing occurred.

Evidence of structures is limited to rock-lined hearths, pits and postholes. A small circular depression (3 ¥ 4 m) and an arc formed by multiple postholes suggests a small structure at Hidden Falls.[16] The large number of postholes in the arc suggests the structure was rebuilt a number of times . Blue Jackets Creek contains the burials discussed above; sites in Prince Rupert Harbor also contain burials by the end of this period.[17]

Many rockshelters and caves were first used in southeast Alaska during the Early Pacific. Dates between 2000 and 3000 BC on shell midden deposits at Yatuk Creek Rockshelter[18] on Prince of Wales Island and at several sites in Saginaw Bay on Kuiu Island[19] are two examples. These sites show a rapid build-up of shell-midden deposits and a broad range of resource use. There is no evidence of chipped stone in these sites.

25 Bone bipoints were used on herring rakes, as barbs on fish hooks, and as arrow points.

Middle Pacific period

The most significant Middle Pacific components on the northern coast are in Prince Rupert Harbor and on the Skeena River where the earliest, well-documented Northwest Coast village is located at the Paul Mason site, lying 160 km (90 miles) from the coast in the Skeena River's Kitselas Canyon. The site contains 12 rectangular house depressions dating to about 1200 BC. Ten of the depressions are arranged in two rows overlooking the river, while the other two structures are above and somewhat separate from the rows. We will discuss this site in detail in Chapter Six.

Of the 11 sites tested or excavated in Prince Rupert Harbor (all large middens), 10 have extensive deposits and thousands of artifacts dating to this period. Of these, the Boardwalk site is both the most distinctive and the best

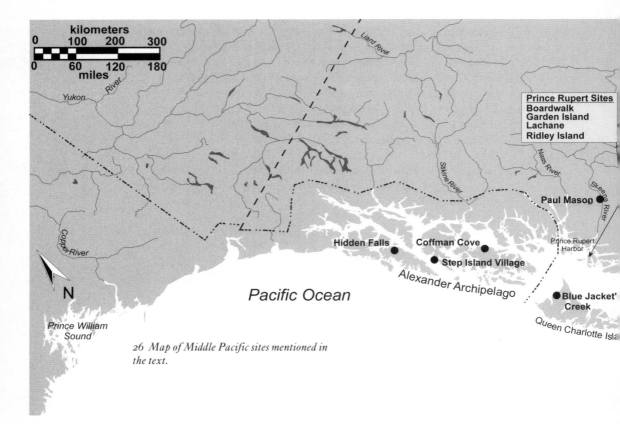

26 *Map of Middle Pacific sites mentioned in
the text.*

understood. Boardwalk may have been a two-row village before the beginning of the
Middle Pacific. The excavations in Prince Rupert Harbor also recovered some 230
Middle Pacific burials that indicate the presence of marked social inequalities in the
harbor by 500 BC, as well as intense levels of warfare or raiding. The Prince Rupert
artifact assemblages follow the general trends described above. They are distinct
from much of the rest of the coast in the almost total lack of chipped-stone tools.
The harbor was virtually abandoned during the last centuries of the Middle Pacific,
the result, perhaps, of warfare, or local ecological changes. In many respects,
however, the Prince Rupert evidence is unique on the northern coast, with
few analogs.

   A number of large shell middens/villages are found in southeast Alaska at this
time, including seven Middle Pacific villages ranging from 700 to 3500 sq. m in
midden area on Kuiu Island. At the multi-component site of Step Island Village, the
large, dense middens contain superimposed living floors, and numerous hearths.
Artifacts are similar to the Early Pacific materials at this site, including bone harpoons, bone awls, heavy but crude cobble tools, and a few fragments of ground slate.
The Middle Pacific deposits at Step Island Village date to between 1500 BC and AD
300. The Coffman Cove site on the northeast side of Prince of Wales Island dates
from about 1500 BC to AD 500. The site is known for the number of ground-slate
artifacts, ground bone, and human burials. Another site on Prince of Wales Island
includes the lowest component at Sarkar Cover Entrance site excavated by Chris
Rabich-Campbell dating to about AD 200.

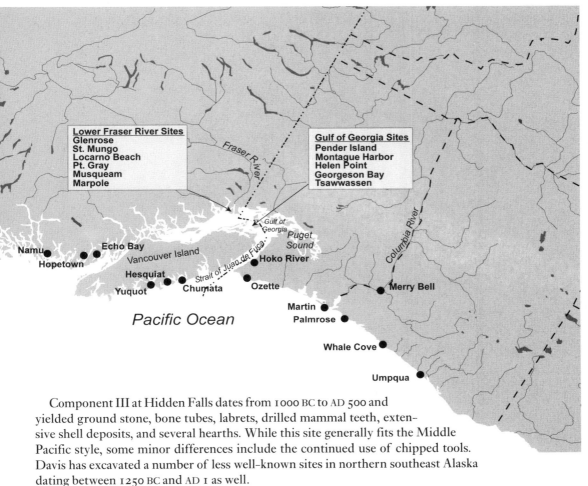

Lower Fraser River Sites
Glenrose
St. Mungo
Locarno Beach
Pt. Gray
Musqueam
Marpole

Gulf of Georgia Sites
Pender Island
Montague Harbor
Helen Point
Georgeson Bay
Tsawwassen

Fraser River

Gulf of
Georgia

Puget
Sound

Namu
Echo Bay
Hopetown

Vancouver Island

Strait of Juan de Fuca

Hoko River

Hesquiat
Chumata
Yuquot
Ozette

Merry Bell

Columbia River

Martin
Palmrose

Pacific Ocean

Whale Cove

Umpqua

Component III at Hidden Falls dates from 1000 BC to AD 500 and yielded ground stone, bone tubes, labrets, drilled mammal teeth, extensive shell deposits, and several hearths. While this site generally fits the Middle Pacific style, some minor differences include the continued use of chipped tools. Davis has excavated a number of less well-known sites in northern southeast Alaska dating between 1250 BC and AD 1 as well.

The Middle Pacific is also when wooden fish weirs become a dominant site type in southeast Alaska. These date mostly after 1500 BC and, according to Madonna Moss and Jon Erlandson, seem to indicate the intensification of salmon harvesting. These sites are often found in the same areas as the Middle Pacific village sites.
Recently, Mark McCallum of the US Forest Service, and Pete Bowers and Bob Betts, contracting archaeologists, have identified a number of archaeological sites in southeast Alaska that do not fit the Middle Pacific at all. These sites date approximately from 1250 BC to AD 1 and consist of tool assemblages dominated by microblades and microblade cores. All of these sites are located on the mainland and islands near the mouth of the Skeena River and may represent an incursion of interior peoples down to the coast at this time.

Blue Jackets Creek is the major site on the Queen Charlottes that spans the period.

Late Pacific period
The Late Pacific settlements in southeast Alaska are comparable with those of the historic Tlingit, and include house-depression villages and defensive sites.

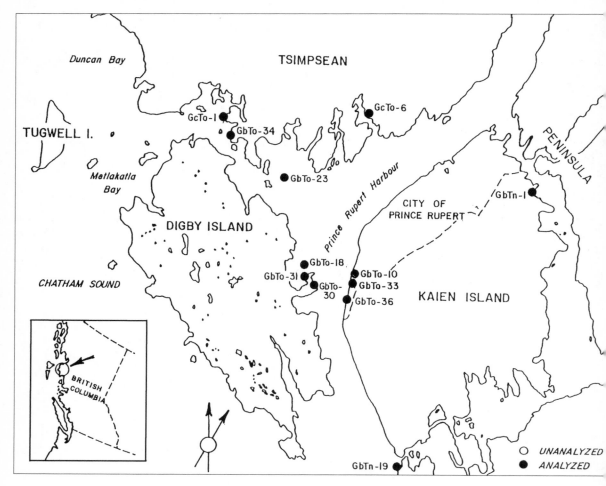

27 *Map of the locations of excavated sites in Prince Rupert Harbor. GbTo 31 is Boardwalk, GcTo 6 is McNichol Creek.*

Numerous Late Pacific sites have been identified but few have been extensively investigated. Exceptions to this include Maschner's testing of nine sites on Kuiu Island and Rabich-Campbell's testing of one on Prince of Wales Island. Artifactual remains from Late Pacific sites in southeast Alaska bear a striking resemblance to the ethnographic period, with a heavy emphasis on ground bone and stone forms identical to those found elsewhere on the coast.

In the Queen Charlotte Islands, most of the archaeological information available after AD 200 comes from Acheson's work on southernmost Moresby where, for the first time, he could describe the last 2,000 years of Queen Charlotte prehistory – a period that has been very difficult to find archaeologically.

Prince Rupert was re-occupied by the beginning of the Late Pacific and Archer has dated a number of village sites that began to form after AD 200. Unfortunately, the Late Pacific deposits of many of the excavated sites were disturbed during the late 19th and early 20th centuries.

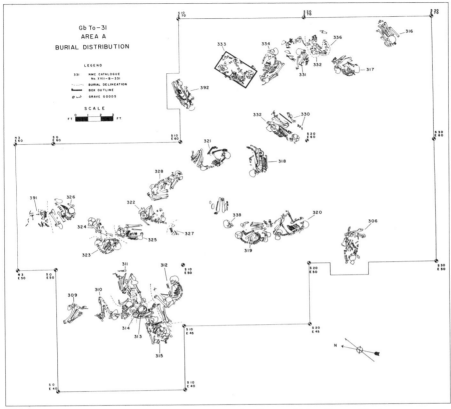

28 Drawing of the distribution of burials at the Boardwalk site in Prince Rupert Harbor.

Central coast

Early Pacific period

There are few sites on the central coast with significant deposits this old. These include Namu on the central British Columbia coast, Bear Cove on the northeast corner of Vancouver Island, Yuquot, in Nootka Sound on the west coast of Vancouver Island and Ch'uumat'a in Barkley Sound, also on the west coast of Vancouver Island.

The usual wide array of bone and antler tools are present in all of these sites. The Namu ground-stone industry is limited to celts and "burnishing stones." Namu lacks the variety of ground slate and ground stone found farther north, particularly ground-slate points. Chipped stone, including cobble tools, macroflakes, and microliths, is present, although microblade cores are absent. Thus, there is again the persistence of very small stone tools, but produced by a different technology. The oldest Yuquot assemblage spans the period from 5000 to 3000 BC and contains only 97 tools. Despite its small size, it is remarkably diverse, with a variety of abraders as well as ground- and chipped-stone adzes and saws. Bone tools include awls, fixed bone points and barbed harpoons, but also valved or toggling harpoons as well (which are not widespread on the coast until the Middle Pacific). The Ch'uumat'a assemblage in Barkley Sound resembles that from Yuquot, but also produced a piece of incised schist in a design that suggests feathers on a wing. Namu contains ash lenses, rock concentrations, and burials by the beginning of this period.

Middle Pacific period

Many of the coast-wide trends of the Middle Pacific are visible on the central coast. There is evidence for houses at Yuquot, in the form of massive hearths. There are also important ways the central coast, especially the west coast of Vancouver Island, differs from other regions. Midden burials are extremely rare in west coast sites, and there are no midden cemeteries, as there are elsewhere, including Namu. Ground-stone celts are rare on the west coast, replaced by shell celts, probably because nephrite was difficult to acquire from its distant sources in southern British Columbia. West coast sites also differ among themselves. Shoemaker Bay, at the upper end of Barkley Sound is in many ways more similar to contemporary sites in the Gulf of Georgia than other west coast sites, while Yuquot has strong similarities to the Prince Rupert sites, rather than Namu, which is geographically closer.

In addition to the geographic patterns, there are interesting patterns of change through time on the central coast. For example, early Middle Pacific components from sites on the northeast corner of Vancouver Island and on the opposite mainland coast across Queen Charlotte Strait, contain composite harpoon heads, bipoints, and abraders and shell tools, including adzes. These assemblages, however, are dominated by another microlithic stone tool industry based on producing obsidian microflakes from bipolar cores. Around 500 BC, this complex was replaced by artifact assemblages more typical of those on the coast in general, and the microlithic industry disappears. Donald Mitchell argues that this change indicates the arrival of Wakashan speakers (the ancestors of the modern Kwakwala speakers of the region).[19]

Late Pacific period

Occupation at Namu becomes much less intense by the beginning of the Late Pacific, probably as the result of siltation in the Namu River. The site's function shifts from being a residential site to being a fishing locality. Assemblage contents from the sites on Queen Charlotte Straits show strong continuities with the assemblages from the late Middle Pacific – they are dominated by bone and antler. Unfortunately, these excavations are not extensive. At Yuquot, the Late Pacific assemblage closely resembles the Middle Pacific, but with increasingly specialized fishing and sea-mammal hunting tackle. Iron cutting tools were present at Yuquot before European contact.

One of the best Late Pacific samples for the west coast of Vancouver Island is from six sites in Hesquiat Harbor, south of Nootka Bay. The sites span the last 1,800 years, though the bulk of the deposits appear to be less than 1,200 years old. While there was geographic variation among these sites in their content, there was little temporal variation, which Jim Haggerty, the excavator, took to indicate continuity with the historic local Hesquiat groups that occupied the harbor.[21] Chipped-stone tools are rare, ground-stone tools are predominantly abraders. Composite toggling harpoons and fish-hook shanks are common artifacts associated with food procurement. There was no ground slate. Iron was also present in Late Pacific deposits in Hesquiat Harbor. Shoemaker Bay II, from the Shoemaker Bay site, on Alberni Inlet, spans much of the Late Pacific and contrasts in some ways with the Hesquiat Harbor sites. Ground-slate and ground-stone tools, including a number of celts, are present as are a wide array of bone and antler tools, including both barbed and composite harpoon heads. Evidently no metal was recovered, suggesting either that the site was abandoned before iron became available, or that the upper end of Alberni Inlet was not on the trade routes along which iron moved.[22]

Southern coast – Gulf of Georgia/Fraser River Canyon

Early Pacific period

The Gulf of Georgia area and the Fraser River Canyon have the largest number of excavated Pacific period components. This time period is known regionally by a variety of local names. Some of these local differences reflect different research methodologies and theoretical orientations among archaeologists, but they also imply important but presently poorly understood local variation in cultural history or ecology.

The Early Pacific in this region is marked by chipped-stone projectile points (perhaps indicating a greater reliance on terrestrial resources than farther north), unilaterally and bilaterally barbed harpoon heads, ground-slate knives and points, incised and decorated ground-slate objects, T-shaped labrets, chipped-stone drills, stone pendants, and abraders. These traits are generally comparable to Early Pacific traits to the north. Microblades or microliths are present at at least one site, Helen Point, in the Gulf Islands. Midden burial was practiced.

Of all the many sites, perhaps the two Pender Canal sites are the most distinctive. Carlson excavated a large cemetery there dating between 2700 and 1800 BC.[23] Among other things, including labrets, the burials contained ten antler spoons with zoomorphic images on their handles. The artifacts from these sites are not yet fully reported, so other comparisons are not possible. The earliest piece of carved antler on the Northwest was recovered at Glenrose Cannery; it too is dated to 2700–2000 BC. Finally, Ham reports evidence for plank houses at St Mungo Cannery dating to 2700 BC (see Chapter Six).[24] There are also Early Pacific structures at Hatzic Rock[25] and the Maurer site,[26] on the Fraser River, above Vancouver.

Middle Pacific period

In the Gulf of Georgia the Middle Pacific is divided into phases: Locarno Beach, which spans a period from 1500 to 600 BC, and Marpole from 600 BC to AD 500.

Locarno Beach is well represented by components from almost 30 sites. Locarno Beach is characterized by the persistence of chipped-stone technology, including stemmed points and flaked semi-lunate tools, as well as the ubiquitous pebble and cobble tools. Most distinctively, microblade cores and blades are present as are microflakes produced by bipolar technology (these of course were absent from this region during the Archaic and Early Pacific periods). Ground-stone tools include ground-slate points and blades, celts or adzes, labrets, netsinkers and abraders. Hand stones (mullers) and grinding slabs are also present. These tools, probably used for grinding nuts or other plant foods, are rare, or completely absent in other parts of the coast to the north. The bone and antler industry includes unilaterally and bilaterally barbed antler points, composite and single piece toggling harpoon heads, bone and antler wedges, and bone blades reminiscent of ground-slate blades. A Locarno Beach wet site component at the Musqueam Northeast site produced

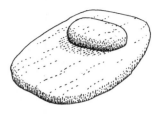

29 *Handstone (upper) and abrasive slab (lower) from Montague Harbour.*

cordage, basketry, knob-topped hats as well as bentwood fish hooks and yew-wood wedges with their withe bands or grommets intact.[27] A second wet component at the Hoko River site on the Olympic Peninsula also contains fish hooks and cordage as well as ground-slate points and microflakes[28].

The initial date of Locarno Beach is subject to some controversy since Carlson places the Pender Canal burials in the Locarno Beach phase, and Ham assigns the possible house remains at St Mungo Cannery to the phase as well. The strongest contrasts between Locarno Beach technology and that of the preceding Early Pacific in the Gulf of Georgia are the microblade cores and blades, the appearance and number of toggling harpoons, and the ground-stone mullers and slabs.

Bone and antler objects with zoomorphic and geometric designs are present. Among these are distinctive slotted antler objects with quite detailed geometric designs, and small skulls or deaths heads. These carvings are rather distinctive, and do not fall readily into the usual canons of Northwest Coast art (Chapter Nine).

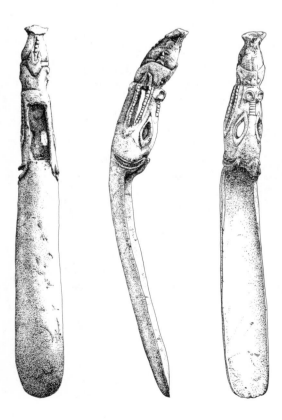

The subsequent Marpole phase is generally regarded among workers in the Gulf of Georgia as marking the appearance of "Classic" Northwest Coast culture in the local area.[29] Both flaked-stone and microblade technology persist. Large, heavy mauls appear, in a variety of forms, including nipple mauls and banded nipple mauls. The variety of toggling harpoons is replaced by large unilaterally barbed harpoon heads. Grinding slabs and handstones continue to be present, however. There is a greater variety of items of personal adornment, including stone and shell beads, as well as objects of native copper.

30 *An Early Pacific zoomorphic spoon from Pender Canal.*

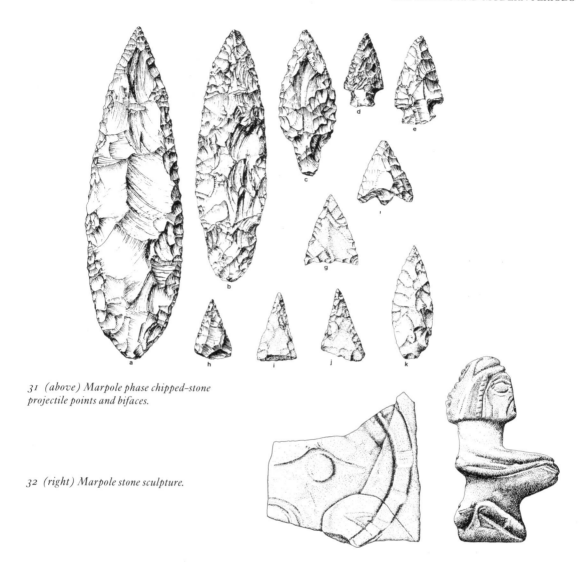

31 (above) Marpole phase chipped-stone projectile points and bifaces.

32 (right) Marpole stone sculpture.

Though no houses have been excavated, Marpole sites contain large numbers of massive postholes as well as small ones, suggesting the presence of plank houses.[30]

Marpole is also characterized by a distinctive tradition of stone and antler sculpture. The most characteristic of these sculptures are anthropomorphic figurines holding or carrying a small bowl. These objects are seldom associated with archaeological sites, suggesting they were cached away from residential areas. Marpole sites are rich in small zoomorphic objects that are clearly within the tradition of Northwest Coast art.[31]

The Middle Pacific is also divided into two phases in the Fraser River Canyon – the Baldwin and the Skamel – which are essentially contemporary with Locarno Beach and Marpole respectively. The Baldwin phase is poorly represented. Components for both were recovered from sites with poor organic preservation, so bone and antler tools are rare. Both phases are characterized by chipped-stone tools, but the

Pl. 65

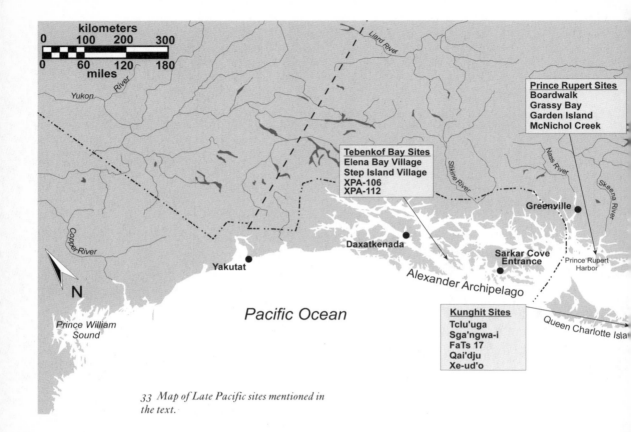

33 Map of Late Pacific sites mentioned in the text.

Baldwin phase, like Locarno Beach, possesses microblades and microblade cores, while the Skamel components do not. Ground-stone tools include adzes and ground-slate points. The Baldwin phase is also marked by a distinctive practice of carving soft stone such as talc, shale, steatite, and schist, producing a variety of zoomorphic and anthropomorphic forms. This trait is absent in the following Skamel phase.[32]

Late Pacific period

The Late Pacific period is known by a variety of names in the Gulf of Georgia, including Developed Coast Salish, the San Juan phase, and Strait of Georgia. While all researchers see strong continuities between Middle Pacific (Marpole) and Late Pacific components in this region, the period between AD 300 and 800 is poorly documented, similar to the situation in Prince Rupert Harbor. This may reflect, at least in part, the methods by which archaeologists classify assemblages and assign them to one or another of the region's archaeological cultures. We suspect that undated components from that 500-year period may have been assigned to either Marpole or Strait of Georgia.

The Late Pacific is characterized by changes in the forms of ground-slate points and blades: they are smaller and triangular in form. There is an increase in the

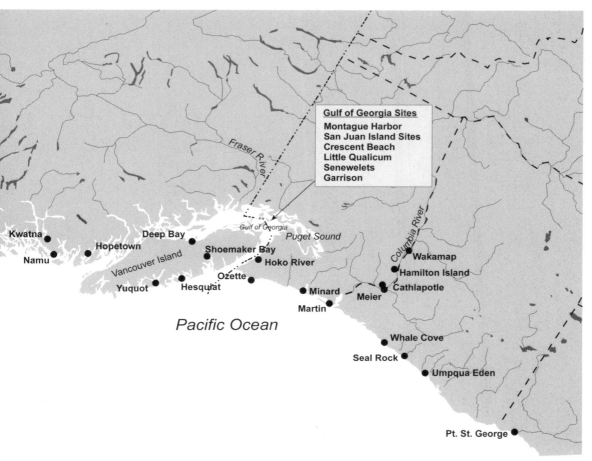

Gulf of Georgia Sites
Montague Harbor
San Juan Island Sites
Crescent Beach
Little Qualicum
Senewelets
Garrison

numbers of composite harpoon valves and of bone bipoints and bone points in general. Ground-stone tools include large celts, and flat-topped mauls (though nipple mauls persist). Bone pins, plain and decorated, are present, as are spindle whorls (which indicate weaving). There is evidence for both houses and fortifications, including ditches and embankments. Absent is the stone sculpture of the Marpole phase. The amount of decorated bone and antler objects is also less, although motifs that are present are as skillfully executed. There are no microblades. This period on the Lower Fraser is marked by large numbers of ground-slate knives, zoomorphic and anthropomorphic effigy pipes, nipple mauls, celts, chipped-stone points, and scrapers, as well as by the presence of semi-subterranean pithouses.

South Coast: outer Pacific coast (Washington and Oregon) and the Lower Columbia River

Early Pacific period

Sea levels were still below their modern positions along much of the outer coast, resulting in few sites dating to this period. One of the better known is Yaquinna Head, which dates to the end of the Early Pacific. The site is located on the promontory of that name on the central Oregon coast that would not be affected by rising sea levels. The period is somewhat better known in the southern portion of the

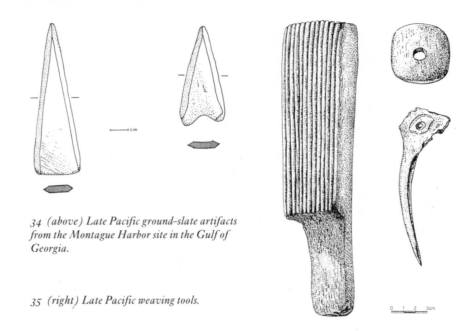

34 (above) Late Pacific ground-slate artifacts from the Montague Harbor site in the Gulf of Georgia.

35 (right) Late Pacific weaving tools.

Puget-Willamette Lowland in western Oregon where a number of sites, including the Flannigan Mound, have dates falling in this period. Most of these sites appear to be small camps or special use sites. Some, for example, appear to be camas processing sites (camas, *Camassia quamash*, is a plant of the Lily family with a nutritious bulb that was important to Native diets through much of Cascadia). The Flannigan site is a deeply stratified mound, but does not appear to be a residential site. There are other smaller mounds in the valley as well. There are a few Early Pacific sites along the Lower Columbia River, generally in the surrounding uplands. Any Early Pacific sites on the river's floodplain are deeply buried.

Middle Pacific
A few sites on the Washington Coast date to the end of this period. The famous Ozette wet site (which dates to the end of the Late Pacific, see below) is associated with a dry midden site whose dates span the last 2,000 years. Other sites whose occupations fall into this period are Sand Point (just south of Ozette), and the Martin site, located on Willapa Bay on the extreme southwestern Washington coast.

The most important Middle Pacific site on the southern outer coast is the Palmrose site, located near the town of Seaside, Oregon.[33] The site is one of several located at the south end of the Clatsop plain of northwest Oregon, and is one of the rare, large, shell middens on the Oregon coast. It contains a large, rectangular house. The structure appears to have been built and rebuilt several times over the period between 350 BC and about AD 400. The Palmrose structure is the earliest well-documented house on the southern Northwest Coast and is slightly later than the Paul Mason village in northern British Columbia. The importance of this will be discussed in Chapter Six.

Middle Pacific sites along this outer coast have extensive bone and antler industries, as well as chipped-stone tools and stone toolmaking debris. They also contain

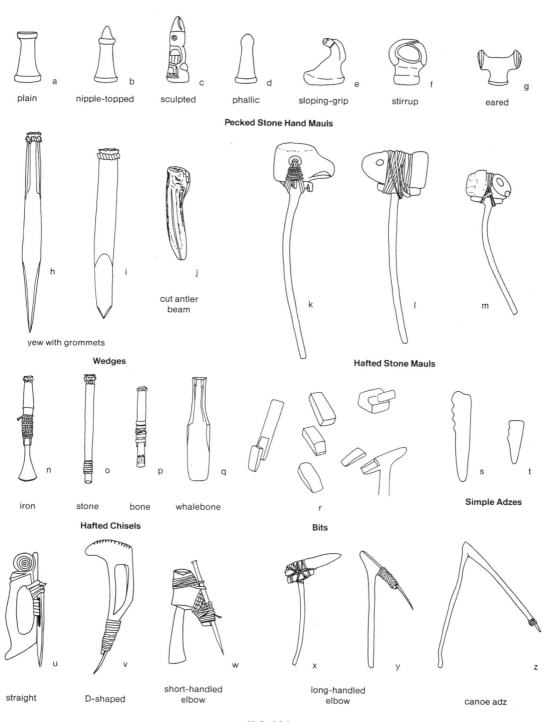

Pecked Stone Hand Mauls

a — plain
b — nipple-topped
c — sculpted
d — phallic
e — sloping-grip
f — stirrup
g — eared

h, i — yew with grommets
j — cut antler beam

Wedges

Hafted Stone Mauls

n — iron
o — stone
p — bone
q — whalebone

Hafted Chisels

r — **Bits**

s, t — **Simple Adzes**

u — straight
v — D-shaped
w — short-handled elbow
x, y — long-handled elbow
z — canoe adz

Hafted Adzes

36 Late Pacific woodworking tools.

grinding slabs and stones, composite toggling harpoons, fish hooks and shell adzes and blades. However, they lack the extensive ground-slate industry found farther north at this time, and while they contain heavy ground-stone tools, such as mauls, these are much rarer than those at sites farther north. They also appear to lack microblades and cores in contrast to the Gulf of Georgia during this period.

The occupants of the Columbia River below the Dalles only begin to emerge into the archaeological record during the Middle Pacific.[34] The oldest dated material below the Dalles is a hearth on the valley floor near Vancouver, Washington which dates to about 1800 BC.[35] Rectangular structures are documented along the lower Columbia by *c.* 300 BC.[36] Pithouses may also have been present.

Late Pacific period

There are a relatively large number of sites on the Washington and Oregon coast that fall into this time period. Of these, the Ozette site, at Cape Alava, near the northern tip of the Olympic Peninsula, is the best known (see box). Ozette has both a wet site, and a dry midden. The wet site is world famous since it contains several plank houses almost instantaneously sealed beneath catastrophic mud-slides. As a result, enormous numbers of organic objects, including house planks, netting, basketry, and tools, were preserved. Ozette provides crucial evidence on many aspects of life on the southern coast for the period immediately before contact.

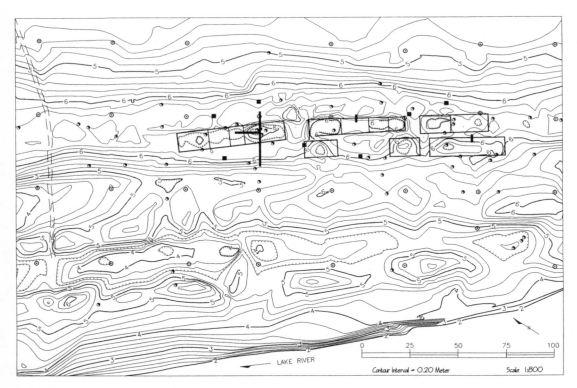

37 Map of the Cathlapotle site on the Columbia River, near Vancouver. The house at the north end of the site is 63m long. This village was visited and described by Lewis and Clark on 29 March 1806.

THE OZETTE SITE AND ITS ART

OZETTE is justifiably one of the most famous archaeological sites in the world. Unique preservation conditions protected virtually all the contents of several Makah houses, including all the wood and fiber artifacts normally lost. Ozette is located on the Olympic Peninsula of Washington State, just south of Cape Flattery, the westernmost point in the continental United States. The site faces out on to the open Pacific, though its beach is somewhat sheltered. The village was a major whaling village for the Makah. Sometime in the early 1700s, part of the village was suddenly buried beneath a massive mud slide triggered by an enormous earthquake. The mud sealed the houses, preserving their contents for the next two centuries. In the early 1970s, the houses began to wash out, as the result of severe winter storms. For the next 10 years, the site was excavated using water and hoses, rather than the traditional trowel, by crews from Washington State University. They recovered basketry, cordage, harpoons, lines, bags, pegs, planks, clubs, boxes and so on – over 40,000 artifacts in all. It took 10 years to recover the contents of three houses.

Ozette provides an unparalleled glimpse into life on the Northwest Coast not too many years before the appearance of Europeans and even fewer years before the first smallpox epidemics. Perhaps most important, the three houses contain the material culture of everyday life, unfiltered through the interests and biases of collectors. At a very fine-grained level, we can see the choices of wood for different purposes (sealing clubs are of yew (Taxifolia brevifolia) since it is hard and dense, bowls of alder (Alnus rubra) and houses of red cedar), while bone and antler were used for handles, which on the one hand is evidence for knowledge of their raw materials, and on the other is an indirect look at their cultural landscape (where they had to go for yew, for alder, which places are closer, farther away). Ozette shows how important and well-made basketry was, from large storage baskets to the decorated hats of the elite. A society of sailors made extensive use of rope and line, and Ozette produced a great deal of cordage.

We can see how the status system affected not only the distribution of tools, but even housekeeping. The earthen floors of the two lower-status houses contain the bones of fish, sea lions and other creatures which were butchered and processed on the floor. The high-status house has far fewer such remains in the floor midden, and contains a decorated box, and other such valuable items. Within the high-status house, whaling tackle is concentrated in the two corners away from the door, the high-status corners, and the ethnographies tell us that harpooning of whales was reserved for men of the elite. We can even see the effects of status on food remains – the shell midden of the high-status house contains the shells of the most nutritious mollusks. Ozette is a guidebook to the archaeology of life on the Northwest Coast, full of information about the things early observers did not notice, or did not care about, or did not understand.

Other residential sites from this period occur along the coast, including the Minard site on Grays Harbor spit,[37] but most are small, or have not been extensively excavated. The Late Pacific is the best represented period along the Oregon coast. The Oregon sites contain an array of chipped-stone tools, including small projectile points, some ground stone, and the usual bone tools.

The Lower Columbia River from the Dalles to the river's mouth has an excellent record for this period. Wakemap Mound, directly across the Columbia River from the Five Mile Rapids site, was the location of a large settlement; and is composed of numerous, superimposed house floors with stratigraphy analogous to the tells of the Middle East.[38] Below the Dalles, there have been excavations that have produced Late Pacific components at Hamilton Island,[39] in the Columbia Gorge; at the Meier site[40] and other sites in the Portland Metropolitan area,[41] and at sites in the Columbia Estuary.[42] Sites in the estuary area are generally similar in their artifact contents to those on the Oregon and Washington coasts, while those upriver have far greater proportions of chipped–stone tools. However, ground–stone mauls, netweights, celts and stone sculptures occur in sites along the river above the estuary. There is evidence at a number of sites of plank houses and also suggestions in the record of pithouses.

Modern period (AD 1775 to the present)

The Northwest Coast has an excellent archaeological record for the period spanning the Early Modern period, the period between AD 1775 and 1850 or so, roughly the end of the fur trade and beginning of the reservation era in the United States. Many Northwest Coast sites have Early Modern (or Historic) components, though these are not often the focus of archaeologists' attentions, and they have relied primarily on the ethnographic and historic records of their research areas. There is also a long tradition among archaeologists working on the coast of trying to link the sites they are excavating directly to the people living in the region. Frederica De Laguna's pioneering work among the Tlingit epitomizes this approach in which ethnographic, ethnohistoric and archaeological data are integrated.[43] We describe another example in Chapter Eight, where we discuss George MacDonald's excavations at a Tsimshian fortress and the linkages between that fortress, the fortress' legendary history and changes in Tsimshian territory during the 18th century.

A number of researchers have excavated Early Modern houses along the coast from southeast Alaska to the Oregon coast.[44] Many of these structures date to the fur-trade period, and the investigators have been interested in seeking the effects of the fur trade and of contact. Rather than seeking to demonstrate cultural continuity, the interest is in what aspects of life changed, in how people responded to contact, and to test the early accounts and the ethnographies. Fladmark, for example, excavated an early fur-trade-era house at the Richardson Ranch site on the Queen Charlotte Islands. Through his excavations, he was able to show that the carving of argellite, a soft black stone in which the Haida produced superb examples of late 19th century Northwest Coast art, began well before the major period of contact on the islands. There had been a debate as to whether argellite carving was entirely the product of the contact period. He also discovered that the house he excavated did not fit descriptions of the "typical Haida" house. Ames has been excavating the Cathlapotle site, a large Chinookan village visited by Lewis and Clark on 29 March 1806 as they headed home from their long expedition. While we can see the replacement of bone with iron tools, it is also clear, for example, that trade with the fur traders and other Euroamericans was easily accommodated by the productive Chinookan household economies.

Finally, excavations at major fur-trading posts, such as Fort Vancouver, near the present-day Vancouver, Washington, and Fort Langely, on the Fraser River above Vancouver, British Columbia provide direct evidence of relationships between Native people and the traders. Archaeology at these posts originally focused on the fur traders themselves, but more recent work has looked at areas occupied by Native people and sought evidence for their activities at the forts. The excavations are often supplemented by careful work with diaries and journals from the fort's occupants.

CHAPTER FIVE

Northwest Coast Subsistence

The coast's rich environment as cause

In this chapter, we discuss the history and evolution of the subsistence economies of the coast's peoples over the last 11,000 years. As with previous chapters, an essential theme is that of regional similarities and local diversity. Since we are also dealing here with the environment, that theme includes regional environmental richness.

The first explanations for the complexity and large populations of the Early Modern period rested on the simple assertion that the Northwest Coast's environment was so rich that hunter-gatherer societies could not help but flourish; they were the inevitable consequence of the rich environment. Salmon were viewed, as they still are, as key resources in that abundance. Researchers in the early part of this century such as A.L. Kroeber and Clark Wissler[1] focused on the central role of salmon in the region's economy as almost defining the region itself. However, early ethnographers actually paid little attention to the environment beyond documenting basic subsistence techniques and giving quite general descriptions.

The notion of a rich coastal environment producing affluent foragers has not been limited to the Northwest Coast. We now know that many groups of affluent foragers developed along coastal strips and, as David Yesner and others[2] have argued, littoral and maritime environments are so productive that large-scale, complex societies are often seen as an almost inevitable outcome after humans began to make use of them. Globally, widespread heavy exploitation of coastal resources does not occur until after the end of the last glaciation, and subsequent rises in global sea levels, with local exceptions. To explain affluent foragers, goes this line of reasoning, one needs only to document the development of rich coastal environments. In this way, the explanatory focus is on the environment, not the people inhabiting it.

For the Northwest Coast, however, things are not so simple. Recent research on the coast has questioned whether the coast's environment has been stable and always rich. Wayne Suttles[3] and Andrew Vayda challenged that idea in the early 1960s, using Northwest Coast Native oral traditions of famines and food failures to support their view that while the coast's environment can be seen as rich overall, it is subject to important variation in time and space, variation that the coast's human inhabitants had to cope with to maintain their large populations, permanent towns and complex societies. It has also been shown that the presence of rich marine environments alone may not be enough to explain the development of complex hunter-gatherers.

More recently, Leland Donald and Donald Mitchell[4] have examined the territories of groups living along the west side of Vancouver Island, including Kwakwaka'wakw and Nuu-chah-nulth, focusing on salmon runs. They discovered first that variation in the numbers of salmon among different groups' territories was

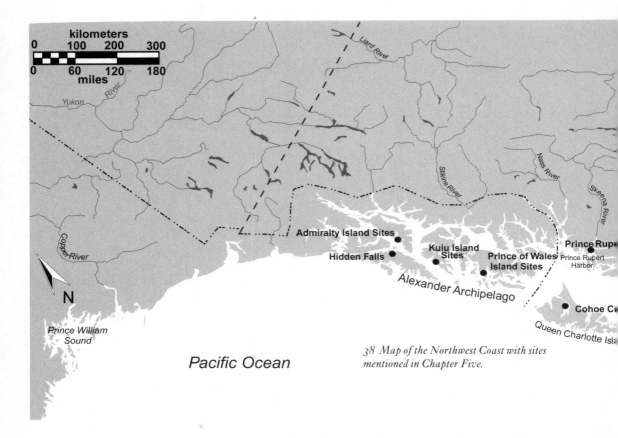

38 Map of the Northwest Coast with sites mentioned in Chapter Five.

so extreme that for some groups failure of their poor salmon runs was probably an ever-present problem. For other groups, however, their salmon resources were so rich that the runs exceeded the capacity of the available fishing technology to fully harvest them. Secondly, it emerged that groups with poor territories were more likely to join confederacies and participate in feasting circles, apparently to mitigate the effects of their territory's poor resources, to get access to a wider area, and to the resources in that area.

The "richness" then of any particular Northwest Coast group's effective environment[5] was the result of the interplay between not only terrestrial and marine productivity, but between the local environment and social organization as well. While it is true, therefore, that the Northwest Coast, as a region, is environmentally rich, locally (the level at which people used the environment), it was subject to extremes, from places that were far richer than could be used, to other places that were quite marginal for human subsistence.

The relationship between marine resources and complex hunter–gatherers also may not be as direct as once thought. These ideas are based on the assumption that people will inevitably exploit rich marine habitats, but this may not be so. Many researchers have observed that neritic resources were increasingly important to the subsistence economy going north along the coast, from Oregon to southeastern Alaska. Randall Schalk shows this trend was not related to an increase in the richness of the ocean, but to a steady decline in the productivity of the land.[6] As terrestrial

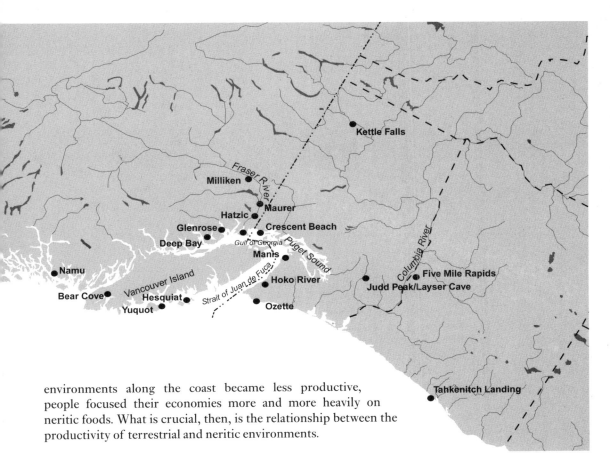

environments along the coast became less productive, people focused their economies more and more heavily on neritic foods. What is crucial, then, is the relationship between the productivity of terrestrial and neritic environments.

Salmon and storage

During the past 25 to 30 years, most students of the coast's history have emphasized two aspects of the Northwest Coast as being the key to the development of the coast's subsistence economy: salmon and storage.[7] Salmon offer a number of advantages to foragers: they are available at predictable times (runs happen at the same time annually), in predictable places and in those once prodigious numbers. Estimates for the annual runs on the Columbia River, the richest salmon river, range as low as 8.2 million fish to as high as 25 million annually.[8] Smaller streams would, of course, have far fewer fish. Salmon also have disadvantages. For storage, they must be processed promptly to prevent or delay rotting. Runs are sensitive to environmental problems, particularly small streams and upper tributaries, while, on large rivers, such as the Columbia and Fraser, the sheer volume of fish protects the run (there were so many fish, that the failure of one run on one tributary would have little noticeable impact on 8 million fish).

Salmon runs, rich in the aggregate, are highly variable species to species, stream to stream, and year to year.[9] They are subject to patterned variation, with some rivers having large runs only every second, third or fourth years.[10] Absolute fish abundance may be less important for patterns of human aggregation, labor

39 Salmon drying house at The Dalles of the Columbia River, about 1844.

organization and settlement patterns than is the temporal clumping of runs. In a good year on the Klukshu River in the southwest Yukon, for example, half the sockeye salmon run passes in 7.5 days, in a bad year (in terms of clumping, not numbers) half go by in only 2.5 days. Such variation in clumping is not predictable.[11] Early European travelers were often impressed by the sheer numbers of salmon drying and smoking on racks and in the houses of Northwest Coast peoples. It was clear that the fish, both fresh and stored, were a mainstay of the diet; they provided a high quality source of fats and protein that were readily stored. However, Northwest Coast peoples exploited a wide array of resources, as we have stressed. There is debate among archaeologists as to whether salmon alone were sufficient to sustain the Northwest Coast's large human populations and complex social organization.

Some archaeologists, including Knut Fladmark, Roy Carlson, and R.G. Matson, have argued that the emergence of intensive harvesting of salmon[12] at some time in the past was the major economic change leading to the development of complex hunter-gathering societies on the Northwest Coast. Gregory Monks has used the humorous term *salmonopia* to describe this emphasis on salmon.[13] Archaeologists and anthropologists afflicted with salmonopia can see only salmon, and are blind to the other resources that were crucial to the coast's Native economies.

In our view, salmon alone were not sufficient to sustain complex societies on the Northwest Coast, nor was the intensification of salmon harvesting alone enough to produce complex societies. As we will attempt to show in this and succeeding chapters, the development of complexity on the Northwest Coast depended on the formation of a subsistence economy that exploited a wide range of resources and habitats. So-called "secondary resources" played as essential an economic role, if not greater, in our view, as did salmon.

Monks has also made the important suggestion that Northwest Coast peoples organized their economies to use not only single resources, but entire food chains. He was studying a fish weir at Deep Bay on the east coast of Vancouver Island used for catching herring. He concluded that the people built and exploited the weir not for herring but to create a habitat attractive to the other fish and sea mammals (such as seals) that hunt and eat herring. In pursuing the herring, these other creatures were exposed to the human hunters who built the weir. In this sense, people on the Northwest Coast manipulated their environment to modify or even create microenvironments suitable for human use. Michael Kew has recently extended Monks' arguments, suggesting that the history of fishing on the Northwest Coast is not a history of adding new fish species to the list of exploited fish, but of adding new environments in which the same fish could be taken. Thus, we need to think not only in terms of particular resources but also in terms of microenvironments and habitats.[14]

Early Modern period subsistence economies

In addition to salmon, economically important fish included flatfish, such as halibut, flounder, and sole. In salmon-poor areas, such as the Queen Charlotte Islands, halibut was a major resource. Cod and herring were among the important schooling fish. In fact, it is certain that herring was more important than present evidence suggests. The herring is a small-boned fish, and until recently on the coast, common excavation techniques would not recover herring bones. Smelt are another significant fish. Of the smelt, eulachon (*Thalicthys pacificus*) was the most

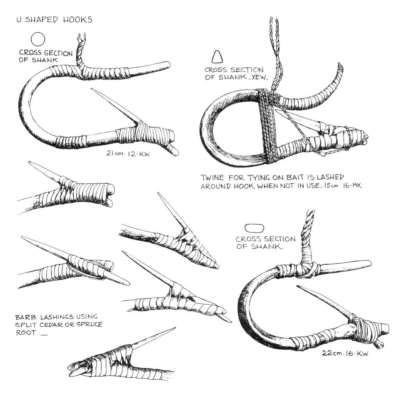

40 *A variety of bentwood fish-hooks and hook barb types used on the Northwest Coast.*
Usually archaeologists find only the bone barb. Hooks such as these have been in use on the coast for at least 3000 years, if not much longer.

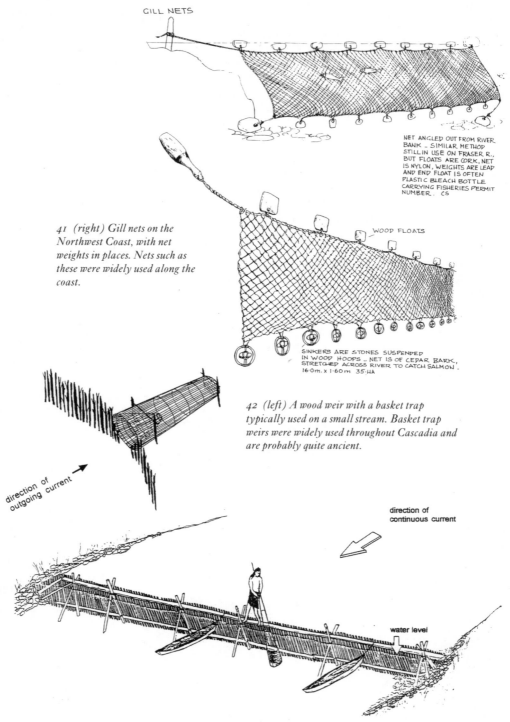

GILL NETS

NET ANGLED OUT FROM RIVER BANK — SIMILAR METHOD STILL IN USE ON FRASER R., BUT FLOATS ARE CORK, NET IS NYLON, WEIGHTS ARE LEAD AND END FLOAT IS OFTEN PLASTIC BLEACH BOTTLE CARRYING FISHERIES PERMIT NUMBER. CS

41 (right) Gill nets on the Northwest Coast, with net weights in places. Nets such as these were widely used along the coast.

WOOD FLOATS

SINKERS ARE STONES SUSPENDED IN WOOD HOOPS — NET IS OF CEDAR BARK, STRETCHED ACROSS RIVER TO CATCH SALMON. 16·0m. x 1·60m 35·HA

42 (left) A wood weir with a basket trap typically used on a small stream. Basket trap weirs were widely used throughout Cascadia and are probably quite ancient.

direction of outgoing current

direction of continuous current

water level

43 (above) A wood weir used on a larger stream or river. Weirs were also used in coastal tidal flats. The fisherman is using a dip net.

important. Eulachon (also known as candle fish because it is so oily it can burn) was a major source of oil (as was herring), and oils are highly prized among peoples dependent on dried foods for long periods of time. A diet heavy in dried foods can lead to constipation and other digestive problems, as well a crucial, even fatal, shortage of fats in the diet. Rendered eulachon oil was very prized and traded widely on the northern coast. The tiny fish ran in late winter and early spring, making them among the earliest fresh foods available. Sturgeon were taken along the Fraser, Columbia and other major rivers. Sturgeon can weigh over 1000 lb, making them well worth the effort of landing them. Evidence for tuna has been recovered in sites on the west coast of Vancouver Island by Allan McMillan.[15] Analyses of the fish remains in archaeological sites sometimes identify well over 20 species of fish.

Fishing techniques were as varied as the fish taken and the habitats in which they were harvested. There were some technological limits. There were no methods, for example, by which large numbers of fish could be netted in the open water. Instead, hooks and line, trolling gear, gigs, and fish rakes were used. Nets were employed in Pls. 10–12 streams and rivers. Nets included dip nets, and gill nets. Weirs and fish traps diverted or stalled migrating fish so they could be netted or speared. Fish were also harpooned, gaffed, speared, and clubbed. The gear and techniques used depended on the fish itself and where the fishing occurred.

Fish were prepared for storage by being filleted or split along their spine and then placed on racks to expose them to sun and wind (the best drying and preserving method) or over a fire to be smoked. Unlike other parts of the world, fish were not salted. The interiors of Northwest Coast houses usually had frames suspended from Pls. 29, 30 their ceilings festooned with foods, including fish, being preserved in the smoke of household fires. Preservation and storage were crucial; a great many resources were stored. The relatively short shelf life of stored salmon (about six months, depending on the species; some dried salmon might last over a year) was an important limiting factor affecting spring subsistence practices.

Deer (*Ocdocoelious*) and elk (*Cervus elephas*, or wapiti as they are known in Canada and some parts of the northwestern USA) were the largest common land mammals along much of the coast. Hunters also sought mountain goats and sheep where they were available, as well as bears, river otters, martin, mink beaver, porcupines, muskrats, raccoons and other small mammals. These creatures were used not only for food, but for industrial purposes as well. The incisors of beavers and porcupines became small blades in woodworking and carving tools. The dense lower leg bones (metapodials) of deer and wapiti were particularly useful for needles, wedges, and chisels. Hunting was done with bows and arrows, deadfalls and other traps. Swimming animals (deer swim from island to island) were ambushed in open water and speared and clubbed.

Harbor seals and sea otters were the most important sea mammals for the coast's economy, but fur seals, sea lions, porpoises, and small whales were all pursued. The basic technique for taking sea mammals was to harpoon them, and then, when the animal tired (after being harpooned the animal would try to flee, but the harpoon and its line attached the struck animal to the harpooner and his boat), to kill it with a lance or club. On land, these creatures can be awkward and easily killed at rookeries where they spend the mating season and periods of time after pups are born. They can also be faster than expected and dangerous to the unwary. Only people of the west coast of Vancouver Island and Washington whaled in the 19th century, although there is recent archaeological evidence for whaling among the residents of Moresby Island in the Queen Charlotte Islands in the Late Pacific period. Otherwise, whales were exploited when they beached. Porpoises and dolphins were also hunted, using the same techniques employed against other small sea mammals. Sea otters were clubbed, harpooned, netted, and hunted with bows and arrows.

Collected foods included both vegetable foods and intertidal organisms such as kelp and shellfish. These latter were the most important. People used a wide range of shellfish, including several species of clams, mussels, and even barnacles. Women and children dug shellfish from intertidal mud flats or pulled them off rocks at low tide. The mollusks were steamed and often smoked and preserved. Dried shellfish meat was a trade item in exchange with groups in the interior, while the shells were made into adz blades and points for harpoons.

Plant foods were more important in the south than in the north. Berries were enjoyed everywhere and dried to provide sweetness in the winter diet. In the more southerly areas, roots and corms, such as those of camas (*Camassia quamash*) and wapato (*Sagittaria latifolia*) respectively, were made into flour. Ferns and bracken were also collected. Acorns and hazelnuts were collected in the few areas where the trees grew. Plants played important industrial roles, particularly red cedar (*Thuja plicata*) which was used for canoes, houses, clothing, baskets, and boxes among many uses. On Vancouver Island, people maintained gardens of Pacific silverweed (*Potentilla anserina*) and Springbank clover (*Trifolium wormskjoldii*),[16] while farther north, people collected kelp and eel grass.

The coast's people manipulated their environment to produce more food. The regular burning of Oregon's Willamette Valley by the Kalapuya is the best-documented case.[17] In the early 19th century, the valley's floor was covered by an oak savanna, a park-like grassland with small stands of oak. As a habitat, it was very productive, producing large quantities of camas and acorns, and supporting large populations of deer. It was this environment that attracted the first settlers along the Oregon trail, and it was entirely the result of burning. Robert Boyd, who has studied Kalapuya burning practices, suggests on the basis of pollen cores, that Native peoples may have used fire to manipulate the Willamette Valley's vegetation for 5,000 years. Nancy Turner, who has studied native plant use on Vancouver Island, has collected accounts and descriptions of deliberate burning to produce a more productive forest environment.[18]

Seasonality and mobility

Food resources were primarily available from early spring through fall, often at the same time but in different places. Berries might be ripe in an upland meadow while salmon were running in the river far below. People had to cope with this complex distribution of resources in time and space. They had to have their work parties where and when the resources were available. In most instances, the food had then to be transported back to where the majority of the group were living. Most groups, as a result, had complicated patterns of movement through a year. The Coast Tsimshian of northern British Columbia are a good example.

In the 18th and 19th centuries, the Coast Tsimshian spent their winters in Prince Rupert Harbor, where they maintained their principal towns. There were probably some 6,000 Coast Tsimshian at this time. In late February or early March, many would go by boat to the mouth of the Nass, 50 km (30 miles) to the north, for the eulachon run, which the Coast Tsimshian controlled. The fish were netted and rendered into oil. At the conclusion of the run, many people returned to the harbor, and then moved to fishing and shellfish collecting camps on the islands west of the harbor where they might remain until late spring, or early summer, by which time the salmon were running in the Skeena River. At this time, the houses in Prince Rupert were disassembled (the massive frames left in place), the planking lashed across canoes to form rafts, boxes of equipment and household goods stacked on the rafts, and almost everyone would remove to the summer villages on the Skeena estuary for the fishing season. At the conclusion of the runs in the early fall, the move would be reversed, and people would return from the summer villages to Prince Rupert Harbor with their household goods and dried salmon for the winter. Other groups had even more complicated annual movements, some moving as many as 16 times. Five to six such shifts in a year was typical in the early 19th century for many groups, while others, often in adjacent bays or even the same bay, did not move at all. Regardless of the number of residential moves, they maintained permanent villages, sometimes in several places.

Production

The household was the basic unit of both consumption and production. People occupied one or more of the large, cedar plank houses that were the primary form of dwelling, their numbers ranging from as few as 20 people to over 100. Households were organized into villages and towns. There was a fairly strong gender-based division of labor, although Madonna Moss suggests that the strength (rigidity) of the sexual division of labor has been exaggerated.[19] Slave labor was important, and

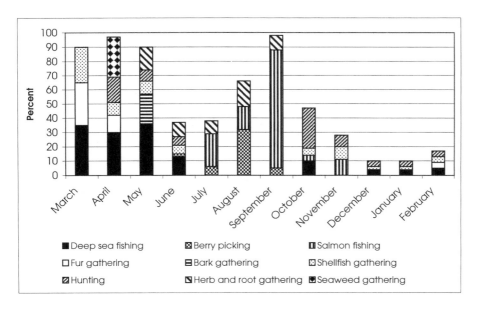

44 The relative amount of time spent on gathering resources among the northern Tlingit based on research conducted by Kalervo Oberg. While patterns varied locally, all Northwest Coast groups had complex annual schedules.

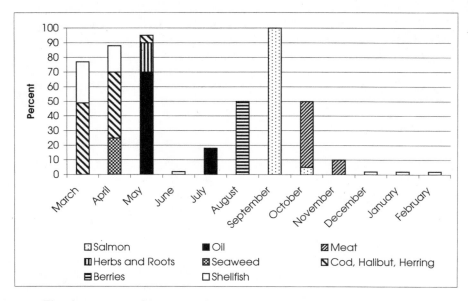

45 The relative amount of time spent each month on storage activities among the northern Tlingit based on research conducted by Kalervo Oberg .

what some have called a "fair amount of specialization" for hunter-gatherers.[20] Households owned estates of corporeal and non-corporeal property. Corporeal property included resources and their habitats, the ground upon which the household's dwellings were built, the dwellings themselves, and the processed food, and wealth produced by the household. Non-corporeal property included the rights to resources, to songs and ritual performances, and to particular animal helpers and spirit beings. Non-corporeal property is commonly termed "privileges" in the ethnographic literature. Households had genealogical depth and maintained oral household histories. In theory at least, household members had equal access to the household's estate.

Patterns of resource ownership varied along the coast.[21] In some areas, usually along the southern coast, they were owned by individuals, while farther north, by the household. Formation of wealth was ultimately dependent upon producing food surpluses, though wealth often took other forms than food. Redistribution through the potlatch and other means was important. There was a strong ethos against hoarding.

The household's subsistence economy focused on the resources that were part of its estate. However, households also participated in a regional economy of trade and exchange (Chapter Seven). The Coast Tsimshian who caught and processed eulachon on the Nass traded the fish and oil with Haida, Tlingit and interior peoples for such things as canoes, copper, and buckskins. Trade routes into the British Columbia interior were called grease trails after the fish oil that was traded along them, and were fortified in places because the trade was so important. On the Lower Columbia, the Chinookans participated in a trade network that ultimately extended east, beyond what is now Yellowstone Park, as well as far to the south and north.

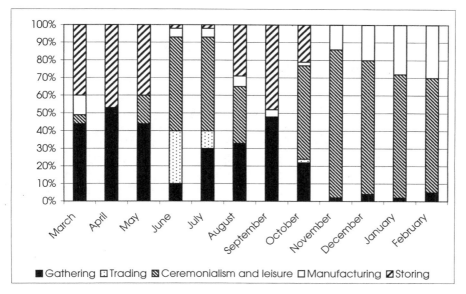

46 The relative amount of time spent each month on important activities among the northern Tlingit based on research conducted by Kalervo Oberg.

The archaeology of Northwest Coast subsistence economies

Archaic period

It is worth recalling from Chapter Three that this is a period of great environmental changes and sharp contrasts with today's conditions. At the period's beginning *c.* 10,500 BC, the coastal plain in the south was much broader than it is today, though the coastline itself was probably as sharp and abrupt. A coastal plain with lakes and streams also extended north from what is now Vancouver Island. Another coastal plain linked the Queen Charlotte Islands to the mainland. By 8000 BC, sea levels had risen rapidly, particularly in the north, sometimes reaching positions much higher than today's, and then receding. Along the southern coast, sea levels also rose quickly, but without major transgressions. The climate became warmer and drier, and plant and animal distributions changed. It is likely then that hunter-gatherer economies, particularly in the north, had to be quite flexible to adjust to what at times were probably rapidly changing conditions. Also, given the environmental differences along the coast, there is no particular reason to expect the same subsistence economy along its entire length.

Evidence for subsistence practices on the coast prior to the Pacific period is quite thin, and there is nothing older than 8400 BC, which is almost two-and-a-half millennia younger than the oldest evidence from the interior (Chapter Three). It is possible, however, to make some educated guesses about what these early people were doing for a living on the coast, and match those guesses against what data are available. There are three general possibilities: they could have been fully maritime, littoral, or terrestrial in their economy (and of course some combination of these three).

If Archaic peoples on the coast were fully maritime we would expect some evidence for sea-worthy boats, boats capable of going out into open water in a variety of conditions as well as evidence of people's capability to exploit a wide range of neritic environments, from high-tide to the deeper waters on the continental shelf. Such evidence would include both specialized fishing and hunting tackle as well as the direct evidence of fish and sea mammals taken from a wide array of marine habitats. This describes a maritime economy geared to take advantage of the full diversity of neritic environments. An alternative is a highly specialized maritime economy in which the subsistence technology and techniques were narrowly focused on fully exploiting a few productive resources. In this case, the range of resources recovered in sites would be quite narrow, with perhaps two or three species completely dominating the assemblages. A littoral economy would look quite different.

The early Archaic peoples of coastal California are an excellent example of a littoral economy. Jon Erlandson[22] reconstructs their economy as focused on terrestrial plant foods and shellfish. A variety of mammals, including deer and seal, were hunted, and some fishing occurred, but Erlandson believes that seeds and shellfish were the dietary mainstays. This is indicated by the presence of shell middens and of milling stones (used to mill plant seeds). There is no evidence for harpoons or other tackle required to take sea mammals from a boat, nor need there be any, since seals can be hunted and killed on land, particularly when they come ashore to pup.[23] However, the capability to kill seals from a boat with a harpoon does not indicate, to our minds, a fully maritime economy.

The third possibility is a terrestrial/riverine economy, perhaps similar to Windust peoples in the southern interior of Washington and Idaho. The Columbia Plateau, particularly its southeastern corner, contains the longest record of human occupation in Cascadia. It has produced a number of sites spanning the period between 11,000 and 6000 BC. The evidence suggests that the region was occupied by highly mobile foragers whose subsistence strategies emphasized the wetter portions of the plateau, including uplands, lakes, streams, and rivers.[24] Windust peoples may have extended down the Columbia to the coast. Windust points are found as far west as the suburbs of Portland, Oregon, and Windust-like material has been reported from the mouth of the Columbia River.[25]

Windust peoples hunted a variety of mammals, including elk, deer, antelope, bison, and rabbits.[26] There is no evidence that they focused on any particular animal, hunting what was locally available. However, they were able to hunt and kill large mammals, such as bison. The role of fishing is unknown for the period before 6800 BC. A single, large net weight was recovered at the Hatwai site in central Idaho, which may date as early as 10,900 BC, and barbed points occurred at Lind Coulee, dating to 7500 BC. The Lind Coulee site was next to a lake at the time it was occupied. The first direct evidence for salmon fishing in the Columbia Basin is from several widely separated sites: Five Mile Rapids on the Lower Columbia; Bob's Point and Umatilla on the Middle Columbia River; Kettle Falls, far up the Columbia River, near Spokane, Washington; and Bernard Creek Rockshelter, on the Snake River in Hells Canyon. Taken together, these sites show fishing for salmon and other fish by 6000 BC. There is no evidence for significant reliance on storage (there is no direct evidence for storage at all). Population levels appear to have been quite low.

Three skeletons provide chemical data on the role of salmon in Windust diets. The oldest is the Buhl skeleton dating to 10,600 BC, and is the oldest skeleton in western North America. The skeleton, that of a young woman, was recovered near the Snake River in south-central Idaho. The evidence suggests that she may have had some minor amounts of marine protein in her diet. That far inland, salmon could be the only source of marine protein. The youngest skeleton is that of a young male, recovered at Gore Creek in south-central British Columbia, and dating to 7500 BC. Salmon appear to have played almost no role in his diet either. The third skeleton, that of a middle-aged man dating to 7800 BC, produced a very different picture. The skeleton was recovered from the banks of the Columbia River, near Kennewick, Washington. Bone chemistry data suggests a diet high in marine protein. However, there is clear evidence for bison hunting in the region at this time. Bison are grazers, and so the chemistry results may be the result of his eating bison meat rather than large quantities of salmon.

Archaic period technology was designed by its users to be flexible. The same gear could be employed against a variety of animals. Hunting and fishing equipment were made from modular parts that could be re-arranged depending on need. For example, the evidence from the Columbia Plateau indicates that hunters used darts armed with different kinds of points mounted on foreshafts. A foreshaft with a stone lanceolate point could be placed on the mainshaft to use against bison; replacing the stone point with a barbed bone point changes the bison dart into a fishing spear. Mount a toggling harpoon point on the same foreshaft and one can harpoon salmon or seals. Several specialized toolkits are unnecessary and there is no evidence for their existence either in the interior or on the coast.

The limited faunal evidence available on the coast suggests that a wide variety of neritic and terrestrial foods were exploited. Chuck Lake on Hecate Island contains the northern coast's earliest preserved shell midden, though other sites, such as Hidden Falls, have some shell deposits and may be decayed middens. Deeply buried shell deposits in Prince Rupert Harbor could also be of this age. The Chuck Lake midden is small, thin and discontinuous, unlike the later massive middens. Intertidal mollusks dominate the shellfish, while both salmonid and non-salmonid fish such as halibut are present in the faunal assemblage. The identifiable mammalian fauna include rabbit, beaver, deer or caribou, sea lion and seal. Except for the rabbit, these are all represented only by teeth, though sea-mammal longbone fragments were found, as were longbone shafts of "medium" and "large" mammals. Halibut are generally found in deep waters, and taken from boats with lines and hooks. The presence of salmon indicates that harvested foods were transported in from elsewhere, probably in canoes, since the site is not near a stream.

The Archaic occupation at Glenrose Cannery produced a small faunal assemblage: 18 mammal bones and 56 fish bones. Despite its size, it is a remarkably diverse assemblage, including elk, deer, seals, canids, beaver, mink, salmon, sturgeon, flounder, eulachon, squawfish, peamouths, and sticklebacks. There are also some shell deposits as well. The fish remains suggest the presence of nets (the eulachon), and fish spears (e.g. sturgeon) and trolling gear, including boats (halibut). Glenrose was right on the Fraser River during the Archaic, and all the mammals and fish, except the halibut, could have been harvested in riverine habitats. The seals could have been harpooned in water, or killed on land. There are no harpoons, however, at Glenrose, only a single barbed point.

Nothing described so far for the coast appears to be beyond the capabilities of the Early Archaic terrestrial hunter-gatherers we described on the plateau. Artifacts often regarded as crucial evidence of a maritime economy, including barbed points and nets, are present in the interior. What about boats? There is only indirect, but quite strong, evidence for boats worldwide by 50,000 years ago. Quite recently, two archaeologists have argued that Clovis people had boats.[27] If so, certainly Windust folk did as well. Fladmark's coastal route hypothesis for the peopling of the Americas requires boats to be feasible. Nevertheless there is nothing to indicate the presence of specialized maritime hunters along the Northwest Coast during the Archaic, rather the data indicate hunter-gatherers similar to those in the interior, but adapted to exploiting the littoral zone, and nearby waters.

There are some data that do not appear to fit this model, however. Bone chemistry analysis of a human jaw recovered by James Dixon[28] in On-your-knees Cave in southeastern Alaska suggests that virtually all the protein in this person's diet came from marine organisms. The site is on an island, so it is unlikely that these results reflect the presence of certain kinds of terrestrial plants. A diet high in marine protein does not, to our minds, contradict our model. Furthermore, the bone chemistry results must be viewed with some caution. They only tell us about protein, not the whole diet, nor do they reveal the exact source of the protein. If Jon Erlandson's reconstruction of the diets of Archaic people along the California coast is correct, bone chemistry analysis would probably produce results quite similar to those from the On-your-knees jaw, missing the important role of plant foods in the early California diet.

There are differences in artifact assemblages between coastal sites and the interior sites. The earliest interior sites contain large stemmed lanceolate points that are generally absent (though not completely so) on the coast. This may reflect an accommodation to hunting a greater range of large terrestrial mammals in the interior. The Early Archaic interior assemblages lack microblades, which could also be an adaptation to particular circumstances on the northern coast. Microblades are present in later Archaic assemblages in the northern interior of Cascadia, and they occur in Pacific period assemblages on the southern coast.

The Bear Cove site on the northeast corner of Vancouver Island may be the major sticking point for our model. Bear Cove's component 1 has a basal date of approximately 7000 BC. However, the faunal remains from component 1 may only date to between 3338–2550 BC. These faunal remains include rockfish, salmon, and a variety of other fish. Over 75 percent of the mammal bones are those of sea mammals, and two-thirds of those are the bones of dolphins. No artifacts that can be interpreted as subsistence gear were recovered, except for a single leaf-shaped point. Many archaeologists view these dolphin bones as evidence for a maritime economy, but questions about porpoise behavior and the dating of the site weaken it as an exception.

There is no evidence on the Northwest Coast at present for an economy like that described by Erlandson for the early California coast, and it is not known how far north beyond San Francisco Bay the littoral pattern he describes extended. It is an open question whether an economy like that could function along the more heavily forested Northwest Coast. However, the warming and drying trend that climaxed around 6800 BC produced environments different from those of the last 6,000 years. The recent discovery of the Indian Sands shell midden near Bandon, Oregon, by

Erlandson and Madonna Moss at least raises the possibility that the California littoral economy could have extended as far north as the southern Oregon coast. The Indian Sands midden dates to 7500 BC.

A final issue to be addressed is the role of storage and salmon fishing in the economy postulated here. First, it is quite likely that some food storage occurred and that salmon were procured for that purpose. It seems unlikely that humans could survive in any numbers along the northern coast, at least, in the absence of storage (though the reader should recall that by 7000 BC the climate was warmer and drier than at present and perhaps storage was less crucial to surviving most winters). In any case, such small-scale storage need not have dramatic consequences in terms of social and economic change. O'Leary's research among the Southern Tutchone peoples in Canada shows that salmon fishing for storage does not necessarily lead to partial sedentism.[29] The basic storage techniques – sun and wind drying, and smoking – have probably been known for many thousands of years, probably at least since the Upper Paleolithic, so significant technological innovations are not required for storage to play a role in Archaic period economies. Finally, salmon could have been taken in large numbers without storage. Mobile hunter-gatherers, particularly those with low population densities, gather periodically to do all the things people do in large groups: trade, gossip, exchange information, gamble, dance, worship, and, most importantly for small dispersed groups, find mates. The everyday group sizes of 25 to 50 people common among such hunter-gatherers are too small to be socially or reproductively viable. Larger aggregations are crucial for finding mates for the young, sharing information, reestablishing social connections and so on. These aggregations would require a food supply. In the 18th and 19th centuries on the Columbia Plateau, huge aggregations formed at the meadows where camas roots were gathered in late summer. Salmon would be ideal for such large but temporary gatherings: 1) their location is predictable; and 2) a large run could not be depleted or dispersed by fishing pressure (game animals will disperse under hunting pressure). Five Mile Rapids, Kettle Falls, and Milliken would be excellent localities for such gatherings, even in the absence of significant reliance on storage. The point here is that we need not invoke storage on a large scale to account for particular instances where we find large numbers of salmon.

Pacific period subsistence economies

Our knowledge of Pacific period economies is far better than for the Archaic period, but it is not as good as one might suspect, given the important role subsistence questions have played in explaining social and cultural developments on the coast. The basic and most important questions being asked by archaeologists about Pacific period subsistence systems are: when did the coast's people begin significantly to increase their production of food, how did they do it, and why did they do it? A related question is when and why did storage become central to their economies? Efforts to answer these questions must draw upon our general understanding of economic changes among hunter-gatherers.[30]

Hunter-gatherers often increase their food production by diversifying their economies. These diversified economies are sometimes described as "broad spectrum," reflecting the sheer number of food resources used.[31] They increase both the numbers and the kinds of organisms they use. These new resources often require more work or time to make it worthwhile to harvest them. Another alternative is for people to focus their efforts on a few productive resources in what is sometimes called a "focal economy."[32] Focal economies often combine a focus on a few, quite productive resources, while continuing to harvest a wide array of other foods. People may choose to do this because the focal or staple resources do not provide everything required for a relatively healthy diet; the staples may be boring to eat; or people may think it too risky to rely on only a few food sources, no matter how productive they are.

Finally, hunter-gatherers may specialize, and rely completely on only a few resources. In this case, there is often no alternative but to gear their technologies and economies to make full use of the few foods or useful environments available. People along the arctic coast have little choice but to specialize in sea-mammal hunting, because that is about all the environment offers these hunter-gatherers.

Why produce more food? One basic reason is to feed more people. This is the most likely cause, over the long run, for increasing levels of food production on the coast. However, people increase the amount of food they harvest and process for other reasons. They may plan to trade the extra food for other things they want. But food can also be exchanged, through feasting and by giving it away, for spouses, pres-tige, and power.[33] Why store food? Again, there is the basic answer – to get through the winter, particularly among populations too large to survive well on whatever is available to harvest through the winter. But people can have other motives. Dried foods can be widely transported and traded. Large accumulations of stores can be used to attract new people and followers to ambitious leaders.

Since the coast is not a uniform place, we should expect to see different patterns of intensification in different places along it as people took advantage of whatever opportunities their local environment provided. If Randall Schalk is correct, for example, we should expect to see differences in how food production was increased between the northern and southern coasts. In the north, where the pro-ductivity of terrestrial environments is low, people would have to emphasize littoral and marine resources in their efforts to acquire more food, while on the southern coast, where terrestrial habitats are richer, they would likely intensify terrestrial resources – such as plants – first. On a smaller scale, increasing food production in a salmon-rich territory might involve increasing the salmon harvest, while in a salmon-poor place, it might include efforts to increase production of other resources, or it might mean having to expand a group's social and economic ties, perhaps by producing some goods that could be traded for food, as the Haida traded canoes for eulachon oil.

Economic data on the coast then are best viewed at three scales, the microscale of a site and its immediate environs, a regional middle scale (e.g. Hesquiat Harbor or the Gulf of Georgia), and then a macroscale that is defined minimally at the level of a subarea (northern coast, central and southern coast) if not at the level of the whole coast itself. The available information often does not permit us to discuss all these dif-ferent scales, but the reader should bear them in mind since they structure much of the following discussion. Economies are regional in scale, but their effects are local, and will vary with local (microscale) differences in ecology. Economic change, such as intensification, is a medium or even macroscale event, with different, local effects in different places. Large, regional samples are the only way to distinguish local responses to purely local situations from local responses to regional developments.

Because there is so much more evidence for the Pacific period, we can only

*33 Yakutat Tlingit guests at a Sitka potlatch, 1904. The elderly man in the middle of the middle
row is wearing a potlatch hat with three potlatch rings, indicating he has given three potlatches.
Two other men in that row are wearing Chilkat blankets, possession of which marked high status
and wealth. Others are wearing nose rings, another marker of high status. Some of the floral
designs are from far to the east, in central Canada.*

34 Chief Tatoosh, a Nuu-chah-nulth chief, wears a knobbed whaler's hat and a fur robe, both markers of his status. The hat, with its whaling scenes, was a common part of high status regalia.

35 "A Young Woman of Queen Charlotte's Islands" 1787. This young woman is wearing two markers of status, her large labret, or lip plug, and her fur or hair robe.

Status

36 Portrait of Chinookan man illustrating the style of cranial deformation practiced along the Lower Columbia River.

37 *Ceremonial Copper, Tlingit, before 1876.*
"Coppers," large sheets of copper beaten to this
distinctive shape were significant markers of
status and prestige during the 19th century.
Objects made of copper were used as status
markers for over 2,000 years.

38 (left) Haida mortuary pole commemorating a high-status person. Like most such monuments, this one is smooth for its entire length, and is topped by a single large carving. Similar poles are visible in plate 40.

Mortuary practices

39 (right) Mortuary monuments at Port Mulgrave, Yakutat Bay, southeast Alaska, illustrating the possible size of some burial poles and boxes. Elaborate burial ritual can produce sizable monuments which leave little or no archaeological record.

40 (below) Memorial poles at Masset, Queen Charlotte Islands, 1910. There are a variety of memorial poles illustrated here, all with a top and bottom figure and potlatch cylinders in between.

41 (above) Grave of Chinookan Chief
Concomoly, Lower Columbia River. The
drawing illustrates the differences in mortuary
monuments and decorative motifs that could be
found along the coast.

Warfare and weapons

42 (far left) Nuu-chah-nulth arrow box lid, collected by Captain Cook in 1778. Engravings are illustrative of West Coast art.

43 (left) Stone club in the form of a sandhill crane. The club is one of a unique cache found near Hagwilet Canyon, B.C. in the 19th century.

44 (right) Copper Tlingit dagger, with the double blade of the traditional design.

45 (below) "Village of the Friendly Indians." There is a fortress or fortified village at the top of the hill. Vancouver's expedition 1791.

46 (above) Carved, wooden helmet collected
by 1888. The helmet may originally have been
plumed. The facial expression may portray
paralysis, or pain from a blow,

47 (below) Tlingit breastplate of painted hide,
first half of the 19th century. The design is
similar to those found on Chilkat blankets. Hide
armour was widely used on the coast.

48 *Helmet mask from the Northwest Coast*
now in the Lowe Museum of Anthropology,
Berkeley.

summarize what is known. A book longer than this one could be written on this topic alone if one were to do justice to all the available evidence and ideas.

Early Pacific period

The Early Pacific is almost everywhere (excluding perhaps the Oregon and Washington coasts[34]) marked by increased use of intertidal resources. Fladmark originally argued that this increase in shellfish eating was an indirect result of the stabilization of sea levels at their current positions at 3800 BC. He believed that the stabilization of sea levels lead to increased use of salmon, which led to increased levels of sedentism (living in the same spot year-round), which in turn led to increased exploitation of other resources, including mollusks. We agree with him to the extent that the expansion in shellfish use was probably the result of people being more sedentary. Sea-level changes and salmon exploitation alone cannot be the causes of this, however. As pointed out in Chapter Four, the appearance of shell middens is coincident in time with the widespread appearance of pithouses east of the Coast-Cascade ranges, sometimes in places where salmon have never gone. We think the appearance of houses marks a shift to greater sedentism and increased food production that occurred throughout Cascadia starting around 4400 BC, and that shell middens are the coast's expression of this change.

Mollusks provide a good example for considering the effects of intensification. Erlandson has argued successfully that shellfish are a fine source of protein; by increasing their consumption of mollusks, therefore, Early Pacific peoples were increasing their protein consumption. But it is open to debate whether or not this was important on the Northwest Coast, since nearly everything eaten was a good source of protein. Perhaps more important is that shellfish have virtually no fats or carbohydrates. While people rely heavily on shellfish to supplement their diets,[35] and the accumulation of shellfish remains does indeed indicate a more intensive harvesting practice, we are actually measuring a change in labor organization and sedentism. Shellfish could be collected not only by the able-bodied but also by individuals such as the elderly and children (those who could not participate in other harvesting activities); we may thus be seeing a change in which previously non-producing members of the community were now encouraged to contribute to the subsistence economy. It is also possible that people were relying less heavily on other sources of protein. In short, while shellfish are a classic example of the kind of resources hunter and gatherers will begin to heavily exploit as they work to increase their food production, interpreting increased production is not always straightforward.

Namu appears to provide the best sequence for the intensification of food production during the Early Pacific. Between 5000 and 4000 BC (Namu 2), the economy was at its most diverse. Shellfish played only a minor dietary role (and the shell deposits are similar to Archaic period shell deposits elsewhere), while salmon and probably herring were economically the most important fish.[36] Other fish were harvested, as were seals, deer, and an array of small mammals. During the next millennium (4000 to 3000 BC, Namu 3), salmon use increased markedly, as did the exploitation of shellfish. At this time, Namu developed a large, dense shell midden. Use of other fish appears to have declined as the economy became more focal. The increase in salmon harvesting may in part have been the result of opportunities provided to fishermen by the stabilization of sea levels and the lower course of the Namu River[37] which probably produced larger runs. This fails to explain why people made that choice, though. During Namu 4 (3000 to 2000 BC), the economy diversified again. Salmon production increased marginally, and people took greater numbers of rockfish, cod, seals, and sea otters. Herring appears to have been a major staple through the Early Pacific. As we point out below, increased harvesting of sea otters and seals may point to people exploiting new neritic environments.

At the beginning of the sequence, at Namu, the economy is relatively diverse. When significant increases in food production occurred, the economy seems to have become somewhat focal, as people elected to expend most of their effort on fewer resources among the total number of foods they were collecting. By the end of the period, however, they probably could not significantly increase their salmon harvest and had to expand their use of other resources and other environments. The major technological change at Namu is the disappearance of microblades and microliths at the end of Namu 2 (4000 BC),[38] at a time when salmon production was increasing. Perhaps the most "specialized" equipment at Namu during the Early Pacific were fish hook shanks, which may have been used as part of halibut gear. In any case, the changes in subsistence do not appear to have been fueled by major technological innovations. Despite the central importance of salmon in the economy of Namu's people, there is also no direct evidence for storage, although storage does not necessarily result in storage features. We will return to that matter below.

Turning to the coast, as a whole, bone chemistry analyses provide a clear indication of the relative importance of marine vs. terrestrial resources during the Pacific period. Chisholm examined some 90 skeletons from the coast dating between 3800 BC and AD 500. In all cases, between 90 and 100 percent of the proteins in the bone (and presumably therefore in the diet) were derived from marine sources, i.e. ocean fish (including salmon), shellfish, sea mammals, kelp etc. It does not reveal what proportion of the diet was from fish, from sea mammals, from shellfish, or a myriad other possible sources. Nor does it tell us about other necessary sources of nutrition and calories. Faunal remains are our only evidence for the relative dietary roles of different marine organisms. These data do show that at the macroscale, littoral and marine resources were the basis for the Northwest Coast diet and subsistence economy by 3800 BC.[39]

The appearance of ground-slate points probably reflects increased use of specialized sea-mammal hunting tackle in place of, or in addition to, the more generalized equipment used during the Archaic period (see above). This does imply a shift towards a maritime economy and perhaps increasing sedentism, and a move away from the more generalized littoral economy of the Archaic.

In the Gulf of Georgia area, the evidence shows a broadly based subsistence economy. The available faunal data do not suggest a significant increase in production of salmon or any other resource during this period. However, these data are from a relatively few sites, some of which were excavated a generation ago, and so the possibility remains that this apparent pattern is the result of our sample. Also, the Gulf of Georgia area possesses a rich, terrestrial environment, and so patterns of economic change may have been quite different there than farther north. One important aspect of these possible differences is use of plants. Gulf of Georgia assemblages contain milling stones well into the Middle Pacific, suggesting a far greater importance of processed plant foods than farther north. Acorns, camas, and wapato were all available in this area, providing oil, protein, and carbohydrates. Efforts at increasing production here might very likely have taken the direction of broadening an already broad resource base. We will return to this point in the discussion of the Middle Pacific.

The Early Pacific economy on the northern coast was also diverse. In southeast Alaska, salmon, herring, and cod were taken in roughly even proportions. Deer, seals, and sea otter were the primary mammals harvested.

Seasonality and mobility

Data on site functions and seasons of occupation are another line of evidence with which to reconstruct subsistence. Glenrose Cannery appears to have been used year-round at this time[40] There is no evidence of residential structures there, however. Nor does it appear to have been a special-purpose site, although it was a good spot for a fish camp. Glenrose may have been used off and on throughout the year by a variety of local groups, or by members of a single group for different, but for overlapping purposes. It was certainly used as a base for hunting as well as for fishing. The seasonality evidence from Namu suggests a fall and spring occupation.[41] From this Aubrey Cannon infers that Namu was occupied through the winter, on the grounds that people would not take and store large numbers of salmon, then move briefly elsewhere and then return to fish for herring. However, there are no reported structures at Namu, though the site does contain hearths and postholes. Burials from this period are concentrated in one area, suggesting a cemetery. In subsequent periods burials were placed behind houses in some areas, thus the concentration at Namu could be taken to at least raise the possibility of a cemetery associated with a structure there. There is also no direct evidence of storage at Namu, except for the large numbers of salmon. It seems perfectly feasible that mobile hunters and gatherers would gather at Namu for a fall fish run, perhaps even erecting structures, dispersing to other available food sources, and returning in the spring. The Namu 2 midden is contemporaneous with the earliest pithouses in the interior, those in Surprise Valley, California.

The Boardwalk site, in Prince Rupert Harbor, appears to have been occupied year-round by 2100 BC,[42] at which time it had also reached its maximum size.[43] However, no houses from this period have been found.

Component II at Hidden Falls does contain a structure, an exposed semi-circle of postholes with an adjacent hearth. Lightfoot concludes that this component was produced by highly mobile hunter-gatherers. The reader will recall that substantial Early Pacific structures were recovered at Mauer and at Hatzic Rock on the Fraser River above its delta. Ham also argues for the presence of substantial structures at this time at St Mungo Cannery in the Fraser Delta. It seems only a matter of time until such structures are exposed in Early Pacific shell middens. However, at present, many Early Pacific sites have an undifferentiated quality; there seems little evidence for special-use sites. Namu is a significant exception to that statement. But it, like Glenrose, may have been used for a variety of overlapping purposes.

We will see in subsequent chapters that the Early Pacific is a rather murky period in a number of respects. Part of this murkiness is the result of the available data (or lack of it). We would argue that regional variation is another cause. As we shall see below, there is good evidence that heavy reliance on salmon and storage developed on the coast by the beginning of the Middle Pacific; this suggests that this change was occurring along the coast earlier as it seems to have been at Namu. There is no reason to assume it happened everywhere the same way, or at the same time. Given the available sample of excavated sites and data, this was a very dynamic period.

Middle Pacific period

It is during this period that we clearly see the emergence of middle-scale and macroscale economies. It is also quite evident that storage plays a significant role in the foundation of those economies. There are a number of lines of evidence that, taken together, support this conclusion, although any single one alone is not very strong. These lines of evidence, together, also point to the regional development of maritime (as opposed to littoral) economies.

Technology

Net weights are present throughout Cascadia in relatively large numbers for the first time. As noted above, they may have been used since before 10,000 years ago, but before 1800 BC they are quite rare in archaeological deposits. After that date, they are relatively more common, suggesting expanded use of nets, and perhaps new types of nets, and therefore, larger catches of fish. Evidence for increases in capacity to take and process food resources is key evidence for intensification. It is interesting to note that although net weights are always relatively rare, divers report them in large numbers along accessible portions of the Lower Columbia River, some quite large in size relative to what are found in sites. Compound harpoons, though again present for a long time, and probably part of the basic toolkit of the region since 11,000 BC, become quite widespread and common, as do ground-slate points and ground-slate objects in general.

In addition to evidence for nets, there is also evidence in southeast Alaska for use of large weirs at this time. These weir sites consist of intertidal stakes numbering from several to many thousands. They represent the remains of traps that were used to capture fish, primarily salmon. Madonna Moss and John Erlandson have mapped and dated over a dozen weirs on Admiralty Island and adjacent areas of northern southeast Alaska. The oldest and largest weir dated to 1800 BC. Maschner has found over 20 weirs and weir complexes on Kuiu Island dating from throughout the Middle Pacific. Most of the southeast Alaska weirs are associated with salmon streams. Recently, both Eldridge and Maschner have identified a number of weirs in central southeast Alaska that may have been associated with herring harvesting. Moss and Erlandson have noted that these large weir complexes probably represent an intensification in the harvesting of salmon,[44] and this may be the case for the herring traps[45] as well.

On the south coast, Morely and Acheson have suggested that a weir dating to 2700 BC was associated with Glenrose Cannery, but that possibility is far less well documented.[46] However, just as there were nets before 1800 BC, so too were weirs likely to have been used before that date. We are not seeing new technology at this time so much as the reorganization of older technology.

Nevertheless, there is evidence for what may have been a crucial technological innovation, and this evidence comes from an intriguing source. Jerome Cybulski, a physical anthropologist with the Archaeological Survey of Canada, has been studying ancient burial patterns on the coast for well over 20 years and has developed a considerable body of data for the coast as a whole. He notes that boxes used as coffins appear in the archaeological record around 1900 BC. Bent-wood boxes made of western red cedar were, along with baskets, the primary container for stored foods on the coast in the Modern period. The sides of these boxes were made from a single cedar plank that was steamed and bent to shape. The bottom was then sewn

Pl. 17

on, and the side and bottom seams waterproofed. Water was boiled in these boxes by dropping in hot rocks. The appearance of these boxes in the archaeological record is the equivalent of the appearance of pottery elsewhere in the world, except that these boxes are far less likely to break, and stack more easily, being square. This is then an extraordinary development. The presence of boxes as coffins indicates that boxes existed at this time and could certainly have been been used as storage and food-processing containers.

A second major technological innovation of the early Middle Pacific appears to have been the rectangular plank house. This development is discussed in detail in Chapter Six. Here it is sufficient to note that these structures were the primary food-processing and food-storage facilities of the Late Pacific and Early Modern periods, and so again, the potential exists for that function earlier in time. At the Paul Mason site, with its 12 houses, Coupland encountered storage pits outside the houses as well as substantial hearth features.

A shift from a generally round semi-subterranean pithouse to a rectangular, surface dwelling (many plank houses did have internal central pits) would mirror similar architectural shifts in the southwestern USA and elsewhere in the world. The change has sociological implications, but of interest here is simply that a rectangular surface dwelling will have a larger internal volume than a pit house of equivalent area. Early houses on the Columbia Plateau had an average floor area of 71 sq m and an estimated internal volume[47] of 39 cubic m while the Paul Mason houses have a floor area of 62 sq m but an estimated volume[48] of 216 cubic m. The square shape would also provide more available area for interior activities, important in a rainy climate. The potential increase in internal volume probably reflects storage and food processing; one must have a "big box" in which to put all the little boxes full of food.

There is also indirect evidence for the presence of large canoes. The deposits in Prince Rupert Harbor contain both salmon and eulachon bones for the first time. At the Ridley Island site, salmon and eulachon bones are present in astronomical amounts in Middle Pacific deposits. Neither fish is presently available in the harbor, both having to be transported a minimum of 50 km (30 miles), implying the presence of canoes sufficiently large to move large amounts of processed foods.

Pl. 13

Faunal remains and ecology
There is some tantalizing evidence for changes in what we are calling the ecology of Northwest Coast subsistence. We are interested here in the particular environments exploited and the mix of resources collected. The reader will recall Kew's important suggestion that increased food production on the Northwest Coast came about, in part at least, through using new environments[49] (not new species). Put another way, intensification occurred as people were able to exploit the same resources in new places.

In Prince Rupert Harbor, for example, the evidence suggests that key new habitats were kelp beds and shallow off-shore banks. The beginning of the Middle Pacific in the harbor is marked by a dramatic increase in the number of faunal remains present in the sites, as well as by an explosion in the numbers of artifacts related to subsistence, including ground-slate points, barbed and hafted bone points, composite harpoons, bone bipoints, and other tools. The increase in mammal bones is particularly marked for sea mammals. Sea mammals were far more important in the economy of the harbor than earlier. Sea otters were the most important sea mammal, not only for food, but for industrial purposes as well. Sea-otter teeth were used as decorative studs in boxes; sea-otter bones were used as tools, and sea-otter hides were also used.

Sea otters are also, we believe, an indicator of exploitation of productive near-shore marine shallows, such as banks, with dense stands of kelp. Sea otters eat large marine invertebrates such as sea urchins, limpets and chitons that themselves eat kelp and seaweed. Where sea otters are present, these environments are rich and support a wide array of organisms, many useful to humans, such as herring and seals. Where sea otters are absent, these habitats are ecologically sterile from the human standpoint. We may recall here Monks' ideas about Northwest Coast peoples exploiting whole food chains rather than just particular resources. Two sites located near such banks, one (Garden Island) in Prince Rupert Harbor, and one (Lucy Island) in Chatham Sound, were first intensively occupied during the early Middle Pacific. This, coupled with the evidence for intensive exploitation of sea otters themselves, suggests that the residents of Prince Rupert Harbor were intensifying not so much their exploitation of sea otters as a resource, but particular productive habitats, of which sea otters were an important member.

Prince Rupert Harbor was abandoned (perhaps not completely) for a period of time between AD 200 and 500, though the process of abandonment may have begun much earlier. While at present the causes are unknown, one possibility is over-exploitation of these shallow, near-shore environments, including the sea otter population, which would cause a decline in the general productivity of these environments for humans. Perhaps the harbor was reoccupied when the sea otter population recovered and the shallows again supported dense stands of kelp and their associated fauna.

There was also important regional variation in subsistence patterns. The economy of the people of the west coast of Vancouver Island (as revealed at Yuquot) had a persistent marine orientation through both the Early and Middle Pacific.[50] In sharp contrast, the Middle Pacific economy of the Queen Charlotte Strait area (including the northeast coast of Vancouver Island and the adjacent mainland) appears to have had a strong terrestrial emphasis.[51] Ironically, during this period, salmon fishing at Namu declined significantly, due, in Cannon's view,[52] to increased siltation in the Namu River, and consequent impoverishment of the river's salmon runs.

The focus on salmon and other maritime resources may be obscuring evidence for plant use and environmental manipulation. Milling stones are present in the Gulf of Georgia through the Locarno Beach phase, while in the Willamette Valley of western Oregon, people had apparently begun to deliberately and frequently burn the valley floor by 3,000, if not 5,000 years ago. They did this to increase the productivity of oak trees and improve conditions for white tail deer. Oaks produce acorns more often and more regularly if they are subject to annual fires that burn off under-brush and that scorch the tree's bark, cleaning it.[53] How far north such practices extended prehistorically is not known, though historically people burned to maintain forest openings and to create good conditions for desired plants as far north as the Skeena River.[54] Milling stones are not present in Marpole assemblages in the Gulf of Georgia, suggesting an economic change away from processed plants around 500 BC.

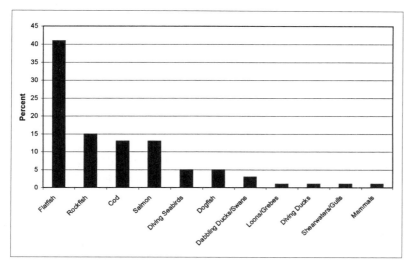

47 Amounts of bone found at the Hoko River rockshelter in northwest Washington. Note the almost complete reliance on fish.

Evidence for intensification of salmon at this time is difficult to see and geographically scattered. Salmon bones appear for the first time in the Prince Rupert middens. The Paul Mason site is located in the Skeena River's Kitselas Canyon, a major salmon fishery, and Coupland reasonably concludes that the site's location indicates that its inhabitants were dependent on salmon; but the site has poor organic preservation and few faunal remains. Matson[55] sees a significant increase in salmon bones at the Crescent Beach site in deposits dating 1800 BC to 1500 BC, a circumstance he argues is definitive proof of the intensification of salmon on the Fraser Delta. Driver, however, reanalyzed Matson's data and concluded that it pointed to an increase in the diversity of the fish being taken.[56] In either case, we seem to be seeing intensification.

In Tebenkof Bay on Kuiu Island in southeast Alaska, Maschner found that while there were many salmon-harvesting weirs dating to the Middle Pacific, the faunal remains from village middens actually showed a decrease in salmon when compared with the Early Pacific. Instead, herring and cod harvesting were intensified, with remains of these two fish numbering in the hundreds of thousands per cubic meter of excavated midden.

Settlement and mobility patterns

Settlement patterns also seem to have changed, at least in some areas of the coast. The appearance of substantial structures indicates some form of partial to full sedentism, again probably depending on local ecological conditions. There is also widespread evidence for the first time for logistical mobility (see Chapter Two) and special-use sites. We have already mentioned much of this evidence in the preceding subsections. Middle Pacific (Locarno Beach phase) settlement patterns in the Gulf of Georgia suggest people placed their camps with access to particular habitats, though, again, what these crucial habitats were seems to have varied locally. Locarno Beach sites on the Fraser Delta seem to have been located with an eye towards productive littoral zones, while the Hoko River locality on the Olympic Peninsula reveals a focus on deep-water environments, with an apparent heavy exploitation of halibut. During the Marpole phase, people may have camped where they were assured access to the salmon runs entering the Fraser Delta.[57]

Late Pacific period
Technology

The beginning of the Late Pacific period is marked by a significant technological shift in many parts of the central and southern coasts. Previously, chipped-stone tools and waste were numerically significant portions of many artifact assemblages. Around AD 500, however, this changes, and chipped stone becomes comparatively rare, almost completely replaced by bone and antler tools, including increased numbers of bone bipoints and varieties of hafted and barbed bone points. Large composite harpoons become common on the west coast of Vancouver Island. The economy of the Queen Charlotte Strait area of the central coast shifted from its Middle Pacific terrestrial focus to a maritime economy like that practiced elsewhere on the coast.

These changes reduced regional variation in artifact assemblages. Some localities, such as Yuquot, Prince Rupert Harbor, and parts of southeast Alaska, never had any numbers of chipped-stone tools in assemblages spanning the Early and Middle Pacific. Now, at the beginning of the Late Pacific, assemblages from these sites are typical of the entire coast in being overwhelmingly of bone and antler.

The reasons for this shift are obscure, although it is probably quite important. It has been interpreted as indicating further intensification of marine habitats and the adoption of the necessary tackle. This interpretation is reasonable but unsupported by extensive studies of changes in faunal remains. Local studies, such as that by Donald Mitchell of the data from the Queen Charlotte Strait (see below), do lend support to the idea.

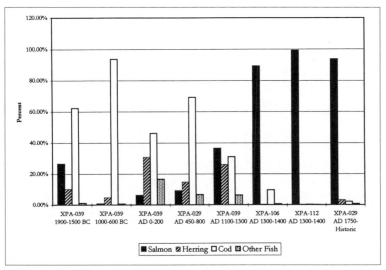

48 Amounts of fish bone found in Tebenkof Bay, southeast Alaska, village sites over the last 4500 years. Note the shift from open-water fish to salmon around AD 1300.

Another technological innovation is less firmly dated, and is quite local in its effects. During the Early Modern period, Coast Salish living in the Gulf and San Juan Islands off Vancouver Island anchored large reef nets placed in channels between the islands through which salmon passed on their way to the Fraser River. Underwater research by Norm Easton suggests that these nets may have been developed sometime during the Late Pacific. Reef nets made accessible large numbers of fish in environments where few could have been taken using previously available tackle.

Faunal remains

Available faunal studies[58] suggest important geographic variation. In Hesquiat Harbor, Gay Calvert found that faunal remains and artifacts recovered over the last 2,000 years varied not with time but with the microenvironment exploited from particular sites, i.e. in their effective environments.[59] She attributes differences in effective environments to socially defined territories, the same pattern described by Leland Donald and Donald Mitchell in their study of salmon catchment described above. The only significant change for the entire 2,000-year period is that the harbor was perhaps originally within the territory of a single social group, but then was divided among several such groups through time, possibly as the result of population growth. A major study of faunal remains in the Gulf of Georgia for the Late Pacific by Diane Hanson[60] also showed significant geographic variation in faunal remains from site to site, including sites where salmon appear to have been quite insignificant.

The Ozette site also shows continuity in the last 200–300 years in at least some subsistence practices. An analysis of the distribution of shellfish remains associated with the three excavated houses at Ozette shows that the members of each house exploited different shell beds,[61] as would be the case if the shell beds were owned as was the practice in the Modern period among the Makah, one of whose villages is Ozette. The Ozette fauna also show the importance of whaling in the Ozette economy.

There was also geographic variation in economic practices in the north. There was considerable continuity in settlement and subsistence pursuits in the central portions of southeast Alaska, but with a general increase in the role of salmon through time.[62] In Tebenkof Bay on the outer coast, there was continuity with the Middle Pacific for the first half of the Late Pacific, with a broad-spectrum economy dominated by cod, herring, and sea mammals, with salmon playing a rather tertiary role. Between AD 1150 and 1350, there was a radical shift to a focal economy based on salmon and supplemented by deer. This change corresponds to a peak in village formation, population, and defensive site construction.[63] Perhaps the most fascinating data are those from the west coast of Moresby Island, in the Queen Charlottes, where Acheson found sound evidence for whaling, a subsistence practice unrecorded among the Haida. Acheson's data span the period between AD 300 and the end of the Late Pacific period.

Settlement patterns and mobility

There is evidence for changing settlement patterns during the Late Pacific. In some cases the changes may merely be increasingly complicated variations around an old theme, but in other cases, the changes may suggest a new theme, such as the development of large, multi-kin-group villages in the north. Very large houses may appear in the south (Chapter Six).

Conclusions

The Archaic occupants of Cascadia appear to have possessed a basic subsistence economy and technology with which they exploited a range of environments, from the drier portions of the Columbia Plateau to the coast's littoral. While it is certainly possible that the coast's earliest occupants had a maritime economy (as we have defined it here), it is not necessary to propose such a specialized economy to explain the available data. Nor is it necessary to have people migrate up or down river. It is most likely that the exposed (now submerged) coastal plain of the Northwest Coast was occupied by these littoral hunter-gatherers as the archaeological record opens. Conditions, particularly in the north, would have favored flexible subsistence strategies over the next several thousand years, as local sea levels fluctuated, sometimes rapidly to extreme elevations, and the climate warmed. It is clear that salmon were exploited. It is also clear that the technological foundations of the later maritime economies were present quite early.

The appearance of shell middens on the coast between 4200 and 3200 BC indicates both an increased emphasis on near-shore resources and probably the appearance of semi-sedentism, at least in some areas. Early Pacific subsistence economies appear to have been quite broadly based, or "broad spectrum," though locally, resources such as salmon may have been relied on heavily. At present the evidence suggests that a storage-based subsistence economy developed all along the coast by 1800 BC, although it could have occurred as early as 2500 BC. Intensification of production appears to have continued throughout the Pacific period. The beginning of the Late Pacific is marked in many areas of the coast by changes in technology and increased use of near and offshore resources (with some interesting exceptions, such as Tebenkof Bay in Alaska).

The record is made complex by the interplay among these regional and coast-wide developments and local ecology. We have stressed in this chapter the crucial role of geographic variation in the environment and in subsistence practices on the coast. This variation makes it more difficult to understand changes through time, but is also absolutely fundamental to understanding those changes. The local archaeological record itself is the result of how people used their local environments – their effective environment. Ownership of territories, for example, was a crucial aspect of the effective environment. At Ozette, because different houses owned different stretches of beach for collecting shellfish, their effective environments were different. Thus, our subsistence record reflects both subsistence and social practices. We will examine the latter in Chapter Seven.

CHAPTER SIX

Households and Beyond

This chapter is about households and houses, places, regions, and continents. In it, we shift through several geographic and social scales, beginning with households and ending with the North Pacific Rim. One of the major themes of this book is local variability, and regional similarities. In this chapter, we consider how those regions came into existence, and the role they played in the development of complexity on the coast. We begin with households, and link them into towns and villages. We then define two kinds of regional organization, one political (polities) and the other economic, cultural and social (interaction spheres) that tied households together into regions. At one point we will also take a tangential look at the development of occupational specialization on the coast.

Houses, households and sedentism

The household is central to understanding the dynamics of Northwest Coast life. We believe that any of the changes we discuss here will either begin, or be felt first in, households. As we have stressed, households[1] were the basic economic and social units of Northwest Coast societies. Northwest Coast households were residential corporate groups:[2] the members lived together, or in close proximity. They held and transmitted common property across generations; the household functioned as an individual in economic production and consumption.

Households are the foundation in most societies for biological and social reproduction, including the enculturation of children. They are the basic unit in both economic production and consumption and for the transmittal (inheritance) of property. In egalitarian societies, family and household social roles are a major route for the acquisition of prestige. It is also within the household in egalitarian societies that individuals are able to impose their will on other individuals. The reorganization of social and economic ties required for the evolution of complexity would require changes in household production, in how much is produced, and in the purposes of production. Households produce both for their own consumption and for trade and exchange. However, evolving inequality would require that household production also be for the purposes of an emerging elite.[3]

Houses were the major possession of Northwest Coast households and served them in many ways: they were the physical manifestation of the household and its social rank; they were theater and stage for social and spiritual rituals,[4] but they were also shelter in the Northwest's dank climate; they were food-processing factories, in which food resources were butchered, roasted, smoked, rendered, dried, boiled, stored, and consumed; and they were the objects of enormous effort and great skill. Their interior arrangements were often a map of the relative status of the household's members. According to George MacDonald, these houses were maps of the

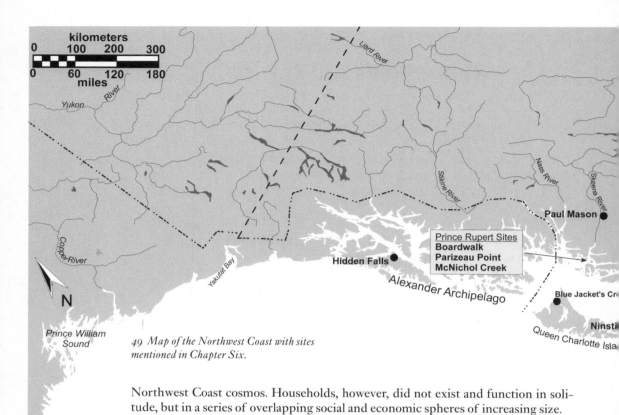

49 *Map of the Northwest Coast with sites mentioned in Chapter Six.*

Northwest Coast cosmos. Households, however, did not exist and function in solitude, but in a series of overlapping social and economic spheres of increasing size.

A town or village[5] usually consisted of several households.[6] The town was the coast's major setting for political and social activities. Households had territories that they exploited during their annual economic round, and they often lived in different parts of those territories in different seasons (sometimes in different towns). This was often accomplished by loading the house's contents onto rafts created by lashing house planks across canoes, and moving to another house frame. Households were socially, politically, and economically linked through trade, exchange, marriage ties, and so on over sometimes vast regions (interaction spheres) by the activities of their chiefs. The relative status of chiefs was measured at the scale of the village within which, and of the region across which, the household maintained its social and economic ties. These differing scales are sometimes marked by differences in art styles, as we will see in Chapter Nine. Understanding these scales is fundamental to an understanding of Northwest Coast history (or that of any region).

The appearance of substantial houses in the archaeological record of any region represents an extremely important event, indicating as it does the formation of the residential corporate group – the household. Such households are in marked contrast to the more fluid family groupings found among generalized hunter-gatherers. Substantial houses also demonstrate the development of some degree of sedentism and of significant economic and social changes accompanying (and causing) sedentism.

Labor organization and specialization are key aspects in the evolution of social complexity. Labor organization (and how much of it there is available) is the primary

Pl. 25–27

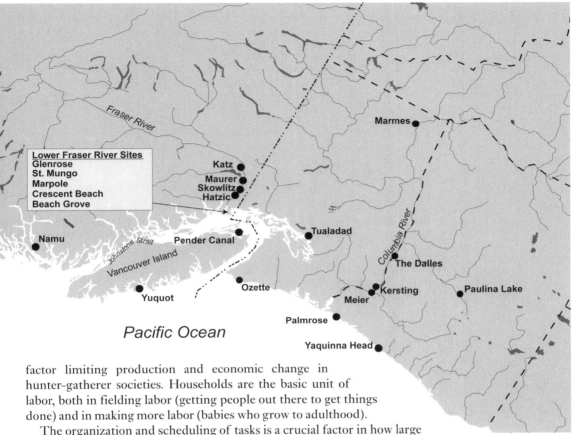

Lower Fraser River Sites
Glenrose
St. Mungo
Marpole
Crescent Beach
Beach Grove

Katz
Maurer
Skowlitz
Hatzic

Marmes

Namu

Johnstone Strait

Vancouver Island

Pender Canal

Tualadad

Columbia River

The Dalles

Yuquot

Ozette

Meier

Kersting

Paulina Lake

Palmrose

Pacific Ocean

Yaquinna Head

factor limiting production and economic change in hunter-gatherer societies. Households are the basic unit of labor, both in fielding labor (getting people out there to get things done) and in making more labor (babies who grow to adulthood).

The organization and scheduling of tasks is a crucial factor in how large a household needs to be. Households will tend to be small where crucial economic tasks can be performed by one or two people over a period of time. On the other hand, where many tasks must be performed at the same time, households frequently tend to be large. In more technical terms,[7] anthropologists identify two kinds of tasks, depending on how they must be done: lineal tasks "can be done by a single person performing a sequence of actions." Automobile repair, for example, is a lineal task. Only one mechanic is often needed to actually repair an automobile, with each task performed following another. Simultaneous tasks, in contrast, must be performed by a number of people at the same time. The musical performance of a band or symphony is a simultaneous task; one can hardly imagine one person playing, in sequence, all the individual instrumental parts to Beethoven's Ninth Symphony, for example. Simultaneous tasks can be either simple or complex. Simple, simultaneous tasks require many people doing the same task at the same time. Before the invention of mechanized grain harvesters, grain would be cut by parties of people in which each person swung a scythe as the harvesters worked across a field. Complex simultaneous tasks involve specialists: all work at the same time, but do different parts of the job, as in playing Beethoven's symphony. We will argue below, and in Chapter Ten, that a crucial development on the Northwest Coast was the evolution of households organized to perform many complex simultaneous tasks, and that specialization also developed on the coast for the same reasons.

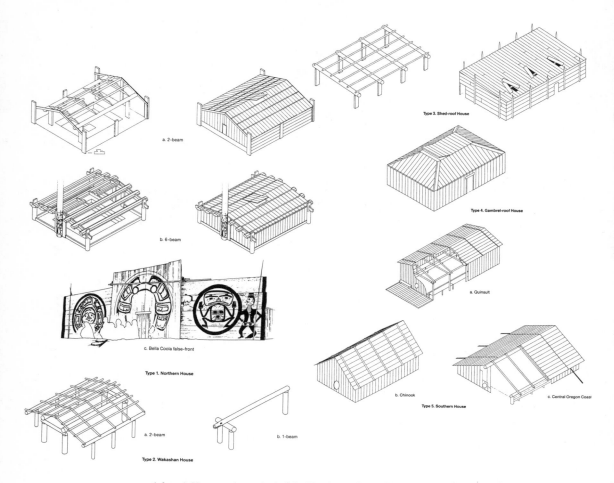

50 (above) House styles typical of the Northwest Coast. Type 1 are northern style houses; type 2 are those found on the west coast of Vancouver Island; types 3 and 4 in the Gulf of Georgia region, as well as on Vancouver Island. Type 5 houses are found on the southern coast.

The size of dwellings indicates the size of the household group, bigger structures housing more people. General increases in house sizes through time suggest an overall increase in the number of people per household. If all of a society's houses are large, then we are seeing the effects of labor organization. If, however, some houses are even larger than others, we are probably seeing the effects of relative household wealth and status.

Another important factor in household size is the simple ability of the house to attract and hold members, irrespective of labor organization. Worldwide, house sizes usually reflect only one of two things: household size (big houses = big households) or household prestige or rank.[8] Larger households within a society are usually richer, or of higher status or both.[9] The greater wealth and prestige are a consequence of having more labor with which to produce wealth, which in turn can be used to attract more labor.

Houses and households on the Northwest Coast

There were four basic kinds of houses in Cascadia: plank houses, pithouses, mat lodges, and long houses.[10] In the Early Modern period, Northwest Coast peoples almost universally lived in some form of plank house. Northwest Coast houses were of post-and-beam construction, a form of construction found around the North Pacific Rim. Though details varied, Northwest Coast houses were usually built by erecting a frame of posts or squared timbers, then sheathing the frame with planks – hence the term "plank house." These planks were split from logs (and sometimes standing trees) using antler and stone wedges. In the north and extreme south (central Washington to Northern California) houses were built with gable roofs, while houses on the central coast had shed roofs. In most areas, floors were earthen, usually clean beach sand, fine gravel, crushed shell, or some other material that drained well. Floors were also sometimes made of planks. In the north and portions of the central coast, some houses (usually of very high-status households) had multi-level interiors made by excavating a stepped pit. This increased the interior volume of the structure without requiring a larger superstructure. Since high-status houses were usually larger anyway, the combination of an interior pit with large house sizes produced structures with vast, impressive interiors. Houses had one or more hearths for warmth, light, and smoke. Above the hearths were suspended racks holding stored foods that were preserved in the smoke produced by the fires. Raised platforms or benches were built against the interior walls of the house. Valuable goods, dried foods, and oil were kept in water-tight wooden boxes and baskets that were stacked on the benches, or stored underneath them.

Pls. 25–31

Pl. 32

Pithouses were semi-subterranean structures in which the walls of the excavated pit formed the house walls. They are widespread in North America and elsewhere in the world, being easily constructed (one needs to dig a hole and roof it), and are warm and snug in cold weather.[11] Their roofs took a variety of forms. Prior to perhaps 500 years ago, they were the most common form of dwelling east of the Inner Mountains, but were also used on the coast.[12] In the northern interior (British Columbia), roofs were substantial, constructed of heavy timbers, poles, and mats

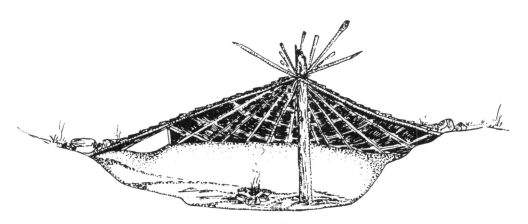

51 Example of early pithouse of the southern interior of Cascadia.

covered with dirt and sod. On the American plateau, the earliest pit dwellings may also have had such roofs, but after 3,000 years ago, the superstructures appear to have been much lighter. The differences in roofs probably reflect differences in winter climate. British Columbia has colder winters, and much heavier snows, requiring stronger roofs.[13] The pits of pithouses varied considerably in depth and diameter.[14] Mat lodges replaced pithouses as the most common structure on the Columbia Plateau by 500 years ago. Mat lodges are light tent-like structures built of poles. Long houses are essentially long mat lodges (some were up to 120 m, or 400 ft long). The term "long house" has recently been applied to plank houses, as well to the mat-and-poles structures. We retain the term plank house to distinguish the two forms, which differ significantly in design.

The shift from pithouses to mat lodges may have been to accommodate larger households, and much greater variation in household size. Very large mat lodges were constructed from the poles and mats of the families living in them, so the structure could easily expand and contract as the household waxed and waned. Pit dwellings would not be so flexible. We postpone answering the question why such flexibility was needed until Chapter Ten.

The interior arrangements of coastal houses provide clues to how the household was organized. On the Early Modern Northwest Coast, the internal living arrangements of houses were structured by the status and economic organization of its household.[15] High-status families lived in the rear or in the corners of the houses, while the lowest-status members generally lived in the front, with intermediate status families along the sides. As different families had different economic specializations, tools and debris associated with those activities tend to be concentrated[16] in those areas of the house occupied by particular specialists.

Northwest Coast houses required considerable labor. How often the structure was repaired and rebuilt is crucial evidence on how long the structure was used, which, in turn, provides clues about the durability of the household occupying it. A repair and rebuilding chronology for one plank house demonstrated that it had stood for perhaps 400 years,[17] indicating considerable time depth for the household(s) that lived in the house.[18] Differential labor costs also point to differences in the relative status of the household.[19] Different styles of house construction may point to several forms of differentiation, including ethnic and regional differentiation.

Villages and towns

Households were tied together in two basic ways: physically by sharing the same town, and socially through kin ties (both blood and marriage). Town size and layout provide information about how households were tied together and the nature of larger-scale political, social, and economic ties. Northwest Coast towns typically contained a row of plank houses facing out upon some body of water. Towns were placed with an eye to fresh water, ease of canoe access, and defense. While not inevitable, the layout of towns often reflected the relative status of the households within the town. The largest houses were those of the highest ranked households; often the highest ranked households lived in the middle of the house row. If the town had two house rows, the front row contained households ranking above those

Pls. 25–28

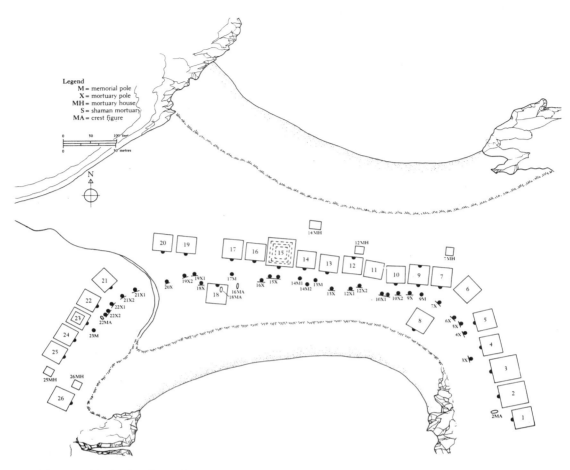

52 Plan map of the Haida village of Skedans on the Queen Charlotte Islands, showing linear village pattern adapted to local landscape. Each house row has a large central high-status house, which is either much larger than the others (houses 2, 3, & 15), has interior terraces (15, 23), or both. House 15, in the middle of the village, is the largest house and has multiple interior terraces. The structure is reported to have been the house of the highest ranking lineage in the community.

of the back row. On the northern coast, small single-row villages usually contained only one extended kin group (a group of households linked genealogically to a single ancestor). Two-row villages generally contained two or more such kin groups. Thus the layout of towns and villages expressed the social relationships, particularly the social status, of the households and extended kin groups living there. Relative house sizes provide clues about both the relative status of households and of the political order of the village (the ranking house chief usually being the ranking village chief).

Town layouts were standardized over much of the coast, particularly along the northern and central coasts. This standardization reflects common elements of Northwest Coast social organization and intense interaction. Town locations were also standardized since a rather particular set of geographic conditions, such as southerly exposure, sand and pebble beaches, and protection from storms, among a number of other characteristics, were important when placing a town.[20]

Sedentism

Sedentism may be one of the most important developments in human history. At least one archaeologist, Peter Wilson of the University of Otago, New Zealand, regards it as more important than the rise of agriculture.[21] Behavioral sedentism is usually defined as people residing in one place for a long time: several years, a generation or more.[22] Sedentism is also a set of social and economic relationships tying people to immobile property. Modern societies are "sedentary" because, while there may be considerable personal movement, our social, political and economic organization is based on permanent places on the landscape. This is social sedentism.[23]Historic Northwest Coast sedentism is a very distinctive form of both behavioral and social sedentism. People might move several times a year, but they often moved the entire town two or three times, taking everything with them. This was made possible by their ready access to water routes, and to canoes large enough to freight everything.[24] Thus, many Northwest Coast groups were behaviorally and socially sedentary, while still retaining some of the advantages of mobility (e.g. access to fresh resources). Sedentism requires a stable food supply throughout the year. In most places this means storage (see Chapter Five). Storage and sedentism usually (as in all things human, not always) go hand-in-hand.

Polities

The use of space is also standardized in polities[25] – a political entity with a boundary and a territory. Polities are the regional expression of politics. Archaeologists recognize the existence of ancient polities minimally through the presence of settlement hierarchies. In a settlement hierarchy there are two or three levels of residential sites. The lowest level is the most common, while the top level has only one, or a very few sites. These top-level sites are distinctive in some way: they are significantly larger than the others; they contain distinctive architecture, a wide diversity of artifacts, or unique features of some kind. For example, the modern Canadian province of British Columbia contains a clear-cut settlement hierarchy, in which the city of Vancouver is enormous relative to all other settlements in the province. The simple presence of such a hierarchy does not necessarily tell the observer about how it is organized politically. In modern Cascadia, none of the primary centers are the official political capitals of their polity, although these cities are the polities' de facto capital – Vancouver is the not the capital of British Columbia, though it is its population and economic center. Victoria, a much smaller city on Vancouver Island, is the capital. While there were no clear-cut polities on the Northwest Coast during the Early Modern period (with the possible exception we have noted of the Coast Tsimshian and Nuu-chah-nulth) there are tantalizing hints of polity formation in the Middle Pacific, so it is necessary to introduce the topic.

Interaction spheres

As originally defined by Joseph Caldwell,[26] an archaeologist working in eastern North America, an interaction sphere is a region with several distinctive local cultures that share values, ceremonials, styles, and other traits. These common features are the result of interaction among the various communities in the sphere. These interactions can be trade and other forms of exchange, shared ritual occasions, and so on. In the late 1960s, George MacDonald[27] suggested that the northern Northwest Coast was such an interaction sphere in that the Haida, Tsimshian, and Tlingit were linguistically distinct (their languages are mutually unintelligible) but they shared a number of social and stylistic traits that suggested intense, long-term interaction. Archaeologists and anthropologists have recognized that some of the stylistic zones discussed in Chapter Nine may represent interaction spheres, though they have not been examined in detail. Large interaction spheres may be common features of complex hunter-gatherers. They are also clearly central to the development of elites in these societies.

There appear to be two routes to increased power and prestige: one is gaining control of the household economy (or that of several households) and diverting it to one's own ends.[28] The other is through participation in the large-scale exchange and trade networks mentioned above in the discussion of sedentism (mobile peoples also have such networks – they may simply be more important among sedentary peoples). One aspect of this is controlling access to one's own territories. Sedentary peoples may need to gain access to resources in another's region.[29] Such access to those resources is commonly through high-status individuals. On the Northwest Coast, one had to ask the permission of a house chief to use resources on that house's territories. While permission was rarely denied, not to ask was a grave insult and grounds for war. High-status individuals, by virtue of participating in large-scale networks, had the social connections through which their followers could gain access to resources elsewhere. On the southern Northwest Coast, major Chinook chiefs often had wives from many places across the region, providing the chief and his followers with a large network of in-laws and access to their territories.[30]

On the Northwest Coast, chiefs participated in large networks in which goods were exchanged (such exchange does not imply an "economic" exchange; Northwest Coast chiefs exchanged wealth for prestige). Some of these networks covered considerable territory.

Archaic and Early Pacific period houses and settlements

It is likely that pithouses were the first houses on the Northwest Coast. This suggestion is not original to us. Archaeologist Hiromi Bifeku proposed in the early 1950s that the pithouse was the earliest dwelling in North America.[31] Pithouses were in widespread use in both North America and northeast Asia (examples more than 20,000 years old have been excavated in Siberia,[32] pit dwellings 9,000 and more years old have been found in Japan,[33] the earliest substantial dwellings in North China are semi-subterranean,[34] etc.[35]). We imagine that pithouses were part of the basic knowledge of North America's first inhabitants. It is not unreasonable to expect that someday an archaeologist may find a Clovis pithouse. Such houses are not hard to build; even with sharpened sticks, a substantial pit can be dug in two or three days. The major problem is finding roofing materials.

The wide geographic distribution of the earliest pit dwellings in western North America supports the idea that they were part of the material culture of the continent's earliest inhabitants. The earliest well-documented pithouses in North America have been encountered in the Aleutian Islands, at a site called Anangula. The structures at Anangula are as much as 1 m (6.5 ft) deep and 5 m (16.5 ft) across, dating to *c.* 6500 BC.[36] The oldest pit dwellings in the continental United States have been found in high mountain basins in southwest Wyoming. They are only slightly younger than the Anangula structures, dating to 5500 – 4500 BC.[37] These structures are small (*c.* 4–5 m or 13–16.5 ft in diameter), and do not appear not to have been repeatedly occupied.

The earliest known structure in Cascadia is the wikiup or windbreak at the Paulina Lake site in central Oregon (Chapter Three). This is the only known Windust-period structure. The structural remains include a central hearth and support posts. The support posts are dated to 9500 BC and one of the posts is rather substantial.[38] James Chatters reports two more wikiup or tent–like structures dating to *c.* 5500 BC in central Washington.[39] Pithouses appear widely on the Plateau after 4400 BC.

There were two patterns of pithouse construction on the Plateau between 4400 and 2800 BC. In the first, spanning the period 4400–3500 BC, pithouse construction appears to have occurred sporadically, here and there. People appear to have built them occasionally, perhaps under certain conditions. Starting around 3500 BC, pithouses were constructed more often, and they became much more widespread, and common in the archaeological record of the region,[40] representing an early period of village formation in the interior that we are calling Cascadia Village 1.[41] We believe that the coastal middens are associated with this pattern.

These early interior settlements[42] probably contained no more than one or two occupied houses simultaneously, though a few sites contain large numbers of house pits, raising the possibility of larger communities. There is no evidence of consistent patterns of settlement layout. Given house sizes, each household probably contained no more than one or two families.[43] These pithouses were usually intensively occupied, as indicated by thick midden accumulations associated with them. Artifact assemblages are generally large and diverse. Houses were sometimes reoccupied several times. They may not have been lived in continuously throughout any given year, but it seems likely they were used annually for many years, suggesting some form of semi-sedentism. The presumption is that these structures were the winter dwellings of households that were dispersed throughout the rest of the year.[44]

The earliest substantial structures on or near the Northwest Coast are both located on the Fraser River above Vancouver, British Columbia. They are contemporary with the peak of house construction in the interior and share many construction details with those dwellings, enough to see them as part of the same phenomenon – a Cascadia-wide shift in residential and settlement patterns to semi-sedentism. The oldest, at the Hatzic Rock site, dates to about 3600 – 3300 BC and is located on the Fraser River above modern Vancouver,[45] as is the second structure, at the Maurer site.[46] While Maurer and Hatzic Rock are the only well-documented early houses on the coast, it is possible that the St Mungo Cannery site, near Vancouver itself, contains evidence of a post-and-beam structure.[47]

The excavations at Hidden Falls appear to have located a small, temporary structure dating to 1800 BC. The structure is indicated by a hearth and a semi-circle of small post-holes.[48] While the Hidden Falls features are clearly not those of a large pithouse or plank house, they do represent the earliest documented structure actually found on the northern coast.

53 Floor map of the Hatzic Rock site house, Early Pacific period.

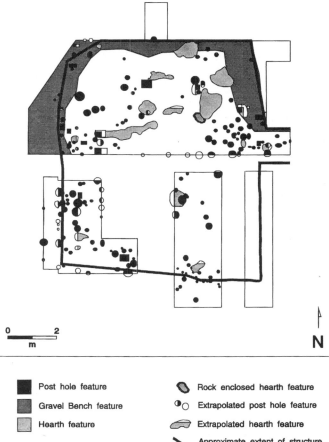

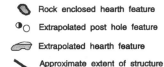

0   2
m

N

■ Post hole feature

▨ Gravel Bench feature

▨ Hearth feature

◗ Rock enclosed hearth feature

◗○ Extrapolated post hole feature

◗ Extrapolated hearth feature

╲ Approximate extent of structure

The presence of cemeteries (Chapter Seven) on the coast during the Early Pacific may also indicate the existence of some form of sedentism. While there may be one at Namu at the beginning of the Early Pacific, the cemeteries at Pender Canal and Blue Jackets Creek date toward the end of the period. Archaeologists generally regard the presence of cemeteries as evidence for either full or partial sedentism, or territories.

In summary, after 4400 BC substantial structures were fairly widespread across southern Cascadia. There was a peak in house construction around 3500–2800 BC after which houses are quite rare in the interior for several hundred years. It is not known whether this break in house construction also occurred on the coast.

Despite the lack of data, we are prepared to speculate about Early Pacific settlements and mobility on the coast. We suspect that settlements were much like those in the interior, rarely larger than two or three structures, with perhaps 10 to 30 people. The size of these settlements was probably limited by the amount of food available when they were occupied, presumably in the winter. Another option would be to place villages as close as possible to where the winter stores were caught and processed.[49] Namu may represent such a settlement. Others are likely in the Gulf of Georgia, where both terrestrial and littoral environments were rich and relatively accessible. But there would always be the risk of local resource failure.

Hunter-gatherers usually buffer such risk by creating and maintaining social ties with people living in other areas to ensure access to other resources when theirs fail. Marriages would be one prime way of accomplishing this. Instead of moving to another village of their own, people could move in with their in-laws for a month or two. It seems likely then that Early Pacific settlements would have had fairly widespread social connections.[50] In many parts of the coast, such ties would be dependent on watercraft (since it would be impossible to move overland), and on people being able to shift around a lot[51] producing a great deal of fluidity.

Middle Pacific period houses and settlements

The Middle Pacific is marked on the coast by major changes in house form and in community structure: by the presence of rectangular houses, probably plank houses, and by formally laid-out villages. The houses in Northwest Coast villages were laid out in one or more rows, with the houses all facing the same direction. These have been termed "linear villages."[52] Linear villages are in dramatic contrast to earlier patterns in Cascadia, in which there is no formal village plan. We shall argue below that these shifts were made possible, at least in part, by the development of larger canoes.

The Paul Mason site is the single most important Middle Pacific residential site. As we described it in Chapter Four, it is a two-row village of small, rectangular houses. The village appears to date between 1450 and 950 BC. In addition to the houses, there are exterior pit features and hearths. There are also two, enigmatic larger structures that are separate from the house rows.[53] The Boardwalk site in

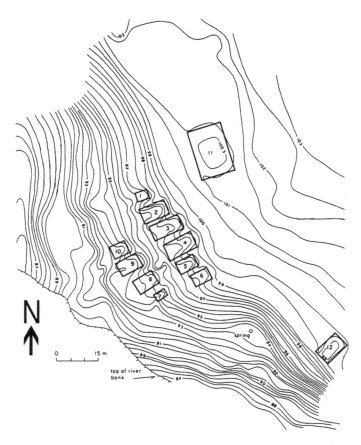

54 *Map of the Paul Mason site, a Middle Pacific village on the Skeena River in northern British Columbia, as described by Gary Coupland. Note that the houses are arranged in two rows.*

Prince Rupert Harbor is probably a two-row village[54] contemporary with Paul Mason, although its dating is somewhat shaky. The site achieved its maximum size at 2100 BC,[55] and the two rows may postdate that time. The back row appears to be associated with burials spanning the lengthy period from 900 BC to AD 200, so it was certainly a two-row village by that time. The only two well-preserved structures are small rectangular dwellings at the rear of the second row, perhaps part of a third row of houses. Both are slightly smaller but similar in outline to the Paul Mason houses. The two structures appear to have been abandoned around 200 BC. There are other two-row villages in the harbor, including McNichol Creek, which dates to *c.* AD 500.

Evidence for structures at Yuquot on northwest Vancouver Island dates to AD 1. A structure (of some kind) at Shoemaker Bay on Barkley Sound is dated to 910 BC. Two-row village layout is not limited to plank houses. The Katz site, on the Lower Fraser River, is a two-row pithouse village dating to 650 BC. The Katz site produced some beautiful examples of carved wooden boxes well within the southern Northwest Coast style.

The Katz site is roughly contemporary with the end of the Locarno Beach phase of the Gulf of Georgia sequence. There is no clear evidence for house form in most Locarno Beach age sites, though Matson may have located the remains of a small Locarno Beach age pithouse in the Crescent Beach site.[56] Marpole phase sites, on the other hand, are rich in structural remains of substantial post-and-beam structures.[57] Matson excavated Marpole structures at the Beach Grove site in the early 1980s that are clearly plank houses.[58]

The best-documented Middle Pacific structure on the south is the large rectangular dwelling at the Palmrose site on the northern Oregon coast.[59] The house seems to have been 20 x 6 m (65.5 x 19.5 ft) in size, considerably larger than any excavated so far in the north.[60] The house appears to have been rebuilt and reoccupied many times, but in three major phases between 800 BC and AD 300. Its excavators suspect the house may have been destroyed periodically by large earthquakes along the coast. The earliest, multi-house village on the southern Coast is located near Portland, Oregon, and dates to AD 1. It contains rectangular structures, but their arrangement is not reported.[61]

Late Pacific period houses and settlements

There are few Late Pacific houses that are more than about 500 years old. After that date, there are a great many excavated structures,[62] including the famous houses at Ozette. Perhaps the best-documented house dating to the end of the Middle Pacific and the beginning of the Late Pacific is the Marpole phase Tualdad Altu house on the Black River, south of Seattle. The house is about 1,600 years old.[63] The house appears to be a shed roof structure of the kind built in the region during the Early Modern period. Jim Chatters, the excavator, discovered evidence for some differences in subsistence pursuits between the east and west ends of the structure. This is the earliest possible evidence on the coast for intra-household specialization in production. Unfortunately, Chatters' data are weak and he was unable to excavate a significant portion of the structure.

There may have been significant additions to village organization in the north. Single-row villages were the dominant village form in the southern Queen Charlotte

Islands and southeast Alaska beginning with the transition to the Late Pacific (AD 300–500). Large multi-row villages appear in both areas after about AD 500 but they are quite rare, with single-row villages being the more common. Additionally, much larger houses – presumably chief's houses – appear for the first time in both of these areas, and perhaps in Prince Rupert Harbor as well, although the data at present are not definitive. The reader may recall that this is the same period in which midden burial ends, the wearing of labrets appears to shift from males to females (indicating a shift from patrilineality to matrilineality?), and warfare intensifies on the northern coast.

Discussion

Plank houses appear to have been present, but rare, all along the coast between 1450 and 800 BC. Given the vagaries of radiocarbon dating, we think these structures probably appeared in a number of areas of the coast at virtually the same time. These developments have several implications.

The first implication is technological. The development of plank houses is clearly part and parcel of the evolution of Northwest Coast woodworking techniques, including the capability of making planks from cedars and other trees. Another contemporary (or slightly earlier innovation) is the kerfed box (Chapter Five). It seems reasonable to conclude that these structures represent the application of box-making skills to the internal post frames we witnessed in the pithouses of the Early Pacific.

A less obvious technological implication is that these houses and villages probably indicate the presence of large freight canoes, which would have been needed to transport the larger volume of winter stores required by the larger settlements. Larger canoes would also make it possible to exploit resources at a greater distance from the towns and carry them home. Finally, large canoes would make possible the Northwest Coast's distinctive form of sedentism, which involved moving entire towns several times a year, and in which households owned several house frames across their territory (although some villages never moved). While we do not know whether that pattern actually existed in the Middle Pacific, it is clear from the burial record that groups had long-lived ties to particular places (see below).

The appearance together of plank houses and of linear villages has social implications. They represent a shift in social organization at at least two levels, the household and the village. At the household level, the change is highlighted by the possible shift from round pithouses to square surface structures.

Shifts from round and curvilinear pithouses to rectangular surface structures have occurred several times in world history, including in the southwestern USA at about the beginning of the Late Pacific period in Cascadia; and in China at the end of the Neolithic, among other places. This shift is usually thought to indicate the appearance of more formally organized or structured households, since square spaces are more easily organized and formally arranged than round spaces. Rectilinear structures create more usable interior space; they can also be more easily packed into high-density communities than can round or curvilinear dwellings. One need only try to draw a series of circles and squares on a piece of paper to see this. Square structures can more easily be expanded than round structures to accommodate increased household size or more possessions. An increase in the diameter of a circular house requires enlarging all dimensions of the structure. Increasing the length of a house does not necessitate widening it, yet a longer house has more floor space. Rectangular houses also make it easier to indicate the relative status of household members. It is easier to segregate or differentiate interior space in a rectangular than a round house. A rectangular table (or house) has a head and a foot (front and back), a top and a bottom. Rectangular structures appear on the coast with linear villages, a form of village layout that could also easily convey information about the relative status of households to anyone who knew the code.

While social changes are one set of reasons for house form to change, functional reasons must also have played a significant role. Rectangular structures met certain crucial functional needs, perhaps arising from the storage economy, and from long-term residence in one place: a sturdy comfortable residence, a dry, spacious place to work (fix tools, make baskets, butcher and process foods etc.), additional space for storage, and the need for a smoke house and drying shed (the ceilings, roofs and racks within Early Modern houses were festooned with smoked foods). In short, people were living in their smoke houses. If the concept of living in one's smoke house is difficult to accept, one need only remember that many of the world's farmers live in or above their stock barns. Differences in status can be one reason to differentiate the space within a house, specialized activities and behaviors are another, especially when many activities are restricted to indoors. Areas can be set off with dividers, or screens, for example, or separated to different ends of the house. These needs were met in a single remarkable structure.

These structures may also indicate the existence of households with considerable time depth during the Middle Pacific. The cemetery behind the Boardwalk houses was in use for at least 700 years. The Palmrose house was erected and re-erected on the same spot several times over 1,000 years. The Late Pacific Meier house was in continuous use for 400 years. We do not expect that the same household necessarily occupied the structure throughout this lengthy period, but nothing precludes that possibility. This is clearly what Tim Ingold meant by social sedentism – people were closely tied to places in the landscape. The apparent short duration of the Paul Mason village is quite interesting then – why might the village have been occupied for only a relatively brief period (less than a century perhaps?).

The small sample of early settlements includes one single large-house settlement – at Palmrose – and three two-row villages. Two-row villages are a distinctive Northwest Coast development which did not arise in the rest of Cascadia. Elsewhere, houses were distributed along the bank of a river, or clustered above a bend in a river. Even very large villages lacked such formally organized space, but were clusters of houses. Two-row villages indicate the operation of formal principles of village layout and organization that were in force irrespective of house form, as is indicated by the Katz site. Whether that principle was ranking of extended kin groups is moot until sufficient data are available to test the notion. It is clear from the burial data reviewed in Chapter Seven that some form of ranking of individuals may have been in operation on the coast by 2500 BC if not much earlier. As with rectangular houses, linear villages permit more houses (and presumably more people) to be packed into a suitable space than a scatter or cluster of structures. They also facilitate the expression of status differentials, as well as other aspects of social organization. Compact settlements are also more defensible than are ones in which

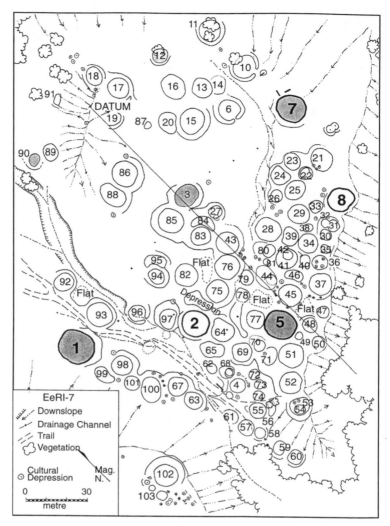

55 *Map of the houses at the Late Pacific pithouse village at Keatley Creek in southern British Columbia. The village layout contrasts sharply with linear Northwest Coast villages, as illustrated by Cathlapotle, Skedans and Paul Mason.*

houses are scattered about. Standardized rules of village or town layout over a vast region suggest both common culture as well as participation in a common social network. The Katz site shows that the principles of village layout applied regardless of house form.

Why have a common code for signaling the relative status of households and even extended kin groups? Colin Renfrew, a British archaeologist, has argued that such similarities over large distances are the result of intense interaction and the need for a common yardstick with which to measure relative prestige and authority among the people participating in the interaction.[64] These developments occur at the same time that we see the rise of the new Middle Pacific elite, and the development of regional markers for individuals (cranial deformation and the wearing of labrets). Coast-wide interaction clearly played a fundamental role in the development of ranking on the coast.

Settlements consisting of a single very large house are a distinctive feature of the southern coast. The largest recorded dwelling on the coast was observed by Simon Fraser in 1798 on the lower Fraser River. The structure was close to 200 m (650 ft) long and was almost 18 m (60 ft) wide. The potlatch house of Chief Seattle was over 160 m (525 ft) long. Early Modern Chinookan houses on the lower Columbia River were commonly 30 m (100 ft) long, but were frequently 60 to 140 m (200 to 460 ft) in length, and as much as 14 m (50 ft) wide. Large houses were not restricted to the southern coast. Mat long houses in the southern interior were sometimes 120 m (400 ft) long as well. Houses on the northern coast were never so large. This in part was the result of how northern plank houses were built. Shed-roof houses (and the narrow, gable-roofed houses of the Chinook) could be extended almost infinitely, without requiring large timbers. Long houses in the interior could also be extended as much as needed. It was also easier to make the houses smaller, by taking down one end, whereas northern houses would have to be rebuilt completely. Southern houses allowed fluctuating household sizes better than did northern architecture (though a household often occupied more than one house). Social organization in the south also facilitated the formation of very large households. This is so because the bilateral systems of the central coast allowed members from both sides of the family to live in one house, making a large corporate group. The patrilineal systems of the southern area, where males could have a series of wives throughout their lives and where all their children were in their corporate group, could also become large, reaching several hundred individuals. The result was that entire communities sometimes lived within a single dwelling. The matrilineages of the northern coast, where residence in a house is based on kinship through the mother's line, were generally much smaller, since their size was limited by the fertility of the female core of the lineage. It is no surprise then that the northern coast developed matriclans that created fictitious kinship ties between biologically unrelated lineages. The result was a social group equal in size to the south coast patrilineages, but one that was divided among several houses.

Specialization

Northwest coast households had complex divisions of labor that relied on part-time and full-time specialists. Complex simultaneous tasks can be performed more efficiently by specialists than by people with more general skills. Even relatively simple, linear tasks can be more efficiently accomplished by specialists.

There is little archaeological information about the development of occupational specialization on the coast. The emphasis among archaeologists has been on status inequality. In the Early Modern period, craft specialists performed their skills usually as part of the household economy, but also for trade or exchange. Most occupational specialists were part-timers. There is little ethnographic evidence for full-time specialization (where artisans support themselves and their families), except for some carvers and painters. Individuals or families could specialize in

almost any activity: basket making, carving, painting, sea-mammal hunting, land-mammal hunting, plank making, net making, fishing etc. Specialization of this kind ensured the presence in the household of skilled individuals who could efficiently accomplish tasks needed for the household economy, and in the larger regional economy. High-status individuals were also specialists, at least in some places. At Ozette, it appears that high-status men were harpooners on the whaling expeditions so important to the Makah prestige and spiritual systems.[65] High-status individuals were also probably carvers in some Northwest Coast societies.[66] There is some, admittedly weak, evidence for specialization at the village level in the Early Modern period. In Chapter One we presented a lengthy quote from Boas' Coast Tsimshian ethnography that suggested that Coast Tsimshian villages at least produced particular objects for use in potlatches. The Haida of the Queen Charlottes produced some of the coast's most famous carvers, and traded canoes for eulachon grease. The peoples on the west coast of Vancouver Island, well supplied with cedar, also traded canoes and logs. The Makah may have traded whale bone.[67] The
Pl. 16   Chilkat Tlingit wove the famous Chilkat blankets that were traded and exchanged almost the entire length of the coast and were everywhere a marker of the highest status.

The archaeological evidence for occupational specialization is thin. An anthropomorphic handle for a carving tool recovered at Glenrose Cannery dating between 2600 and 1300 BC certainly seems to indicate the importance of carving, though that does not necessarily mean specialization at that early date (Chapter Nine). Several zoomorphic spoons, dating to 2140–1740 BC, from the Pender Canal site display high levels of carving skills, suggesting specialized carvers.[68] Another, different, but tantalizing hint at specialization of about the same age comes not from the coast but the interior. Jim Chatters recovered a shell adz blade, or celt, on the floor of a pithouse dating to 2300 BC in interior Washington State. The adz blade was made of marine shell, therefore originating on the coast. Making shell celts was a specialization during the Early Modern period. This of course does not mean it was also a specialization 4,500 years ago, but the process of making a shell adz blade is long, involved, and difficult, requiring considerable knowledge, skill, and practice.

The presence of boxes, plank houses, and nephrite adz blades in the early years of the Middle Pacific certainly means that there were part-time specialists in carpentry and woodworking, as does the appearance of boxes and plank houses. Production of the nephrite adz blades themselves was also probably a specialization. The earliest direct evidence for specialization on the coast is a well-made copper sheet dating to 600 BC recovered in Prince Rupert Harbor. The sheet was made by hammering and annealing the copper. A. Coutre, the metallurgist for the National Museums of Canada, concluded that the skill required clearly indicated specialization.[69] Several Middle Pacific period carvings and grave goods from the Gulf of Georgia also indicate specialized carvers (Chapter Nine). However, no one has studied these materials with that question in mind. Chatters also thought he detected specialization in subsistence pursuits in the house at Black River, where the distribution of faunal materials suggested a specialist in hunting terrestrial mammals around AD 600.

The presence of specialists in building houses also indicates that the households themselves were organized around full- and part-time specialists. Household organization had developed to accomplish complex simultaneous tasks. This represents a major rearrangement of Northwest Coast economic organization, which appears to have crystallized around 600 BC–AD 1.

We have no archaeological evidence for village- or regional-level specialization in production with one exception. It is possible that Parizeau Point, a site in Prince Rupert Harbor, was used for heavy-duty woodworking, in contrast with the Board-walk site (the two are part of a site complex) where finer work appears to have occurred.[70] The absence of such evidence is in some ways as interesting as its presence. For example, the major source in North America for dentalium – a species of deep-water mollusk – is the west coast of Vancouver Island. Dentalium was highly prized from the coast to the high plains for beads. Because of this, one might expect to find dentalium-rich sites on the Vancouver Coast. None are known. This may be telling us something about the site sample from Vancouver Island, or about dentalium production.

Regional Dynamics

Polities, trade and interaction spheres

Wayne Suttles, looking at patterns of cranial deformation, labret wear, social ties, similarities in art styles and so on, suggests that there were two broad interaction spheres on the coast in the Early Modern period: the north and south coast.[71] Within the south coast region, however, he thinks that five smaller spheres existed: the central British Columbia coast and adjacent portions of Vancouver Island; the west coast of Vancouver Island and northwest Washington State; an extended Gulf of Georgia region along the eastern side of Vancouver Island and the southwest coast of British Columbia extending to the southern end of Puget Sound; the Lower Columbia River and adjacent coastline; and the last region including the northern Californian and southern Oregon coasts. Suttles believes these interaction spheres may have been somewhat ephemeral, shifting their boundaries through time, even appearing and disappearing. The archaeological evidence, presently scanty as it is, suggests these spheres had considerable antiquity. Donald Mitchell, for example, demonstrated more than 20 years ago that the Gulf of Georgia region has been stable for several millennia.[72]

Archaic period interaction spheres

The earliest evidence for what may be a cultural distinction between northern and southern coasts is the presence of microblade technology on the northern coast during much of the Archaic. This difference between the two regions has led many workers to postulate that the coast was originally occupied by at least two cultures or cultural traditions. Whatever its cause, the distinction existed, and the northern coast has remained the most distinctive region of the coast for the last 9,000 years.[73]

Obsidian sourcing is a line of evidence crucial to this discussion. Obsidian is volcanic glass, and is highly prized as a raw material for making stone tools. There are many obsidian sources in Cascadia, which has seen extraordinary volcanic activity over the past 30 million years or so. The obsidian from different flows can be identified since each will have a distinctive mineralogical "signature." The signature may result from the presence of minerals not present in other obsidians, or in distinctive proportions, or in the chemistry of the obsidian.

Roy Carlson has developed a series of maps based on "sourcing" (locating the flow from which the obsidian originated) a large geographic and temporal sample of obsidian artifacts.[74] The north coast obsidian from the Archaic are all from Mt Edziza in northwest interior British Columbia. Obsidian is rare on the southern coast during the Archaic period. The interior of southern Cascadia also appears to have been part of a regional network of obsidian exchange that may have stretched from south–central British Columbia to southwestern Idaho and across to the eastern slope of the Cascade Mountains.

The presence of Olivella shells in the Archaic period burials at the Marmes Rockshelter indicates some exchange between coast and interior. Other marine shells occur in Archaic components in the interior, on the Canadian and Columbia plateaus. The shell appears to have moved up the Columbia and Fraser rivers from the coast.[75] It seems most likely that it was exchanged from person to person along the routes. We do not know what was exchanged downriver, though something,

THE ARCHAEOLOGY OF NORTHWEST COAST HOUSES

Excavations and analyses of houses have become an increasingly important part of Northwest Coast archaeology over the past 10 years. Excavating these structures is not easy; an individual house may require years. However, houses provide invaluable information.

The excavated houses at Ozette are the best current examples of what can be learned from Northwest Coast structures. The disaster that befell these houses and their inhabitants – but preserved the structures – is described in Chapter Four, as are the unusual techniques required to dig at Ozette. Since the excavations ended in the early 1980s, analysis of the enormous quantity of artifacts, faunal remains, and so on has been undertaken by a number of individuals, most of whom conducted this research as part of their Ph.D. work at Washington State University.

The heart of this work has been detailed computer maps of three of the structures: houses 1, 2 and 5, showing the detailed distributions of structural features (postholes, etc.) artifacts, and faunal remains (including shells). Stephen Samuels used these data to show that house 1 (located in the front row of houses at Ozette) was clearly a higher-status house than either 2 or 5, both in the back row. The researchers at Ozette developed a model of the interior layout of a Makah house, and then have evaluated the distributions of different kinds of archaeological data against that model. Samuels and his colleagues, David Huelsbeck and Gary Wessen, have gone on to compare the contents of the three houses. They have discovered some fascinating things. The high-status house at Ozette was kept cleaner that the lower-status structures. These two contain far more animal and fish bones than does the high-status structure. Within the high-status house, the northeast corner is relatively tidier than the rest of the structure. It is also this same corner that held the highest proportion of decorated shell objects. There were differences in diet among the inhabitants of the houses. Those in house 1 appear to have eaten more salmon and halibut, while those in the lower-status structures ate more widely available fish. The people of house 1 may have eaten more whale meat. There are even differences in the proportions in which shellfish were eaten. It is clear then that the status differences that organized Northwest Coast societies in the Early Modern period structured life to the point where they are clearly discernible in the archaeological record.

The researchers have also been able to show, using the distribution of seal-hunting gear, that high-status individuals specialized in sea-mammal hunting. Jim Chatters, in his excavations of Sbabadid, a late 18th- to early 19th-century plank house on the Black River south of Seattle, perhaps obsidian, certainly was. We have also said that there may be cultural commonalties between the southern interior and the southern coast in burial practices during the Archaic.

The number of people living in Cascadia and how they moved across the land-scape would have determined how patterns of interaction and exchange developed during the Archaic. These early populations were doubtless quite small, and scattered along the coastline. It seems likely that very small groups could easily have become isolated. Social ties would be needed across large areas, so people could find mates, and develop the connections needed to protect them from local resource fail-ures. Many of these links followed the rivers, as indicated by the movement of marine shell. On the coast, the rugged landscape and forested mountains make it likely that maintaining these ties depended upon the quality of available boats. Periodic gatherings of a few score to a few hundred people (even just every few years) could offset the isolation, making it possible for people to find mates, share

was also able to show, using the distribution of artifacts, that there were sea-mammal hunting specialists present.

Ames' excavations at the Meier site, near Portland, Oregon, have produced evidence similar in some ways to that from Ozette and Sbabadid. It appears that at Meier, high-status individuals may have specialized in some aspects of woodworking. It is clear that the most expensive (in terms of time or effort) objects are concentrated in the north end. It also appears that most food processing occurred away from the high-status end of the house.

Ames has also been quite interested in the amount of work these large wooden structures represent. Using the board foot (the modern system of estimating the amount of lumber required in a house – a board foot is 1 ft square, and 1 inch thick; a typical modern, North American house for a single family takes 10,000 to 12,000 board feet of lumber), he estimated the amount of lumber in the Meier structure and in other houses on the coast. These structures represent a tremendous amount of labor investment. Many of these structures have enough wood in them to build a small housing development. High-status houses, such as house 1 at Ozette, are larger than lower-status houses. This difference can be seen in the lumber estimates. House 1 at Ozette required more than 28,000 board feet, while house 2 needed 18,000 board feet. At the Haida village of Ninstints, high-status houses required more than twice the lumber of lower-status houses in some instances. What is interesting about these figures is that the high-status structures also required more lumber per capita. They were not just bigger because they held larger households (which was usually the case); they also required more work by household members to construct.

The Meier house has been reconstructed using computer graphics techniques by Darin Molnar. The computer reconstruction of the interior gives some sense of the size of one of these dwellings. The use of computers in house reconstruction was pioneered at Ozette by Dale Croes, Jonathan Davis, Samuels and others. Computers are absolutely necessary given the size and complexity of these dwellings.

Another question pursued in the Meier research was how long one of these structures might stand. By examining the numbers of postholes and other features left by the house frame, Ames used estimates of how long different types of untreated wood might last in contact with the ground to estimate that the Meier house stood for almost 400 years (and in that time required somewhere between 500,000 and 1,000,000 board feet of lumber to maintain).

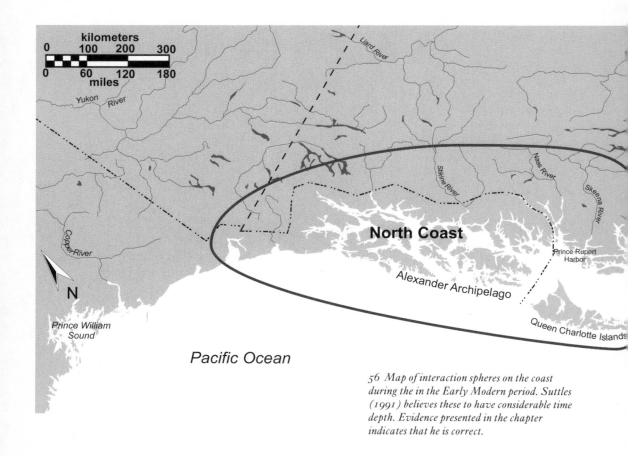

56 *Map of interaction spheres on the coast during the in the Early Modern period. Suttles (1991) believes these to have considerable time depth. Evidence presented in the chapter indicates that he is correct.*

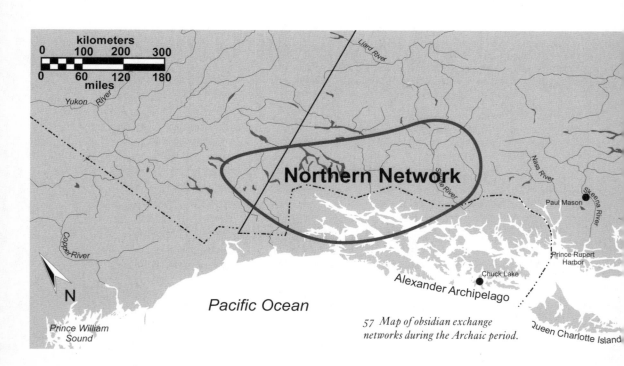

57 *Map of obsidian exchange networks during the Archaic period.*

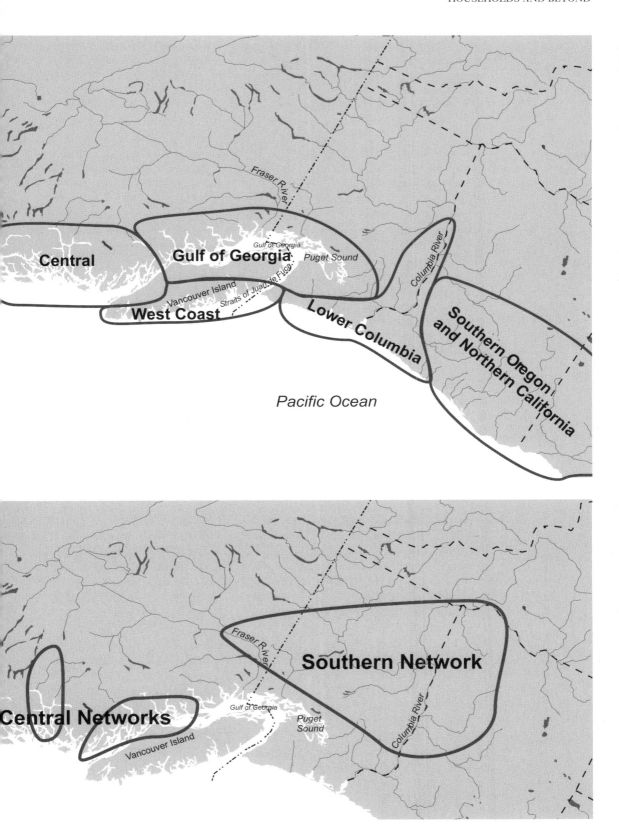

information and the like. We suggested in Chapter Five that early evidence for heavy use of salmon could actually be the result of such periodic gatherings in places that could support large numbers of people during brief periods of time.

Pacific period interaction spheres

There are three distinctive obsidian exchange regions during the Early Pacific: the northern coast; the central coast, centering on Namu and extending into central interior British Columbia (following the rivers through the coast range); and what might be termed a "Southern Cascadia" obsidian exchange network extending well into central Oregon and eastern Washington State. The northern region is not as well defined as the others since there are technologies in the north (as in Prince Rupert Harbor) in which chipped lithic tools played almost no role, unlike those farther south, and obsidian was unnecessary.[76] The south region may have come into existence as early as 4000 BC,[77] if not earlier, since it may have been the source of the Olivella shells at Marmes.

The obsidian networks of both the central and southern coast persist through the Middle and Late Pacific periods. Interestingly, they do not overlap as they did at the beginning of the Early Pacific. During the Middle Pacific the southern system includes portions of the east coast of Vancouver Island, and at least one site on the west coast.[78] By the middle of the Late Pacific, however, the southern system was restricted to sites in the Gulf of Georgia. In part, this probably reflects the major technological changes that occurred in Johnstone Strait by AD 500 which included the virtual abandonment there of stone tools. The central and southern obsidian exchange networks conform somewhat to two of Suttles's social interaction spheres: the central coast and inner coast. The virtual absence of obsidian on the west coast of Vancouver Island and northwest Washington State is also interesting. We noted the distinctiveness of the material culture of that region in Chapter Three, including the use of shell celts. This may be a reflection of the west coast interaction sphere.

The southern obsidian exchange network also corresponds closely with the distribution of antler and clay figurines discussed in Chapter Nine. Distinctive antler figurines have been recovered from sites extending from the central coast to the lower Columbia River and east of the Cascade Mountains. These figurines date primarily to the Late Pacific period.

Turning from the southern sub-regions, there is evidence for north–south distinctions in a number of traits by the Middle Pacific. To anticipate Chapter Nine, the northern and southern regional Northwest Coast art styles probably existed by AD 1, if not several hundred years earlier. North–south regionalization is also indicated by the distributions of whalebone club styles, and, of course, by the evidence from the regional patterns of cranial deformation and labret wear, which crystallizes around 500 BC to AD 1.

The intensity of social interaction is also indicated by the common principles of house and town organization operating through most of the coast by the end of the Middle Pacific. We described these as part of a common yardstick to measure social prestige. The yardstick was in use along most of the coast.

The Northwest Coast as a whole

It also clear that the whole Northwest Coast was a single interaction sphere during the Pacific period. Some of this interaction was through exchange of raw and finished products. Copper, which may have been acquired in southern Alaska, was a widespread status marker at contact and probably had been so for more than 2,000 years. The nephrite for celts was located in two or three quite restricted localities in southwestern British Columbia and northwestern Washington (near the wonderfully-named town of Cedro Woolley) on the Skagit River and in the Gulf of Alaska. Nephrite celts were crucial to northwestern woodworking and carpentry and were traded from southeastern Alaska to Oregon. Dentalium is accessible only on the west coast of Vancouver Island, but was traded throughout Cascadia and the high plains of central North America. Dentalium appears in the interior at the beginning of the Pacific period.[79]

The Northwest Coast participated in exchange linkages that ultimately included the entire continent. For example, stone clubs are found from the southern Northwest Coast far into southern California. Northwest Coast rock art shares features with rock art found far into the interior. In the north, the trade in eulachon grease extended well into the northern interior on well-defined trails. Some of these trails had fortifications to guard crucial crossroads. Other trade moved up river on the Skeena, where narrows were defended and tariffs charged.[80]

One of the major connections between the southern coast, southern interior, and the rest of North America, was the trade fair at the Dalles on the Columbia River.[81] The Dalles fair was probably the largest such fair in western North America. It was supported by the salmon available at what was once the finest salmon fishery in the world. The Dalles fair was linked to a trade fair in southwest Idaho, to trade routes extending south in California, east to Yellowstone, and thence, ultimately, to the East Coast. There were three other major centers in the interior including Kettle Falls on the Columbia, and at the confluence of the Fraser and Thompson Rivers in British Columbia. Both were major fishing locations with access to broad regions in the interior.[82] The fourth was located near the eastern end of a major pass across the Cascade Mountains from Puget Sound.

There is no evidence of such trade centers on the coast, but trade and exchange must have occurred whenever people gathered for potlatches, and other ceremonials. It also occurred where large numbers gathered to harvest resources, as at the mouth of the Nass for the spring eulachon runs. Trade and exchange were probably continuous. It is clear from the testimony of the early European explorers and fur traders that the people of the coast were expert traders.[83]

Polities

There is little evidence for the formation of polities on the coast during the Pacific period, at least not of polities that included several households or villages. During the 18th and 19th centuries, there were "great chiefs" in several regions of the coast,[84] including among the Coast Tsimshian, Nuu-chah-nulth and Chinook. However, there is nothing to suggest they were more than extremely influential house chiefs. There is evidence, nevertheless, from both the Middle and Late Pacific periods of site hierarchies which may suggest experiments – short-lived ones – in polity formation.

For example, the Boardwalk site is quite unlike other residential sites in Prince Rupert Harbor in a number of ways, including the presence of most (but not all) of the richest group of burials. It is also the richest site of the nine excavated in the harbor in terms of the diversity and range of artifacts recovered from it. All the copper was recovered from Boardwalk.[85] The artifacts suggest that a wider variety of

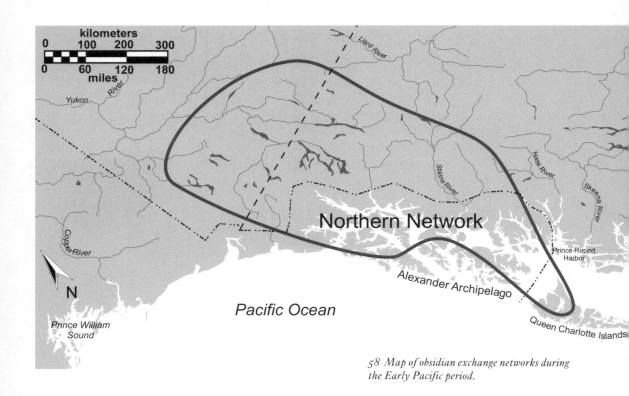

58 Map of obsidian exchange networks during the Early Pacific period.

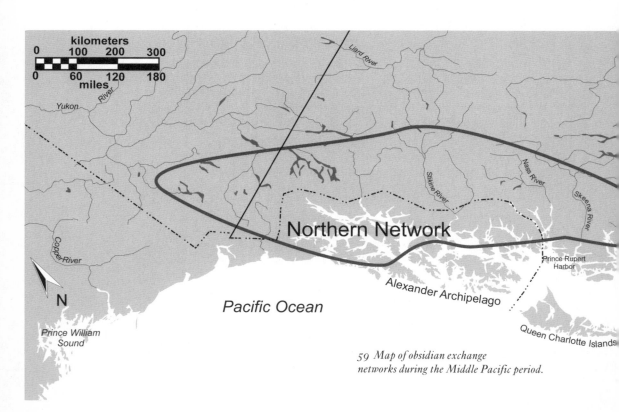

59 Map of obsidian exchange networks during the Middle Pacific period.

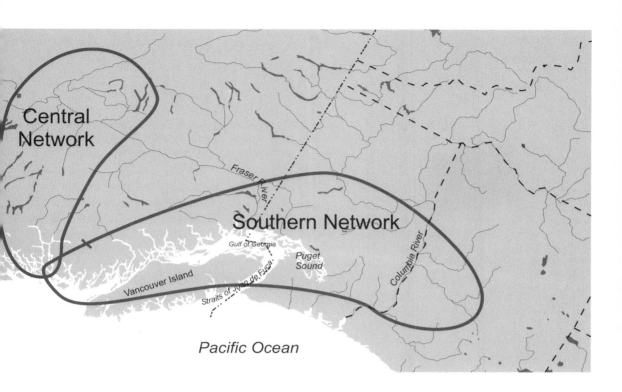

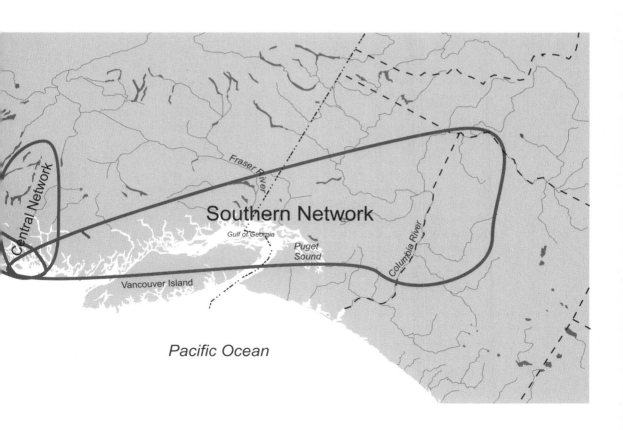

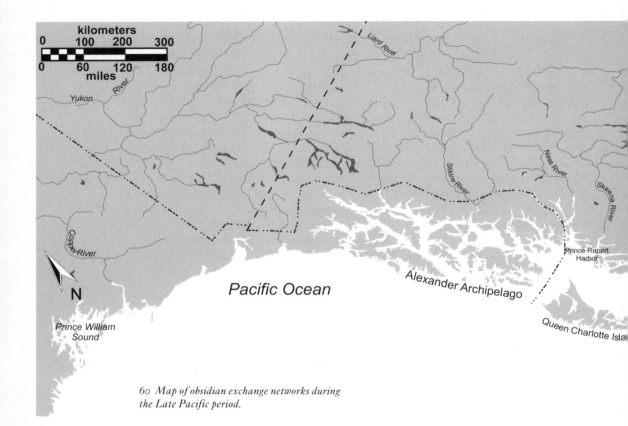

60 Map of obsidian exchange networks during the Late Pacific period.

tasks occurred at Boardwalk than at the other villages. Boardwalk also seems to have been the location for fine woodworking, in contrast to its immediate neighbor, Parizeau Point, where heavy-duty carpentry tools occur. There is one particular set of house floors that presently have no parallel north of the Gulf of Georgia. Part of this is the result of sampling, but the distinctiveness of Boardwalk suggests the possibility of a site hierarchy.

The Marpole midden in the Gulf of Georgia appears to have been similarly distinct, though the site was extensively destroyed prior to the initiation of arch-aeological research in the region. It has produced an extraordinary number of decorated artifacts, unlike any other in the Gulf region (see Chapter Nine). Finally, the Scowlitz site (discussed in chapter Seven) also seems to be distinctive in the scale and number of burial mounds associated with it (though mounds occur elsewhere). These sites, and others, may be telling us of attempts at creating polities.

Discussion

There is little direct evidence about structures on the coast before the Middle Pacific. We have speculated that Early Pacific residential patterns were semi-sedentary, with people spending part of the winters in small villages of pithouses, similar to those found during the Early Pacific in the interior.

In contrast, there is evidence for several major changes by the beginning of the

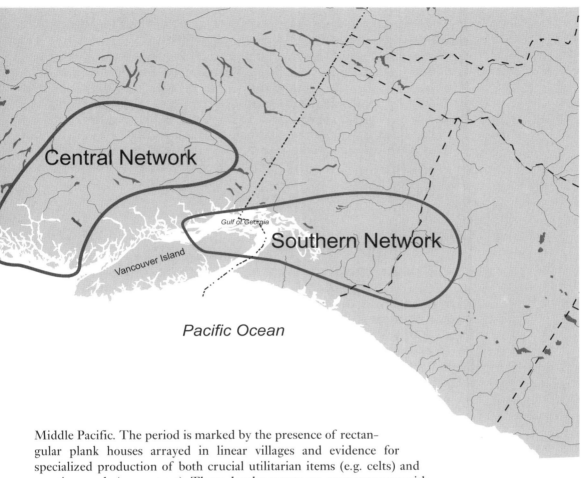

Central Network

Southern Network

Gulf of Georgia

Vancouver Island

Pacific Ocean

Middle Pacific. The period is marked by the presence of rectangular plank houses arrayed in linear villages and evidence for specialized production of both crucial utilitarian items (e.g. celts) and prestige goods (e.g. copper). These developments are contemporary with the evidence for the development of a storage economy (Chapter Five) and the ranking of individuals (Chapter Seven). We also argue that there is indirect evidence for the appearance of large, seaworthy canoes.

We suggested that the appearance of plank houses indicated changes in social organization, given the capacity of rectangular structures to express status differences within the household. With the evidence for specialization, it also seems quite likely that the appearance of these structures indicates the development of households organized around complex simultaneous tasks, as we discussed in the introduction to this chapter. It was this form of labor organization that permitted Northwest Coast households to use their environment effectively, and to solve the problems posed by resources that were available at the same time, but in different places; in other words, to take full advantage of the coast's environmental richness (Chapter Five). It was this organization then that was one of the key solutions to the problems of local resource variability.[86]

Turning to regional patterns, there is evidence for the existence of interaction spheres, particularly in the south, as early as the Archaic period. It is likely that long-distance interaction was partly a consequence of the normal mobility of foragers

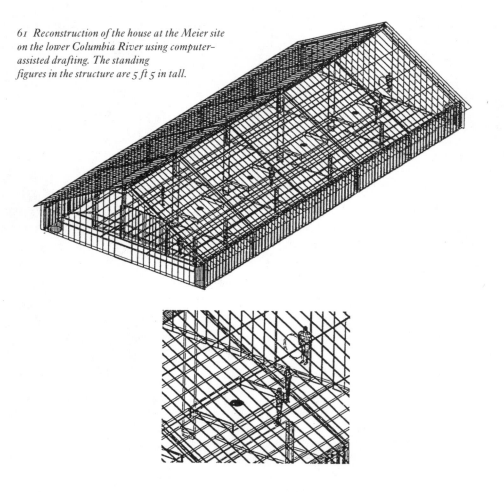

61 Reconstruction of the house at the Meier site on the lower Columbia River using computer-assisted drafting. The standing figures in the structure are 5 ft 5 in tall.

and their need to maintain far-flung social ties, particularly along the Northwest Coast of the Archaic period. These ancient interaction spheres began to crystallize into the regions of the Early Modern period by the beginning of the Early Pacific, and appear to have stabilized in their historic form by the beginning of the Middle Pacific.

In short, the evidence presented in the previous chapter and in this one indicates that major technological innovations and social and economic reorganization occurred on the Northwest Coast around 1800 BC.

CHAPTER SEVEN

Status and Ritual

Introduction

It is clear from the previous chapters that Northwest Coast societies became complex around the beginning of the Middle Pacific. The one aspect of social complexity we have not looked at yet is inequality. We do so in this chapter.

Social inequality was a permanent and pervasive part of Northwest Coast life during the Early Modern period. The evolution of that inequality – when it developed, where, and why – is one of the central issues for Northwest Coast anthropology and archaeology. This chapter addresses where and when, leaving questions of how and why until Chapter Ten. In order to explain how inequality developed on the coast, we must also address issues of gender, geography, and slavery, as well as differences in power and prestige.

Ranking and stratification on the Northwest Coast

Northwest Coast societies were ranked and stratified.[1] Ranked societies are those in which there is differential access to prestige, authority, and in some societies, power. There are fewer high-ranked statuses than there are people to fill them. These statuses may be achieved (individuals earn them) or ascribed (people are born to them). What is important here is that these high statuses are permanent aspects of the society's social organization. In egalitarian societies, there are also differences among people in their relative prestige and authority, but these differences, by and large, are not permanent because they depend on individuals' personalities and abilities. Leaders have no power; they must persuade their followers to follow. All known human cultures differentiate their members in some way or another. Age and gender are universal ways by which this is done. Kinship is another. In an egalitarian society these differences are not assigned permanent differences in prestige or authority. In ranked societies, some statuses are assigned such permanent differences. However, in both ranked and egalitarian societies, all members of the society have equal access to the society's basic resources.

Stratified societies share some features with ranked societies: there are fewer positions of prestige and status than there are people to fill them. There are, however, some profound differences. The two most important differences are first, in stratified societies, there is differential access to basic resources: that is, some individuals have access to basic resources (those upon which health, reproduction, and even life depend) and others do not; and second, some individuals or groups have power over others. Such power can take many forms and routes but, fundamentally, it means that a person or group can make another person or group do what they do not want to do. In all human societies, some individuals exercise personal power over their

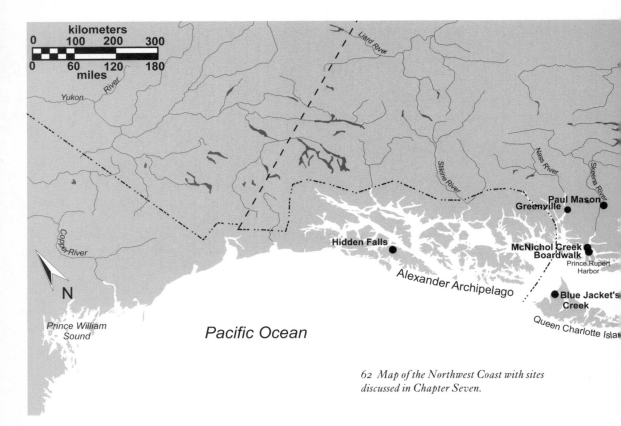

62 *Map of the Northwest Coast with sites discussed in Chapter Seven.*

peers by virtue of their strength, their ability to manipulate social relationships, and so on. In stratified societies, these differences are institutionalized and are permanent parts of the social order. In these circumstances power takes on new forms.

The societies of the Northwest Coast were stratified in that there were two classes, free and slave. Ultimately, free individuals, especially chiefs, had the power of life and death over slaves, who had to do whatever they were told to do. Free people on the other hand were essentially ranked. There were three ranks of free people, the chiefly elite ranking highest, then individuals who held some wealth or social stature, and were related to the elite. The lowest were "commoners" – people who were free, but held no rights in a household. Free people could ignore their chiefs. Chiefs could be quite authoritarian, and act with great dignity and pomp, but they had little or no power to make people do their bidding. Chiefs had to wheedle, cajole, or persuade their people to do what they wished. This is not to deny that chiefs had great influence, and, on a regional basis, they formed a distinctive elite class.[2]

The basis of a chief's authority was his (or her) household. A chief's prestige depended on how productive and rich their household's estate was and whether the chief was able to use that wealth to participate in local and regional exchange systems. In most parts of the coast, the potlatch was the crucial ceremonial in these exchange networks, and chiefs were expected to participate in potlatches, both as host and guest. Chiefs had to have wealth to function as chiefs. A person with high inherited rank, but no wealth, had little influence, while a rich, though lower-

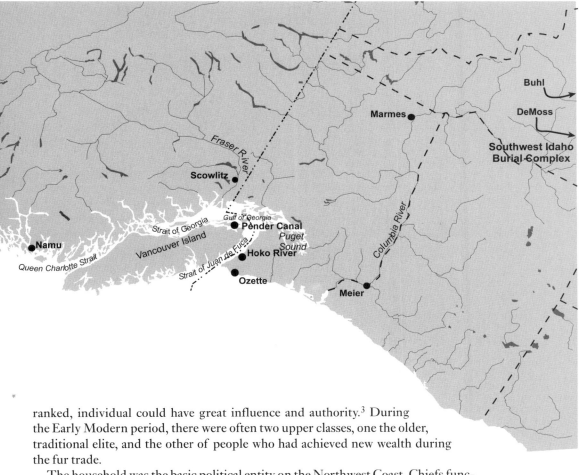

ranked, individual could have great influence and authority.[3] During
the Early Modern period, there were often two upper classes, one the older,
traditional elite, and the other of people who had achieved new wealth during
the fur trade.

The household was the basic political entity on the Northwest Coast. Chiefs functioned in a series of larger arenas, including the village or town, the region in which
they lived, and sometimes even at even larger geographic scales (Chapter Six), but all
chiefs, no matter how far their influence stretched, were basically house chiefs. All
chiefs were rooted in their house and dependent upon their house[4] for support and
resources – to produce the wealth they needed in order to behave as chiefs. In the
19th century, there were no polities on the coast larger than the house.

The evolution of ranking and stratification on the coast cannot be understood
apart from gender and geography. Both women and men could be born to high
status, and, although men were commonly house chiefs, women occasionally held
that position. High-status women exercised enormous influence, authority, and
great prestige in their own right. Marriage ties were the fundamental means by
which the overlapping social ties central to maintaining high status were established
and maintained. Free-born women were often occupational specialists who produced goods essential both to the household's domestic economy and for its external
exchange relationships.[5] The archaeological record suggests that a person's region
of origin was as important as gender in defining the social status. During the past
3,800 years, it has always been possible to identify whether a high-status person was

Pls. 14, 15, 34–36

a man or woman from either the northern or southern coasts (see below). This surely indicates the important role both women and men played in the regional exchange systems.

As with gender and geography, slavery is a key part of the history of inequality on the coast. Slaves[6] were either war captives or the descendants of war captives. Slaves performed a wide array of tasks, from being the body servants of members of the elite to hauling water, chopping wood and doing whatever else was necessary. Slaves worked for the benefit of their high-status owners and for their household. Slave labor was outside the sexual division of labor, so slaves could be assigned whatever tasks needed doing, irrespective of their sex. Treatment varied: they could be treated as a member of the family or traded or even killed at the whim of their owner.[7]

Measuring status archaeologically

Archaeologists employ many lines of evidence to determine whether ancient societies were ranked, stratified, or egalitarian. These methods rest upon the definitions of all three. Ranking is differential access to prestige and authority, but equal access to resources and the means of production. Stratification is, at root, differential access to resources and the means of production. In ranked societies, leaders are unable to exercise power over their colleagues, while in stratified societies, elites can and do exercise power. So archaeologists look for evidence for differential access to prestige, authority, and power, and for evidence of control over production, however it might be done.[8] One key measure of prestige and power is access to wealth and sumptuary goods. Wealth goods are available to anyone who can afford them, while sumptuary goods are restricted to people of the appropriate status. Such items are usually quite costly in the amount of effort or skill they represent. A huge earthen mound may have required little skill, but represent the work of a large number of people, while only one artisan was necessary to carve a jade pendant, but each is costly in its own way. Wealth and prestige goods are often of exotic or rare raw materials: raw materials not locally available, or only in small amounts. Diamonds in the modern world are an excellent example of all of these. They are found in only a few places, so they are exotic. They usually represent a great deal of effort, both in their mining and in the skill required to split them.

Burials and mortuary ritual are among the best sources of such evidence. While the treatment of the dead in mortuary ritual does not always reflect the status of that person in life, there is generally a connection. As Paul K. Wason puts it: "most variation in mortuary treatment *within a social group* relates to differences among people as to their 'place' in society. This can be expressed as the composite of someone's statuses, the social personae."[9]

There are many elements to mortuary ritual, including treatment of the body, the nature of what Wason calls the "disposal facility (grave, crypt, coffin, etc.)," what accompanies the burial (grave goods and grave furniture), and the biology of the deceased (sex, age, disease, and nutrition).[10] The basic dimensions of an individual's social personae are their sex and age, so when archaeologists look at a burial, we seek first to determine the sex and age of that person. We then examine how the other dimensions of mortuary ritual are distributed according to age and sex. We are also

Pl. 37

interested in the proximics, or spatial organization, of burials: are they scattered across a region, or do they occur in cemeteries? Do certain classes of burials occur in all cemeteries, or only some? Do certain classes of graves occur only in parts of cemeteries? Burials are not the only sources of such evidence. We also analyze the distributions of costly items in occupation sites, and across regions.

Finally, we see if there is evidence for the exercise of power. Sometimes, this is quite clear cut. In the famous Shang dynasty tombs near Anyang, in China, members of the ruling house were buried with scores of other people, probably retainers. These burials clearly indicate the presence of a stratified society – no leader in a ranked society could possibly arrange the deaths of hundreds of followers. A more common line of evidence is the apparent ability to command labor, which is evident through monumental architecture, such as the pyramids, or the Great Wall of China. However, establishing command of labor is usually not so clear cut. On the Northwest Coast, for example, we look at the size of houses, and their cost in labor and wood (see box in Chapter Six).

The best evidence for evolving status distinctions on the coast is provided by a large number of excavated burials spanning the period between 4400 BC and AD 1000. As discussed in Chapter Five, when middens appear on the coast, they contain burials. The practice of interring people in middens persisted until approximately AD 1000, although midden burials actually become increasingly rare after AD 500.

Funerary practices on the coast and adjacent parts of Cascadia appear always to have been rather varied and sometimes quite elaborate over the past 11,000 years, even when the rest of the archaeological record makes it clear that social groups were egalitarian. While some of this elaborateness is no doubt due to the social standing of both the living and their dead of the time, it must also reflect aspects of culture such as religious beliefs.

Grave goods usually regarded by Northwest Coast archaeologists to indicate high social status include items made of copper, shell beads,[11] ground-stone beads, carved pendants, scallop-shell rattles, lanceolate flaked-stone points and large ground-stone points, earspools and earrings, shell bracelets,

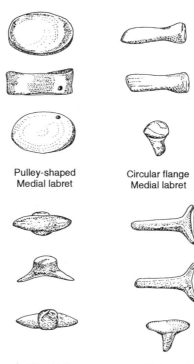

Pulley-shaped
Medial labret

Circular flange
Medial labret

"Top Hat"
Medial labret

"T" shaped
Medial labret

63 Labret styles typical of the Northwest Coast.

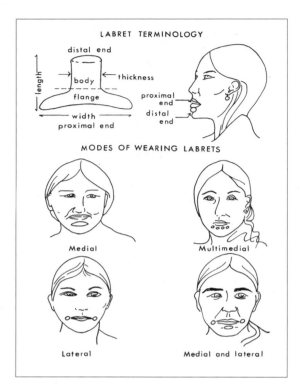

LABRET TERMINOLOGY

MODES OF WEARING LABRETS

64 Figure illustrates the variety of ways in which labrets could be worn.

carved-bone brow bands, whalebone clubs and zoomorphic objects. Evidence for social ranking also includes the energy and labor invested in the grave, including such features as the presence and size of rock cairns capping the grave, the presence of a wooden coffin and so on. Most individuals on the Northwest Coast were buried in the flexed, or fetal position.

However, the most crucial evidence about status on the coast is that provided by labrets and by the practice of cranial deformation. Labrets are large lip plugs. They were worn by free women on the northern coast during the contact period.[12] A girl's lower lip was slit, to receive a small T-shaped labret. As the girl matured, the labrets she wore increased in size. There were two forms of labret worn on the coast: *medial labrets* worn in the lower lip below the mouth, and *lateral labrets*[13] worn in the cheeks of the face, next to the molars. Only medial labrets were worn during the Early Modern period. Among the medial labrets, button or spool labrets were worn in the fleshy portion of the lip; while T- or hat-shaped labrets were worn in the more muscular lower portion of the lower lip and rested against the lower incisors. Labrets were made of stone, bone, and wood. Stone labrets caused a distinctive pattern of abrasion on the outside surfaces of the teeth behind them, a pattern called "labret wear." Labret wear also probably caused tooth loss. Archaeologists working on the coast infer high-status from either the presence of a labret with a burial or the presence of labret wear on the teeth. That assumption however needs to be made cautiously. During the 19th century, all free women on the northern coast wore labrets. What differed with social status was the size of the labret; high-status women wore large labrets[14]. During the Early and Middle Pacific periods labrets were worn by both women and men. The historic pattern appears to have developed after AD 500.

Frequently labret wear is the only evidence that an individual wore a labret in life. It is not unusual to excavate an interment in which the individual displays labret wear on the teeth, even though no labret (or even other grave goods) is present in the grave. Wearing labrets was always uncommon, though it is difficult to estimate the frequency of labret wear in a population because of tooth loss during life and after death. Jerome Cybulski, a physical anthropologist of the National Museums of Canada, who has analyzed the vast majority of Northwest Coast burials, believes

Pl. 14
Pl. 35

that some of this tooth loss is probably the result of labret wear, but cannot prove it. Cybulski has suggested that the presence of a labret as a grave good marks achieved status (a status one acquires during one's lifetime, based on one's accomplishments), and the absence of a labret (tooth wear present, no labret) points to ascribed status (a status one acquires by virtue of one's birth).[15] He reasons that with ascribed status, labrets were heirlooms and passed on to the living, while with an achieved status, a person acquired the right to wear a labret during their life, but did not pass that privilege on to their heirs. This is difficult to demonstrate; labrets often occur in a variety of non-mortuary archaeological contexts such as middens, house floors, and so on – curiously enough, often broken. It also assumes that labrets were always status markers, which may not be the case.

Cranial deformation was practiced on the southern and central coast during the Early Modern period, and was generally associated with free or high status. Several forms of cranial deformation were customary, depending upon where one was on the coast.[16] Cranial deformation is accomplished by binding a young child's head in a particular way so that as the bones of the head grow, they take on the desired shape. This practice was widespread in the world and was sometimes inadvertent (the result of placing a child in a cradle board so the back of the head becomes flat, for example). The growing brain accommodates itself so there is no effect on cognition (though it may cause serious damage to the auditory canal leading to the ears). Common forms of cranial deformation on the coast were flattening the forehead, flattening the back of the head (and a combination of the two), and wrapping the head so as to flatten it all the way around.

Pl. 36

Both labret wear and cranial deformation are traits of the living individual. They were not part of funerary ritual, and therefore are direct evidence of status in the Early Modern period. Grave goods, on the other hand, are placed in a grave as part of funerary ritual, and funerary rituals may have little to do with the social status of the dead. All things being equal, however, no matter the reason for placing grave goods with the dead, costly items (costly in time or labor) are usually associated with high status. But funeral ritual can disguise status differences. Many stratified societies make no distinctions among the dead. In contrast, modifications of the body are connected directly to the individual's life.

Labrets have a number of advantages as an indicator of social role or status. The wearing of labrets is a permanent and visible modification of the face, and so can be an unambiguous status marker – one wears a labret or one does not. Differences in labret size will also be quite visible. Cranial deformation is only somewhat less unambiguous. People on the Northwest Coast wore few clothes, and so labrets and cranial deformation would be visible, even when someone was nude. In some parts of the coast, facial tattooing was also associated with high status. Medial labrets are more visible when a person is viewed from the

65 Drawing of a box burial from Prince Rupert Harbor.

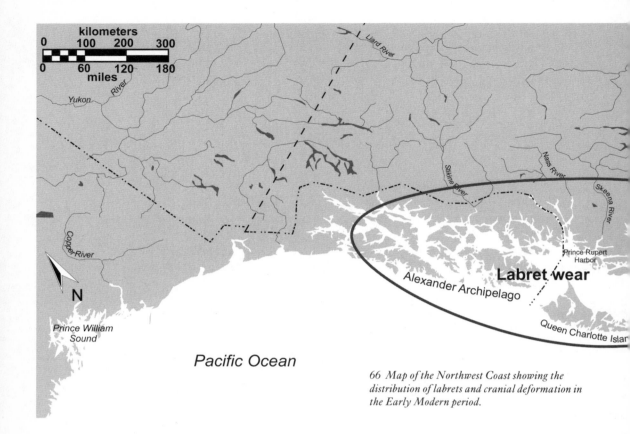

66 Map of the Northwest Coast showing the distribution of labrets and cranial deformation in the Early Modern period.

front than lateral labrets. As we shall see, in the Early Pacific, both medial and lateral labrets were worn: in the Middle and Late Pacific, only medial labrets. The evidence suggests that for the last 4,000 years on the coast it was important to distinguish certain individuals in as clear-cut a fashion as possible. It also became important in the Middle Pacific to indicate from what region of the coast people originated and to mark their gender. In the Middle Pacific, a female wearing a labret was probably from the south coast. In the Late Pacific, such an individual was from the north coast. Why the region of origin for women was so important is not known, but we will return to the topic at the end of this chapter, and in Chapter Ten.

The spatial distribution of graves can also provide useful evidence about status differentiation. Graves may occur in cemeteries, or they may be scattered across the landscape. The presence of cemeteries is thought by archaeologists to indicate partial or full sedentism, territoriality or the presence of corporate groups with long-lasting ties to particular places. The distribution of individuals, funerary practices and grave goods within and between cemeteries can be telling evidence about social and political organization. As already discussed in Chapter Six, the relative sizes of houses and the layout of villages were also used as indicators of rank. Pl. 34 Finally, items of costume could sometimes be used. Knob top hats (woven of basketry) have been recovered at wet sites such as Ozette and Hoko River. Historically these were worn only by high-status individuals.

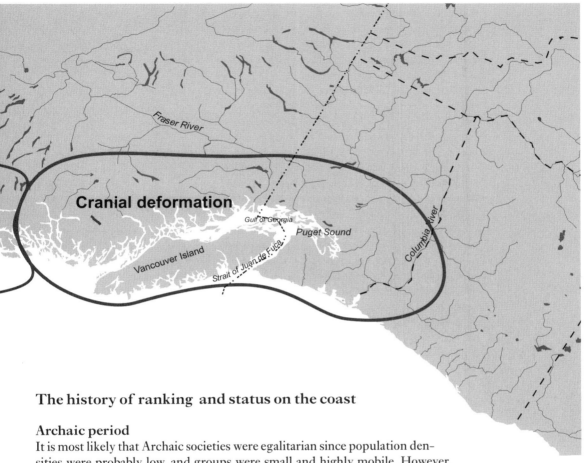

The history of ranking and status on the coast

Archaic period

It is most likely that Archaic societies were egalitarian since population densities were probably low, and groups were small and highly mobile. However, there is no direct evidence, one way or the other, on this topic for the entire coast during this period.

Data from the interior of southern Cascadia suggest that a tradition of relatively elaborate burial practices existed in the region from the beginning of the Archaic, with special treatment of some individuals as part of that tradition. The roots, then, of social inequality on the coast and across Cascadia may be quite ancient.

The earliest Archaic burials are all in southeastern Cascadia, and include the Buhl burial and at least 10 individuals buried in Marmes Rockshelter. Another 15 burials at Marmes date to the Late Archaic and Early Pacific and are discussed in the section on the Early Pacific. Early Archaic burial practices included both interment and cremation. At least five individuals at Marmes were buried as part of a single cremation burial, dating to *c.* 9500 BC. Cremation burials can be quite costly, particularly in the wood needed to completely burn the bodies to ash[18] in the funeral pyres. The interments for the period, including five at Marmes and the older Buhl burial, all contain grave goods, including Olivella shell beads, stemmed lanceolate points, other bifaces and chipped-stone tools, cobbles, and bone tools such as needles and pins. The young woman in the Buhl burial, for example, had a lanceolate point placed beneath her head and a bone needle and pin. Some of these grave goods were "expensive," in that they required time or skill in their making or use. The bone needles, for example, are quite small and delicate. Olivella beads were probably also quite valuable. Olivella is a genus of marine mollusk presently found in waters along the Pacific Coast from Baja California to the Gulf of Georgia, and so the shells were most likely traded from the coast.

The only well-documented Late Archaic burials are from the DeMoss site in south-central Idaho, where 22 individuals were recovered associated with 236 large, well-made bifaces. The DeMoss burials may represent the earliest documented cemetery in Cascadia, and date between 5000 and 4700 BC. In southwest Idaho, Max Pavesic, an archaeologist at Boise State University, has reconstructed what he calls "The Southwest Idaho Burial Complex (SWIBC)" which is characterized by very elaborate funerary practices. The complex dates *c*. 3200 BC to 2500 BC. Individuals were buried in flexed positions. Grave goods include red ocher, olivella shells, large well-made bifaces, large side-notched points and caches of bifaces and blanks, dog skulls, bone and shell beads, pipes, hematite crystals, and bone, chipped-stone and ground-stone tools. The significance of these burials is that they show that elaborate burial practices were not limited to the coast, and they clearly precede evidence of social stratification on the coast by perhaps one to two millennia.

Taken in the overall context of the Archaic period, these burials do not indicate pervasive social inequality. However, they do suggest differences in relative wealth, or at least prestige, among people even at an early date. The DeMoss cemetery raises the possibility of the existence of corporate groups in Cascadia by the end of the Archaic. In short, the stage may already have been set for the development of ranking and stratification.

Early Pacific period

Cemeteries appear on the coast perhaps as early as 4000 BC and certainly by 2500 BC. A concentration of burials in one area of Namu may be the earliest one, while cemeteries are undoubtedly present at Blue Jackets Creek on the Queen Charlotte Islands and on Pender Canal in the Gulf of Georgia by the latter date. These cemeteries are marked by considerable diversity in burial practices, though lacking cremation. Differences in interments include some people being buried in an upright, seated posture, while others were laid on their sides, curled in a fetal position. Grave goods range from everyday, utilitarian items such as the points for fish spears to such valuables as bone dagger blades. At Pender Canal, several individuals were buried with horn spoons. The spoon handles were carved in Northwest Coast style (see Chapter Nine) zoomorphic motifs, including wolves. Several of the spoons were apparently resting on or across the individual's jaws, as though they had been placed over their mouths. Others at Pender Canal were each buried with a clam shell bowl. Those with the spoons or bowls were placed in the seated posture, while the seated individuals at Blue Jackets Creek were covered in red ochre. They also displayed labret wear. Roy Carlson believes the spoons and bowls were placed in the graves as part of ritual feasting at funerals, rather than just as status markers. Other people, of course, were buried without grave goods, and many people were probably not buried in cemeteries at all. Gender was central to the definition of high status on the northern coast in the Middle Pacific. However, its role in the Early Pacific is difficult to determine.[19]

A position of labret wearer clearly existed on the coast during the Early Pacific. Labret wear is present on individuals at all three sites, including a male at Namu, dated to 4000 BC, the earliest evidence on the coast for labret wear.[20] What that position represents in terms of social organization is an open question. Use of labrets was widespread along the North Pacific Rim at this time; the Namu burial is contemporary with a labret recovered on the Kamchatka Peninsula.[21] Labrets are not restricted to burials on the Northwest Coast but occur in residential sites, the earliest being from Hidden Falls II. Access to labrets was restricted to perhaps 10 percent of the population,[22] but they were worn by adults of both sexes equally. Labret wear has been found on adults ranging in age at death from their mid-20s on up.

Early Pacific patterns of labret wear differed from those of later periods in some important ways. Both lateral and medial labrets were worn, and the medial labrets may have been smaller than those of later periods, at least at Pender Canal. Finally, labret wear was geographically more widespread on the coast than in later times.

In sum, cemeteries appear to have been present, both on the coast and elsewhere in Cascadia, during the Early Pacific. A social position of "labret wearer" seems to have existed, although we do not think that this necessarily indicates the kind of social ranking of later periods.

Middle Pacific period

Midden cemeteries are much more common and widespread along the coast during the Middle Pacific, except along the outer Pacific coast of Vancouver Island, Washington State, and Oregon, where midden burials are relatively rare. The two largest samples of excavated Middle Pacific burials are from the Gulf of Georgia on the southern coast, and Prince Rupert Harbor on the northern coast. Systems of ranking evolved throughout the Middle Pacific. The north–south distinctions of labret wear–cranial deformation emerge, as does the geographic marking of gender. Distinctions in relative wealth and prestige become much sharper after 500 BC. In addition to ranking, slavery may also have emerged by the beginning of the period.

"Labret wearer" continued to be a special status among peoples in the Gulf of Georgia between 1800 and 650 BC (Locarno Beach phase), but grave goods are relatively rare during this period, limited to stone and shell beads, pendants, and red ochre.[23] The exception is Pender Canal, where broken labrets and ear spools were also present in the deposits.[24] This may mean that wealth and perhaps even status differences were not particularly strong.[25] Labrets were still worn on the southern coast during this early part of the Middle Pacific (Locarno Beach phase) by both men and women equally. The labrets were larger and more complex in form than those of the Early Pacific, but labret wear was still restricted to a limited number of people.[26] In contrast to these evident continuities with Early Pacific practices, there are no seated burials, nor any carved spoons or clam-shell bowls.

The nature of high status changed in the Gulf of Georgia after 650 BC (Marpole phase) with the clear emergence of a wealthy elite that included more people than the older, "labret-wearer" status. Labret wear ceases, completely replaced by cranial deformation. There is a marked increase in the number of midden burials, as well as in the differences in the costliness of grave goods. Grave goods are associated with about 15 percent of interments, and include dentalium beads (sometimes in the thousands), copper artifacts, carved pendants and brow bands, scallop-shell rattles, large flaked- and ground-stone points.[27] The carved brow bands appear to may have been made by specialized carvers (Chapter Nine),[28] suggesting that the bands were valuables, or even sumptuary goods,[29] made specially for the elite. Grave goods are

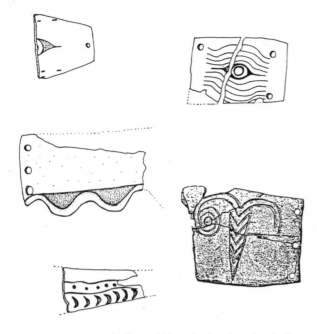

67 Carved Marpole phase brow bands. These may represent the work of specialists.

associated with all ages, including children, and both males and females. High-status graves are not restricted to any particular cemeteries. The age distribution of grave goods suggests that status was ascribed. However, about three times as many males as females have grave goods with them, indicating a strong male bias in access to higher status in the Middle Pacific, in contrast with the Early Pacific. Overall, the proportion of males to females in these cemeteries is 0.98 male:1 female.[30]

The same basic patterns are also present on the northern coast at this time. In Prince Rupert Harbor, less than a third of adult burials contain any grave goods at all. The distribution of graves and grave goods suggests four broad categories of people. The largest category comprises the people who were not buried in the midden cemeteries, but whose bodies were disposed of elsewhere. Given the number of buried individuals, this first class must have been by far the largest. As we will see below, it may have included slaves and perhaps low-status free people. The next category are those buried in the midden cemeteries but without grave goods or other forms of special treatment (boxes, cairns, etc.). This group includes males and females of all ages from children to the aged. Both the third and fourth categories are burials with grave goods or special funerary treatment. Grave goods include copper tubes and sheets; shell bracelets, beads, and gorgets; amber beads; labrets; dog burials; bone daggers; a variety of more mundane items made of bone and antler (tubes, pendants, punches, awls, etc.), as well as burial boxes studded with scores of sea otter teeth. In the third class of burials, the grave goods are those made of bone and antler, while the fourth includes the copper items, labrets, shell artifacts, the amber beads, in other words, the things made of exotic raw materials or that were costly in labor or skill. The copper artifacts particularly would have been extremely expensive, since they represent the work of specialists. The origin of the copper is unknown, though southern Alaska is the most likely place. The source of the amber is also unknown. This fourth class of grave constitutes 8 percent of all adult burials in the harbor, and most are virtually from a single cemetery at one site, the Boardwalk site. This class of burials appears in the harbor around 500 BC. Class three burials are less restricted, occurring in three sites.

The distribution of grave goods across gender and age categories shows strong degrees of ranking. It also suggests that high rank was probably ascribed. Gender played a crucial role in status distinctions in the north. Among the buried adults, the sex ratio is almost 2:1 in favor of males; the ratio among those with grave goods is 3.25:1; while among labret wearers it is 6.3:1. The sex ratio among class four burials is 8.5:1. On the other hand, the sex ratio in the third class of burials (grave goods made of bone and other locally available materials) is almost balanced, 1:0.7. In this group, women and men are both buried with items such as dagger blades. Additionally, two of the women in this group are accompanied by grave goods that are completely unique among graves in the harbor, a harpoon and a ground–slate point worn as pendants.[31] Ages range from young adults to aged individuals, while among the class four graves, the youngest male was perhaps 12 years old, and others were teenagers, quite young to have achieved high status. In sum, a minority of the population was buried in the midden cemeteries, and an even smaller minority was accorded special treatment in their burials. Higher statuses were generally more available to men than to women, except in the second highest-ranking group. Women, though a distinct minority, were also present in the highest-ranking group. Membership in the highest rank ranged from the young to the very old, indicating that the positions were inherited. Finally, the burials of the highest-ranked individuals were restricted to certain cemeteries in contrast with practices in the south at this time.

The wearing of labrets was especially restricted. After 500 BC, as the sex ratio indicates, labrets were worn almost exclusively by men (in contrast to the earlier north coast pattern at Blue Jackets, and on the south coast). Beyond that, pains were taken to ensure that stone labrets, as a sumptuary good, were not widely available for wear. About half the labrets recovered in Prince Rupert Harbor were found in graves. However, labrets are also found in dumps and other archaeological contexts. Many of these had been deliberately broken, some snapped in half, others smashed around their edges, making them unwearable. Why a valuable labret would be discarded in the first place is an interesting question, but the destruction of sumptuary goods, as a way of establishing or raising their value, is not an uncommon practice around the world and was often done on the Northwest Coast during the Early Modern period. The point is that such behavior is almost always associated with permanent social ranks.[32]

While it is clear that there was ranking of individuals on the northern coast by the middle of the Middle Pacific, this is not reflected in house sizes. Several archaeologists have mapped late Middle Pacific house floors on the Queen Charlotte Islands,[33] in southeast Alaska,[34] Prince Rupert Harbor,[35] and the Paul Mason site.[36] The houses are almost all uniformly small, suggesting that individual households were not commonly ranked, in contrast to practices during the Early Modern period. There are, however, the two rather large house depressions at Paul Mason, that are somewhat separate from the rest, although clearly part of the village. These, which are unexcavated, could represent a number of things, including the large houses of high-status households. On the other hand, extended corporate groups, such as kin groups, may have been ranked. Three of these villages, two in Prince Rupert Harbor, and the Paul Mason site, are two-row villages. Two, Boardwalk in the harbor, and Paul Mason, are the earliest villages on the northern coast, dating to the middle of the Middle Pacific, while the third, McNichol Creek, dates to the end. There is no equivalent information for the south coast at this time, though houses and single-row villages are known for the Marpole phase (see Chapter Six).

The evidence is clear for warfare and raiding in the Gulf of Georgia and in Prince Rupert Harbor at this time (see Chapter Eight). Several individuals found in Prince Rupert Harbor appear to have been bound and decapitated. Middle-aged females are the most common of these victims. Other individuals were found in what Cybulski calls "unconventional" burial postures.[37] Most burials are flexed; these are quite loosely extended. Most of these particular burials predate 1700 BC and are therefore more than 1,000 years older than the set of burials with evidence for ranking. These data could be read as evidence for slavery in two ways. The bound individuals were killed in the course of raids as not being worth enslaving, or alternatively, as slaves who were killed as part of ritual disposition of wealth. These inferences remain quite speculative, however. On the southern coast, the skeletons of two scalped females predating 250 BC have been recovered. They were buried in an anomalous location and burial posture, leading the analyst to speculate that they may have been killed as slaves.[38]

Cybulski[39] has suggested that the sex ratio of the Prince Rupert burials may indicate slavery. Slaves were not buried in the Early Modern period; their bodies were thrown out (hence the interpretation of the "unconventional" postures), sometimes into the sea, and so they would not be present in any cemeteries. If he is correct, some 25 percent of Prince Rupert's female population were slaves during the Middle Pacific, and in the south, either slavery was far less important, or involved men and women equally, given the balanced sex ratio of Marpole burials. We think

BURIAL MOUNDS ON THE NORTHWEST COAST

BURIAL MOUNDS, or mounds of any sort, are not usually associated with the Northwest Coast. Mounds occur widely throughout the Middle West and eastern parts of North America, but burial mounds also occur in at least two areas of the southern Northwest Coast: the Lower Mainland area of southern British Columbia, and the Willamette Valley of western Oregon and in the Columbia River Gorge of western Oregon and Washington. The absence of mounds between these two areas may reflect the archaeological sample, rather than funerary practices. While some mounds are simple earthen mounds covering single burials, in other instances, the mounds cover stone cairns and boulder alignments. The more elaborate mounds also contained elaborate grave goods, including copper objects. Skeletal remains often displayed cranial deformation. There are differences between the two areas. In British Columbia, the mounds contain single burials, while in the Willamette Valley, they contain multiple burials. Some Willamette Valley mounds are not burial mounds. While excavations of burial mounds began in the late 1850s, and continued sporadically into the 1980s, the excavations of the mounds at Scowlitz on the Fraser River represent the first significant excavations of a Northwest Coast burial mound in several decades.

The Scowlitz site is important to Northwest Coast archaeology for a number of reasons. The most obvious is that it provides evidence for a poorly known and understood funerary practice on the coast – burial mounds. Another, and ultimately more important, reason is that it represents a model of cooperation between Native peoples and archaeologists. The excavations at the Scowlitz burial mounds were begun at the invitation of the Sto:lo tribal council. The Sto:lo are Coast Salish (there are 12 Sto:lo bands, including the Scowlitz band) living along the Lower Fraser between Hope, British Columbia and Vancouver.

Concern for this site developed when erosion began to threaten parts of it and because a section containing the burial mounds is not part of the Scowlitz Reserve. The ultimate plan is to use the archaeological data as a basis for changing the boundaries of the Reserve to include the archaeological site. It was on this basis that the Sto:lo Tribal Council contacted the University of British Columbia and work began. Scowlitz is not the only example of such cooperation along the Northwest Coast between Native peoples and archaeologists. Jerry Cybulski's excavations at Greenville (indeed, much of his analytical work over the last 25 years) has been done with the active participation of Native peoples. His excavations at Greenville were at the behest of the Nishga band council.

	Male	Female
North	Labrets	Neither (Almost)
South	Cranial Deformation	Cranial Deformation

these ideas need to be viewed cautiously, however, and conclude that slavery is a possibility, but not demonstrated.

Status and gender on the Northwest Coast show a clear geographical patterning in the Middle Pacific, particularly after *c.* 500 BC and the presence of cranial deformation in the south. As the table shows, one could readily identify the region of origin of any high-status individual on the coast as one encountered them.

A labret-wearing male was from the north coast, a woman with cranial deformation from the south. A labret-wearing northern woman was probably of remarkably high status. Labrets were worn medially and were larger than previously, i.e., they were more visible. It is quite clear then, that patterns of interaction along the coast were such that it was important to identify where a high-status person came from. We will address this issue in more detail in Chapter Ten.

It is sufficient to say here that by *c.* 500 BC a coast-wide system of ranking of

Scowlitz is a village site. There are 18 house depressions generally facing out over the Harrison River. Behind, and in some cases, among and in the house depressions are at least 37 earthen mounds and cairns. Most of these features sit on a ridge behind and above the house depressions. Two of these features, mounds 1 and 23, had been excavated by early 1995.

Mound 1 is quite large. It is isolated from the rest, standing on a high knoll south of the major concentration of mounds and house depressions. The mound's base is rectangular, and is 12.5 m (41 ft) x 11.5 m (38 ft) and is 2.7 m (8 ft) high at its center. Its volume is estimated at 164.1 cu. m. The mound appears to have been constructed in a single building episode covering a burial cairn. The mound was built by placing culturally sterile clays over two concentric boulder alignments surrounding the central burial cairn. Both alignments were square, the outer measuring 7 m (23 ft) on a side, the inner 3.5 m (11.5 ft). The alignments were one to two boulder courses high. Within the inner alignment was the burial cairn composed of over 200 boulders. These constructions were built on a levelled surface that had been covered with a thin layer of grey clay. The cairn itself covered a small burial pit containing the skeleton of an adult male. He was in a flexed position. Grave goods included four flat perforated copper disks resting near the lower face. Four abalone shell pendants and the fragments of a copper ring were also found near the head. Roughly 7,000 cut and ground dentalia shell beads were also recovered. This is one of the richest burials yet encountered on the Northwest Coast.

In contrast, mound 23 is 9 by 10 m (29 x32 ft), and 1.4 m (4.5 ft) high, containing only about 53 cu. m of material. It is part of a large cluster of cairns and mounds at the north end of the site. Mound 23 was built using midden material from the site itself. The mound's base was formed by a retaining wall almost a meter high and a meter wide built of compacted midden materials. Within this wall was a cairn covering a small burial pit. The ground surface had been levelled and covered with a thin layer of yellow clay. The soil was quite acidic, so no bones, or other organic materials were preserved. There were no other grave goods.

Mound 1 is dated to about AD 500 while mound 23 dates to about AD 850–950, right at the end of the period of the Midden Burial Complex.

The skeletal materials recovered from mound 1 were reburied the day after they were excavated, though a small number of bones, and the original grave goods, were kept for analysis. They were replaced by new items of copper, shell, and leather.

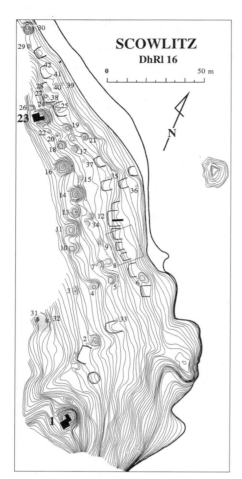

68 *Map of the houses and mounds at the Scowlitz site on the lower Fraser River.*

individuals was well developed. High-ranked individuals had access to rare or exotic materials, such as copper, as well as to the work of specialized artisans. There is little or no evidence, however, that they exercised much if any power. This circumstance fits most definitions of ranking. Additionally, in the north, it is possible that extended corporate groups were also ranked. As we shall see in the following section, there are differences, at least on the northern coast, between the system of ranking that emerged in the Middle Pacific, and the forms it took during the Late Pacific.

Late Pacific period

Ranking went through a number of marked changes during the first centuries of the Late Pacific that are reflected in rapidly changing funerary practices along the coast. In what is the most dramatic shift in mortuary ritual in the 11,000-year prehistory of Cascadia, the practice of midden burials ends by AD 1000–1200, all along the coast (and starting as early as AD 500–600). It was replaced by the practices of the Early Modern period, which included disposition of corpses away from villages, often through exposure. In the 18th and 19th centuries, the bodies of high-status people were wrapped and then often placed in a canoe or some other container that was then placed on a rack, platform, pole, or tree. Wealth and prestige items would be put in the container with them, sometimes even slaves. These practices, although well described historically, have left virtually no archaeological record. They are also not the only changes.

The most elaborate burials of the Pacific period were burial mounds constructed along the lower Fraser River, and perhaps elsewhere in the Gulf of Georgia, around AD 1000. Burial mounds also occur in the Willamette Valley and along parts of the Lower Columbia River, where they have produced status goods.[40] Limited excavations of mounds in the Gulf of Georgia were conducted at the beginning of this century,[41] but curiously, not pursued. More recent excavations at the Scowlitz site on the Fraser River, however, are unparalleled.

Scowlitz is the site of a village with at least 18 house depressions. The site commands a dominating view down the Fraser River at its confluence with the Harrison River.[42] Behind and in some cases among and in the house depressions are scores of earthen mounds and rock cairns. Most of these features sit on a ridge behind and above the house depressions. Two of these features, mounds 1 and 23, had been excavated by early 1995.[43] These features represent significant investments in labor and clearly were placed to maximize their impressiveness (see box).

Scowlitz itself is a distinctive form of cemetery, though not completely unique. Thus, there is a regional distinction between people buried in mound cemeteries, and those who are not. There are villages, like Scowlitz, with mound complexes, and those, much more frequent, without. This suggests the possibility of the ranking not only of individuals and households, but perhaps villages and towns as well, with the implications for regional political organization that we discussed in Chapter Six.

Changes in status and funerary ritual took a different course in the north, if the Greenville burial ground is at all typical. Greenville, on the Nass River, is the only well-documented Late Pacific cemetery in the north and offers sharp contrasts both with Scowlitz, its southern contemporary, and with Middle Pacific cemeteries in near-by Prince Rupert Harbor. The site dates between *c.* AD 500 and 1290, with a majority of burials post-dating AD 1180. The Greenville graves lack grave goods of the kind found in Middle Pacific graves in Prince Rupert Harbor. At Greenville, there are only burial boxes, some dog remains, and elderberry[44] in the graves. Labrets were worn exclusively by females. Thirty-nine individuals were excavated, of whom nine, all females, had evidence of labret wear.[45] This clearly indicates the beginning of the historic pattern of labret wear on the northern coast. It may also point to the beginnings of matrilineality in that region.

Between *c.* AD 500 and 1000 large houses appear in Prince Rupert Harbor,[46] the southern Queen Charlottes,[47] and southeast Alaska.[48] These large houses suggest   Pl. 32

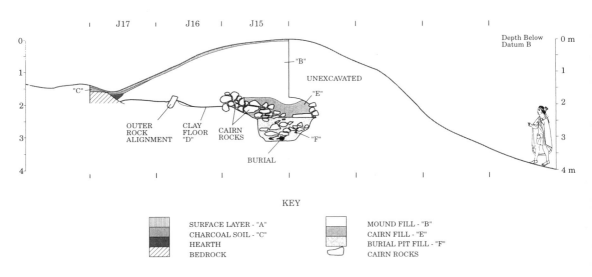

69 *Cross-section of the main mound at the Scowlitz site.*

the ranking of households and that household chiefs were able to attract large numbers of followers. In short, it seems certain that the historic system of ranking emerged on the north coast by AD 1000. We will address possible causes in Chapter Ten.

Discussion

The roots of permanent inequality on the Northwest Coast may lie in the Archaic. In southern Cascadia distinctions were drawn among individuals in burial treatment quite early. The late Archaic and Early Pacific periods appear to have been marked by what we are calling "experiments" in ranking along the coast, and across the Columbia Plateau, where the strongest indicator of ranking may be the Southwest Idaho Burial Complex. Some form of status differential appears to have existed on the coast from the beginning of the Early Pacific in the position of "labret-wearer." We have not attempted to define that status, although it appears to have been limited to perhaps 10 percent of the population, and was open to both men and women. Labrets have considerable time depth in the North Pacific, and were worn as status and geographic region markers from the Northwest Coast to the Kamchatka Peninsula. Thus, the origins of the practice and the status may lie elsewhere than on the Northwest Coast.

"Labret wearer" as a status appears to have merged into an emerging and expanding elite around 500 BC. The newer elite included more people, with a distinctly male bias in its higher ranks. It was much wealthier, with a wider array of prestige markers, including exotic items clearly requiring specialized production, such as copper. The new elites were regional, as indicated by the appearance of cranial deformation in the south and the restriction of labret wearing to the north. While this pattern developed after 500 BC, it continued to evolve and change.

During the Late Pacific in some parts of the south, an increasing elaboration of the ranking systems is reflected in the mounds at Scowlitz. Mounds 1 and 23 may indicate the emergence of regional leaders, or at least of individuals who could command considerable wealth and labor far beyond that of their contemporaries. In contrast, in the north, burial ritual simplifies, though it is clear from house sizes that significant differences in household ranking had emerged during the early centuries of the Late Pacific. The wearing of labrets makes its final shift, to women. And then, all along the coast, the ancient burial practices of interment were replaced by new ones.

CHAPTER EIGHT

Warfare

Introduction

In December 1860, a Russian Naval Officer, Lieutenant Commander Golovnin, was visiting Sitka, a Russian fort and capital of Russian America in southeast Alaska. While looking out from the parapets he noticed a great commotion starting in one of the Tlingit houses below the fort. Suddenly the wall planks pushed out and he saw Tlingit running to other lineage houses, returning shortly in full battle armor and carrying weapons. Quickly the Russian fort fired several cannon rounds over the clash and the Tlingit dispersed. Intrigued by this event, Golovnin set out the next day to interview the participants.

Through these interviews he found that the conflict had erupted because the Sitka out-sang the Yakutat and the Yakutat attacked to avert their public humiliation. Apparently, during a potlatch in 1859, the Sitka out-sang the Yakutat in the Yakutat area. During the following year the Yakutat sent some people north to the Copper River to learn more songs from the Athapascans living there. When another potlatch was held in 1860, the Sitka started singing Aleut songs they had learned from sea-otter hunters employed by the Russians; again the Yakutat could not compete. They had come armed in preparation for an attack if they were again defeated. The result was 13 Sitka wounded, 2 critically, and 5 Yakutat wounded. The Russians suppressed the conflict because "blood vendettas begin after such incidents, and wars will go on, perhaps for several years..."

Such was the nature of warfare among the Tlingit and on much of the Northwest Coast during the Early Modern period. The protection of status, and revenge for the loss of status, were so important to the maintenance of Northwest Coast society that conflict and ultimately war often erupted. Powerful and high-ranking war leaders led their lineages and clans on raids that might involve hundreds of warriors in dozens of 18-m (60-ft) war canoes. Large palisaded defensive constructions, full body armor, and sophisticated weaponry were united with well-honed tactical skills to make the Northwest Coast natives effective soldiers. But was this always the case? Are there any data from prehistory that would allow us to formulate a different picture of Northwest Coast warfare? In this chapter, we present an archaeological analysis of the evidence and potential causes of warfare on the Northwest Coast. Using a variety of evidence, including skeletal, archaeological, and ethnographic data, we demonstrate that warfare has a long but variable history on the Northwest Coast and that the historically recorded accounts were probably a remnant of the prehistoric pattern.

Brian Ferguson, a cultural anthropologist whose research has focused on the causes of warfare, has attempted to explain Northwest Coast conflicts from the perspective of conflict over scarce material resources. He justifies his lack of interest in symbolic and social explanations for warfare by reasoning that given the hazards of

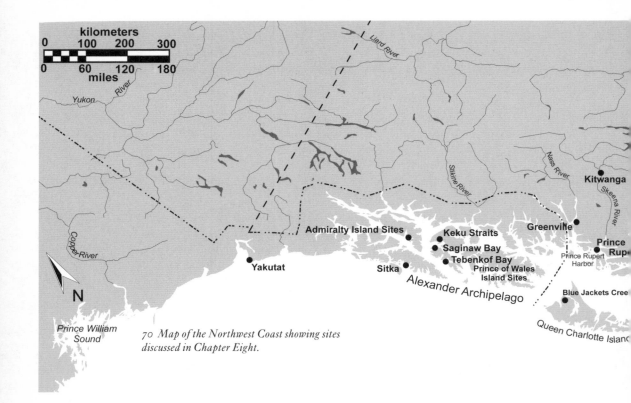

70 *Map of the Northwest Coast showing sites discussed in Chapter Eight.*

war, practical considerations were probably more important than in other less life-or-death matters. He believes that by emphasizing economic goals, he is not ignoring the variety of other reasons entering into decisions to go to war. However, in his view, motivations such as the quest for status, prestige, or acquisition of ceremonial titles are constant cultural norms whereas warfare is not. In other words, wars occur only sometimes, not constantly, while people were always competing for status, prestige, and titles, and so such competition cannot explain when and why wars occur.

We take a somewhat more generous view of the historic record. We believe that people will fight over anything that they consider important to their social or economic survival. This does not take away from the fact that the original, historical cause of Northwest Coast warfare may have been scarcities of food or land during remote time periods. But all the ethnographic data indicate that there were many reasons why people might participate in warfare. Revenge wars, wars to capture slaves, fights over women and infidelities, and wars for access to desirable foods, territory and trade routes are cited as the primary causes of Northwest Coast warfare in the literature of the Modern period.

Revenge wars are conflicts that develop because of some perceived wrong, insult, or aggressive act and are the single most common cause in the ethnographic literature. Ivan Veniaminov, a Russian Orthodox priest who lived in southeast Alaska in the 1820s, best described this type of conflict. He maintained that "a Kolosha [Tlingit] does not seek out blood: he only exacts blood for blood."[1] This was also the

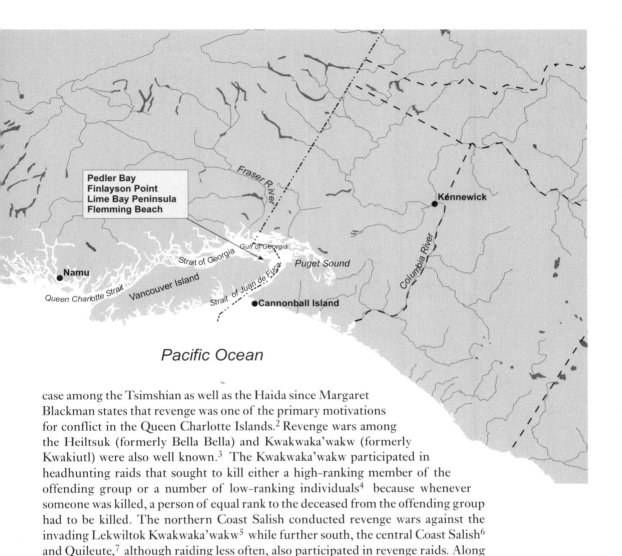

Pedler Bay
Finlayson Point
Lime Bay Peninsula
Flemming Beach

Fraser River

Kennewick

Gulf of Georgia

Strait of Georgia   *Puget Sound*

Columbia River

Namu

Queen Charlotte Strait   *Vancouver Island*

Strait of Juan de Fuca   *Cannonball Island*

Pacific Ocean

case among the Tsimshian as well as the Haida since Margaret Blackman states that revenge was one of the primary motivations for conflict in the Queen Charlotte Islands.[2] Revenge wars among the Heiltsuk (formerly Bella Bella) and Kwakwaka'wakw (formerly Kwakiutl) were also well known.[3] The Kwakwaka'wakw participated in headhunting raids that sought to kill either a high-ranking member of the offending group or a number of low-ranking individuals[4] because whenever someone was killed, a person of equal rank to the deceased from the offending group had to be killed. The northern Coast Salish conducted revenge wars against the invading Lekwiltok Kwakwaka'wakw[5] while further south, the central Coast Salish[6] and Quileute,[7] although raiding less often, also participated in revenge raids. Along the Columbia River and further south, revenge wars often ended in payment or enslavement of the offenders, the victors taking payment from the losers without any change in territory. This form of conflict was common among the Chinookan-speaking groups of the lower Columbia, as well as the Tillamook, Lower Chihalis, Lower Cowlitz, and Tualatin.[8] Overall, nearly every explorer, missionary, and ethnographer has discussed and described the importance of revenge wars in maintaining status and prestige in Northwest Coast society.[9]

The capture of slaves for labor and wealth was a common and critical motive for conflict.[10] Kamenskii stated[11] that warfare provided the Tlingit with wealth in the form of slaves and argued that "the Tlingit himself considered it demeaning to perform dirty work...this was the duty of slaves or at least women." Slave raiding was also standard practice among the Haida, who raided up and down the northern Northwest Coast against the Tlingit, Tsimshian, Heiltsuk, Kwakwaka'wakw, and other Haida. Among the Tsimshian, Garfield[12] noted that "raiding parties were

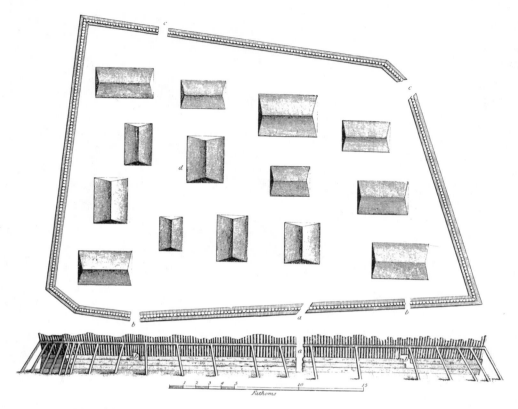

71 Map of the Tlingit fort at Sitka as drawn by Lisiansky in 1804. This fort withstood a bombardment by the Russian navy only to be abandoned when the Tlingit ran out of supplies.

organized for the capture of slaves or to avenge a wrong or injury inflicted by another group," and that "raiding for captives, either to be returned to their relatives for ransom or kept as slaves, was profitable." The northern, central, and southern Coast Salish groups needed to be constantly on the defensive because the Lekwiltok Kwakwaka'wakw were avid slavers. Traded to the Haida or Tlingit, Salish slaves often ended up nearly 1,000 km (over 600 miles) from their home. The taking of their people prompted a number of southern Coast Salish revenge wars against the Lekwiltok.[13]

The Chinook of the Lower Columbia also raided for slaves, but they were more famous for their participation in the slave trade, being the middle men between the Columbia Plateau and the Northwest Coast.[14] Most of the southern groups spent more time being raided and enslaved than they did raiding and they do not appear to have been active slave raiders. Slaves in these villages were usually acquired through trade. Early battles between the Tillamook and the Chinook and the Tillamook and the Tualatin have been recorded, and there is evidence that they may have involved the slave trade.[15]

De Laguna mentions that quarrels over women are traditionally cited as a cause of group fissioning and emigration, which may often lead to war. It has been reported that the Eyak had many Tlingit wives, which were "always (frequently?) stolen..."[16]

This often led to wars between the Tlingit and their northern neighbors. Garfield[17] states that "in myths illicit love affairs are also related to the cause of trouble between groups" and argues that female slaves that were Tlingit, Haida, or interior Tsimshian often became Tsimshian. Many conflicts occurred over adultery according to Veniaminov. Southern Northwest Coast wars fought over infidelities, theft of women, or incest are much less reported.[18]

In 1852, on hearing that the Hudson Bay Company had built Fort Selkirk in the interior to promote trade, Chief Chartrich (Shotridge) of the Chilkat Tlingit led a war party over 480 km (300 miles) into the interior, destroyed the fort, and effectively ended competition.[19] In fact, intense competition for access or control of trade and trade routes seems to have been a motivation for many wars during the Modern era. Wooley has argued that many of the early historic conflicts over trade might be explained by the effects of depopulation and stresses that resulted from unrelated groups congregating at important trading locations.[20] The Chilkat and many other groups on the north coast controlled coast–interior trade routes and prohibited direct interaction between the interior Athapascans and the coastal Europeans, creating effective monopolies.

A good example is the mouth of the Nass River, where a number of intense wars were fought over the spectacular eulachon run that occurred there every spring (see Chapter Five). Eulachon oil was prized because it was not only excellent for the long-term storage of fish, but was also an important commodity in trade, especially with the interior. Boas recorded a number of stories about exterminatory raids between the Tlingit and Tsimshian over this region where the Tsimshian eventually won and pushed the Tlingit northward.

More along the lines of Ferguson's arguments described above, food shortages and territorial expansion are also described as a reason for conflict, only much less common than other reasons. The Heiltsuk certainly participated in warfare during times of food shortage as did the Nuu-chah-nulth.[21] The Kaigani Haida expansion into Tlingit territory (southern Prince of Wales Island), and the Tlingit expansion northward into Eyak territory are recorded in Tlingit and Haida oral traditions. Tsimshian oral history suggests that there were a series of territorial shifts just prior to historic contact, including evidence that the Tlingit once resided in Prince Rupert Harbor, later being pushed out by the Tsimshian expanding down the Nass and Skeena Rivers.[22]

Other considerations in Northwest Coast warfare

One of the more salient aspects of Northwest Coast wars are the incredible distances traveled to conduct them. The Haida not only fought their closest neighbors, the Tsimshian, southern Tlingit, and Heiltsuk, but also raided Kwakwaka'wakw, Coast Salish, and Nuu-chah-nulth villages over 600 km (375 miles) away.[23] These long-distance excursion wars were not limited to the northern coast, since Tlingit war parties raided as far south as the Strait of Georgia for revenge and slaves. On the southern coast the Kwakwaka'wakw regularly conducted slave raids against the southern Coast Salish groups on the south end of Puget Sound.

Northwest Coast wars probably affected the demographic histories of the groups who participated. Boyd[24] states that the extermination of whole villages can be seen in the traditional tales of the Haida, Tsimshian, and Nuu-chal-nulth who conducted territorial wars with a high mortality rate. The Nuu-chal-nulth were known to attack and annihilate a neighboring Nuu-chal-nulth group in order to take their lands and primary fishing locales. The Lekwiltok Kwakwaka'wakw drove the northern Coast Salish out of their traditional territories and villages between the Salmon River and Cape Mudge.[25] These kinds of shifts probably occurred in early prehistory as well but are difficult to identify in the archaeological record.

Two final points in explaining warfare on the Northwest Coast are important to this discussion. The first is that it appears wars were never fought for a single reason. Disagreements over insults or infidelities often escalated into revenge wars that could last for decades. While these wars might result in the total annihilation of one

---

NORTHWEST COAST WEAPONS OF WAR AND ARMOR

The bow and arrow was widely used in warfare and was the primary weapon before the introduction of firearms. The bow was usually made of yew and reinforced with sinew although many were simply made of wood. MacDonald states that the Saskatoon berry bush provided the best arrowshafts but was rare on the coast, thus a brisk inland–coastal trade was conducted for arrowshafts. Although the cedar shafts of the coast worked well, they were easy to break off. The Saskatoon berry shafts were very strong and did much more internal damage while being removed. Evidence for the introduction of the bow and arrow is rare, small arrowpoints on the southern coast and a proliferation of bone bipoints on the north coast being some of the only data. All evidence points to a post AD 200-500 date for its introduction.

Pl. 44

Daggers were the most common weapon for hand-to-hand combat in the historic period. Old ethnographic examples are of whalebone and copper, and archaeological examples made of chipped stone or ground slate are 3,000 years old. They are distinctive in that both the oldest and youngest examples often have one long blade and one short blade, and because the blades are often fluted.

The **war spear** made up the third part of a warrior's weapons. The spear was usually 1.8–2 m (5 to 6 ft) long and was described as "a knife tied on the end of a stick." These were thrusting spears, not usually thrown. Among the Tsimshian, spears as long as 5.5 m (18 ft) were used from the tops of palisaded forts. Spear-like points occur in many contexts from the Middle Pacific and later.

The **stone war** club is dramatic evidence of the type of hand-to-hand combat that occurred on the north coast, particularly the Tsimshian region, during the Middle Pacific. These large and heavy clubs were carved in elaborate effigies of birds, fish, animals, and humans. A cache

Pl. 43

of 35 clubs was found in 1898 by Johnny Muldoe in Hagwilget Canyon and since that time a number of others have been found along the northern British Columbia coast and on the Queen Charlotte Islands.

Several types of **armor** were used on the Northwest Coast. The most substantial was made of wooden slats sewn into an articulated cuirass, which was worn over a leather shirt. Slats were also sewn into leggings and sleeves to protect the lower arms and legs. Another type of

Pl. 47

armor was made from doubled or even tripled leather from a large animal like a sea lion or elk and reinforced with wooden slats. Sometime stones would be glued to the outside with fish glue until the leather became hard.

Above the armor a **wooden visor** was worn around the neck. It was made of a curved piece of wood joined with leather. It had a mouth hole, breathing hole, and slits for the eyes. Huge

Pl. 46

wooden helmets fitted above the visor and added considerably to the warrior's height. Some of these helmets were up to 10 cm (4 in) thick.

All armor, visors, and helmets might be carved and painted in fantastic images of grotesque

Pl. 48

human faces, bears, or other motifs. It was reported that early Russian musket balls would bounce off Tlingit armor at 20 feet. While later muskets and then rifles could penetrate the body armor, none had enough force to do damage to the visors or helmets.

50 (above) Housepost, Nuxalk. Adz marks are visible on the post, the canoe prow, and the roof beam. Such marks were considered to "finish" the surface, in contrast, with European preferences for a sanded, smooth surface. This piece illustrates the rounded, sculptural carving style of the central British Columbia Coast.

Carved
Monumental
Figures

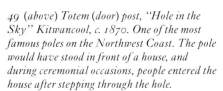

49 (above) Totem (door) post, "Hole in the Sky" Kitwancool, c. 1870. One of the most famous poles on the Northwest Coast. The pole would have stood in front of a house, and during ceremonial occasions, people entered the house after stepping through the hole.

51 (right) House post at Musqueam, 1898. It is illustrative of the Central Coast Salish carving style, in contrast to that illustrated in Plate 50. The figure is supposed to represent a famous warrior named Capilano. The man next to the pole is identified as Capilano III, the great-nephew of Capilano.

Masks

52 (top left) Tlingit cedar mask of a woman wearing a labret, 19th century. The labret is quite large , so presumably she held very high status.

53 (left) Tlingit copper mask with shell inlay, dating c. 1850. This mask displays the high level of metal-working skills present along the coast.

54 (above) Coast Tsimshian stone transformation mask. One of a pair of identical masks, the eyes of this one are closed; the eyes of the other are open. One of the finest examples of Northwest Coast stone sculpture.

55 (*above*) *Closed transformation mask. The mask represents a wolf; when the snout is opened a man's face is visible.*
(*left*) *Early studio portrait of a dancer with a wolf transformation mask. He holds a staff in the form of a two-headed sea monster.*

56 (*below*) *Studio photograph of a dancer with a whale-shark mask.*

57 (left) Sauvie Island figurine . This figurine is a marvelous example of the Lower Columbia idiom, and is a variant of the human figurines found elsewhere on the coast. Highly stylized figurines of clay are also recovered in this same area (near Portland, Or.).

58 (right) Bone Carving, Chinook, Cascades. The motifs and style of these adz handles illustrate elements of the Lower Columbia River style of Northwest Coast art. The position of the hands is common to carved figurines all along the coast.

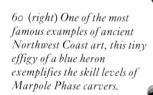

59 (right) Standing owl, Sauvie Island.

60 (right) One of the most famous examples of ancient Northwest Coast art, this tiny effigy of a blue heron exemplifies the skill levels of Marpole Phase carvers.

62 Late Pacific comb in the form of a wolf, Maple Bank site, Gulf of Georgia.

61 Human figurine from Suchia Island epitomizes the bone and antler figures from the central and southern coast.

63 (far left) Human figurine from Anutcix, central British Columbia coast.

64 (left) Seated stone bowl figurine. While this figure displays many "classic" traits of the Northwest Coast idiom, it was found in the interior of British Columbia, near Lillooet.

65 (right) Tsimshian antler club, 1882. This club is similar in form to one recovered archaeological at the Boardwalk site, and which dates between c. AD 1 and AD 500.

**Northwest Coast
Art Objects**

66 (below) Curtis photograph of Northwest Coast dancers wearing a variety of bird masks. The costumes and masks were often far more elaborate than the bare masks seen today in museums.

67 (*left*) *Coast Salish* Sxwayxwey *figurine, collected in 1882. It probably represents a dancer wearing a* sxwayxwey *mask. Such masks were worn among the central Coast Salish as part of a cleansing ceremony in the 19th century.*

Varieties of Northwest Coast Art

68 (*right*) *Carved cedar representation of a portion of a whale's dorsal fin, decorated with some 700 sea otter teeth. This whale saddle was recovered at Ozette, and is presumed to have played a role in ceremonies surrounding whaling, a ritually significant activity among the Makah and other whaling peoples on the coast.*

69 (*above*) A *painted Nuu-chah-nulth panel dating to c. 1850. Objects such as this were produced by professional artists working on commission for the local elite. From left to right this one shows a lightning snake, thunderbird, and wolf, with a salmon below in the thunderbird's talons.*

70 (above) Petroglyph of Tsagaglalal – "She who watches." She overlooks what was once Celilo Falls, the prime salmon fishery on the Columbia River, and Wakemap mound, site of a major village. She is also a prime example of the Columbia River style of Northwest Coast idiom, exemplifying the southern formline.

Rock paintings

71 (left) Long Narrows style petroglyph of X-ray figures and concentric circles. Near The Dalles, Oregon.

or more participants, there is little evidence that these wars often resulted in a shift in territory. Expansionist wars, when they were conducted, were generally done by the most populous and strongest group in a region, and the group that had the greatest subsistence resources in their own territory. This brings us to the second point, that to be successful combatants, a group had to have the numbers, wealth, and resources before going to war. Those in need had the greatest need but had neither the wealth nor the numbers to launch raids against those who could have alleviated their poverty.

The archaeology of Northwest Coast warfare

There are three lines of evidence that archaeologists generally use to identify warfare in prehistory.[26] The most obvious is found as skeletal injuries or evidence of death caused by violence; clues might include broken bones from club blows or projectiles embedded in one or more bones. Another line of investigation is defensive sites and fortifications. Defensive sites are seen either as small villages on bluff-tops, or as villages with palisaded enclosures or trench-embankment features. Few excavations have occurred at defensive fortifications. What little excavation has been done revealed only the approximate dates of occupations, and that the activities performed at these sites, and the foods eaten while they were occupied, were approximately the same as those in villages without defensive constructions.[27] The final line of evidence for violence and war are tools or weapons that could only be useful for conflict. The problem is that these types of artifacts are usually found in low numbers and most tools had more than one clear purpose. When all three types of data are combined, we have enough information from a number of sites throughout the Northwest Coast region to discuss the prehistory and evolution of conflict.

Pl. 45

Pls. 42–44, 46–48

Archaic period (10,500 to 4400 BC)

There is little archaeological evidence for conflict on the Northwest Coast during the Archaic. The recent discovery of the "Kennewick Man," with a fragmented projectile embedded in his hip is the only obvious early case.[28] A number of middle Archaic burials on the southern Columbia Plateau may also have skeletal injuries from violent conflict as well.[29] Given the nature of the archaeological sample, these few examples mean little since we have no control over our sample size. But the mere presence of individuals with evidence of violent injury indicates that the Archaic social landscape was not a peaceful one.

Early Pacific period (4400 to 1800 BC)

It is during the Early Pacific that we begin to see more evidence of conflict and warfare. An individual dating to 2900 BC at Blue Jackets Creek was buried with two carved bone blades or points. A male skeleton at Namu dating to 2200 BC was recovered with a bone point or blade tip in his backbone. In Prince Rupert Harbor, some individuals dating to the end of the Early Pacific appear to have been bound and decapitated. In his analyses of the skeletal materials recovered from Early Pacific sites, Cybulski concluded that fully 21 percent display some form of trauma that he attributed to interpersonal violence (another 7 percent display trauma from other causes). Most of the individuals with violence-related traumas were recovered at Namu. There is little or no evidence of violence at Blue Jackets Creek. Cybulski notes that these injuries include depressed skull fractures from club blows, facial and anterior tooth fractures, defensive forearm "parry" fractures, defensive fractures of the outer hand, disarming fractures of the forearm and hand, and instances of decapitation. In southeast Alaska there are two bluff-top sites dating to about 2200 BC that in later times would be considered defensive fortifications, but it is not known whether they were used as such in the Early Pacific. These data suggest some conflict during the Early Pacific.

Middle Pacific (1800 BC to AD 200/500)

During the Middle Pacific the intensity of warfare increased markedly on the north coast while the incidence of interpersonal violence is much lower on the southern coast, particularly the Strait of Georgia. Cybulski concluded that over 32 percent of the individuals in north-coast burials (primarily from Prince Rupert Harbor) carry evidence of wounds. Another 16 percent show other forms of trauma and injuries. In all, over 48 percent of the north-coast skeletal population for the Middle Pacific displays some form of trauma. In strong contrast, only 14.8 percent of the south-coast population carries evidence of trauma, and only 6 percent of south-coast individuals display indications of violence. These data indicate important differences in lifestyles between the southern and northern coasts during the Middle Pacific. In the north, people were far more likely to be injured, and very likely to be injured by conflict.

In the Prince Rupert Harbor sites males show high levels of trauma, including parry fractures of the forearm and depressed skull fractures, and there are obvious weapons such as bone and stone clubs, bipointed ground-stone objects, and ground-slate daggers.[30] On the Queen Charlotte Islands the presence of several "Prince Rupert-style" effigy stone war clubs in non-village locations is evidence that relations between the islands and the mainland were not always peaceful. There is no direct evidence for conflict on the islands at this time.

Except for the evidence for trauma in the Gulf of Georgia area mentioned above, there is very little other evidence for Middle Pacific conflict on the southern Northwest Coast, supporting the inference that warfare was far less important there during the Middle Pacific than in the north. While one might speculate that these differences reflect different tactics, there is no evidence to support such thinking.

Late Pacific and Early Modern periods (AD 200/500 to 1850)

During the Late Pacific evidence from burials suggests that levels of warfare for the entire coast approached those of the northern coast during Middle Pacific times. This suggests that north-coast patterns of warfare may have spread south sometime around AD 500. However, Cybulski's sample is too small presently to separate out north and south coasts, so regional patterns are obscured.

The single most important Late Pacific evidence for conflict on the Northwest Coast is the presence of defensive fortifications and bluff-top villages. Mitchell notes that refuges composed of walls and ditches enclosing temporary shelters were often located near villages in the Late Pacific on the southern Northwest Coast.[31] In Queen Charlotte Strait, "conflict is suggested by the presence of fortified sites..." He also points out that in the Strait of Georgia, sites with trench embankment features are widely distributed. He argues that intense and severe warfare must have been common to justify the considerable labor investment in construction and maintenance of these features.[32] Almost nothing is known of these southern North-

Pl. 43

west Coast trench-embankment sites. Keddie has dated a couple of trench- embank-
ment sites in the Victoria area of the Strait of Georgia. These sites include the
Peddler Bay site (DcRu 1) that dates to AD 400, Finlayson Point (DcRu 23) dating to
AD 800, and the Lime Bay Peninsula Defensive Site (DcRu 123), dating to AD 800.
Another dated site is Flemming Beach, near Esquimalt (DcRu 20 and DcRu 21).
This is a large shell midden bounded by two defensive locations. The main shell
midden has a basal date of over 4,000 years ago, but the trenched-off defensive sections of the site date to around AD 800 to 1000.[33] Cannon Ball Island near the Ozette
site may also have been a defensive site with a maximum date of 200 BC – AD 200.
Moss and Erlandson have pointed out that several archaeologists have recognized a
pattern in the distribution of defensive sites – that they are often found on the edges
of historically known territorial boundaries.[34]

On the northern Northwest Coast the presence of numerous defensive sites indicates that warfare was common and widespread. Historically, these defensive
fortifications were impressive. Large palisades that might have contained several
houses were built on headlands or rocky bluffs with difficult access. A Tlingit fortification west of Prince of Wales Island was described by De la Boca y Quadra in
1779 as "situated on the summit of a high hill, so precipitous in its sides that they
used wooden ladders to get up to it...."[35] Captain Cook described a similar Haida
hilltop fortification on Graham Island in 1778 and Newcombe recorded several
dozen similar Haida defensive locales. In August 1779 Vancouver[36] described a
number of defensive locations near the Keku Straits in central southeast Alaska as:

> ...the remains of no less than eight deserted villages...all uniformly situated
> on the summit of some precipice, or steep insular rock, rendered by nature
> almost inaccessible, and by art and great labor made a strong defense....
> These fortified places were well constructed with a strong platform of wood,
> laid on the most elevated part of the rock, and projecting so far from its sides
> as to overspread the declivity. The edge of the platform was surrounded by a
> barricade of raised logs of wood placed on each other.

On the central Northwest Coast, historic sites were less often palisaded but many
villages were placed in defensive locations. On several occasions the Vancouver
expedition camped on what appear to have been abandoned defensive sites. Bell
described a Nuxalk village in 1793 as "situated on a bare rock about fifty yards from
the mainland...not more than three or four hundred yards in circumference."[37]

During the Late Pacific defensive sites were being constructed on inaccessible
bluff tops throughout southeast Alaska and the Queen Charlotte Islands.[38] Dozens
of these defensive locations have been securely dated and many more identified.
The majority of these defensive sites were constructed between AD 900 and 1200.
This is the global climatic phase known as the medieval climatic optimum, a time of
quite mild climate in the northern hemisphere. The widespread incidence of
warfare across the Northwest Coast at this time does suggest that some region-wide
processes were at work.

Few artifacts of war are known. In the Early Modern period, war equipment
included armor, helmets, bows and arrows, spears, clubs, and daggers.[39] In 1792
Khlebnikov, a Russian naval officer, described a battle between the Yakutat Tlingit
(who were hunting for Chugach (Pacific Eskimo)), and Aleuts and Russians, where
12 on each side were killed:

The Kolosh [Tlingit] were wearing war dress consisting of wooden armor tightly wound about with whale-gut. Their faces were covered with masks made to resemble the faces of bears, seals, and other mammals striking for their fearsome appearance. On their heads they had tall, thick wooden hats joined to their outer clothing with straps. Their weapons consisted of spears, arrows, and two-ended daggers.[40]

Tlingit armor consisted of up to three layers of hide reinforced with wooden slats; it provided protection against spears, arrows and knives and was also adequate protection against musket balls. On the south coast, early travelers first met Concomally, a major Chinookan chief, shaking musket balls out of his elk-hide armor.

THE TLINGIT REVOLT AGAINST THE RUSSIANS AT SITKA

By 1800 the Russian America Company under the command of Alexander Baranov was making powerful inroads into southeast Alaska, ultimately building a fort called St Archangel Michael, at present day Sitka. The American and British traders considered this permanent settlement with apprehension as they feared it would curtail some of their trading practices. The Americans and British bartered for furs with the Tlingit directly while the Russians used Aleut hunters to gather their skins, moreover, the Americans paid a much higher bounty than the Russians could afford, thus getting most of the sea-otter pelts. The Tlingit looked on the Russian fort as direct competition with their trade system and as theft of lands owned by Tlingit. Thus on 18 or 19 June 1802, the Tlingit revolted and the Russian fort at Sitka was burned and all its inhabitants killed. Although the Tlingit had every reason to deter Russian settlement in their homeland, it is also suspected that the Americans and British encouraged them.

At the time of the attack Baranov was in Kodiak. In the summer of 1804 he returned with four vessels, 120 Russians, 800 Aleuts and Kodiak islanders, and 300 kayaks to take revenge on the Sitka Tlingit. Two vessels were sent straight there while two others went through inside waters and shelled and burned a number of Tlingit villages including Kek and Kuiu. Baranov arrived in Sitka Harbor to find Captain Lisiansky with the *Neva*.

The Tlingit had, by this time, constructed a large, palisaded fort at the head of a bay so shallow that the large ships could not draw near. Over several days there were a number of skirmishes with casualties on both sides. Finally, the Russians began shelling the fort with cannon fire. Upon receiving no return fire, the Russians attempted a landing in order to take the fort.

On 1 October, the Russians landed with 5 cannon, 150 guns, sailors from the *Neva*, a number of Russians from the company and several hundred Aleuts. Laying down a heavy barrage of fire, they approached to within a short distance of the fort. Suddenly the Tlingit returned fire with their own cannon and muskets, wounding all the sailors from the *Neva*, many of the Russians, including Governor Baranov, and routing the Aleuts. Several of the Russian ships took damage as well.

The next day Captain Lisiansky on the *Neva* pounded the Tlingit fort with cannon fire, only to be discouraged as the Tlingit ran outside to collect the cannon balls as they bounced off the palisade. For the next several days the Tlingit sued for peace, giving up a number of hostages but refusing to leave the fort. After several days of negotiations, the Tlingit fort was abandoned in the middle of the night on 7 October. The Aleuts had been raiding all the Tlingit food storage areas in the forest behind the fortress and they were running short on powder. Thus the Tlingit revolt was effectively ended, and New Archangel (Sitka) was built on this site.

Lisiansky later reported that very few of his cannon balls had penetrated the palisade and he found abundant stock of cannon balls inside the fort. He was further amazed at the layout and construction of the palisade. The Tlingit retreated to Chatham Strait where they built another fortress. The effectiveness of the Tlingit revolt and fear of their skill in warfare kept the Russians from any further expansion for the next 50 years. The Tlingit who participated in the taking of the Russian fort were reportedly from many different clans and lineages and may have included some Haida as well. This was probably the largest alliance of clans and lineages in all of Tlingit history.

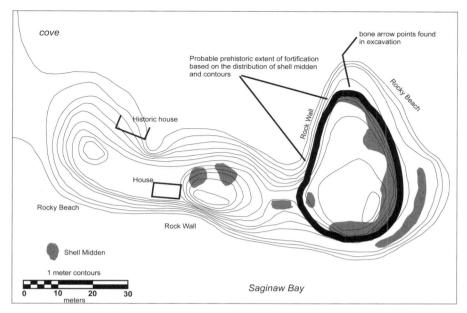

72 Map of a Late Pacific defensive site in Saginaw Bay, Kuiu Island, southeast Alaska. The line of the palisade can be determined by the distribution of shell midden since refuse was usually dumped next to the walls.

Material items of Northwest Coast warfare do not generally survive in the archaeological record except bone, polished, or chipped-stone arrow and spear points, bone or polished-slate daggers, and bone or ground-stone clubs. Northwest Coast archaeologists have debated the meaning of these finds and there is some discussion as to whether or not they demonstrate conflict as opposed to hunting or ceremony. A recent experimental study of Northwest Coast projectile points has provided new insights.

Nathan Lowrey replicated armor in all the styles represented on the Northwest Coast, as well as bows and arrows with points of ground slate, chipped stone, and bone using ethnographic descriptions as a model. He found that slate and chipped-stone points fractured before fully penetrating most styles of armor while bone points punched through the armor.[41] Stone projectile forms and styles are quite variable on the Northwest Coast while bone projectiles are similar across broad regions. These bone points are relatively long and slender, with a wedge-shaped base, and have been found outside the palisades of defensive fortifications. While having a long history on the Northwest Coast, a proliferation in numbers may correlate with the arrival of the bow and arrow in the region.

In Maschner's view, the bow and arrow probably altered inter-village politics and altered warfare strategies.[42] This is seen in the apparent change from hand-to-hand combat to bow-and-arrow wars. The construction of cliff-top, palisaded, or embankment/trench-surrounded defensive forts, villages, and refuges is the most obvious aspect of this change. Hand-to-hand combat continued, however, as shown by both the skeletal evidence and descriptions of engagements in the oral traditions of coastal peoples, particularly in the north.

Investigating Northwest Coast Warfare

Two projects on the northern coast exemplify research on Northwest Coast warfare. The first is the Kitwanga Fort Project conducted by George MacDonald and based on a single site with a detailed oral history. The second is the Kuiu Island Project conducted by Herb Maschner, which takes a regional and temporal approach to warfare.

The Kitwanga Fort Project[43]

The early spring eulachon runs on the Nass River were crucial to the economy of the northern Northwest Coast. Though the runs themselves were owned and controlled by the Coast Tsimshian who wintered in Prince Rupert Harbor, the fish and their rendered oil were widely traded along the coast and well into the interior. The grease moved inland along well-traveled routes known as "grease trails." Sometimes crucial points along these trails were fortified. The most famous of these forts is the fortress at Kitwanga.

The Kitwanga fortress, or Ta'awdzep, is located at a crucial branching of the grease trail running up the Skeena River, and also plays a central role in the oral traditions surrounding *Nek't*, a Tsimshian warrior. The fortress was placed atop a flat-topped, relatively steep-faced hill located out in the middle of the Skeena floodplain, but close to the river itself. The fortress was investigated and reconstructed by George MacDonald in 1979. Based on dendrochronology, use of the fortress spanned the entire 18th century. There is also evidence of a prehistoric occupation of the fortress as well, though this is undated. MacDonald made use of both archaeological, ethnohistoric, and ethnological information in his reconstruction.

The walls were a typical Northwest Coast palisade, with log walls slopping outwards supported by poles. Fastened to the outside of the palisade were spiked logs, made by trimming logs and their branches to sharp ends. These could be rolled down on attackers, or form an abatis work that attackers would have to penetrate to enter the fort. Within the fortress were perhaps five large plank houses. The houses had large storage pits, and escape hatches, including a large trap-door. The fortified area was perhaps just under 1000 sq. m.

According to MacDonald's informants, the Ta'awdzep was first built during the "Haida wars." which were probably among the wars of the last millennium. The fortress that MacDonald investigated appears to have been a response to intensified warfare during the 18th century, which preceded the arrival of Europeans, but continued well into the period of the fur trade, certainly further escalating conflict along the Skeena.

Southeast Alaska: The Kuiu Island Project[44]

For four seasons an archaeological survey and testing program was conducted in Tebenkof Bay on Kuiu Island in southeast Alaska. One of the goals of the project was to model the relationship between Northwest Coast warfare and political and economic changes.

The construction of defensive sites in Tebenkof Bay began about AD 500 but did not peak until after AD 900. A typical defensive site in Tebenkof Bay is XPA-188, located near the most important salmon stream in the local area. Dated to between AD 1160 and 1285, this site is an isolated island in the only channel leading to this stream. The island has vertical rock walls on all sides, making it nearly impossible to safely land a boat. The top has been leveled, and the entire island is covered in shell midden. This site also has the highest density of salmon bone of any location in Tebenkof Bay, indicating that it was probably a storage area as well.

Four recently investigated defensive sites in Saginaw Bay on the north end of Kuiu Island are similar in appearance to those in Tebenkof Bay. One of these, XPA-061, has been known for many years but remained uninvestigated because its vertical rock walls were impassable. When the summit was finally reached in 1994, dense shell-midden deposits were found covering its surface. Many areas seem to have been leveled, and some areas appear to have stone-fronted terraces. The site dates to between AD 1440 and 1650, but evidence indicates that it was utilized historically as well. A long span of use can also be inferred for XPA-289, another defensive site identified in Saginaw Bay. This site dates to AD 500–800 and also to AD 1250–1600. It was probably not used in the recent past. Over 2 m (6.5 ft) of highly stratified shell midden deposits indicate that the site was occupied for a long time. The distribution of the midden deposits is a good indicator of the location of the palisade, as garbage was often dumped along the walls. At XPA-289 these deposits also follow the contours of the hill and there is even some evidence for a second fortification on the center hilltop. Either rocky beaches or natural vertical rock walls surround the islet itself. In terms of the region's geological history, the land has risen at a faster rate than the sea level, although the low area on the west end of the islet was probably submerged at the time of occupation as it is less than 1 m (3 ft) above sea level at present. Interestingly, a bone point with armor-piercing capabilities was found in an excavation on the outside of what is thought to have been the site's palisaded area. Both XPA-061 and XPA-289 are typical of defensive sites found throughout southeast Alaska. Defensive sites in southeast Alaska, like those on the southern Northwest Coast, were often located near villages, or sometimes constituted the village itself, although this was not always the case as many sites were suitable for village location but were not defensible, and vice versa.

Both defensive sites and village sites are important to our understanding of the rise and maintenance of Northwest Coast warfare. The majority of defensive sites in southeast Alaska date between AD 900 and 1200 but a few date between AD 400 and 900 as well. This is the same date range as the majority of village sites.

Village sites also provide significant evidence for warfare in this region. The very structure of historic Northwest Coast houses with thick plank walls and roofs made them defensible. These types are visible in the Late Pacific archaeological record by the presence of large, rectangular house depressions with 70 to 300 sq. m of floor area. The first large, typically Northwest Coast villages occur in Tebenkof Bay between AD 300 and 500. This is approximately the date they appear in the Queen Charlotte Islands and shortly after they occur in Prince Rupert Harbor. They are often in defensible locations or have a defensive refuge in close proximity.

Changes in village location can be a measure of conflict. Maschner found that Middle Pacific villages are located on convoluted shorelines in the center of Tebenkof Bay allowing easy access to all of the area's subsistence harvesting zones. Open-water visibility out from these villages is poor. Late Pacific villages, as well as all the defensive sites, are located primarily in the northern part of the bay on long, straight shorelines with poorer access to resources but more defensibility and much better visibility.

Since all Northwest Coast raids were conducted over water, defensive considerations can be measured by the quality of the visibility out from a village. Thus, in order to understand better what cultural considerations were responsible for these different settlement strategies, Maschner used a geographic information system to model and compute the amount of open water visible from each Middle and Late Pacific village. He found that Late Pacific villages have over three times the amount of visible surface water than those of the Middle Pacific. Thus, sometime between AD 300 and 500, villages moved from highly convoluted shorelines in the middle of the bay to long, straight shorelines in the northern part of the bay. This transition included a reduction in the accessibility of intertidal resources and open-water resources, and made the sites more vulnerable to seasonal storms. But this appears to have been a trade-off in favor of sites that were much more defensible.

Maschner also found that Middle Pacific villages were about the size that would be expected for a single lineage occupation while the much larger size of the Late Pacific villages suggests the amalgamation of a number of lineages, as was recorded in the Early Modern period. This can be seen by the average size of the Middle Pacific villages, which is almost exactly the same as the average area inhabited by a single lineage house in the Late Pacific villages. Thus, Late Pacific villages appear to be the result of a number of independent lineage-based villages coming together to form a single village. This process of amalgamation, as well as the shift from village locations emphasizing subsistence maximization to locations better suited to defense, and the beginning of defensive site construction, occurred at the same time as the introduction of the bow and arrow.

These changes are mirrored to some extent in the subsistence economy. Maschner found that subsistence from the Early Pacific through the Middle Pacific and into the Late Pacific showed only minor variations on a generalized theme. This theme included primarily cod, herring, some salmon, and many sea mammals and shellfish. But halfway through the Late Pacific, at approximately AD 1150–1350, there was a switch to a subsistence based on salmon and deer.

What could explain this change? Did the prehistoric inhabitants over-fish the bay and harvest too many sea mammals, or was there some other cause for the switch? There is no evidence of over-harvesting and it may not even have been possible with a prehistoric technology. Further, the primary salmon stream in the bay, Aleck's Creek, which is barely 4 m (13 ft) wide and 1 m (3 ft) deep, had an early 20th-century salmon run of over 500,000 while Tebenkof Bay as a whole produced over 1,000,000 salmon each summer. As little as 20 years ago herring spawned in Tebenkof Bay in volumes measured in thousands of tons. There is no evidence for over-exploitation of the local waters in any category of data.

When harvesting strategies are considered, a more plausible explanation is possible. In the Early Modern period, open-water fishing for herring and cod, as well as sea-mammal hunting, was performed by small task groups who would go out in groups of 2–4 people. As was pointed out in Chapter Five, an effective salmon harvest requires that large numbers of people participate so that the fish can be processed before they spoil. Thus, salmon were harvested by entire villages moving to a major salmon stream for a short time and returning with the catch. Deer were hunted around the village. Since small task groups are more vulnerable to attack than whole villages, this shift in subsistence can perhaps best be explained by a change in the political environment, one that was causing an increase in warfare and defense.

While the total population of Tebenkof Bay never reached more than 350 people, it is interesting that the change in subsistence occurs at the same point as the peak in regional construction of defensive sites and at the exact time of the peak in local population.[45]

Discussion

Warfare on the Northwest coast during the Modern period was conducted for many reasons and at a number of scales. Taking these rich and detailed descriptions back into the past is nearly impossible, but a few generalizations are warranted. These include the realization that wars are most common during times of social, political, or economic stress. It is during stressful periods that people will more often choose violence over some other means of conflict resolution. But it is also during times of stress that the strongest and most powerful groups will take advantage of small, less intimidating villages to increase status and prestige through acquisition of wealth, slaves, and other goods.

During the Archaic there is certainly evidence for violence. But the scarcity of data for conflict, or anything else in the Archaic, leaves us little room for conjecture. In the Early Pacific there is more evidence, especially at the end of the period. This was a time of increasing sedentism and perhaps increasing territoriality. It was also a time of rapid environmental change. These changes in settlement and landscape may certainly have increased tensions between individuals and groups, creating the potential for conflict.

It is in the Middle Pacific that evidence for warfare becomes more prevalent. This was a time of economic intensification, with a greater emphasis on salmon and other storable species (Chapter Five). This was also the time when there were much larger houses and villages, probably composed of multiple kin-groups (Chapter Seven) and there is clear evidence for status and ranking. Numerous skeletal injuries and the presence of weapons best suited to hand-to-hand combat are evidence that these transitions to greater complexity came at some social and political cost.

At the beginning of the Late Pacific there were a number of changes, including the formation of large households and towns composed of many different corporate groups. There were technological changes as well, with a greater use of the bow and arrow, an increase in heavy woodworking tools, and the construction of fortifica-tions. The rise of the Late Pacific is seen in every regional cultural chronology on the Northwest Coast by a break or significant change in the archaeological record. To describe a few of these changes, it is chronicled in the Middle to Late Pacific transition in southeast Alaska, village abandonment and then reoccupation of Prince Rupert Harbor, the rise and development of large villages during the Graham Tradition of the Queen Charlotte Islands, and further, the changes that mark the decline of Marpole culture and the development of the Straits of Georgia culture type.

The introduction of the bow and arrow as a weapon of war corresponds with a number of these changes. First, we see a transition from hand-to-hand combat to more of a siege warfare using defensible locations and fortifications, although the Modern record indicates that hand-to-hand conflict continued as well. We also see a shift from small houses to large houses, indicating that increasing conflict may have had a role in the formation of large, corporate households. This is also the time when the wearing of labrets shifted to being exclusively a female practice, suggesting shifts in social organization with the consolidation of villages.

There was a proliferation of defensive site construction after AD 900 that corresponds to a proliferation of village formation in many areas of the Northwest Coast. On Kuiu Island this escalation of warfare eventually led to a complete shift in subsistence from open-water fishing and sea-mammal hunting to salmon and terrestrial mammals. This time period was also an apparent peak in population throughout the Northwest Coast region (Chapter Four).

During the Early Modern period warfare was as pervasive as it was in the Late Pacific, with one notable difference. By the time explorers and ethnographers began recording evidence for war, the populations of the Northwest Coast had been substantially reduced (Chapter Two). One result of population decimation probably included less competition for territory and subsistence. The reason wars continued, even without competition for the basics of everyday life, was either because old wounds truly do never heal and revenge wars are difficult to stop, or more likely, the act of war was so intricately woven into Northwest Coast systems of wealth, status, and prestige, that, regardless of the changing circumstances, the maintenance of rank through aggression was such a conservative social institution that it was difficult to abandon.

CHAPTER NINE

Northwest Coast Art

The Northwest Coast art style is one of the most distinctive and famous in the modern world. It is also one of the oldest. Examples of Northwest Coast art such as masks, totem poles, carved boxes, and woven blankets can be seen in many of the world's museums. In fact, by the early 20th century, there was more Northwest Coast art in museums across the world, some 500,000 objects by one estimate,[1] than there was on the entire coast. In some parts of the coast, along the Lower Columbia River, for example, production of art ceased during the 19th century. In other areas, among the Kwakwaka'wakw and Haida, for example, art continued to be produced[2] in small amounts (the Kwakwaka'wakw continued to raise totems into the 1920s, for example), but the social and ritual contexts of the art were repressed by the new Canadian government, beginning in 1888.[3] The style made an explosive return in the 1960s. This was fueled by two quite different developments: the reassertion of Native rights in the 1960s and an extraordinary conjunction of the work of two individuals: the great Haida carver Bill Reid, and the art historian, Bill Holm. We will use Bill Holm's concepts to explain some fundamentals of the Northwest Coast art style necessary to understanding its history.

Before going on to that discussion, it is important for the reader to understand some fundamentals about the archaeology of Northwest Coast art, or of any art style for that matter. In the 19th century, Northwest Coast art was pre-eminently a carved art; western red cedar (*Thuja plicata*) was its major medium. While there was stone sculpture, rock art and some carved bone and antler, the overwhelming majority of decorated objects were of wood. Wood does not survive except under extraordinary circumstances. One such circumstance is the Ozette site (see Chapter Five). Among the facts learned at Ozette is that wooden and fiber tools made up well over 90 percent of the artifacts recovered there. In other words, archaeologists, when they find stone, bone and antler objects in Northwest Coast sites, are finding less than 10 percent of the material culture of the people who lived at that site. When the primary medium for an art is wood, that means that few objects in the style will be recovered. Thus, we have no ancient masks, totem poles, boxes, and almost none of the other wooden objects that fill museum cases. Carved wooden objects are occasionally recovered from sites, like Ozette, where the deposits are sealed in a wet, low-oxygen environment that slows or prevents decay of plant fibers. These 'wet sites' are crucial to our knowledge of the archaeology of Northwest Coast technology because they produce basketry, cordage, netting, fish-hook shanks,[4] and so on. These sites are themselves rare.

Most of our knowledge of the history of the Northwest Coast art style comes from stone sculpture, from small bone and antler objects that are preserved well in shell middens, and from rock art, both petroglyphs and pictographs (petroglyphs are designs pecked into stone, pictographs are designs painted on stone). Rock art is found here and there along the coast, sometimes in quite inaccessible locations, and is seldom easily dated. We depend on small stone sculptures, and especially those of bone and antler. However, these objects are also rare. In one example, Ames studied over 10,000 artifacts from Prince Rupert Harbor dating from the entire Pacific period, of which less than 180, 1.8 percent, had any kind of decorative motif on them. Of that number, only 20 had zoomorphic or anthropomorphic designs, the rest were geometric (zoomorphic designs are based on animal forms; anthropomorphic on humans; and geometric designs include motifs based on rectangles, circles, triangles, lines and so on).

In what is probably the most thorough study of the archaeology of Northwest Coast art to date, Margaret Holm[5] examined the full corpus of excavated zoomorphic and anthropomorphic items recovered from sites in British Columbia through the late 1980s. Her total sample was 243 objects for the last 4500 years (her study did not include geometric designs). Her sample excluded sites in Alaska, Washington (except Ozette and Hoko River) and Oregon (except a few objects from the lower Columbia River). One hundred and fifty objects were recovered from sites in the general Gulf of Georgia region and 29 from the central and northern British Columbia coast. These figures, coupled with those from Prince Rupert Harbor, suggest the present limitations of the archaeological record of Northwest Coast art. These proportions are probably typical for the entire coast. As a result, we have available for study a very small sample of decorated objects, representing a tiny fraction of the potential total number of objects that carried designs.

The kinds of objects archaeologists recover are not the kinds of objects commonly collected in the 19th and early 20th centuries. Occasionally stone sculpture was collected, but small antler and bone objects were seldom of interest to those who bought Northwest Coast art for collectors and museums in New York, London, Berlin and St Petersburg. Some kinds of objects found by archaeologists do occur in collections, horn spoons for example, but generally they do not.

Pl. 40, 49   Totem poles illustrate the problems. They are the most famous examples of Northwest Coast art, so famous in fact that they are now sometimes stereotyped as being typical of all Native peoples in North America,[6] when in fact they were not even erected in all parts of the coast. There is also debate over when totem-pole carving began. Some scholars think that the widespread carving of poles was entirely the result of the availability of metal tools during the Early Modern period. The earliest recorded observations of what may be totem poles were made at Clayoquot (among Nuu-chah-nulth) on the west coast of Vancouver Island in 1788, in the Queen Charlotte Islands among the Haida in 1790 and 1791, and Yakutat among the Tlingit of southeast Alaska in 1791, suggesting that poles were erected in some places on the northern coast at contact. Philip Drucker, a cultural anthropologist well known for his work on the coast's peoples, concluded in 1948 that the widespread carving of totem poles predated European contact. He also concluded that iron was used on the coast for carving tools well before the development of trade with Europeans, arguing that the iron originated in Asia.[7] Are totem poles recent or ancient?

While the skills needed to carve a pole are certainly ancient on the coast, actually carving a pole with the traditional tools (adzes of stone, shell and beaver incisor) would have been a slow, arduous process, so even if poles predate contact by any length of time, they would probably have been rare. Metal objects dating before contact have occasionally been recovered from sites along the coast, including

Ozette on the Olympic Peninsula and Cathlapotle, on the Columbia River, near Portland, Oregon (see Chapter Five). The latter site produced an iron adz blade dating to AD 1400–1500 (though in a geographic area that did not traditionally carve totem poles). It is unlikely that this was the only iron adz on the coast at this time, though at present, it is the only one known. So, it is possible that the tools to make poles were available on the coast 200 to 300 years before the first European voyages.[8]

Archaeologically, how could we know poles were erected in more remote times? Short of finding one in a wet site, the only direct archaeological evidence would be the hole in which the pole was set, and it would be difficult to prove that that hole was for a totem pole and not some other, substantial post, possibly part of a house. Another, perhaps more likely, line of evidence would be the depiction of a pole in the art we do find. In the 19th century, figures were sometimes carved holding a carved pole. However, no figurines holding totem poles have ever been found.

Finally, in dealing with art, archaeologists are faced with the problem of what does the word art actually means. As this chapter is being written, archaeologists are struggling mightily with that very problem: how do we understand the meaning of ancient symbolic systems? At some fundamental level, we cannot know the meanings that motifs and designs held for the people who made them. However, that does not imply that we cannot read the clues people left behind. The crucial clues are those of context and association: what are the decorated objects associated with and what condition are they themselves in (are they always whole, broken, are they always found in graves, never in graves, always in houses, never in houses?)? Other clues include the methods and techniques used in making the objects, associations among particular motifs themselves and among the motifs and their execution (is a motif always deeply carved, are certain other motifs only found on stone?).

For all the reasons outlined above, archaeologists have emphasized the development of the Northwest Coast art style in their research. One needs only a single object to demonstrate that a particular motif or technique existed by a certain date. What is far more difficult is to determine the role or roles played by the art style in ancient Northwest Coast society and culture. The art may not have played the same role among Native peoples 4,000 or even 2,000 years ago that it played during the Early Modern period. The very small sample of decorated ancient objects also makes it difficult, at present, to study geographic variation in the style.

Up to this point, we have discussed the Northwest Coast art style as if it were a single style, but in actuality, there were several during the Early Modern period, depending on region, medium, and purpose. In the next sections, we will sketch some aspects of geographic variation along the coast, the functions of the art in the 19th century, and introduce some basic elements of the style. After that introduction, we will turn to the archaeology of the art. The reader looking for a primer on the 19th-century art is urged to turn to the works cited in the bibliography.

The idiom of Northwest Coast art

Bill Holm, in his seminal and definitive study, *Northwest Coast Indian Art*,[9] describes the style as an idiom, as a form of expression, which is a better way to think of it than just as a style. The idiom was used in two intimately tied spheres of Northwest Coast life: spiritual and socio-political.[10] In the spiritual sphere, decorated objects were used by shamans as part of their regalia and accouterments, displayed and used in healing and divining performances. In the socio-political realm, decorated objects displayed the crests that validated the status, rights, and behavior of upper-class individuals as well as of entire households and extended kin groups. The animals and beings portrayed in the art were spirits who may have come to a shaman in a trance, or whose powers were part of the estate of a household. Though the art then played key roles in Northwest Coast life, motifs were also widely used as decoration. The best artists were specialists, some of whom, at least, were title holders. Some carvers were so famous that they worked from commission to commission, moving from place to place with their entire family.

Basic concepts

The art includes animal or zoomorphic motifs, with humans included among the animals. But geometric designs are actually far more common archaeologically and were widespread on basketry; some geometric designs on bone and antler tools and small rocks may imitate basketry or clothing designs. The geometric designs have received far less attention than those of the zoomorphic art.

Holm distinguishes between *representation* and *composition*, representation refer-ring to how the artists presented the creatures that are the subjects of Northwest art, and composition to the rules governing how the designs and shapes were organized. Composition then refers to form. We would also add here *technique* to include such things as selection of raw materials, methods, and styles of carving. The rules of representation in Northwest Coast art have been known for a long time:[11] the art is *stylized* rather than *naturalistic*. In portraying animals, it emphasizes particular parts of the body, especially the head, which is often large relative to the rest of the crea-ture. Animals are split, sometimes at the head, sometimes at the rear, so the creature is shown in two profiles. Split details are not always shown in their anatomical

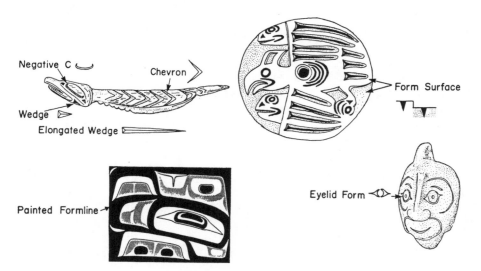

73 *Basic design elements in Northwest Coast art.*

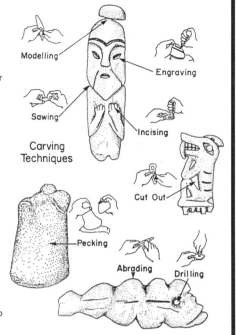

CARVING TECHNIQUES (based on Margaret Holm)

Sawing: shaping features in stone with a sawing motion.

Modeling: defining features with gentle contours that create rounded, sculptured forms.

Pecking: shaping features in stone by striking with an angular stone.

Abrading: shaping features in stone, or other materials, by rubbing or scraping the object with a coarse stone, such as pumice or sandstone.

Relief: the projection of sculptured figures and forms from a flat, background surface.

High relief: forms are almost fully lifted from their background and are modeled in three dimensions.

Low relief: a small portion of the volume of a form is raised from the background surface.

Incising: defining features with a thin, carved, line. The line is a positive feature.

Engraving: defining features by cutting away portions of a surface. An engraved line reveals an area that has been cut out, and is a negative feature.

Two-dimensional block engraving: cutting away background to leave a raised primary form. The cut-away area is a negative feature.

Inlaying: Filling a carved out, or carved away area with material cut to shape. Inlay can include copper, shell (e.g. abalone), or other material.

relationship to the rest of the body; sometimes they are completely displaced. The motifs are usually symmetrical, at least at first and even second glance.[12] There is a continuum in how naturalistic a motif may be from quite naturalistic (it is quite easy to identify the creature being portrayed, at least at the level of "this is a wolf") to the motif being quite stylized (it is impossible to identify the creature or even to recognize body parts and assemble them visually into an animal).[13] This continuum is governed by how the motif relates to the space in which it is placed. A key aspect of composition in Northwest Coast art is the complete use of space (not necessarily filling it, but using it). In a representational portrayal the creature may be arranged in the available space in such a way that it retains its anatomical integrity. In another instance it may be artistically dismembered and the entire space filled with its parts, arranged to fill the space, not to display anatomical linkages.

Creatures are often *skeletonized* or shown in X-ray view. Ovoids are sometimes used to indicate crucial joints; the vertebral column is also frequently depicted as a series of connected ovoids. Ribs and other skeletal elements are also commonly portrayed. This particular aspect of the art may be quite ancient.

Bill Holm's particular contribution to the study of Northwest Coast art has been his recognition of the rules and elements of composition in the two-dimensional art of the north, including the importance of *formlines* to create negative and positive space, particularly in the northern style. Formlines are the broad lines, varying in width, that define and outline areas within a design, and sometimes the entire design. Holm describes what he terms the formline system:

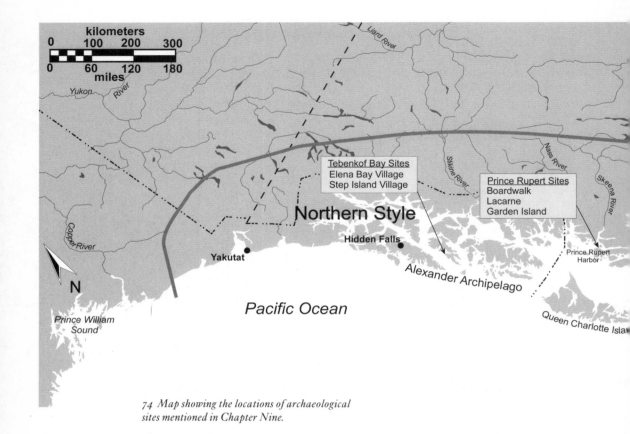

74 *Map showing the locations of archaeological sites mentioned in Chapter Nine.*

> ...the formline system provided that creatures be portrayed by representing their body parts and details by varyingly broad "formlines" which always joined to present an uninterrupted grid over the designed area.... Formlines joined one another in a limited number of juncture types, which were designed to permit smooth transitions...[14]

Primary formlines are often connected, so as to flow through and around the entire design. When a piece is painted, primary formlines are most often black. In carving, they are raised by carving away material around them. Margaret Holm expands the concept of primary formline to include *formsurface*.[15] There are also secondary formlines, and free-floating formlines (eyes and ovoids) within the space created by a primary formline. Bill Holm believes that the northern development of formlines grew out of painting, given the resemblance between a carved formline and a painted line. He has recently distinguished between a northern formline tradition – that just described – and a southern tradition, in which the formlines are uniform in width, and animals' bodies are defined by use of incised crescents, "T"s and wedges.[16] He regards the northern and southern formlines as parallel developments from a common tradition on the coast.

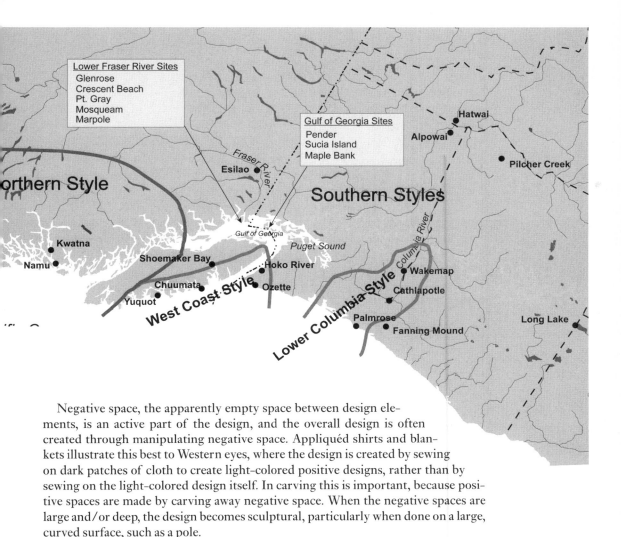

Negative space, the apparently empty space between design elements, is an active part of the design, and the overall design is often created through manipulating negative space. Appliquéd shirts and blankets illustrate this best to Western eyes, where the design is created by sewing on dark patches of cloth to create light-colored positive designs, rather than by sewing on the light-colored design itself. In carving this is important, because positive spaces are made by carving away negative space. When the negative spaces are large and/or deep, the design becomes sculptural, particularly when done on a large, curved surface, such as a pole.

Bill Holm's insights on composition are particularly important to archaeologists wanting to trace the history of Northwest Coast art. While it is difficult for us to penetrate the meanings of ancient symbols and systems of symbols, we can discern the rules by which designs were formed and space used, whether that space is an ancient courtyard in the Yucatan, or the handle of a 4,000-year-old antler spoon from British Columbia. We also see how the rules were executed. Holm proposes that the style developed from an ancient, two-dimensional style, marked by T-shaped reliefs, incised crescents, use of negative space to create positive space, the Northwest Coast eye and skeletonization. Formlines developed, in his view, as a consequence of painting, based on the similarity of a painted line and carved formlines. Carved sculpture developed from the application of this flat, two-dimensional style to rounded surfaces.

Techniques include not only the carving techniques listed in the box (which are applicable to antler, wood, bone, and stone), but such things as choices of raw material, processing steps in the treatment of raw materials before carving (for example,

Pl. 51

specific steps required for working antler, as opposed to working red cedar), and posture (e.g. how tools are held: Northwest Coast carvers use adzes rather than knives, thus they cut towards their body, rather than away from it).

Geographic and tribal variation

Pl. 49

Pl. 50

The northern style is marked by the use of formlines and adherence to the compositional rules rediscovered by Bill Holm. The northern style (sometime called the "classic style") is the basis for much of the modern Northwest Coast art we see.[18] The northern style reached its apogee among the Haida, Tlingit, and Coast Tsimshian, but is also exemplified by the works of artists among the Kwakwaka'wakw, Haisla, Haihais, and Nuxalk. The art of other groups to the south share many common features but is different in a variety of ways, including the southern formline. Creatures are also less likely to interlock, and they are generally less stylized than in the north. There was considerable variation within this southern style, with the art of the peoples on the west coast of Vancouver Island differing from that of the Coast Salish peoples of southern British Columbia and adjacent Washington State, while the art of the peoples along the lower Columbia River was perhaps even more distinctive. The reason for this variability is as yet unknown, but these stylistic regions correspond to the geographic distribution of other traits (Chapter Seven) and may point to the existence of ancient interaction zones.

In the north, there was little variation at the tribal level in the execution of flat, two-dimensional designs, such as those on boxes, while there was much more variation on large sculptures such as totem poles. There was considerable variation among individual artists in both flat and sculptural compositions. To the south, there were greater degrees of variability among local groups and individuals, and less art may have been produced in the south during the Early Modern period.[19]

The archaeology of Northwest Coast zoomorphic and anthropomorphic art

Origins: The Archaic period (10,500 to 4400 BC)

As we see in the next section, designs well within the Northwest Coast idiom are present as early as 2500 BC. What little data there are for the Archaic period indicate that Northwest Coast art probably developed from much older art traditions in western North America itself. Once again, the archaeological record for the interior portions of Cascadia is more informative than that of the coastal regions. The earliest carvings in Cascadia appear to be several soapstone beads recovered at the Pilcher Creek site in eastern Oregon.[20] These beads predate 7500 BC. The site is located near a source of soapstone, and David Brauner, the excavator, believes people camped at Pilcher Creek to mine the soapstone for the pendants. No other examples of these beads have been recovered in Cascadia. Further, they are only roughly carved, probably at a preliminary stage in their production, so we cannot use them to discern the presence of "proto-proto-Northwest Coast art" design elements. What the Pilcher Creek objects do show us is that carving has great antiquity in Cascadia.

75 *Petroglyph panels at Long Lake, Oregon. The panel on the left is 1 m high. This is the oldest dated design in or near Cascadia.*

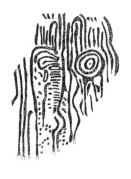

What is probably the single most important (certainly the largest) design motif dating from the Archaic period in western North America comes not from Cascadia, but from the northern Great Basin area of south-central Oregon, where Mary Ricks and William Cannon have investigated a large rock art panel at the Long Lake site.[21] The panel predates 5800 BC and consists of complex, interlocking curvilinear designs that were deeply pecked into the rock surface, creating strong positive and negative surfaces. The Long Lake panel thus displays some of the techniques and perhaps even compositional rules found in Northwest Coast art several millennia before the emergence of designs that are recognizably Northwest Coast. Further, the depth of the motifs creates the effect of sculpture. Had the panel, particularly the section in the figure, been pecked *around* a piece of stone, rather than across a rock wall, it would be hailed as an elaborate piece of sculpture. Northwest Coast stone sculpture could easily have developed from an earlier rock-art tradition related to the Long Lake tradition. Some compositional traits, such as the deep negative space, could also have been adapted to antler and wood carving. In addition, the panel displays the technique of pecking to shape stone long before its widespread use in toolmaking in Cascadia.

The Long Lake panel suggests considerable effort in the production of "art." The exposed portion of the panel is 3 m (9.75 ft) long; its complete length is unknown, but is thought to be considerable. It is 1 m (3.25 ft) high, pecked into hard basalt. In contrast the Pilcher Creek beads are carved from soft, easily carved soapstone. The Pilcher Creek site itself, however, appears to have been occupied regularly as a camp at which the soapstone was quarried, probably as part of an annual round, so production of the beads may have been a regular activity.

Tools suitable for woodcarving are also widely present during the Archaic period. Antler splitting wedges indicate that some carpentry took place. Engraving and incising tools of chipped stone also exist. Bone tools, such as harpoons and slotted points, were carved to shape. This does not demonstrate widespread effigy carving, but does indicate its potential. The skills, techniques, and tools were there.

Early Pacific period (4400 to 1800 BC)

What is perhaps the earliest zoomorphic object from the Northwest Coast is a concretion from the Boardwalk site. Dating between 3800 and 2500 BC, it may represent a fish; it is incised in a cross-hatched motif (perhaps representing ribs and backbone, according to MacDonald[22]). These may also be geometric designs.

The earliest dated anthropomorphic figure on the Northwest Coast is an antler handle dating between 2600 and 1300 BC recovered at Glenrose Cannery.[23] It is clearly associated with the St Mungo (or Charles) phase deposits. The back of the

76 Middle Pacific antler comb from the Garden Island site, Prince Rupert Harbor, British Columbia.

figure is slotted, probably to receive a beaver incisor. Historically, these incisors were used as small adz blades in carving. Thus, appropriately, one of the earliest examples of Northwest Coast art is probably the handle of a carving tool. The figurine has a large face and head, while the rest of the body (lacking legs) is proportionally smaller. The hands rest on the chest, the arms bent against the figure's sides. The figurine has a topknot, a common feature of anthropomorphic and zoomorphic figurines on the southern coast through the Pacific period. The face is dominated by a positive t-shaped and joined brow and nose (another common feature of Northwest Coast anthropomorphic figures). The positive nose and brows were made by carving away antler around them. The mouth and eyes are also positive (raised) and oval in shape. The figure appears to be bearded. A similar, though less fully carved handle was recovered from the Lachane site in Prince Rupert Harbor. Unfortunately it cannot be dated. It too has a topknot, hands resting against the chest, beard or pointed chin, and almond-shaped eyes with raised outer edges.

The Glenrose figurine also has small holes at the position of the earlobes, so it may have been worn as a pendant, or perhaps had a wrist thong. The holes may also have carried inlays, such as abalone. This may suggest the wearing of earspools as personal adornment at this early date on the coast. Historically, ear decorations were associated with high status.[24]

Pl. 30   The antler spoons recovered at the Pender Canal sites are the most significant evidence for Early Pacific art (Chapter Seven). Full descriptions and illustrations of these spoons are not yet available. However, drawings have been published of which one dates to *c.* 2140–1740 BC.[25] It is therefore generally contemporary with the Glenrose handle. Antler and horn spoons were made and used on the coast well into the Modern period, and the handles were commonly decorated or carved. The Pender spoons are the earliest examples of this tradition. They are "scoop spoons," to distinguish them from spoons which are ladle shaped.

The figure (fig. 76) shows an animal, probably a wolf, joined at the mouth with a fish. The wolf identification is based on the pointed ears, and the flaring nostrils and nose (compare with wolf comb in Plate 62). The wolf's vertebral column is probably represented by the raised notches along the creature's nose. The eyelids are positive, a raised flat rim around the hole (which may have held inlays) for the iris. The eye is elliptical and pointed at either end. The lips and edges of the ears are also positive. The wolf's head is hollow, leading Carlson to suggest that it, and other hollow effigies from the Gulf of Georgia in later periods, actually represent masks. As he admits, this idea presently is pure speculation. Another Pender Canal spoon has ovals present at a joint. One could also speculate that the ovals forming the paired, flaring nostrils of the wolf in fig. 30, which lead to the spinal column, also represent the hip joints, thus indicating the presence of other compositional elements of Northwest Coast art (animals bent over themselves, animals dismembered and design elements placed illogically, and polyvalence – a design having multiple meanings, in this case nostrils and hip joints). This speculation illustrates both the attraction and difficulties in analyzing ancient art; it is limited only by the knowledge and imagination of the analyst.

Both the Glenrose handle and the Pender Canal spoons fall within the Northwest Coast idiom, displaying representational elements of that tradition as well as at least one compositional aspect: the creation of positive forms through the creation of negative areas by carving away material. This is particularly clear in the antler handle. The spoon, with its interlocked fish and wolf, anticipates features of the northern style. Margaret Holm concludes that by the end of the Early Pacific, the techniques of carving, deep engraving, modeling, inlaying, and cutting out sections of antler were present. Motifs present in the Gulf of Georgia in this early period include humans, mammals, birds, fish, and backbones and ribs.

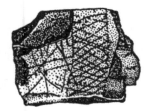

77 An incised stone from the Early Pacific midden at the Step Island Village site in Tebenkof Bay, Kuiu Island, southeast Alaska.

Expanding our scale, these are not the only Early Pacific decorated objects in Cascadia. Stone objects with incised geometric designs that may date as early as 3800 BC have been recovered at the Esilao site near the Fraser River Canyon not far from the coast. Maschner found an incised stone with geometric designs at the Step Island Village site in southeast Alaska dating to 2200 BC. Also in southeast Alaska, Stan Davis identified both an incised stone and incised bone in Early Pacific deposits at the Hidden Falls site. A bone artifact (perhaps a pin) from the Hatwai site on the Clearwater River in the interior was incised with what appears to be an elegant vine or plant motif. Plant motifs are extremely rare. The Hatwai artifact was associated with a house that dates to *c*. 3200 BC, and is the earliest carved bone artifact in Cascadia. Ground-slate artifacts incised with geometric designs occur at the near-by Alpowai site in deposits dating between 3200 and 2500 BC.

The artifacts from Pender Canal and Glenrose Cannery do not tell us much about the origins and early evolution of the Northwest Coast art tradition, except that it already existed by *c*. 2100 BC. The stone objects from Step Island, Boardwalk, Esilao, Alpowai and elsewhere indicate that incising geometric designs on slate and other stone was a widespread practice across Cascadia in the Early Pacific period. Decorated bone objects existed in Cascadia by 3200 BC. In order to understand the early evolution of the Northwest Coast idiom, we need some decorated objects from the coast and elsewhere earlier than 2100 BC. At present, the Long Lake panel remains unique. It seems to us that the Northwest Coast art tradition probably derived from even more ancient traditions of carving and incising, and traditions of composition in western North America; it is, in other words, the local manifestation of those traditions. Its emergence at 2000 BC may also be only the local manifestation of cultural developments across Cascadia at that time and therefore not explainable solely by reference to events on the coast.

Middle Pacific period (1800 BC to AD 200/500)
There is a much larger corpus (27 objects) of Middle Pacific art than from the Early Pacific, though again, most are from the Gulf of Georgia region, with significant examples from the Oregon coast and the northern British Columbia coast.

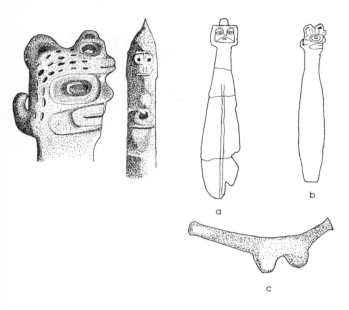

a

b

c

78 (far left) Middle Pacific period whale bone club pommel from the Boardwalk site, Prince Rupert Harbor. Many designs elements common to 19th-century art on the northern coast are present on the club, including the use of formlines to structure the design.
(left) Whalebone club styles: a) full-face southern style, b) northern face in profile style; and c) "Slave killer" or scimitar style of the southern coast and California.

Northern coast

There is little material from the northern coast for this period. Most was recovered in Prince Rupert Harbor, where ten objects can be relatively firmly dated. These include a wolf comb (decorated combs are an innovation in the Middle Pacific), which bears a strong resemblance to the wolf on the spoon from Pender Canal, including their pointed ears and almond eyes. The ribs are clearly present. Margaret Holm regards the cut-out spaces formed by the upper and lower legs as significant compositional innovations associated with this piece. This comb, and several other objects, were recovered from residential contexts. The only zoomorphic object directly associated with a grave in Prince Rupert Harbor is a raven pendant carved from micaceous schist. The execution of the pendant displays considerable skill. However, except for ribs indicated on the bottom surface, the raven is not distinctly Northwest Coast. It was recovered in the chest area of the skeleton of an adult male and dates to 640 BC.

A large whalebone club dating to AD 1 displays crucial aspects of developed Northwest Coast style. It was recovered from a cache of objects buried in the burial area at Boardwalk, but not directly associated with any particular burial. Ethnographically, whalebone clubs were status markers (Chapter Seven). The face is formed of three ovoids created by a wide primary formline. The two upper ovoids contain the eyes, while the lower ovoid the mouth, which is itself an ovoid created by a formline or form surface. The formlines of the face interconnect. The handling and creation of space in this design is basically the same as that in the two-dimensional designs found on boxes and housefronts in the 19th century. There are of course differences: the style continued to evolve; but the fundamental rules of composition are the same. Interestingly, the formlines are uniform in width, and are therefore more similar to the southern formline tradition than to the northern formline, though this object was recovered in the north. The human head is surmounted by an animal, whose tail turns up at the end. The human wears a nose ring, an ethnographic status marker. The nose ring is a U-form, as are the eye, ears, and tail of the creature.

We believe this is the earliest evidence for the use of primary formlines on the Northwest Coast. It is also the earliest evidence for their use in this manner, which is a crucial aspect of the compositional rules of the northern Northwest Coast style.

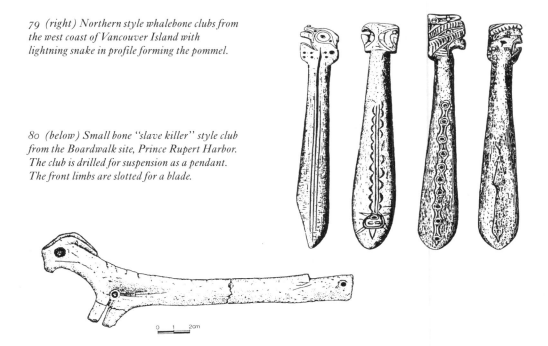

79 (right) Northern style whalebone clubs from the west coast of Vancouver Island with lightning snake in profile forming the pommel.

80 (below) Small bone "slave killer" style club from the Boardwalk site, Prince Rupert Harbor. The club is drilled for suspension as a pendant. The front limbs are slotted for a blade.

Ames was the first to view this club in this way, since the motif was essentially wrapped around the pommel of the club; we figuratively unwrapped and laid it flat. This places the use of primary formlines on the northern coast a thousand years earlier than George MacDonald or Margaret Holm have done.[26]

There are two basic styles of club on the Northwest Coast. One, carved of whalebone, had a broad, paddle-shaped blade, and a decorated pommel. The second club style is a scimitar-shaped club of ground stone, usually slate. These are widely known as "slave killers." In the first style (A) there are two subtypes (A1 and A2) which differ in their pommels. In A1 clubs, the face on the pommel is viewed in profile. In A2 clubs the face is seen full face. The face on the pommel of A1 clubs may be that of a thunderbird, sometimes surmounted by another being, such as the lightning snake (style A1a) or it may be anthropomorphic (A1b). The Boardwalk club then is the earliest A1b club. In the second subtype of whalebone club (style A2), the face is always human. Type A1a clubs were made on the west coast of Vancouver Island and traded widely along the coast and into the interior during the Early Modern period. One has been recovered as far east as Spokane, Washington. Subtype A1a is thought to be a more northern style, while style B clubs are found in the southern Northwest Coast.

The ground-slate clubs (style B) usually terminate with a generalized mammal head, which could be a deer or seal or some other creature. These clubs have one or two adz blades on their lower surface, located where the legs of a quadruped would be. These clubs are distributed from southern California at least through the Gulf of Georgia region. They were probably status markers. Two miniature bone examples were recovered from Boardwalk, on the northern Coast, and date between AD 1 and 500. The utility of either club type as weapons seems low,[27] though the whalebone ones were widely worn on the coast and described as weapons by European travelers.

Pl. 66

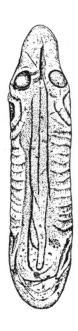

81 Concretion carved into the form of a monster, Prince Rupert Harbor. Northwest Coast style "art" was not limited to wood and bone.

Slate is brittle and would shatter easily. A wooden sword in the shape of the "slave-killer" club, with adz blades mounted along its length, would be a nasty weapon, as would a hard wood (or hardened wood) version of the whalebone clubs. There is no evidence for such weapons, except that the small antler style B clubs recovered at Boardwalk are each slotted for a small blade, though they seem too small to have been a weapon; they were most probably large pendants. These club styles and their distribution are important evidence for regional interaction. During the Early Modern period, clubs of the first style were carved on the west coast of Vancouver Island and traded widely. The second style is generally found on the southern Northwest Coast.

Other decorated objects recovered from residential deposits in Prince Rupert Harbor include a small anthropomorphic pendant (which MacDonald suggests is shamanic) and the anthropomorphic handle similar to the Glenrose handle. A carved, red cedar handle (probably for a bowl) from wet-site deposits at the Lachane site is interpreted by MacDonald as a sea creature. It shows the use of formlines, particularly on the head. The object dates to 600 BC.

At Hidden Falls in southeast Alaska a number of incised stones were recovered. Stan Davis found designs ranging from geometrics to stick-figures. One was ground in a flattened egg shape and polished smooth. It had three rows of tree-like stick figures, each row with four figures. Each of the rows was separated by an incised line. These incised stones date to the later half of the Middle Pacific.

In the Early Modern period, sea-otter teeth were used as decorative studs on the sides of bentwood boxes. A number of the Middle Pacific period interments at Boardwalk appear to have their coffins decorated in this manner, since some graves contain hundreds of sea-otter canines associated with box outlines.

Central coast
There are few decorated objects from the central coast of British Columbia that can be firmly dated to the Middle Pacific period, and these few date to the period's end. This probably reflects the small site sample. There is a similar dearth of such materials from the west coast of Vancouver Island. The only anthropomorphic or zoomorphic figurines recovered from Yuquots date to the historic period, except for a whalebone club fragment, while no decorated artifacts are reported from Hesquiat. An incised stone was associated with the Shoemaker I deposits at the Shoemaker Bay site. Recent test excavations at DfSi 4, Ch'uumat'a, a site located

on Barkley Sound, produced what may be a comb. At the base of the deposits, the crew also recovered the fragment of a large feather, carved from schist. The site dates between 2400 BC and AD 1000. At this writing, the investigators, McMillan and St Claire, are still in the preliminary phases of their work.

Southern coast

The Middle Pacific record for art on the southern coast is quite rich, particularly in three areas: the Gulf of Georgia, the Lower Fraser River, and the northwest Oregon coast. The Lower Columbia River also contains a rich record of art, but it is less easily dated and will be discussed in the section on the Late Pacific. We will turn first to the Gulf of Georgia, where the Middle Pacific is divided into the Locarno Beach and Marpole phases.

Locarno Beach phase (1500 to 600 BC)

The sample from this phase is small, 14 objects in all. Among them are two spoons from the Musqueam Northeast site. The deposits associated with the spoons date between 1300 and 530 BC. The spoons are generally similar to those recovered at Pender Canal, but they have features that Margaret Holm sees as close to formlines, including positive and negative U-forms and T-shapes. These design elements are, in her interpretation, isolated (they are not connected by primary formlines), a trait she regards as typical of Coast Salish art. The Locarno Beach spoons are also the same scoop-shape as those recovered at Pender Canal. Locarno Beach phase art also, and uniquely for the coast, includes death's heads, as well as antler objects with deeply carved geometric designs. There are also anthropomorphic figures from this period.

The earliest carved wooden object from the Northwest Coast was recovered at the Hoko River site (see fig. 83). It appears to date to *c.* 1000 to 800 BC[28] and so is slightly older than the bowl handle from Lachane in Prince Rupert Harbor. The artifact is the handle of a mat creaser (used to make fiber from cedar bark), on which is carved two crested birds touching beaks. The birds are thought to be pileated woodpeckers

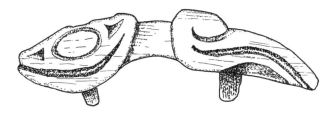

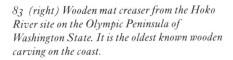

82 (above) Red cedar box handle from the wet site deposits at Lachane, Prince Rupert Harbor, dating to the late Middle Pacific. The handle displays form lines, use of wedges and the stylized rendering typical of the northern style.

83 (right) Wooden mat creaser from the Hoko River site on the Olympic Peninsula of Washington State. It is the oldest known wooden carving on the coast.

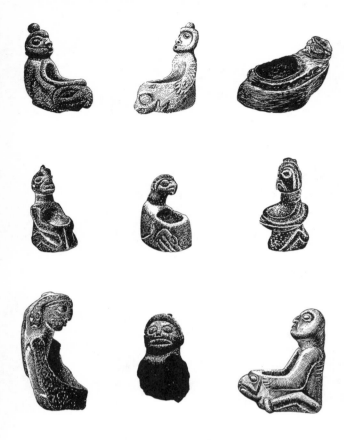

84 Marpole phase stone bowls, Gulf of Georgia region. Stone bowls and figurines are often thought to be distinctive traits of the Marpole phase in the Gulf of Georgia. However, many have been found in poorly controlled contexts, so they may not be restricted to Marpole.

or kingfishers. The handle was painted (and is the first evidence of painting); there are black stains from a lignite-based pigment on the crests and eyes of the birds.

The effects of sample size on our ability to trace the histories of particular motifs is illustrated by the distribution through time of ovals or circles used to mark joints (elbows, knees, etc.). This fundamental motif in Northwest Coast art is present on one (perhaps two) examples of Early Pacific art from Pender Canal, but on none from the Middle Pacific. This suggests that the motif was relatively rare, and that we are simply lucky to have the one early example. If we had not found that one, the motif would not be present in the archaeological record until the Late Pacific and archaeologists might conclude that the motif is a late addition to Northwest Coast art. Thus, it is possible that many design elements, and even compositional rules, are much older than we can document. The classic Northwest Coast design elements documented for the Locarno Beach phase are U-forms and T-shapes (though the reader may recall that formlines are present in Prince Rupert Harbor at 600 BC). In her inventory, Margaret Holm identified humans, mammals, birds, fish, skulls, and lightning snakes as Northwest Coast motifs present during the Locarno Beach phase.

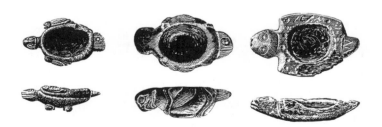

85 Marpole phase stone bowls, Gulf of Georgia region. Some stone bowls also have a much wider geographic distribution than the Gulf of Georgia.

Marpole phase (600 BC to AD 500)
The Marpole phase is marked by a dramatic increase in the number of decorated artifacts and decorated types of artifact in the Gulf of Georgia. Margaret Holm assigns 28 artifacts from her total sample to the Locarno Beach phase (including three from Prince Rupert Harbor), but 102 for Marpole (including Yuquots and Prince Rupert Harbor). Of those, 48 have been recovered from the Marpole site itself. Unfortunately, this site has seen little scientific excavation, and much of it is now destroyed. The large size of this sample does make it possible to draw some conclusions about art during the Marpole phase in the Gulf of Georgia.

86 (above) Marpole phase stone bowls, Gulf of Georgia region.

87 (right) Marpole phase stone figurine.

In the Marpole sample, Holm observed differences in the skills with which designs were executed. As we noted at the beginning of this chapter, anyone could produce art, but there were part-time and full-time carvers, specialists in the production of Northwest Coast art. Holm suggests that the quality of some of the carving implies the presence of such specialists. Carlson speculates that the carving skills and control of composition displayed by the Early Pacific spoons recovered at Pender Canal indicates specialists at that early time. That may be, but the Marpole sample is big enough that the contrast in skills is clear and can be used to support Holm's inference. Further, these skills seem focused on particular classes of artifacts. Brow bands are uniformly well made, with deeply engraved motifs (including both zoomorphic and geometric) while pendants vary in their quality. Interestingly, pendants are quite restricted in the motifs they display, being limited to birds (in profile) or humans (viewed from the front).

Marpole stone sculpture is also quite standardized; virtually all of it is stone bowls which fall into four classes (see below). An examination of these objects led Margaret Holm to conclude that the quality of these bowls was also uniformly poor, relative to the work invested in bone and antler. There are a few well-made bowls, but none of them are from well-dated contexts, so they may be Marpole in age, or younger.

Pl. 65

Stone bowls are present on the Northwest Coast into the Modern period, but those of the Marpole phase are distinctive. They fall into four classes defined by Wilson Duff: upright human figures with arms enfolding a circular bowl; stone bowls with a human face looking outward; bowls with zoomorphic features added; and zoomorphic figurines or effigies to which bowls have been added. Some of the best executed of these bowls are from undated contexts, and so may post-date Marpole. In many of these the bowls are quite small, and probably were pigment bowls. Some may have had no utilitarian purpose. The steatite bowl in fig. 86 is only 10 cm (2.5 in) high, and was originally covered in ochre; the bowl held by the human in fig. 87 has no basin.

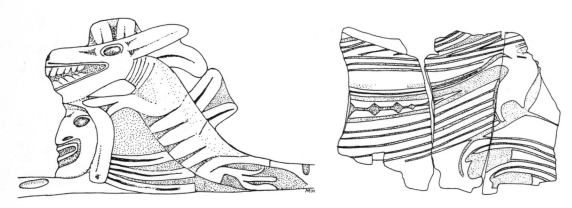

88 (left) The Skagit atlatl. In terms of form and design, this is perhaps one of the most complex prehistoric carvings from the coast, and dates to approximately AD 350.

89 (right) Fragments of a carved kerfed box from the Esilao site in southern British Columbia, late Middle Pacific period.

Marpole phase art (in the Gulf of Georgia) contrasts sharply with earlier periods in the kinds of motifs employed. Humans (anthropomorphic motifs) are ubiquitous; birds, lightning snakes, rib and back bones, and feathers are also present. Notably absent (except for lightning snakes) are the zoomorphic mammal motifs present in the much smaller earlier samples. The Marpole phase sample is large enough that this absence certainly represents a distinctive quality of Marpole art. What it means beyond that is impossible to say, but we will take the issue up again in Chapter Ten. Turning to composition, a wide array of design elements are present in Marpole art, including formlines, T-shapes, wedges, Salish eyes, and chevrons.

Pl. 61

Perhaps the most famous example of Marpole art is the small pendant (or plug) in the form of a blue heron, complete with the heron's plume. One of the anthropomorphic pendants is also an excellent example of the eye form that Margaret Holm calls the Coast Salish eye. The most important wooden example of Marpole art is the Skagit River atlatl (spearthrower), so named because it was originally dredged from a distributary of the Skagit River near its mouth.[29] It dates to the very end of the Marpole phase, to *c.* AD 230–450. The atlatl was carved by a superb artisan from a piece of western yew (*Taxus brevifolia* Nutt.). It displays a complex image of a creature described variously as a sea monster and as a lightning snake (the descriptions are not mutually exclusive) surmounting a human face. The creature has a wolf-like face with inlaid eyes. The eyes are flanked by wedge forms. It has plumes rising from the head and backbone. The combination of a human and a "monster," particularly a sea creature, is a common feature of Northwest Coast iconography, and oral traditions are replete with "sea chiefs," beings who can transform themselves into a variety of sea creatures as well as humans, and who exercise considerable power over the productivity of the oceans, as well as over human affairs. The carving clearly shows us what may have existed widely in wood at this time. Knut Fladmark even suggests that it shows that the skills to carve totem poles existed by this date, even if we have no evidence for poles.

Another example of what may have been common is a charred box from the Esilao site, on the Fraser River. The box was recovered from a pithouse that post-

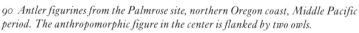

90 *Antler figurines from the Palmrose site, northern Oregon coast, Middle Pacific period. The anthropomorphic figure in the center is flanked by two owls.*

91 *(right) Carved digging stick handle from the Palmrose site, northern Oregon coast, Middle Pacific period.*

dates AD 1. It was elaborately and deeply carved in curvilinear designs, which Margaret Holm regards as being well within the traditions of Coast Salish carving and composition. Given this evidence and the roughly contemporary evidence for sea-otter tooth decorative studs in Prince Rupert Harbor, the practice of decorating and carving boxes clearly existed by *c*. AD 1.

Northwest Oregon and the Lower Columbia

The Palmrose site, near Seaside, Oregon has produced a remarkable collection of Middle Pacific decorated objects. They are associated with the remains of a large, rectangular structure, probably a plank house that was occupied several times between 700 BC and AD 200. Overall, the collection is quite reminiscent of Marpole material, though with some distinctive features of its own. It also shares characteristics of later sculpture along the Lower Columbia River.

The only effigies are of humans and birds. The anthropomorphic effigy in fig. 90 is seen in full, face front view, with positive eyes, and a T-shaped nose and brow, which is consistent with much earlier human effigies on the coast and with very late anthropomorphic designs from the Lower Columbia River. The owl motif is a consistent design in this region through time and is quite similar to the owl effigy from the Pender Canal site dating perhaps 1,000 years earlier. The clearest example of Northwest Coast composition in this collection is the formline ovoid on an antler digging stick handle. The formline is uniform in its shape, and so may indicate the presence of the southern formline tradition by this time. Below the ovoid, there is a carved constriction, separating the design field from the rest of the handle. Such a constriction is common on spoon handles and antler and bone clubs farther north. The shape of the ovoid suggests it is an eye, and so the motif is probably a face wrapped around the end of the handle (recall the human head on the whalebone club from Prince Rupert Harbor). The assemblage also includes a number of deeply incised handles with geometric designs, reminiscent of some carved antler objects from the Locarno Beach phase of the Gulf of Georgia. These data seem to suggest close contact between the Oregon coast and the Gulf of Georgia during this period.

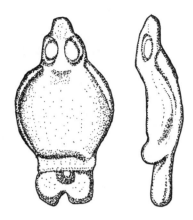

92 *Raven pendant from the Boardwalk site, Prince Rupert Harbor. This is the only zoomorphic item directly associated with a grave in Prince Rupert Harbor. Middle Pacific.*

Discussion of Middle Pacific art

By AD 1, the Northwest Coast art idiom was well and strongly established. There are examples of formlines from Prince Rupert Harbor in the north to Seaside, Oregon, in the south. The implications of this fact for our understanding of regional interaction were explored in Chapter Six. Suffice it to say here, it clearly shows that carvers had considerable contact. These commonalties may obscure some local and regional differences. For example, much Marpole art appears to be directly or indirectly associated with burials. In Prince Rupert Harbor, by contrast, among the 230 excavated Middle Pacific burials (Chapter Seven), only the raven pendant (and whatever designs were on the coffins) was directly associated with a burial, and the whalebone club indirectly. The Palmrose materials were recovered from a house, as was much of the Prince Rupert Harbor art. At present, these differences remain impressionistic. However, they suggest that the roles played by art in different areas of the coast may have only incompletely overlapped, with art in the north more closely associated with the emerging status system (Chapter Seven) while in the Gulf of Georgia it appears always to have been associated with funerary ritual. Margaret Holm notes that decorations on highly visible objects, such as browbands, are more deeply and better carved than those on objects that would have been less visible. This may suggest that in the Gulf of Georgia, art was also acquiring a role in the status system. Her analysis further suggests the presence of specialist carvers by that date.

Another impression we have is that decorated objects tend to be concentrated at a relatively few sites. Put another way, decorated objects occur at many sites, but only a few sites produce decorated objects in any number. Among these sites are Palmrose, Marpole and Boardwalk. Among these, both Palmrose and Boardwalk are virtually unique on their sections of the coast. Palmrose is unique in its region, while one or two other Prince Rupert sites may be similar to Boardwalk in the relative concentration of art. However, outside Prince Rupert Harbor, on the northern coast, Boardwalk has no excavated (at least fully reported) analogue (Blue Jackets Creek on the Queen Charlotte Islands is a possibility), particularly in southeast Alaska, but this may be a product of sampling. If we consider the large amount of excavation that has been conducted in Prince Rupert Harbor and the small number of art objects found, then it is quite possible that not enough has been excavated in southeast Alaska for even one to have been found.

Margaret Holm also strongly argues that the regional Coast Salish style of Northwest Coast art existed by this time. This implies long-term ethnic and linguistic stability on the coast. The presence of the full formline face in Prince Rupert Harbor may point to the emergence of the full northern style by this time as well.

Late Pacific period (AD 200/500 to 1775)

Many researchers, one of us included, have commented on the relative paucity of decorated objects during the Late Pacific period.[30] This is ironic, since this period probably represents the full "Northwest Coast" pattern. The diminution in the number of decorated objects is particularly marked in the Gulf of Georgia. For her study, Margaret Holm analyzed 102 Marpole phase objects, but only 77 for the Late Pacific. Comparing the Marpole phase with the Late Pacific period in the Gulf of Georgia, she studied 92 Marpole phase objects from 13 sites (for a mean of 7 objects/site); for the Late Pacific, her sample included only 28 objects from 8 sites (mean of 3.5). But if we exclude the Marpole site from our calculations (since it is so unusual in the number of decorated objects found), there are 44 Marpole phase objects from 12 Gulf of Georgia sites in Margaret Holm's sample, with a mean of 3.7 objects per site. These calculations suggest that the apparent reduction in art during the Late Pacific is due to first, the absence of an excavated site like the Marpole midden in the late sample, and second, the smaller number of excavated Late Pacific sites overall in the Gulf of Georgia region. The question becomes not why there are fewer decorated objects but why there are fewer sites. This may be the result of the patterns of archaeological research, or the destruction of Late Pacific sites, which may be more exposed to development than earlier sites which may sit away from current coastlines.

The absence of a site like the Marpole site in this period may be due to important differences in cultural practices between the Late Pacific and the Marpole phase in the Gulf of Georgia area. The beginning of the Late Pacific is marked along the coast by the cessation of midden burials and, presumably a shift to the Early Modern period practice of placing the dead at some distance from residential localities. As a result, archaeologists have encountered relatively few Late Pacific burials in contrast to hundreds of Middle Pacific ones. If Marpole art had a significant role in funerary ritual, the change in those practices alone might account for the apparent decline in art after the Marpole phase.

These temporal contrasts become even more marked when the admittedly small Prince Rupert sample is examined. While scanty, there is no decline in the number of decorated objects between the Middle Pacific and Late Pacific periods in the harbor. This is particularly intriguing since Boardwalk was probably not a residential site during this period. Burial practices also changed on the northern coast, with a cessation of midden burials, with no evident effect on the number of art objects recovered.

On the other hand, the Late Pacific corpus of decorated objects from the Gulf of Georgia is less well controlled by archaeology than that of previous periods. Holm had to expand her sample by using objects in private collections. As we shall see along the Lower Columbia River, almost none of the stone sculpture from that area has reliably documented contexts.

North coast

Two objects from Prince Rupert Harbor show that the northern style of Northwest Coast art existed in its 19th-century form by AD 1000 to 1200. One, an antler pendant, is engraved with an ovoid and a negative C. The other, a comb fragment, displays a complex formline design in which it is exceedingly difficult to identify the creature represented.

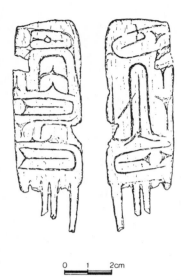

93 (left) Comb fragments from Prince Rupert Harbor, dating to the Late Pacific. They display form line composition and are quite stylized since it is not possible to recognize what the motif represents.

94 (above) A Late Pacific incised stone showing a fish possibly processed for storage and a geometric pattern similar to a "raven's tail" design. The artifact is from the Step Island Village site in Tebenkof Bay, Kuiu Island, southeast Alaska.

0   1   2cm

Maschner found an incised pebble from Step Island Village in southeast Alaska dating between AD 900 and 1150 (fig. 94). This pebble is interesting because on one side it appears to have a salmon without a head. On the other is a complex geometric design that the local Tlingit think might be a weaving pattern called "raven's tail."

Throughout southeast Alaska there are numerous pictographs and petroglyphs that are assumed to date to the Late Pacific period. These include seemingly random distributions of zoomorphic, anthropomorphic, and geometric designs on intertidal boulders to carvings placed to mark territorial boundaries. Territorial boundaries are seen at the Cow Creek site where large spirals are pecked into cliffs near the three entrances to the waters leading to this Late Pacific village. Some paintings, such as the sun symbol from Saginaw Bay, have no known correlates.

Central coast
A small sample of decorated artifacts have been recovered from sites on the mainland of the central coast. These display a number of isolated design elements, such as the split-U on the composite harpoon valve illustrated in fig. 95b. In this sample are a large, anthropomorphic figurine and a pendant carved from antler that is also
Pl. 64   an anthropomorphic figurine. These figurines are similar to figurines recovered to the south, both in the Gulf of Georgia and along the Lower Columbia River.

Once again, there is virtually no art recovered from the west coast of Vancouver Island. Shoemaker Bay II produced an incised rock; a design that almost appears to be leaves.

South coast
Gulf of Georgia / Fraser River
Motifs clearly fall within the traditions of Coast Salish art, both in terms of repre-
Pl. 62   sentation and composition. Margaret Holm regards a comb from the Maple Bank site as perhaps the best example of this. The comb was recovered from sediments that date to AD 700. The wolf or dog possesses the upturned snout typical of

portrayals of these canids in the 19th century. Other Modern period features include the crescent marking the wrist joint, and the long tapering claws. Holm notes that it is a quadruped, a typical motif in historic Northwest Coast art, but absent in Marpole art. She also stresses what she terms its "lively pose" and naturalistic carving, also a feature of some Coast Salish work. This comb is similar in some ways to the wolf comb from Garden Island in Prince Rupert Harbor, particularly the cut-out limbs, which also occur at Pender Canal and on the engraving from Ch'uumat'a in Barkley Sound.

The single most important collection of decorated materials from any coastal site was recovered from Ozette (the figures above on the numbers of decorated objects and sites containing such objects do not include Ozette). The site has recently been dated to the early 1700s. Perhaps 300 to 600 decorated objects (mostly of wood) were recovered among some 42,000 catalogued items. The Ozette artifacts provide us with a clear view of the range of decorated items present in Northwest Coast

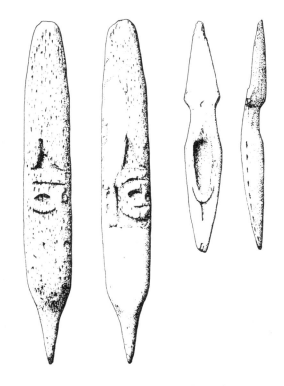

95 *Late Pacific artifacts from the central British Columbia coast. a) is an engraved whalebone spindle or shuttle, and b) is a toggling harpoon valve with a T-form*

houses, from seal clubs and whaling gear, to planks and the famous "whale saddle" and effigy of a whale's dorsal fin studded with sea-otter teeth. According to its investigators, objects that were always decorated include clubs, tool handles, weaving and spinning tools and combs, while harpoon shafts, loom posts, boxes, and bowls were commonly decorated. Sea-mammal hunting gear (including harpoons) was decorated but land-mammal tackle was not.

Wayne Suttles has suggested that for the Coast Salish (Ozette was occupied by Makah), objects that converted raw materials into wealth were decorated. Margaret Holm uses this observation to explain why both the Makah at Ozette and the Salish decorated weaving tools, and to suggest that it also explains the decoration at Ozette of both sea-mammal gear, which certainly converted raw materials into wealth and prestige among the historic Makah, and woodcarving equipment. Her speculation could be applied elsewhere on the coast.

Small anthropomorphic figurines, similar to those recovered on the central coast, also occur in the Gulf of Georgia area. These figurines are important to one of the basic themes of this book, by providing us with evidence of regional interaction discussed in Chapter Seven. In the Gulf of Georgia area, they appear to date around AD 1000. They are carved out of antler, and Margaret Holm lists these common characteristics: a short skirt; well-defined arms, legs, and feet; a head that appears to

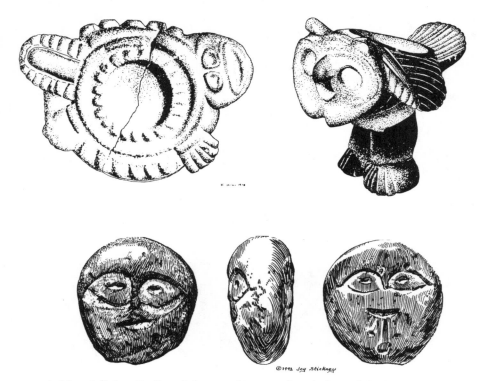

96 (above left) Late Pacific period zoomorphic mortar from the Lower Columbia Rivier region. It may represent a beaver.

97 (above right) Owl effigy with inset mortar, from The Dalles area on the Lower Columbia River. Ht 4.5 in. Late Pacific.

98 (above) Anthropomorphic carving recovered at the Meier site, near Portland Oregon, near the rear wall of the structure.

reflect cranial deformation; clear indications of hair, sometimes elaborately coiffured; ear ornaments; indications of tattooing on the body; and skeletonized portrayal of the body. Holm observed regional variation, but the basic themes are quite consistent. Some also display genitalia, either male or female. Perhaps the best example from the Gulf of Georgia area is one recovered on Sucia Island, in the San Juan Islands. The recovery contexts for these artifacts have not been studied.

Pl. 63

Whalebone clubs are a second class of object important to defining regional interaction spheres. Those recovered in the Gulf of Georgia area are in the west coast style, suggesting they were traded in. Ground-stone zoomorphic clubs also occur in the Gulf of Georgia, reaching the northern end of their distribution.

As in previous periods, many decorated objects have been recovered in the Fraser River canyon, including an anthropomorphic effigy pipe, and a spindle whorl decorated with eyes on one face and snakes on the obverse. When spun, the eyes or snakes would appear to whirl around and down the hole. It has been suggested that the spindle whorl was actually a shamanic device, used to induce trances, though as noted above, the Coast Salish decorated weaving equipment. Unfortunately this quite extraordinary piece was recovered from a collapsed trench wall at the Milliken site, and so its precise age is not known.

Interior British Columbia

Sites in the interior of British Columbia, usually burial sites, have produced a number of decorated objects that clearly show affinities with Northwest Coast art. Some of them may be trade goods, but others were produced by local artisans.[31] This contrasts with the interior areas of southern Cascadia, where such items are much rarer.

Washington–Oregon Coasts / Lower Columbia River

There are no sites on the outer southern coast comparable with Palmrose in the Middle Pacific. Occasional carved objects do occur, but they are rare. The largest corpus of art comes from the Lower Columbia River, from the Dalles to the river's mouth. Little of this material has been recovered in controlled archaeological investigations and much of it is in private collections. The vast bulk of this material is stone sculpture.[32]

The stone work bears some similarities to Marpole art: it is virtually all birds and humans, though an occasional fish and mammal occur. Stone bowls fall into three of the four Marpole bowl types, lacking only the anthropomorphic figures holding a bowl. However, there are anthropomorphic figures holding not bowls but columns (or penises). These figures are generally similar to a few figurines from the Gulf of Georgia and the west coast of Vancouver Island, though they differ in detail. Stone bowls are well executed and many equal the skill displayed to the north. There is also   Pl. 60 a local tradition of freestanding stone sculpture, both inside houses and outside. Some of these are quite large; one, in a private collection, is 1.2 m (nearly 4 ft) tall and covered with red ochre.

Antler, bone, and pumice carvings also occur, as do ceramic figurines. The antler and pumice carvings bear strong resemblances to some presumably Marpole-age steatite figures from the Gulf of Georgia, though these latter have poor provenance. They are also clearly part of the complex of figurines discussed above, sharing the basic traits of that complex. Ceramic anthropomorphic figurines are distinctive to the Lower Columbia River region. Faces are indicated by simple lines, though the arrangement of the hair is sometimes carefully indicated. They also represent (and are virtually the only expression of) the only Native ceramic tradition on the Northwest Coast.

Whalebone and zoomorphic clubs occur in a variety of contexts, mainly funerary ones. A whalebone club recovered from the Fanning Mound site in the central Willamette Valley marks the southern extent of their known distribution. Its pummel is in the southern, full-face style. What may be the largest single concentration of whalebone clubs on or near the Northwest Coast was recovered near the Wakemap Mound site. The clubs had been burned in a pit, or thrown into the pit after burning.[33] This is the only example of this context in the region covered by this book. Style B zoomorphic clubs are quite common and are of both the single and double adz variety, and represent a generalized mammal.

The Lower Columbia River shares a number of features with art to the north, particularly in the Gulf of Georgia region, including the southern formline; use of contrasts between negative and positive space, and of broad positive lines to define facial features (eyes and mouths) on some bone figurines and rock art. Split-Ts   Pls. 58, 59 define noses and brows (an ancient Northwest Coast motif) and raised eyes. How-   Pls. 71, 72 ever, Chinookan art as portrayed in early paintings and drawings is distinctive as

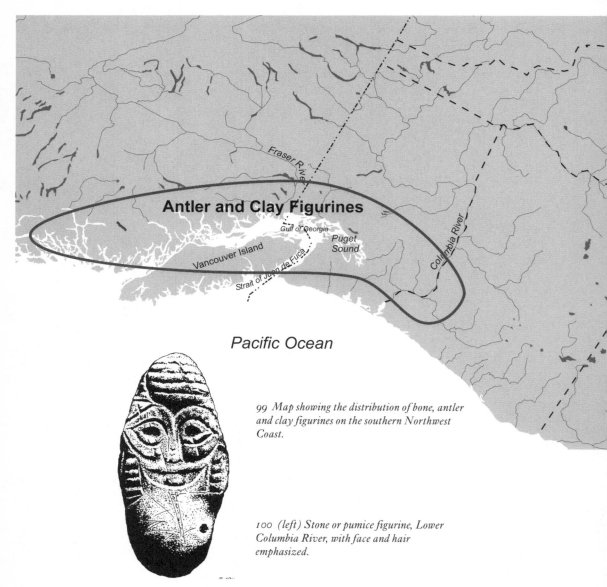

Antler and Clay Figurines

Pacific Ocean

99 *Map showing the distribution of bone, antler and clay figurines on the southern Northwest Coast.*

100 *(left) Stone or pumice figurine, Lower Columbia River, with face and hair emphasized.*

well, making use of large painted geometric designs, much more so than to the north. Large carvings did exist, and shared some features with Salish and west coast art, particularly with Salish guardian spirit figures. There are also carvings similar to the Coast Salish Sxwayxwey mask, which otherwise has no analogues on the coast.

Pl. 68

    There are two major areas along the Lower Columbia River where decorated items have been recovered: the combined metropolitan areas of Portland, Oregon and Vancouver, Washington; and the area of the Dalles at the east end of the Columbia River Gorge. The contexts in which art has been recovered differ between these two areas: in the Portland area, and downstream to the river's mouth, objects are found in residential contexts, while above Portland, to the Dalles, they have been recovered in graves.

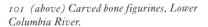

101 (above) Carved bone figurines, Lower Columbia River.

102 (right) Carved antler figurine from the Yakima Valley of central Washington State. This is the most easterly of recovered figurines, and the most elaborately carved. The Yakima Valley is in the Columbia Plateau, but close to mountain passes giving access across the Cascade mountains to Puget Sound.

The development and origins of Northwest Coast art

This section has a very bold heading, one which we cannot really live up to. However, some comments are possible. Our intention is first to summarize what is known about the history of representation, composition, and technique, and then to hazard some discussion of the art's evolution.

Representation

The earliest art is generally quite naturalistic. Some of the most complexly stylized (and completely uninterpretable) motifs are not present until the Late Pacific period. In fact, the corpus of decorated objects lacks many of the stylized representations generally considered diagnostic of the idiom. This may reflect the regional sample, which is small and almost entirely from the south, where the art was less stylized than in the north. As we noted at the beginning of the chapter, many people's expectations of the entire idiom are based on the northern style.

Both anthropomorphic and zoomorphic figurines are present from the Early Pacific on. The variety of creatures expands in later periods but this may simply reflect larger samples in the later periods. There are shifts through time and space. The Marpole phase and the Lower Columbia River lack the mammals present elsewhere in both the Early and Late Pacific periods, but birds are commonly portrayed.

Composition

The available art of the Archaic period does not display any distinctively Northwest Coast rules of composition, though the rock-art motif at the Long Lake site demonstrates that deeply cut negative and positive spaces and curvilinear designs are quite ancient in western North America. By the middle of the Middle Pacific, primary formlines are present from Oregon to Prince Rupert Harbor and, in the case of the whalebone club at the Boardwalk site, were clearly being used to structure a composition. However, formlines in the north may not have taken on their Early Modern period form until AD 1000 to 1200. Polyvalent meanings, or "visual punning,"[34] are clearly present in the Middle Pacific period, and possibly even in the Early Pacific. Margaret Holm sees evidence for Coast Salish-style compositions in the Gulf of Georgia during the Marpole phase. It seems likely that the rules of composition of Northwest Coast art crystallized by AD 1. That they were maintained over the next two millennia with only minor changes represents a significant research problem. Artistic stability, which might imply cultural stability, needs explanation.

Techniques

Carving is quite ancient in Cascadia. The early antler carvings show that most of the basic carving and woodworking techniques existed in the Early Pacific period, if not earlier. It is not until the Middle Pacific period that sites commonly contain a range of heavy-duty woodworking tools. The early development of stone working methods may simply have been accomplished by transferring antler carving skills to soft stone, such as soapstone and steatite. The rare wooden objects, such as the Hoko River mat creaser, the Lachane handle, and most importantly, the Skagit atlatl, demonstrate the high quality of woodcarving skills in use during the Middle Pacific period. Knut Fladmark and his colleagues (who dated the Skagit atlatl) suggest that the skills shown are commensurate with carving large wooden pieces, such as totem poles.[35] As noted at the beginning of this chapter, there is no evidence for poles prior to AD 1788. Stone sculpture seems to flourish during the past two millennia, though the basic pecking technique was in use by 7000 BC. Stone sculpture was perhaps fueled by application of the grinding and pecking methods used to make heavy stone tools, such as mauls, pile drivers, large adz blades and so on. A key question in the development of Northwest Coast art, and in the evolution of technique, is when did metal tools become available along the coast? The presence of an iron adz blade at Cathlapotle at AD 1400–1500 suggests that such tools were being used along the coast well before contact with Europeans as argued by Philip Drucker 50 years ago.

While the data are thin, three regional styles appear to be present by sometime between AD 1 and 500 – north coast, Gulf of Georgia and Lower Columbia River. It is likely then that the others, including west coast, were present as well. The Gulf of Georgia and Lower Columbia River styles have been linked to the modern Coast Salish and Chinookans respectively. The distribution of whalebone club styles and the figurine complex also suggests the formation of regional interaction spheres by this time. The figurines are particularly interesting in this regard since they represent a distinct phenomenon of the south coast macroregion, while within that complex, there are local differences between the Gulf of Georgia and the Lower Columbia River.

There is suggestive evidence for craft specialization in carving in the Marpole phase, if not earlier. Margaret Holm sees the skills required to execute the deeply incised designs on Marpole brow bands as such evidence. The skill invested in the Skagit atlatl also suggests a specialist. As we have seen elsewhere, there is good evidence for specialization in working copper by c. 500 BC as well, lending support to this date for specialization in woodworking. The evidence for bent-wood boxes may also indicate the development of high levels of woodworking skills as early 500 BC.

This information does not tell us what the ultimate "origins" of the art idiom are: where did the rules of composition and representation originate, where did the motifs come from? The most likely answer is that they came from the Northwest Coast, developing out of more ancient local traditions.

This view is probably that of most workers on the coast today, but that has not always been so. During the first half of the 20th century, a number of scholars argued that the ultimate origins of the basic rules and motifs derived from Chinese art of the Shang and Zhou periods (between c. 1800 and 300 BC),[36] even to the point of suggesting migrations from Asia to the Northwest Coast. A less extreme version of this school of thought has been to postulate that peoples living around the North Pacific Rim shared, in more remote times, a common cultural substratum, or what a French historian might call an ancient mentality, from which similar art idioms derived. Kwang-Chi Chang is the most recent advocate of this approach, suggesting all the cultures of the northern Pacific Rim, from the Chinese to the Maya, shared a common mentality, based on shamanism,[37] and that the similarities that he sees among these cultures derive ultimately from these ancient, shared beliefs. In his model, shamanism was brought into the Americas by its earliest inhabitants, who undoubtedly originated in northeast Asia. The difficulty with such an approach is its selectivity, a focus on apparent similarities, some so general that they might reflect the behavior of all humans, without regard for differences (the similarities are due to common heritage, the differences dismissed as the result of subsequent history). In the 1920s and 1930s it was easier to argue that Native peoples in North America shared ideas with peoples in East Asia, since at that time, many thought the Northwest Coast had been occupied for only 2,000 or 3,000 years. Now that we realize people were here for much longer, Chang is forced to suggest that these ideas have lasted 12,000 to 15,000 years, or that there have been multiple migrations into North America much more recently.

We do not want to deny the clear evidence for some very interesting commonalties between the Northwest Coast and the northeast coast of Asia (from Japan to Kamchatka): labrets, and post-and-beam houses are but two. Others include rod armor. There is also evidence for a flow, or at least a trickle, of people and ideas back and forth across the Bering Straits[38] during the past. Recently, items of Norse manufacture dating to c. AD 1100[39] have been found in the Canadian arctic– but the people who owned those objects did not suddenly begin to produce Viking art. In any case, we know little of this flow: what actually moved across the straits, how it moved, and why. We do not know its direction: labrets could have as easily originated on the Northwest Coast and diffused to Asia, as vice versa. However, the assumption always seems to be that the flow is from the seemingly more complex, the civilizations of Asia, to the apparently simpler and more primitive, the hunter-gatherers of North America. It is not surprising that archaeologists and anthropologists generally reject such theories, with their implications of superiority and inferiority. Finally, even if we accepted Chang's view, that there was a 20,000-year-old, deep, cultural substratum shared by all peoples around the North Pacific Rim, it still does not explain the evolution of Northwest Coast art, any more than it explains Chinese culture, and the development of the Shang dynasty.

Roy Carlson and George MacDonald may be correct in their view that the roots of Northwest Coast lie in shamanism, and this may provide insights into the meaning of the art. However, it does not tell us how and why it developed the way it did: why the regional differences developed (unless shamanism in each area was practiced differently); why the rules of composition seem to have been tighter in the north than in the south, why the southern art was generally more naturalistic, why there was a southern and a northern formline, rather than just one, and why there seems to have been more variability in the art in the south, among many other questions we could ask.

The idiom clearly developed hand-in-hand with the evolving status system (the practice of shamanism on the coast probably changed through time as well). Regional exchange and interaction were central to the development of the status system, and regional differences in the art reflect the same impetus that led to the regional marking of people by labret wear, cranial deformation, and tattooing. The full idiom of Northwest Coast art emerged during the Middle Pacific at the same time as the ancient status of "labret wearer" was being absorbed into the new, wealthier elite of the Late Middle Pacific. The presence of specialists must also have profoundly affected the history of the art, through the development of techniques and refinement of tools and knowledge not otherwise possible, and perhaps even the development of local "schools" of specialists.

The production of art by specialists might also have affected how objects were evaluated by their audience. During the Early Modern period masks and other carvings were displayed and were central parts of rituals. Competition among elite members and the specialists who produced the objects (these individuals may very well have been one and the same[40]) might have rapidly led to the formalization of the rules of composition and even to more highly stylized forms.

Then why the differences between north and south? Does this imply that there were no specialists in the south, where the art seems to have been more variable, more naturalistic? It may imply fewer specialists, though there is certainly evidence for specialists in the Marpole phase. It suggests a somewhat different role for the art in the south, where it may have played a greater part in funerary ritual than in the north. We will return to these questions in the last chapter.

CHAPTER TEN

Summary and Conclusions

In our introduction we outlined three basic themes in this work: that hunter-gatherers have dynamic histories; that to understand the archaeology of the coast, we need to understand the relationships between local variability and regional similarities and between local environmental variability and regional richness. Last, that cultural evolution is ultimately the result of the decisions people make. These themes are the framework within which we were to explain the evolution of complex hunter-gatherers on the Northwest Coast. Briefly returning to these themes in this final chapter accomplishes that goal.

We have stressed throughout this work that the peoples of the Northwest Coast have a long and dynamic history. This is not a history in which societies and cultures along the coast simply became more and more similar to their Early Modern form, until, at last, that was achieved at some point in the Late Pacific period. History on the coast has been history like anywhere else in the world, a matter of stops and starts, shifts and tacks. There have been periods of relative peace, and periods marked by conflict; there have been periods with relatively rapid technological and economic changes, and periods of seeming stability, periods in which the ground rules by which people made their decisions stayed the same, and periods in which those ground rules changed.

This is not to say that there have not been continuities in the coast's history. There have been. There is no evidence for massive replacements of peoples. People have moved around on the coast, expanded their boundaries, lost territories, but there is no suggestion of wholesale replacement of peoples. The coast itself, the necessity of making a living from the sea, has also imposed continuity on the coast's peoples. Some places on the coast seem always to have been productive, others not. Virtually all the resources exploited 10,000 years ago were exploited 200 years ago. What changed was the economic organization and intensity with which they were harvested. The idioms of the coast's art show continuities across the last two millennia, suggesting strong cultural continuity during a period marked by the end of midden burials and major changes in the social organization. The patterns of historic change and continuity can be seen regionally as well. For example, there are virtually no alterations in subsistence-related artifacts in Prince Rupert Harbor during the Middle and Late Pacific periods, when there are major changes elsewhere on the coast, along Johnstone Strait, and in the Gulf of Georgia, for example. This, of course, also relates to our second theme, local variability and regional similarity.

A key factor in the coast's history has been the pattern of local diversity and regional similarity, of local environmental variability and regional richness, a pattern the coast shares with the rest of world. Throughout the book, we have seen how diversity and similarity have shaped our perceptions of the coast's history, as well as that history itself. We saw, for example, how interaction and exchange may have created regions on the coast. We also argued in Chapters Five and Six that one of the key social innovations of the Middle Pacific is a household organization that could take full advantage of both variability and richness. That innovation was fundamental to the evolution of social complexity on the coast, and leads us to our third theme, which is basically how and why cultures change, and how and why social complexity developed on the Northwest Coast.

At some level environmental changes must be fundamental to the history we have presented. Which environmental changes, however, remains an open question. Clearly, the development of mature forest stands, rich in cedars, around 2500 to 1200 BC was crucial because they provided the raw materials for houses, boxes, and canoes. But perhaps the shift to a cooler, wetter environment at the end of the post-glacial warm/dry period at 8000 BC was actually the major change, echoing down through the centuries. We know little about the history of the North Pacific as an ecosystem, and it seems likely that changes in the ocean are as basic for understanding the evolution of a maritime people as are changes in terrestrial environments. However, it seems that the crucial changes must have been those that led to increasing levels of environmental richness that was accessible to humans, given the available technology, and which, at the same time, affected patterns of environmental variation. Among these were the stabilization of sea levels and probably salmon runs around 4000 BC, the development of productive shallow neritic and estuarine environments, and the formation and spread of the rainforest and availability of trees such as red cedar that could be made into vast houses and seaworthy canoes.

The coastal environment imposed limits and made demands on the coast's peoples. It provided them with the raw materials for many of their economic and social decisions; it also shaped the short- and long-term consequences of those decisions. Chief among the challenges posed by the environment was variation and it is this variation that is basic to understanding the development of the coast's several levels of economy. The coastal environment was not uniform, but varied, sometimes profoundly, from place to place and from time to time. We saw in Chapter Six how social arrangements in the form of household territories might smooth out some of that variation. We have also suggested that by the Middle Pacific, households had to be parts of regional economies to sustain themselves at the economic levels required for participation in the coast's social systems. But at the root of it all, effective exploitation of the coast's environment required households capable of performing a variety of tasks all at the same time, some tasks requiring specialization, others made more efficient through specialization. It was this household organization that solved the problems in scheduling that local environmental variation caused and that, at a basic level, produced the subsistence wealth that sustained Northwest Coast societies and their systems of ranking. In short, while the Northwest Coast's environment was rich, the large households permitted people to take advantage of that richness.

We cannot say what caused these households to form. What we are saying is that once they did, they had an advantage over other forms of domestic organization that might have existed on the coast at the end of the Early Pacific. Plank houses clearly suggest social sedentism and notions of property. They represented a significant cost in labor and skill, so their benefits must have been considerable, such benefits not being limited to the utilitarian functions of houses. What was the nature of this advantage? There are many possibilities which are not mutually exclusive. They may have produced more food, and so attracted people during periods of shortages; they may have simply produced more people, who then themselves lived in such houses; they may have enjoyed higher prestige than other household forms, leading people to want to live in such households; or the increased numbers and ridged walls may have offered more protection from enemies. These kinds of reasons are what we mean by evaluation of consequences as being central to cultural evolution. We do suggest that, given the coast's environment and the available technology, economies based on such households could support larger regional populations than could economies either not based on corporate group households, or based on smaller households.

The appearance of linear villages implies the development of some form of regular community organization. The arrival of such villages may be linked to the changes in household organization, but was not dependent on them. The Katz village on the lower Fraser River was a two-row linear village of pithouses, for example. These patterns also appear to crystallize sometime between 1800 and 1200 BC, but do not become common until the Late Pacific. Population growth is certainly an important element in these shifts in organization.

The available data on demographic patterns suggests visibly rapid population growth beginning by 4000 BC and peaking on the entire coast by AD 500–900. There are differences in the curves for the north and south coasts that may indicate differences in their demographic histories. The data are too general to permit us to say whether population growth was the cause or the result of the economic and subsistence changes along the coast. What we can say, however, is that the Cascadia-wide changes – the appearance of pit structures by c. 4300 BC, their widespread use after 3900 BC, and the development of a storage-based economy after 1800 BC – coincided with population growth throughout the entire region.

Technological changes were also crucial, both those that were complete innovations, and those that represented expanded or new uses for older tools and techniques. Some crucial toolkits and skills were probably part of the technological base of the coast's first peoples. These may have included making nets, using antler wedges for splitting wood, barbed points for fishing and hunting sea mammals, and knowledge of ground stone and watercraft. We have presented at least indirect evidence for all of these during the Archaic. We also believe that basic techniques for storage – smoking, freezing, and wind and sun drying – were also known to the continent's earliest peoples. We base this belief on the simple grounds that it is inconceivable to us that people could have survived late ice-age winters without such basic knowledge of how to keep food through the winter. If this is so, then the development of the storage-based economy represented a shift in emphasis, a shift to much heavier reliance on storage, rather than the appearance of a new technology.

There were crucial technological innovations. The most important, in our view, were the development of the ground-stone celt or adz blade sometime before 1800 BC, perhaps from antler and shell predecessors, and the skill to make planks and kerfed boxes. Antler and bone wedges and chisels were probably part of the original toolkit of the coast's first people, making it possible to split and shape wood. Ground-stone adz blades, however, made it easier to fell trees, make planks, and to hollow out large logs for seaworthy canoes. Shell and stone adzes of several sizes permitted the development of a complete carpentry.

We have likened the development of box-making technology to the development of pottery elsewhere in the world – watertight boxes allowed the storage of everything from oil to hard-smoked fish pemmican. They also facilitated boiling water, making it possible to make soups and gruel, which in turn, make some plants more digestible and meals more nutritious. The boxes had important advantages over pottery: they stacked more easily, were more transportable and far less likely to break if dropped. Plank houses were simply the application of these skills to the internal frame of the older structures on the coast, such as that at Hatzic Rock.

Of equal importance, to our thinking, was the development of large, seaworthy canoes that were capable of transporting large loads over long distances of open water, as well as for hunting big sea mammals and fishing in deeper waters. They also made possible the distinctive forms of behavioral and social sedentism that existed on the coast in the Early Modern period. Northwest Coast people were able to move towns and their peoples as needed, rather than having always to disperse to resources as pedestrian hunter-gatherers must. Large population aggregations could be maintained year round, but in different places.

Weather on the Northwest Coast is predictably unpredictable. Watercraft and their crews had to have the competency to handle bad conditions safely. It seems plausible that boats of some form were present from the start. However, small- or even medium-sized canoes do not have the full set of capabilities we are describing. Large, seaworthy canoes were highly prized in the Early Modern period. Those with them could travel, trade, and raid over enormous distances. Those without were limited in the kinds of waters they could cross or exploit. We believe that much of the regional and coast-wide dynamics we have described were the result of the presence of large, seaworthy canoes. The admittedly quite limited evidence available suggests these craft were present on the northern coast by AD 1, if not earlier. Since the requisite carpentry skills appear to have existed a millennium earlier, we belief such craft were in use by the early Middle Pacific. Given their value, we expect them also to be present on the south coast by that time as well.

Other important technological innovations (or improvements) include the use of ground slate for points and knives at the beginning of the Early Pacific. Ground slate appears to be an essential part of sea-mammal hunting tackle in much of the world, seemingly having a number of advantages over chipped lithics. Together with seaworthy boats, large harpoons and lances armed with ground-slate points enabled the coast's people to exploit large sea mammals effectively. Toggling harpoon heads expanded the range of neritic animals that could be harpooned. The spread of toggling harpoons along the coast may reflect adjustment to time stresses arising from intensification of production. New nets, or novel use of nets, must also have played important roles in the coast's technological history. Improvements in fish-processing techniques may have increased the amount of food that could be stored.

A discussion of technology brings us logically to subsistence, though we have already touched on some aspects of it. Here again, change involved the changing roles of old resources rather than some entirely new ones. The people of the coast had, for example, exploited salmon from the beginning. The issue then becomes, when and why did salmon begin to play a major role in economies along the entire coast? One part of the answer lies with the development of the storage-based economy, some time around 1800 BC, and which we have suggested was probably the result of population growth that occurred throughout Cascadia. Salmon is a high-quality, readily dried and stored resource. Another part of the story is the evolution of the large households, and the third part of the answer rests with the development of regional economies on the coast, which, given the evidence for the development and continuity in interaction spheres, also probably occurred around that time. Though we discussed them separately, the two may be the same phenomenon – regional economies based on food-storage by households. Increased production appears to have involved greater reliance on mass harvesting techniques, such as nets and weirs, as well as the exploitation of new habitats along the coast, and even the creation of new habitats by the construction of weirs and by burning vegetation.

The regional economies were formed within the framework of the interaction spheres that probably began to develop during the Archaic. The obsidian networks provide excellent evidence for the presence of exchange well back in the Archaic period.

Increased production of salmon did not occur in a vacuum. Northwest Coast societies made use of a wide range of resources. If salmon alone were sufficient to sustain Northwest Coast populations and to support their social systems, we would expect to see widespread specialization in salmon production. While there may have been such specialization at the local level here and there, what we see more often are economies geared to exploit a wide range of resources and habitats. We also witness considerable variation from place to place and time to time in which resources were crucial. It is at the regional level that there is economic uniformity: salmon are important regional resources, though not at every locality (and not necessarily in every region). Increasing levels of production appear to be linked to storage, to larger populations and to sedentism. Once again, the crucial events appear to have occurred at the beginning of the Middle Pacific. These events were not limited to the coast, but occurred across Cascadia. Efforts to increase production appear to have begun perhaps as early as the Late Archaic, and continued throughout the Pacific period, particularly during the Middle and Late Pacific periods.

Throughout Chapter Four, we observed regional differences in artifact assemblages, particularly at places such as Yuquot and Prince Rupert Harbor, and suggested that these differences might be the result of availability of raw materials (little good tool stone, more bone tools). It is also possible that these differences indicate economic differences. We discussed Robin Torrence's theory that technologies that are time stressed as a result of scheduling conflicts will become more complex as a result. The implication of this for technological variation on the coast is that economies in places such as Yuquot and Prince Rupert Harbor were generally more time stressed than other places throughout the Pacific period. When we see the technological shifts at the beginning of the Late Pacific in the Gulf of Georgia, we are witnessing evidence of an increase in time stress produced by scheduling conflicts. These conflicts in turn would have been the result of intensification of food production and expanding the diet. These ideas are speculative, but suggest a possible explanation for technological shifts on the coast during the Pacific period.

A final part of the developments during the Middle Pacific was specialization. We see the presence of specialists most clearly in the grave goods found in elite burials, including the copper in Prince Rupert Harbor and the fine Marpole brow-bands in the Gulf of Georgia. This specialization might seem to be the result of the development of the elite. However, it appears more likely that part-time specialization developed as part of the new household economy of the Middle Pacific. This seems particularly the case with carpentry. Indeed, there is some evidence of a linkage between high social status and woodworking – the two going together. Specialization probably arose as part of the shift in household organization towards accomplishing complex simultaneous tasks. Exchange through the regional interaction spheres, and the rise of an elite would also have encouraged specialized production. One of the least understood aspects of specialization on the coast is the degree to which not only individuals, but towns and regions were production specialists linked through wide webs of social and economic ties.

This brings us to social status. The evolution of ranking and stratification among Northwest Coast societies is at the heart of any understanding of the coast's cultural history. Yet, we have shown that burials appear to have been an idiom for the expression of status differences in Cascadia since at least the middle of the Archaic, if not even earlier. Thus, inequality on the coast is quite likely to have grown from earlier systems of social differentiation rather than developing from earlier, completely egalitarian societies. There was clearly a special position of "labret wearer" as early as 2500 BC, if not before. Northwest Coast systems of ranking, then, were a likely modification or amplification of older patterns. The earlier system of marking differentiation provided a seedbed from which the new system developed. It provided a marker of status, the labret, and it seems most likely that labret wearers formed the core of the new elite. The system of ranking that developed became stratification when slavery became an institution along the coast, even if slaves were held in only small numbers. Once again, it looks as though the changes from the older form of status system to a ranked, and then to a stratified, system began $c.$ 1800 BC, perhaps indicated by the changes in burial patterns at Pender Canal around this time. However, stratification probably emerged $c.$ 600 BC and spread throughout the region after AD 1.

In the Early Modern period, social stratification was most visible on the coast at the regional (interaction sphere) level. It was at this scale, and that of the village, that the relative social stature of chiefs was measured. Gender also clearly had a regional dimension. It is therefore reasonable to conclude that the evolution of elites and of interaction spheres were closely linked.

The obsidian evidence shows that large-scale exchange networks existed on the coast by at least 10,000 BC. The currently available evidence suggests that stable interaction spheres developed around 1800 BC, and persisted into the Early Modern period. At first, elite status was signaled on a coast-wide basis by labret wear for both sexes. By AD 1, this uniformity had broken down with the appearance of cranial deformation on the south coast. In the north the wearing of labrets continued, but only as a privilege first for males, then for females. Cranial deformation patterns varied along the south coast, permitting quite fine-grained identification of where an elite individual had originated. The development of cranial deformation is probably one of the most important changes on the Northwest Coast after 1800 BC.

The elite were also inextricably tied to their households. The only resources they could confidently command were those of their household. Their status at the village and regional levels was usually that of their households. While we have speculated that there may have been experiments in polity formation during the Middle Pacific, these experiments, if they occurred, did not persist (with the two possible exceptions of the Coast Tsimshian and the Nuu-chah-nulth).

The changing nature of rank and stratification on the coast was probably the result of the interplay among the emerging household and village organization (indicated by linear villages and plank houses) and the older status distinctions marked by labret wear. High-status individuals may have been the core of the new households, and used the stores and other wealth produced by the new economy to further their own ends, and to perpetuate their new status. There is clear evidence for greater wealth in the burials after 600 BC.

Like status differentials, aspects of the Northwest Coast art traditions clearly predate these social and economic changes. Art too evolved with the changing circumstances. It appears to have had somewhat different histories in different parts of the coast, differing histories obscured by the evident role of the art in interaction across the coast and among the coast's elite. The Northwest Coast regional idioms seem to emerge after 1800 BC, and take on much of their historic form by AD 1. Northwest Coast art played many roles in the life of the coast during the Early Modern period. It seems likely that it took on those roles with the development of large households, the chiefly elite and the regional interaction spheres.

There were thus at least two parallel trends through all of this that interacted, but were somewhat distinct. The new economy produced a new household form, based on large households with complex divisions of labor. These households participated in larger spheres of interaction and exchange. At the same time, an old, distinct status evolved into a new elite, tied to household production but operating at a regional scale. Differences in resource bases led in part to differences in relative wealth and status among households and therefore in their chiefs, but so too did different levels of participation in the larger scale interaction spheres.

We believe the linkages among the household, social status (including gender) and regional dynamics lie through household production and specialization. Households participated in regional economies through the activities of their chiefs, but probably also through trade and exchange. The production of goods rested in the hands of full- and part-time specialists, some of whom were probably high-status embedded specialists. It is an open question whether households needed chiefs to function. In other words, were chiefs necessary for the household economy to operate effectively, and were they necessary for households to operate at the regional level? The answer to the first question is probably no; the answer to the second question is a very qualified yes. The presence of the elite may have produced larger interaction spheres. However, the point here is that the household and regional economies of the Northwest evolved along with an elite and the elite evolved along with the economies. Why did ranking and then stratification develop on the Northwest Coast? The answer lies in the ability of individuals in the late Early Pacific and early Middle Pacific to take advantage of the productivity of the coast's new household organization to compete for prestige. Warfare also certainly furthered these trends as a route to acquire prestige and resources.

Warfare was endemic, particularly on the northern coast, from sometime after 2300 BC. Conflict was probably a major factor in the development of an elite, and of slavery. Slavery may either have grown out of raiding, or have been a cause for raiding. Slaves provided an emerging elite with labor that elite individuals could command, since chiefs could not coerce free individuals to obey them. The apparent different histories of warfare on the north and south coasts suggest somewhat different histories for the two areas, otherwise linked by participation in the same overlapping interaction spheres. Patterns and intensity of warfare changed through time. Early and Middle Pacific warfare appears to have been primarily hand-to-hand combat, while in the Late Pacific fortresses and moats were present, indicating sieges, an inference supported by oral traditions in the north. The introduction of the bow and arrow may have been one reason for these changes in tactics and intensity. In the north, this second phase of warfare was also contemporary with the shift in the wearing of labrets from men to women, and the appearance of large houses, suggesting these changes happened together.

It is also during this time (AD 500–1000) that mortuary practices reached one of their most costly forms, in the mounds at Scowlitz, and then changed – with the cessation of midden burial. If burials, and their accompanying rituals, played major roles in the marking or establishment of status, as virtually all archaeologists working on the coast now assume (as do we), then a change in burial ritual has important implications for how social ranking was marked and displayed. Ranking and stratification were most clearly measured at the regional level. The change in burial practices was a coast-wide event, indicating that its cause, whatever it may have been, was operating at that scale. This reasoning suggests that the cause was a coast-wide change in how status and prestige was displayed. One possibility is that we are witnessing the development and rapid spread of the potlatch, the combination feast and give-away through which high status was confirmed and increased during the Early Modern period.

The Northwest Coast is a place of extraordinary beauty on a grand scale, with precipitous mountains, great rivers, dark forests with gigantic trees, and, just out of sight, off to the west, the unimaginably huge North Pacific. In this book we have presented an archaeological history of the people of that coast, a history that ends just as the modern world begins, but a history that spans 13,000 years, and includes everything that all histories include. It is important to recall here, at the end of our account, that this grand history is the result of people all along the coast, and elsewhere, for that matter, making ordinary, daily decisions, wanting and hoping for certain kinds of things to happen, and acting on those intentions. These actions had consequences and outcomes, some intended, some unintended. What we have described is the cumulative story of those outcomes.

Notes to the Text

Prelude *(pp. 10–12)*

1 What follows is based upon Pethick 1978, Gibson 1995, Cook 1794.
2 Arima 1983.
3 See Boas 1898.

Chapter One *(pp. 13–42)*

1 John Brown, a Gitksan elder speaking to the ethnographer, Marius Barbeau, in Kispiox, British Columbia 1920, quoted in Cove 1987, 49.
2 Suttles 1990, 11, comments within brackets ours.
3 Kwakwala is the language spoken by the Kwakwaka'wakw.
4 Lee and DeVore 1968, 11.
5 Cohen 1989.
6 Franz Boas, *Tsimshian Mythology*, 196, 274.
7 Cope 1991.
8 We wish to avoid a lengthy presentation of what is a very large literature. The reader is referred particularly to, Winterhalder 1980, Boyd and Richerson 1985, Cosmides and Tooby 1987, Durham 1991, Mithen 1991,1996, Smith and Winterhalder 1992 for many of the ideas underlying this section.
9 This discussion of culture is based on Durham 1991.
10 Learning in a social context from others. Culture requires society.
11 Paraphrasing Durham 1991, 8. Boyd and Richerson (1985) argue that the transmission of cultural traits from generation to generation is the key process in cultural evolution, while Durham argues it is the process of evaluation of decisions by their consequences. We leave that issue for another place.
12 Mithen 1996.
13 Mithen 1990.
14 Hayden (1990, 1992b) for example, argues that social inequality among hunter-gathers arises when the environment rich enough, or subsistence techniques productive enough to ease the strong prohibitions generalized hunter-gatherers usually have against personal aggrandizement, and that the presence of aggrandizers who will pursue their own advantage is simply part of the normal variation in human nature which is repressed in some societies.
15 Mithraism was a major rival to Christianity in the first and second centuries AD. It was particularly strong in the eastern Roman Empire and in the Roman Army. It shared some features with Christianity as Christianity took shape, including a strong duality between good and evil.
16 This may seem trivial, but agriculture is the product of exactly this situation. Hunter-gatherers began using and manipulating plants in certain ways for immediate purposes, without the realization that 2,000or 3,000 years in the future, this activity would lead to farming. They could have no knowledge of this outcome, so it could not be their intent, yet agriculture is the result.

Chapter Two *(pp. 43–56)*

1 Moulton 1990, 21: "a Cloudy morning Som rain the after part of last night & this morning. I could not Sleep.for noise kept by the Swans,Geese, white & black brant, Ducks, &c. on an opposite base, & Sand hill Crane, they were emensely numerous and their noise horrid." Journal entry of Clark, 5 November 1805. Spelling and punctuation his.
2 The crucial papers are Suttles 1962 and 1968. The latter paper was part of the *Man the Hunter* volume, and remains the basic statement on the variability of the coast's environment. Schalk's paper (1977) can be taken as a follow-up to Suttles' 1968 work, but dealing specifically with salmon.
3 This description is based primarily upon Fladmark 1975, Suttles 1990,and McKee 1972.
4 Much of the discussion in this section derives from Redmond and Taylor 1997.
5 The following discussion is based upon Suttles 1990, Alaback and Pojar 1997, Pojar and MacKinnon 1994 and the atlas maps in Schoonmaker, von Hagen and Wolf 1997.
6 See for example Boyd 1986, Turner 1991, Turner 1997.
7 A third zone, the benthic (the ocean floor) is of little direct relevance here. Much of the following discussion is based on Suttles 1990.
8 See, for example, Salmon 1997.
9 The following discussion is based upon Warner et al. 1982; Clague 1984, 1987, 1989; Clague et al. 1982; Blaise et al. 1990; Hutchinson 1992; Luternauer et al. 1989.
10 The term "transgression" means that an ocean or sea has risen to a level above current sea levels.
11 Much of the following discussion is based on Hebda and Whitlock 1997, but see also Heusser 1960,1985; Heusser and Heusser 1980; Heusser et al. 1981; Barnowsky, Anderson and Bartlein 1987; and Whitlock 1992, as well as references therein. The bibliography of Hebda and Whitlock is particularly useful. Hebda and Mathewes 1984 discuss the relationship between the maturation of large stands of red cedar and the development of woodworking on the coast.
12 Heusser 1985, Heusser and Heusser 1981.
13 Boyd 1985, 1991.
14 Dobyns 1983.
15 Ramenofsky 1987.
16 Campbell 1989.
17 Haggerty and Inglis 1984.
18 Much of this discussion is based on Cybulski 1994. Cohen 1989 provides an excellent discussion of hunter-gatherer health, both presently, and prehistorically.
19 Lambert 1993.
20 Cohen 1989.

Chapter Three *(pp. 57–86)*
1 Hopkins 1967.
2 Hopkins 1996; Hopkins et al. 1982.
3 Hulte'n 1937.
4 West 1996; Hoffecker et al. 1993, and Hopkins 1996 argue that the western edge of Beringia is east of the Lena River, more likely east of the Kolyma River of far northeast Asia.
5 Guthrie 1990.
6 Colinvaux 1986.
7 Guthrie 1990.
8 Goetcheus, Hopkins, Edwards & Mann 1994.
9 Elias 1996, 115–117. While the ice sheets began to melt and retreat before about 14,000 years ago, there seems to have been a substantial lag in the tempo of sea-level rise.
10 Hoffecker et al. 1992.
11 Fladmark 1983.
12 Holmes 1996.
13 Fladmark 1979.
14 Mann and Peteet 1994.
15 Maschner et al. 1997.
16 Mochanov 1977, Mochanov et al. 1983.
17 Kuzmin et al. 1994, Kuzmin 1994, Kuzmin and Tankersly 1996.
18 Mochanov 1977.
19 Dikov 1977, 1979.
20 Hoffecker et al. 1993.
21 Holmes 1993.
22 Ackerman 1996.
23 Holmes et al. 1996.
24 West 1981.
25 See chapters by Ackerman in West 1996.
26 Kunz and Rainer 1996. Although the Mesa Site has at least one date in the mid 11,000 range, the remainder of the many dates from this site are after 10,500 years ago.
27 Goebel et al. 1991.
28 Gruhn 1961.
29 Bedwell 1969.
30 Ackerman 1968.
31 Davis, 1989.
32 Alaska Department of Parks–Office of History and Archaeology 1989.
33 Ackerman et al. 1985.
34 Hobler 1978.
35 as argued by Acheson 1991.
36 Fladmark 1986
37 Fedje et al 1996
37 Coupland 1996a
38 Bowers & Betts 1995, Smith & McCallum 1993.
39 Fladmark 1982; Clarke 1978.
40 Cannon 1991.
41 Cannon 1991.
42 Carlson 1979.
43 Matson 1976.
44 Borden 1968, 1970, 1975.
45 Lyman 1991.
46 Samuels 1993.
47 Newman 1966 reports on Cascadia Cave, while Daugherty et al. 1987a, and 1987b report on Layser Cave and Judd Peak.
48 Cressman et al. 1960.
49 V. Butler 1993, pers. comm.
50 Butler 1961.
51 Leonhardy & Rice 1970, Matson 1976.
52 Carlson 1983, 1990a, 1990b, 1996a, 1996b.
53 Carslon 1996a, Connolly 1998.

Chapter Four *(pp. 87–112)*
1 Cybulski 1990.
2 Athapascan is a language family whose speakers are concentrated in central Alaska and Interior British Columbia. However, there are five Athapascan languages spoken on or near the southern coast. These five are most closely related to northern Athapascan languages in Alaska. Clearly, the ancestors of these people migrated into the area from Alaska. When is not known. Tying languages to the archaeological record is extremely difficult, perhaps even impossible.
3 Chartkoff and Chartkoff 1984.
4 Hebda and Whitlock 1997.
5 The term midden actually refers to accumulated organic debris; in that sense a compost heap is a midden. The word was originally applied in Scandinavia where "kitchen middens" were thought to be accumulations of organic debris produced by food processing as well as by other domestic activities. Midden deposits are dark gray to black in color and greasy when wet. A shell midden is a midden that contains shell. It can also contain rocks, lenses of soil, sand and other non-organic matter that was brought in by the site's inhabitants, or by natural processes. Northwest Coast middens contain lenses of fine sand which, in some instances, are the remnants of housefloors that were covered in sand, and in others, were deposited by tidal waves, or tsunamis, produced by large earthquakes.
6 These are the least-productive littoral regions on the coast generally. Highly productive areas are very localized along these coastlines.
7 As assemblage size increased, we would expect there to be increasing numbers of rare tools that we had not seen in earlier, but much smaller assemblages. However, if we look at inventories of bone and antler tools for the Archaic from all of Cascadia, we can be more confident that some of these tool forms are appearing for the first time.
8 See, for example, Møllenhus 1975.
9 See, for example, Acheson 1991 and McMillan 1996.
10 Hebda and Whitlock 1997 and citation therein.
11 Cybulski 1991.
12 Davis 1989.
13 Coupland 1985a, 1988.
14 Moss et al. 1996.
15 Okada et al 1992, Maschner 1992, Ames 1998.
16 Davis 1989.
17 Severs 1973, 1974; Cybulski 1994.
18 Mobley 1984.
19 Maschner 1992.
20 Mitchell 1988, 1991.
21 Haggerty 1982.
22 McMillan 1996, McMillan and St. Claire 1982.
23 Carlson 1991, Carlson and Hobler 1993.
24 Ham et al. 1982.
25 Mason 1994.
26 LeClair 1976.

27 Archer and Bernick 1990.

28 Croes 1995.

29 E.g. Matson and Coupland 1995.

30 Mitchell 1971, 1991, Burley 1980.

31 Borden 1968, Duff 1956.

32 Borden 1970, Mitchell 1991.

33 Connolly 1992.

34 See Pettigrew 1990.

35 Wessen and Daugherty 1983.

36 Jermann et al. 1975.

37 Roll 1974.

38 Strong, Schenk and Stewart 1930; Butler 1956, 1960; Caldwell 1956.

39 E.g.Dunnell and Campbell 1977, Minor et al. 1989.

40 Ames et al. 1992.

41 Ames 1994 and bibliography therein.

42 Minor 1983.

43 DeLaguna 1953, 1960, 1972,1983; De Laguna et al. 1964.

Chapter Five *(pp. 113–146)*

1 Kroeber 1939, Wissler 1917.

2 Yesner 1981, 1987, Renouf 1991.

3 Suttles 1962, 1968, Vayda 1961.

4 Donald and Mitchell 1994.

5 Effective environment refers to the parts of a group's total environment that it actually uses and thinks about.

6 Schalk 1981.

7 Salmon are anadromous; they reproduce in fresh water, laying their eggs sometimes far from the ocean. The fry, once hatched, spend some time (it varies from species to species) in their natal stream before migrating to the ocean. Once in saltwater the fish feed and achieve maturity. This may take between two to six years depending on the species. During this period the fish were inaccessible to native fishing techniques. The fish eventually return to the streams that they were born in to spawn and die. The massive return migrations of adult fish up the streams and rivers are called salmon runs. The fish follow differences in water chemistry to trace their route back to the same place they were born to lay and fertilize their eggs. Unlike Atlantic salmon, Pacific salmon seldom survive spawning. They stop feeding when the runs begin and undergo hormonally triggered changes that have the effect of slowly breaking down their flesh as they work upstream. At least one species, Pink salmon, literally begins to rot alive when it enters fresh water.

8 Schalk 1987.

9 Schalk 1977, Kew 1992.

10 Kew 1992.

11 O'Leary 1985.

12 This process is generally termed "intensification" by archaeologists. Intensification of production means to increase production per capita.

13 Monks 1987.

14 Kew 1992.

15 McMillan 1979. It seems likely that tuna fishing occurred in periods of warm seas, or "El Niños" as they are known.

16 Boas 1921. Boas describes gardens for these plants along the intertidal zone in some areas. Their rhizomes were sometimes heaped in large piles as part of potlatch displays. Cinqfoil is one of the few indigenous plants on the Northwest Coast for which there are ethnographic descriptions of gardens.

17 Boyd 1986.

18 Turner 1996, and references.

19 Moss 1993.

20 Donald and Mitchell 1988.

21 Richardson 1981.

22 Erlandson 1994.

23 See Lyman 1989.

24 Ames 1988.

25 The Young's River Complex, recovered from land surfaces along the Young's River, near Astoria, Oregon (Minor 1984).

26 Atwell 1989.

27 Englebrecht and Seyfert 1994.

28 Carlson 1997.

29 O'Leary 1985.

30 The reader who wishes to pursue these issues in more detail is urged to begin their reading with Robert Kelly's very fine 1995 book on hunter-gatherers.

31 Flannery1969.

32 In the original definition of focal economies (Cleland 1976), people depend on a relatively few resources.

33 Hayden (1990, 1995) argues that these are the primary reasons hunter-gatherers increase food production. The argument that social demands can lead to increased food production was first made for the Northwest Coast by Weinberg (eg 1973), who pointed out that the historic Northwest Coast economy, with its heavy dependence on salmon, was probably as much the result of the coast's social history as cause of it. The exchangeability of food, wealth, and prestige on the coast was well recognized by Suttles (1960), Vayda (1961) and Piddocke (1965) in their functionalist analyses of potlatching. More generally, Barbara Bender argued in her seminal 1978 paper that domestication of plants may have been a consequence of social demands placed on hunter-gatherer production by an emerging elite. It is this thread that Hayden has developed.

34 E.g. Lyman 1991.

35 Erlandson 1994.

36 Cannon 1991.

37 Cannon 1991.

38 Carlson 1996a.

39 Chisholm et al. 1982, 1983; Chisholm and Nelson 1983.

40 Matson 1976.

41 Cannon 1991.

42 Stewart and Stewart 1996.

43 Ames 1998.

44 Moss, Erlandson and Stuckenrath 1990.

45 Monks 1987.

46 Eldridge and Acheson 1991.

47 Ames 1991a.

48 Ames 1996a.

49 In more technical terms, people exploited new resource patches, not new resources. Technology was adapted to the new conditions by modifying it, not through new inventions.

50 Dewhirst 1980, McMillan 1996.

51 Mitchell 1988.

52 Cannon 1991.

53 Shipek 1989.

54 Turner 1996.

55 Matson 1992.

56 Driver 1993. Driver argues that Matson did not control for the volume of excavated fill in his calculations. See Lyman 1991 for a discussion of the relationship between amount of fill excavated and the diversity of artifact and faunal assemblages.

57 Mitchell 1991.

58 E.g. Ford 1989, Ham 1983, Hanson 1991, Moss 1989, Saleeby 1983.

59 Calvert 1980.

60 Hanson 1991.

61 Wessen 1982.

62 Moss 1989.

63 Maschner 1992.

Chapter Six *(pp. 147–176)*

1 The recent focus on household archaeology on the Northwest Coast stems from two papers published in 1985. The first, by Coupland, introduced the idea of household archaeology into the regional literature (Coupland 1985a). The second, by Ames 1985, discussed the concept of the Domestic Mode of Production (Sahlins 1972) in terms of Northwest Coast households. The best available summary of Northwest Coast household economies is that of Mitchell and Donald 1988 in which they review the economies of all major Northwest Coast tribal groups using available ethnographic, ethnohistoric, and archaeological data. Their review does not, however, include groups along the Washington, Oregon, and northern California coasts, or the Chinook along the Lower Columbia River. Discussions of Chinookan economies can be found in Saleeby 1983, Hajda 1984, and Boyd and Hajda 1987. Norton 1985 is also a crucial source on Northwest Coast economies. The term "household archaeology" was introduced into the discipline by Wilk and Rathje 1982. One issue for archaeology is the conflation of domestic group and household. In this matter, Hendon 1996 provides guidance: "I use *household* and *domestic group* interchangeably to refer to the task-oriented, co-resident, and symbolically meaningful social group that forms the 'next bigger thing on the social map after an individual [Hammel 1984]', a group that archaeologists have tried to study based on the remains of houses .... [a]lthough ethnographic research shows that co-residence, domestic activities, and the household are not necessarily isomorphic, they often are. The assumption is a practical necessity for archaeology and is accepted here" (Hendon 1996, 47 *emphasis* hers).

2 Hayden and Cannon 1983.

3 There is an extensive literature on household production, particularly for peasants in modern third-world economies, including debates over Sahlins' Domestic Mode of Production. The discussions in Fricke 1989, Gallant 1991, and Wilke 1991 are all useful here. Archaeological discussions of household economies and the development of complexity out of household economies are little informed by this literature. Gallant's discussion may be the most directly applicable to archaeological cases, since he employs both archaeological and historical data in his reconstruction of Greek peasant household economies of the Classical period. The central question is how emerging elites gain control of household production. We will return to this issue below.

4 See, for example, Marshall 1989.

5 In English, the word town indicates that the settlement possesses a political organization, while villages have none. Therefore, most Northwest Coast settlements were towns.

6 The number of households in a single settlement could vary from one, occupying several houses, to many. There were also settlements with a single house. These are not well understood. In the case of the Meier site, which contained one, large very substantial house, Ames has applied the term villa, in the sense that the structure was the center of production in much the same way that Roman villas were the center of agricultural production.

7 The following discussion, and quotations, is based on Wilk and Rathje 1982 622–623.

8 Netting 1982.

9 Donald and Mitchell, in their seminal 1975 paper, showed a close correlation among the relative status of Kwakwaka'wakw households and household size, which, in turn, was predicted by the productivity of the salmon stream in their territory. Netting (1982) shows the relationship holds more generally across a variety of ethnographic examples.

10 Suttles 1990 describes the several types of Northwest Coast house, while H. Rice 1985 provides a thorough discussion of house types on the Intermontane Plateau. Vastokas 1966 provides detailed information about the construction of Northwest Coast houses. See also papers in Coupland and Banning 1996.

11 Hayden et al. 1996 has recently argued that on the Plateau, they were heated primarily by body heat of the occupants. He also argues that people were jammed tightly into the structures.

12 Barnett 1944. In one of his examples, a Coast Salish household occupied both a plank house and a pithouse, with the chiefly family in the pithouse.

13 Ames 1991 reviews the archaeology of pithouses on the Intermontane Plateau in detail. See also Chatters 1989 for a similar review, but with a more limited geographic focus.

14 Some were as much as 2 or more m deep; others merely 50 cm (hardly a pit at all). Diameters ranged from 3–4 m to structures that were more than 20 m across. There was no necessary connection between diameter and depth. In fact, some very deep houses were not particularly wide.

15 See, for example, Marshall 1989.

16 There has been little archaeological work on specialization at the household level on the coast and how it might appear archaeologically. However, Chatters 1988 and Smith 1996 do grapple with the issue.

17 Ames et al. 1992. The estimates were based on the number of times particular posts and timbers had been replaced and on the length of time red cedar posts would last in the ground without rotting.

18 Ames 1996b.

19 Ames 1996b.

20 Maschner and Stein, 1995.

21 Wilson 1988.

22 Ames 1991a reviews the dimensions of sedentism. Definitions vary, from a minimal definition that some members of the residential group live at the settlement for at least one year, to others demanding that people live there for at least a generation. See Ames 1991a, Kelly 1992, and Rafferty 1985 for reviews of these various definitions.

23 Ingold draws this useful distinction between behavioral and social sedentism (Ingold 1987, 169). Soffer 1989 suggests that social

sedentism might be the more difficult to establish archaeologically, but given the difficulties archaeologists face in establishing behavioral sedentism (e.g. Edwards 1989b) social sedentism is actually probably easier to establish.

24 During some seasons of the year, household members might disperse out to camps to collect particular resources, approximating the kind of semi-sedentism of many hunter-gatherers, who might spend one or two seasons in a village, and then disperse for the rest of the year. Most hunter-gatherers might form large aggregations once a year, but on the Northwest Coast, they could move the aggregation from place to place. Some recent discussions about Northwest Coast sedentism (e.g. Arnold 1996) misunderstand this fundamental quality of Northwest Coast residential patterns.

25 Highly specialized and segmented societies such as the modern world are governed – the segments coordinated – through political institutions. Egalitarian societies have politics, but no specialized political institutions, and no political specialists. Politics here are understood to mean the social means by which resources (economic, social, and others) are controlled and allocated in a society. Stratified societies are hierarchical, and the social strata at the top maintain their position through their control of politics, by controlling the authority to rule. Or, more simply, by maintaining a monopoly on power. This authority is commonly exercised over some territory and its inhabitants. Such a territory is called a polity. Polity is a neutral term that does not specify the particular political arrangements of a given society, as do terms such as nation state, republic, or empire. Polities associated with ranking are commonly termed chiefdoms, while those associated with stratification are states. It is widely assumed that stratification is always associated with polities and with formal political institutions. The Northwest Coast was stratified to a degree but lacked clear-cut polities.

26 J.Caldwell 1964.

27 MacDonald 1969.

28 See Feinman 1996, and Hayden 1996 on somewhat different approaches to this issue. Hayden and Schulting 1997 discuss the role of interaction spheres and the development of regional elites on the Columbia Plateau after *c.* 1500 bp. They argue that the interaction sphere is the result of the presence of elites. We would reverse that, and argue that the interaction in pre-existing exchange networks is crucial to elite formation.

29 Northwest Coast households owned the rights of access to resource localities, or to particular resources. Resource ownership has played an important role in models of the development of inequality on the Northwest Coast (e.g. Matson 1983, 1985, 1989, 1992; Coupland 1985a, 1985b, 1988b; Kelly 1991, 1995). Richardson 1981 remains the definitive review of patterns of resource ownership on the coast, while Ames 1996 has discussed the issue. Differential access to resources is also fundamental to one of the major schools of thought about the origins of complex societies, what is sometimes called the integrationist school (see Haas 1982).

30 Hajda 1984 sees these ties as fundamental to Chinookan success along the Lower Columbia (see also Boyd and Hajda 1987 for a further development of the argument). Basically, the Lower Columbia River, and adjacent portions of the Oregon and Washington coasts were a small unitary interaction sphere, based on these extensive affinal ties.

31 Befuku 1951.

32 E.g. Shimkin 1978.

33 Aikens and Higuchi 1983, Imamuri 1996.

34 Chang 1988

35 The earliest structures on the North Pacific Rim appear to be structures associated with Early Ushki occupation at Ushki Lake, on the Kamchatka Peninsula. The radiocarbon dates are *c.* 14,000 to 15,000 bp, including their sigmas. These dates are too old to calibrate. These appear to be shallow pit structures. The largest is *c.* 100 sq. m, with a floor defined by charcoal. There is also a burial associated with this occupation (Dikov 1996). Another structure at Ust–Timpton, at the confluence of the Timpton and Aldan Rivers in the interior of the Russian Far East, is dated to *c.* 10,500 BC. The remains of the structure includes posts (Mochanov and Feedoseeva 1996).

36 McCartney and Veltre 1996 have recently expressed caution about whether these features are houses. Maschner has reviewed all of the field notes and drawings and is convinced of the authenticity of the houses.

37 This discussion is based on Eakin 1987, McKern 1987, Newberry and Harrison 1986, and Harrell and McKern 1986.

38 Connolly 1998.

39 Chatters 1986.

40 The earliest documented pithouses in the region were found at the King's Dog site in the Surprise Valley of northeastern California (O'Connell 1975). There are perhaps 20 structures at King's Dog. O'Connell excavated one structure rather fully. It was about 8 m across and perhaps 50 cm deep. It was associated with well-developed midden deposits, suggesting the house was occupied for a relatively long time. The roof appears to have been supported by as many as seven central posts. These houses date to *c.* 4400 BC. Pithouses have been excavated in southern Idaho (Green 1993), in Washington State and Oregon (reviewed in Ames 1991a) and in central British Columbia (Wilson1992). Most of these, however, date between *c.* 3700 and 2600 BC. After *c.* 2600 BC, house-pit construction on the Plateau virtually ceases for several hundred years.

41 Chatters 1989a, 1996a. Chatters, and Ames 1991a, both reviewed these data independently, and came to superficially similar conclusions: that there appear to be have been two major phases of house construction on the Plateau: the one we are terming Cascade Village 1, and a second, beginning *c.* 2300 BC and continuing until contact. Chatters, however, argues that the first phase is entirely restricted to the period between *c.* 3800 and 2600 BC, and does not accept an earlier period of sporadic construction. Part of the difference reflects the samples used; Chatters' sample of pithouses is restricted to the Columbia Plateau, while Ames' is drawn from throughout Cascadia.

42 These early structures in the interior tend to share a number of characteristics: 1) their mean size is 8 x 8 m; 2) their pits are rather shallow; while some may be as much as a meter deep, they are usually around 50 cm deep; 3) some (perhaps one out of four) have earthen benches one to two meters wide around their interior circumference; 4) where entries can be identified, they are at ground level, rather than through the roof; some have entry ramps cutting through the interior bench (and one, at Hatiuhpah (Brauner et al. 1990)) appears to have an entry tunnel); 5) there appear to have at least two types of superstructure: those requiring no internal supports (a light exterior frame of poles, perhaps) and

those with interior roof supports. In structures with interior roof supports, they either have one or four or more; 6) the excavation of the pit itself was frequently into the slope of a hillside, or river bank, so that the excavated dirt could be thrown down slope to create either a platform or to build up the rim of the pit; 7) excavations were often placed in order to expose gravel at one end of the house, probably to ease drainage. Gravel appears to have been brought in for this purpose for one house at the Baker Site (Wilson 1992) in British Columbia.

43 There are several formulas for estimating household size from floor area. Using a formula developed by Cook's formula (Hassan 1982) Ames estimated a mean household size of about 12 people for these structures. Recently, Hayden (Hayden et al. 1996) has proposed a formula based on 2.5 sq. m of floor area per person, producing a mean household of 18 people for one of the structures. Having excavated several of them, and watched people work in them, that seems too high.

44 Some, such as those at the Baker Site, may have been occupied at other times. There is no reason why house construction would be limited to one season. Archaeologists, however, generally assume the houses were occupied sometime between mid-Fall and late Spring.

45 The Hatzic Rock structure was not, strictly speaking, a pithouse. It was built by excavating a flat platform into a gentle slope. The excavation was just deep enough to encounter gravel at one end. The house appears to have had an exterior drainage ditch to carry off water. It had an earthen bench about 2 m wide at one end (above the gravel). The excavators found a large number of postholes which probably represent the posts supporting the roof. There are five or six major exposed clusters of postholes (some rectangular), suggesting that the roof may have at least five or six interior supports at any one time. There are several hearths, which tend to cluster near the bench. The house was clearly repaired or rebuilt several times (Mason 1994).

46 Schaepe (1998) recently completed a re-analysis of the recods and artifacts from the Maurer site excavations. his study was finished too late for inclusion in our text. He reconstructs the house as being 7.5 x 5.0 m, and 3 to 4 m deep. In contrast to the previous analysis by LeClair (1976), he reconstructs the house walls as vertical and suggests there is evidence for planking. He did not attempt to reconstruct the roof, though he suggests it may have been similar to early Modern houses in the region. He also detected activity areas on the house floor, with production activities at both ends of the house and the central area a living zone. The single, central hearth produced two reliable charcoal samples dating to approximately 2900 BC. The house appears to be contemporary with some of the earlier houses in the interior, and the first period of village formation there. The site has produced microblades, which have raised questions about its age. Alternatively, microblades at Maurer and at somewhat earlier sites (Layser Cave and Judd Peak Rockshelter) in Washington may raise questions about the utility of microblades as temporal markers on the southern coast. In any case, there is no evidence that the structure was rebuilt or reused.Neither structure appears to be a plank house of the types found in the region in later periods (shed-roofed structures) nor are they similar to the forms of pithouses found in central British Columbia in the Early Modern period. However, to our minds, both have many important features in common with the contemporary, Early Cascade structures in the interior and represent a local variant of what we called Cascadia Village Pattern I. Maurer, for example, is essentially Hatwai house 1 extended from 8 to 11 m in length, with 6 rather than 4 support posts, and these spread a little farther apart. The two structures share an internal entry ramp, an earthen bench, an internal pit about 50 cm deep, and a generally rectilinear shape. The major differences are that the Hatwai house lacked an internal hearth, and the posts probably rested on large flat stones. Hatzic Rock is one of many structures in Cascadia built on a platform rather than a pit. It also possesses an earth bench (at one end), had an excavated floor platform, exposed gravels, multiple interior posts, and a side entrance. Like the Hatwai houses, it had large stone anvils set into the house floor.

47 Leonard Ham, a contract archaeologist, tested portions of the site in the early 1980s and felt he had discovered features indicating the presence of a shed-roof house of the style erected by the Coast Salish in the Early Modern period. His claims remain controversial, since he did not expose enough area to confirm the presence of structures or their form. The presence of large postholes alone cannot be taken as evidence of plank houses, at least not at this time period (Ham et al. 1986).

48 Davis 1989a.

49 There is a long-term debate in archaeology over the causes of sedentism (see Rafferty 1985), with two schools of thought, one of which Binford (1983) has disparaged as "the Garden of Eden" theory – people settle down where resources are rich enough to permit it. What he criticizes is the notion that hunter-gatherers will become sedentary when conditions are right, in other words, they will try and not be mobile. The other extreme argues that people will try and stay mobile, unless forced into sedentism (e.g. Hayden and Cannon 1982), which may have bad side effects. This can be called the "Sedentism is Hell" school, to balance the Garden of Eden.

50 Kelly 1995 provides an excellent general review of hunter-gatherer buffering mechanisms.

51 Hunter-gatherers travel a great deal; to visit relatives, to check out conditions in distant areas – in other words to keep their finger on the pulse of their world. Such information is central to their ability to make decisions about where foods are in season, their conditions and so on.

52 Watanabe 1992.

53 The Paul Mason structures were built on earthen platforms made by excavating into a hillside and presumably throwing the earth forward. The berms (low ridges) between the houses formed as midden accumulated between them. Two houses provide data on internal arrangements and architecture. The structures appear to have had gabled roofs supported by a row of posts down the middle of the interior. The two partially excavated houses each have two hearths, suggesting two to four families. There is no evidence for sleeping platforms. There is minimal evidence for wall construction. The short section of exposed exterior wall had two side-by-side post holes. This pairing could indicate at least one replacement of the wall post, or the use of multiple parallel posts in the wall, a form of construction quite unlike anything historically. The houses do not appear to have been rebuilt many times, since there is only one set of exposed postholes per floor. This would indicate that the actual span of occupation was far shorter – perhaps one or two generations with no reoccupation – than the 400 years indicated by the span of the associated

radiocarbon dates. In any case, it is reasonable to regard these as "plank houses" of post-and-beam construction. The earliest documented planking was recovered at the Grant's Anchorage site by Bjorn Simonsen, a British Columbia archaeologist (Simonsen 1973). The planks were charred and date *c*. AD 1. The technology (stone adz blades) and the skills to make planks certainly existed when Paul Mason was occupied (Chapter Five). Gary Coupland, presently of the University of Toronto, conducted the excavations at Paul Mason as part of his Ph.D. research (Coupland 1985a, 1988a). Coupland has stressed in his interpretations of the Paul Mason data that none of the houses there are significantly bigger than any others. In Early Modern period villages in the same area, one or two structures, those of the highest status households, were much larger than the rest. From this he concludes that there were no significant rank differences present at Paul Mason, and by extension, elsewhere on the northern coast at this early date. We do not think there is enough data to support his conclusions, nor do we think the data that are available support him. If we ignore the two outlying structures for the moment, Paul Mason does conform to the common layout of an Early Modern northern Northwest Coast village (except the front row is quite small). While it is true that there is little variation in house size, the largest houses in both rows are either in the middle or near the middle of their rows. Indeed, the largest of the 10 houses in either row are in the middle front of the village, where the houses of the highest status households would be in the Early Modern period. However, if house 11 is included in the analysis, it is markedly larger than any of the other structures at the site. We know nothing about either this or house 12, and so have no basis to exclude either. If house size alone indicates ranking, then house 11 indicates some degree of social ranking at Paul Mason, though its position is certainly anomalous.

54 This conclusion is based on seasonality studies (Stewart and Stewart1996) and Ames' analysis of how the site formed (Ames 1998).

55 Ames 1998. If the site was a village at the time, it was a pithouse village, if we are correct.

56 Matson et al. 1991.

57 E.g. Mitchell 1971.

58 Matson et al. 1980.

59 An earlier structure, dating to *c*. 1400 BC, is reported at Yaquinna Head, on the central Oregon coast (Minor 1991). The feature may not be a house, however.

60 This structure conforms closely in some of its details – its proportions, and the reported manner in which its hearths were built – to very Late Pacific–Early Modern period houses that have been excavated in this same region (near Portland, Oregon). Settlements in this area varied from single, large dwellings housing the entire community to double-row villages of small structures. The Palmrose house, then, indicates considerable continuity with the Early Modern period.

61 Jermann et al. 1975. The site may also contain pithouses, though structures in the region had cellars in the Late Pacific, and the cellars could be mistaken for house pits.

62 The largest sample of excavated plank houses on the Northwest Coast is for the Late Pacific on the Lower Columbia River where at least 11 Late Pacific – Early Modern period structures have been excavated. This is in sharp contrast with many other parts of the Northwest Coast. However, excavating houses, particularly the

size of some of these, is an extraordinarily time and money consuming process.

63 Chatters 1989b.

64 Renfrew 1986.

65 Huelsbeck 1989.

66 Ames 1996 reviews the evidence for occupational, craft and skill specialization among upper-class individuals on the coast.

67 Huelsbeck 1988.

68 Carlson 1991.

69 Ames 1997, Coutre 1975.

70 Ames 1997.

71 Suttles 1990b.

72 Mitchell 1971.

73 In a massive trait–element study, Jorgensen concluded that the northern coast subarea was perhaps the most distinctive cultural region in western North America (Jorgensen 1980).

74 Carlson 1994

75 Galm 1994

76 Obsidian use also continues in the north, but the use of chipped-stone tools is more sporadic that to the south. Moss et al. 1996 provide one example of an Early Pacific component from southeast Alaska

77 Galm 1994.

78 McMillan 1996

79 Galm 1994

80 Allaire and MacDonald 1971, MacDonald 1984

81 Teit 1928 contains an excellent discussion of this trade fair.

82 Galm 1994, Hayden and Schulting 1967.

83 Gibson 1992 has perhaps the best discussion of the European experience in trading along the coast during the fur trade era.

84 See discussion in Ames 1996.

85 This is unlikely to be the result of sampling given the relatively large number of burials investigated at several other sites in the harbor. See Ames 1997.

86 It might be argued that this scenario depends upon our speculation that there was a shift from pithouses to plank houses at the beginning of the Middle Pacific. That is not the case. Pithouses were an alternative house form available to the coast's people, which were constructed into the Early Modern period on the coast under some conditions (e.g. Barnett 1944). All that our argument requires is the availability of the two alternatives at the beginning of the Middle Pacific. And that condition existed. Our argument lays out the various advantages plank houses had relative to pithouses in the coast's natural and social environment.

Chapter Seven (*pp. 177–194*)

1 We use Fried's definitions of egalitarian, ranked, and stratified (Fried 1967).

2 Our claim that Northwest Coast societies were stratified rests on two arguments. First, chiefs had the power of life and death over slaves, and slaves lacked any access to the means of production. Second, the chiefly elite was maintained through marriage practices whereby high-status people married high-status people. The precise nature of "class" on the Northwest Coast has eluded easy definition for a long time. Wike's discussion of class among the Nuu-chal-nulth in 1958 has not been superseded, although Donald's recent work (1997) is for us definitive. Central to the discussion (see also Ruyle 1973 and commentary) is how slaves

were used by chiefs and their role in the household economy. One area of debate is the power of chiefs over the free members of their households and communities. Ames (1995) has discussed the role and powers of Northwest Coast chiefs in some detail. In that work he stated that there was no evidence for chiefs using slaves to violently enforce their will. There are, however, some references in ethnohistoric accounts of precisely that. Jewitt, in his daily journal of his captivity and enslavement by Maquinna, the Nuu-chal-nulth Great Chief at the beginning of the 19th century (Jewitt 1807), describes how Maquinna twice, within a single month, used Jewitt and his fellow slave, Thompson, as body guards while Maquinna slept. In the first instance, Maquinna feared for his life, according to Jewitt. No fish had arrived (it was mid-April) and people were hungry, and Maquinna feared his own people would kill him. In May, Maquinna was told "three of his captains" intended to kill him and once again Jewitt and Thompson, armed with pistols and cutlasses, were set over Maquinna while he slept. Both of these events occurred early in Jewitt's captivity and appear not have been repeated. Jewitt also observed in his other account(Jewitt 1967) that slaves were forced to fight in battles. Gilbert Sproat, in his description of Nuu-chal-nulth life written in the 1860s (Sproat 1868) makes two observations about slaves: "A master sometimes directs a slave, on pain of death, to kill an enemy, and the slave dare not return without the head of the person" (Sproat 1868, 91). Sproat makes this comment in the context of a discussion of the absolute power chiefs have over their slaves. Maquinna certainly had absolute power over Jewitt, who was well aware that he owed his life and continued existence to Maquinna, and would die quickly following Maquinna's death. Jewitt was particularly impressed by one account he was told of how the Nuu-chal-nulth had killed some sailors off another vessel. Sproat also writes "The chief has no officers, except his slaves, who could enforce obedience in his own tribe" (Sproat 1868, 114). In other places, however, Sproat notes that chiefs have little power, their "authority is rather nominal than positive" (Sproat 1868, 113). He also wondered what the legal implications of a chief using a slave as an assassin would be under Canadian law, since, to his knowledge, such an event had never actually occurred during the period of which he wrote. Donald discusses the Tlingit chief Shakes who, in the mid-1840s, had a retinue made up entirely of slaves (Donald 1997). However, this is noteworthy for its very rarity. Spier and Sapir, in their ethnography of the Chinookan Wishram near the Dalles of the Columbia, state that chiefs were obeyed without question, though they do not describe how that obedience was enforced (Spier and Sapir 1930). Schulting (1995), citing Curtis, states that the Wishram had a class of assassins who might be slaves, though Sapir and Spier make no mention of that. These are the primary sources for arguments that Northwest Coast chiefs had coercive powers over their own people, and they must be weighed against many comments that chiefs had little or no direct power over free members of their household (see Wilke 1958, Ames 1996). It is clear, however, that chiefs did have absolute power over their slaves. A second area of debate is over the contribution of slaves to the Northwest Coast economy and whether slaves were kept primarily as status markers or because their work contributed directly to the wealth that chiefs needed to function successfully. A related issue is the time depth of slavery on the coast (see note 6 below). The basic position among Northwest Coast anthropologists has been that slaves were kept

primarily for the prestige conveyed by owning them, not for their contribution to production. We follow Donald (1985, 1997) in this, and argue that slaves represented an important addition to household production (see also Ames 1996).

3   Sproat 1868.

4   The word "house" has three meanings: the structure or dwelling itself, the household that lived in one or more dwellings, and the House, the named, multigenerational corporate group. In this work, house with a lower case "h" is the structure, with an upper case "H" the House. In the north, the chief's name was also the name of the house (the structure) and the House. See Ames 1996a, 1996b.

5   Norton 1985.

6   Most investigators believe slavery has had considerable antiquity on the coast. There is debate as to whether the scale of it reported in the Early Modern period was the result of an expansion of warfare and slave trading due to the fur trade or whether it represents an older pattern. Mitchell (1985) reports for some groups as few as 1 or 2 percent of the population were slaves, while among others as many as 30 percent of the population were slaves during the early 19th century. Jewitt, in his account of life among the Nuu-chal-nulth, states that half the household of Maquinna, the Nuu-chal-nulth chief whose slave he was, were slaves, or perhaps 50 people (Jewitt 1967). Panowski (1985), however, is in a minority in her argument that prior to contact, all slaves were war captives, and that slavery by birth was the result of the fur trade.

7   Ames 1996 and references therein. Donald 1997.

8   There are full and rich literatures in anthropology and archaeology on social inequality and how to establish its existence archaeologically and how to measure it. We cannot hope in a work such as this to treat these issues more than superficially. However, our discussion rests upon Fried 1968 and Berreman 1981. The reader is referred to Ames 1996a, 1996b; Maschner 1991; Maschner and Patton 1996 for our individual views. Wasson's (1994) discussion of the archaeology of rank is also an excellent place to begin investigating the wider literature.

9   Wasson 1994, 69 *emphasis* his.

10 Wasson 1994, table 4.1, 71.

11 Shell beads were most often made from *Dentalium* and *Olivella* shells. Dentalium was acquired along the west coast of Vancouver Island and traded widely across North America. Olivella was traded north from California.

12 Moss 1993.

13 Keddie 1981.

14 Moss 1993.

15 Cybulski 1991.

16 Cybulski 1975.

17 Footnote deleted.

18 Schulting 1995.

19 One problem is determining the sex of the Blue Jackets skeletons. The two analyses came to quite different conclusions: in one, the sex ratio was almost 1:1 (Murray 1972), the other 2.6:1(Cybulski 1993).

20 We are discussing stone labrets. It is fully possible that everyone else wore labrets made of materials that did not produce labret wear, such as wood or bone. They may also have worn them in such a way that did not cause wear on the teeth. In the former situation, the question then arises, why some people wore stone labrets, while everyone else wore softer ones. The question then

is one of the raw material (why stone vs. organic labrets) and is, fundamentally, little different from asking why a few people wore labrets and many did not. The second possibility can be addressed by looking at the archaeological record to see the relative proportions among labret styles. If the vast majority of labrets are spool labrets, then that would support the idea that most labrets left no tooth wear. Unfortunately, such evidence is not currently available for the entire coast. We do have limited data from Prince Rupert Harbor. Of the 10 documented stone labrets, three are spool labrets that would not leave wear. If this very small sample is representative, about a third of labret wearers would not display labret wear on their teeth. In all burial samples, the proportion of individuals displaying labrets is rarely more than 10 percent, so that error would have only a marginal affect. Of course, this requires testing by looking at labret samples from the entire coast.

21 Dumond and Bland 1995. Dikov 1994 mentions labrets at Ushki lake dating to c. 10,500 BP.

22 Cybulski 1991.

23 Burley and Knusel 1989.

24 Carlson 1995, personal communication.

25 The opposite argument could also be made: that status differences were so strong and pervasive that they did not need to be marked in funerary practices. This is weakened by the fact that there is no other evidence in Locarno Beach sites for such pervasive status differences.

26 This discussion is based on Cybulski's analysis of human remains from Crescent Beach (Cybulski 1991), where only 6 percent of the population have evidence of labret wear, but the sex ratio of labret wearers was 1.3 males: 1 female.

27 Burley and Knussel 1989.

28 Holm 1990.

29 Sumptuary goods are items, usually of costume, whose use or wear is restricted to elite individuals, on pain of some sanction. Valuables, on the other hand, are simply very costly, and so are accessible only to the wealthy.

30 Based on figures in Cybulski 1993.

31 All of the preceding discussion is based on Ames 1998.

32 Wasson 1994.

33 Acheson 1991.

34 Maschner 1992.

35 Archer 1996, Coupland 1996.

36 Coupland 1985.

37 Cybulski 1979.

38 ARCAS 1991.

39 Cybulski 1989.

40 E.g. Laughlin 1942.

41 E.g. Hill-Tout 1930.

42 Ames would like to thank Dana Lepofsky and Michael Blake for the chance to tour Scowlitz in October 1996. This description is based in part on that visit, as well as on Thoms 1995 and Blake et al. 1994.

43 A second field of mounds had been discovered by fall 1996. The site presently has no known parallels anywhere in northwestern North America.

44 In Coast Tsimshian mythology, the elderberry is a symbol of mortality See Cove 1992.

Chapter Eight (pp. 195–218)

1 Veniaminov 1984, 432; Ferguson 1984.

2 Blackman 1990, Barbeau and Benyon 1987.

3 Hilton 1990, 314, Codere 1990.

4 Codere 1990, 359; Boas 1921, 1375; 1966, 109.

5 Kennedy and Bouchard 1990, 443.

6 Suttles 1990, 465.

7 Powell 1990, 431.

8 Franchere in Thawaites 1904-1907, 6:330-331; Henry in Coues 1897, 2:855, 867, 879-880, 905, 908; Scouler 1905, 279; Minto 1900, 311; Silverstein 1990, 542

9 Holmberg 1985 [1855-1863], 22; Krause 1970, 169; Niblack 1970, 340; Swanton 1970, 449.

10 Mitchell 1984, 1985; Donald 1983, 1984; Mitchell and Donald 1985; DeLaguna 1983, 75.

11 Kamenskii 1985, 29-30.

12 Garfield 1939, 267.

13 Suttles and Lane 1990, 488; Brown 1873-1876, 1:70-72; Curtis 1907-1930, 9:14-16.

14 Seaburg and Miller 1990, 560

15 Franchere 1967, 117; Mallery 1886, 26.

16 De Laguna 1983, 77; Birket-Smith and De Laguna 1938, 149.

17 Garfield 1939, 272-273

18 See Arndt et al. 1987, 2,11-12; Veniaminov 1984; Golovnin 1983, 89; and Tihkmenev 1979, 352, for examples.

19 De Laguna 1990, 209; Davidson 1901

20 Wooley 1984; Wooley and Haggerty 1989

21 See Boas 1916; Hilton 1990, 314; and Drucker 1951 for the full descriptions.

22 Wooley and Hagerty 1989 and Barbeau and Benyon 1987 have provided the most information on these conflicts.

23 Blackman 1990, 246.

24 Boyd 1990, 136.

25 Swanton on the Haida 1905, 364-447; Boas on the Tsimshian 1916, 124-145; Sapir and Swadish on the Nuu-chal-nulth 1955, 336-457.See also Drucker 1951, 333 and Taylor and Duff 1956.

26 Lambert 1993; Cybulski 1990, 1994.

27 De Laguna 1960; Mitchell 1980; Moss 1989; Maschner 1992.

28 Our comments on the Kennewick specimen are based on new reports and discussions with its discoverer, James Chatters.

29 Ames et al. 1998.

30 Fladmark et al. 1990, 234.

31 Mitchell 1990, 348. See also 1981, 114,117.

32 Mitchell 1990, 355.

33 Keddie in Moss and Erlandson 1992, 84.

34 Moss and Erlandson 1992, 84.

35 As referenced by Wooley 1984, 4.

36 Vancouver 1984, 1386.

37 Vancouver 1984, 934.

38 Acheson 1991; Moss 1989; Moss and Erlandson 1992; Maschner 1992.

39 Emmons 1991.

40 Khlebnikov 1973, 8-9.

41 Lowrey 1994.

42 Maschner 1991, 1992, 1997

43 Based on MacDonald 19??.

44 Based on Maschner 1992, 1997.

45 Based on 4 sq. m per person in a house.

Chapter Nine *(pp. 219–248)*

1   Cole 1985.

2   E.g. Jonaitas 1993.

3   Potlatching was made illegal in Canada in 1885, and was not legal again until 1951 (Cole and Chaikin 1990).

4   See, for example, Dale Croes' report (Croes 1995) on his excavations at Hoko River, where wooden fish-hook shanks are the most common artifact.

5   Margaret Holm 1990.

6   There is a marvelous scene in the Nelson Eddy - Jeannette MacDonald movie, *Indian Love Call*, in which Eddy, as a Canadian Mounted Policeman, sings to MacDonald with what is supposed to be a Blackfoot village behind them. The village, of teepees, is surrounded by the Canadian Rockies, and there is a row of totem poles in front of the teepees.

7   Totem poles probably began as decorated interior house poles, which were present in virtually all areas of the Northwest Coast at contact. Poles were not erected by the Kwakwaka'wakw on the northern end of Vancouver Island until the late 19th century, and they weren't common there until the 20th century. Poles were never erected along the Pacific coasts of Washington and Oregon, or along the Lower Columbia, while paintings of the interiors of Chinookan houses show extensive carving and painting.

8   The possible presence of metal tools on the coast prior to contact is an old issue (see Quimby 1985, for a discussion). The source of such metal would ultimately have been East Asia, either through long-distance trade, or from Chinese and Japanese vessels swept across the north Pacific. 5estimates that hundreds of such vessels may have been washed ashore on the coast. The other issue would be the source of the skills to make iron tools. There is, at present, no archaeological evidence for metalworking on the coast, only the finished products.

9   Holm 1965. The reader should also consult Holm's 1990 article on art in the *Handbook of North American Indians*, Volume 7 (Holm 1990). Boas' *Primitive Art* (1927) remains the fundamental work. Jonaitas has edited a number of Boas' other publications on Northwest Coast art into a useful volume, as well. Her conclusions are particularly useful (Jonaitas 1996). Her bibliography is also an excellent tool for research on Northwest Coast art.

10 See Jonaitas 1986.

11 E.g . Boas 1927.

12 Northwest Coast artists often made the right and left sides of "symmetrical" designs slightly different, in ways that sometimes require the object to be examined closely to discover the asymmetry, though the eye and brain may be aware of it.

13 The creatures on Chilkat blankets, for example, are extremely difficult to identify.

14 B. Holm 1990, 606–607.

15 Margaret Holm defines formsurface: a connecting, uniform surface whose perimeter is marked by an engraved line or by a conjunction with another lower surface. The primary formsurface stands out in a precise relief. There may also be secondary and tertiary formsurfaces. Two-dimensional block engraving is used to create complex designs with several formsurfaces (M. Holm 1990, 55).

16 B. Holm 1990, 613.

17 M. Holm defines formlines thus: "a continuous positive line delineating the primary features in a design. A formline may be a painted line or a raised line created by engraving the surrounding space. Formlines often swell and diminish as they interact with other elements in a composition" (M. Holm 1991, 55).

18 The northern style has often been regarded as the "high style," the most developed, or advanced, of the coast's regional styles. In 19th- and early 20th-century ideas of progress, cultures and their artifacts developed from the simple to the more complex. Hence, early views were that the more naturalistic Coast Salish and West Coast styles were more similar to the original Northwest Coast style than the more complex, stylized, northern art (see Jonaitas 1995 for a discussion of some of these points). Collections of Northwest Coast art have often favored objects in the northern style (including Kwakwaka'wakw art), though this is also due in part to the low production of southern art (Suttles 1983). In any case, the northern art is now the stereotypical "Northwest Coast art" of the wider European cultures of North America, and has received most of the focus of scholarship and display. Native artists in the south are presently working to revive their regional styles.

19 The reader should examine B. Holm for his discussion of regional and tribal-level variation in art on the coast. Suttles addresses the issue of art "production" in the south (Suttles 1983).

20 Brauner 1985.

21 Ricks 1995.

22 MacDonald 1983.

23 Matson 1976.

24 E.g. as among the Wishram (Spier and Sapir 1930).

25 Carlson 1991.

26 MacDonald 1983, M. Holm 1990.

27 In some ethnohistoric accounts, these are described as weapons. Lewis and Clark (Moulton 1990) observed wooden versions of iron swords among the Chinook.

28 Croes 1995.

29 This discussion is based on Fladmark et al. 1987.

30 See Suttles 1983.

31 These materials are discussed in Stryd 1983, Richards and Rousseau 1987, and Schulting 1995.

32 The best sources on Lower Columbia River sculpture remain Wingert 1952 and Peterson's Portland State University MA thesis (Peterson 1978). It is very ironic, given the widespread interest in and importance of Northwest Coast art, that two (M. Holm 1991, Peterson 1978) of the three monograph-length works dealing with its archaeology are MA theses. The third work is Carlson's 1983 edited volume.

33 Butler 1957.

34 McMillan and Nelson 1989.

35 Fladmark et al. 1987.

36 Jonaitas 1995 reviews these ideas and their fate in a very useful essay.

37 Chang 1995.

38 Fitzhugh 1988.

39 McGhee 1984..

40 Ames 1996 argues that at least some carvers were members of the elite.

Sources of illustrations

Figures

HDGM = Herbert Maschner principal artist
KMA = Kenneth Ames principal artist

The Northwest Coast maps used throughout this work were drawn by HDGM, based on Wayne Suttles and Cameron Suttles, 1985, *Native Languages of the Northwest Coast*. Western Imprints, The Press of the Oregon Historical Society, Portland, Oregon.

KMA: 3, 33 (Original courtesy of George MacDonald), 63 (from Coupland 1988a), 93, 94; 96, 98 and 108 (redrawn from MacDonald 1983); Drawing by Heidi Anderson: 22, 30; Courtesy Michael Blake: 79, 80; From Boas, 1907: 95; From Butler 1958: 119; Courtesy of Scott Byram: 50, 51; Courtesy Dale Croes: 100; Drawing by Steven Dwyer: 92, 110; Courtesy Archaeology Press, Simon Fraser University: 15; Barbara Hodgson courtesy of Archaeology Press, Simon Fraser University: 38, 39, 43, 111, 116, 117; Courtesy of Museum of Archaeology and Ethnology, Simon Fraser University: 37; From Fladmark 1970. This excerpt was originally published in BC Studies 6/7 (Fall/Winter 1970), and is reprinted with the permission of the publisher. All rights reserved: 12; From Fladmark 1986, reproduced by permission of the Canadian Museum of Civilization, Hull, Quebec, Canada: 13, 26, 28, 31, 32, 36; Courtesy of Brian Hayden: from Hayden 1997: 65; Drawn by Margaret Holm. Used courtesy Margaret Holm: 86, 87, 88, 103, 104, 105; Courtesy Dept. of Sociology/Anthropology, University of Idaho: 60; Lisiansky, 1804: 82; Used courtesy George MacDonald: 34, 77, 91, 97, 109; HDGM: 1, 2, 4 (redrawn from Croes and Hackenbergher 1988), 7, 9, 19, 40, 46, 67, 73, 76, 81, 85, 89, 115; HDGM and KMA based on Carlson 1994: 68, 69, 70, 71; Courtesy A.R. Mason: from Mason 1994: 62; MDGB: 55, 58; MDGB after Croes 1995: 57; after Oberg 1973: 52, 53, 54; Darin Molnar: 72; Reprinted by permission of the Musqueam Band, courtesy Margaret Holm: 78; Courtesy Oregon Historical Society: 47; From Connolly 1992. Used courtesy Museum of Anthropology, University of Oregon, and T.J. Connolly: 106, 107; From Peterson 1978, drawing by B. Momi: 112, 114, 118; Drawing by Mary Ricks. Used courtesy of Mary Ricks: 90; Courtesy Royal British Columbia Museum. Ground slate from Mitchell 1971, chipped stone projectile points from Calvert 1970. This excerpt was originally published in BC Studies 6/7 (Fall/Winter 1970), and is reprinted with the permission of the publisher. All rights reserved: 20, 23; Courtesy Royal British Columbia Museum: From Keddie 1981: 74, 75; from Mitchell 1971: 23, 41; Courtesy Royal British Columbia Provincial Museum: From

Duff 1956: 101, 102; Redrawn from Smith, 1930: 120; Courtesy Smithsonian Institution Press: from Holm 1990: 29; from Mitchell 1990: 35; from Suttles 1990: 42, 59; From *Indian Fishing: Early Methods of the Northwest Coast*, Hilary Stewart, 1977. University of Washington Press. Used courtesy of Hilary Stewart: 48, 49; Drawing by Joy Stickney: 18, 25, 113; Courtesy University of Utah Press: From Connolly 1998: 17; Courtesy of the University of British Columbia Press, Vancouver: from Ackerman 1996: 10, 11; from Hutchings 1996: 14; from MacDonald 1983: 61; from Mitchell and Pokotylo 1996: 16; Map prepared by US Fish and Wildlife Service, used courtesy Wapato Valley Archaeological Project: 44; Courtesy of James C. Woods: 8.

Plates

Lowie Museum of Anthropology, University of California, Berkeley: 48; Museum für Völkerkunde, Staatliche Museen Preussicher Kulturbesitz, Berlin: 20, 65, 67; Photograph by Werner Forman, British Columbia Provincial Museum: Frontispiece, 38; Courtesy British Museum: 17; Haddon Collection, Cambridge: 52, 55, 56, 66; Photograph by Roy Carlson: 9, 60, 62, 63; Photograph Ursula Didoni. Linden-Museum, Stuttgart:16; Photograph by Adrian Dort: 2, 3, 4, 5, 6, 7, 8; Photograph by C.F. Feest: 49; Photograph by Ray Hill: 70; Photograph courtesy Margaret Holm: 61; Lomonsov State University, Moscow: 47; American Museum of Natural History: 10 = Negative # 338687, 11 = Negative # 41629F, 14 = Negative # 338660, 26 = Negative # 42264 (Photographs by E. Dossetter),15 = Negative # 42270, 24= Negative # 12134, 51 = Negative # 411787 (Photographs by H.I. Smith), 32 = Negative # 24482, 40 = Negative # 3290 (Photographs by T. Lunt), 33 = Negative # 328740 (Photograph by E.W. Merrill), 44 = Negative # 330987, 330986 (Photograph by Rota), 46 = Negative # 128008 (Photograph by A. Singer), 50, 69; Museum of the American Indian, New York: 53; Painting by Paul Kane. Illustration courtesy Stark Museum of Art, Orange, Texas: 1, 13, 31, 36; Oregon Historical Society: 25, 26, 27, 29 (Drawing by John Webber of the Cook expedition, 1778), 30, 34 (Drawing by Josfl Cardero, 1791), 35 (Drawing by George Dixon), 39 (Drawing by Fernando Brambila), 41, 45, 58, 59; Wingnalt Museum, The Dalles, Oregon: 71Museum of Ethnography, St Petersburg: 19, 21; Royal British Columbia Museum: 18, 43; Smithsonian Institution, National Anthropological Archives, 12 = photo no. 56748, 37; Staatliches Museum für Völkerkunde, Munich: 23; Vancouver Museums and Planetarium Association, Centennial Museum, Vancouver: 64; Museum für Völkerkunde, Vienna: 42; Thomas Burke Memorial Washington State Museum, University of Washington: 57.

Bibliography

The following bibliography includes not only the works cited in the text, but also books and articles that an interested layperson could read to follow up on a particular topic, or which were written primarily for a lay audience. These works are indicated in the bibliography with an asterisk (*). The great bulk of the vast Northwest Coast literature has not been written for the lay audience, with the notable exception of the seemingly endless list of beautifully illustrated books on 19th and 20th century Northwest Coast Art. We list only one of those (Brown 1998). Its theme (and the galley exhibit it accompanied) is the evolution of Northwest Coast art from the 18th century to the present, and so the book fits with the theme of our Chapter 9. These art books aside, there are not many works about the cultures of the Northwest Coast for the non-specialist.

We have starred works that we thought interesting and accessible, including Swan's 1854 account of his life on Willapa Bay (*The Northwest Coast*), and Ivan Doig's, *Winter Brothers*, his 1982 reflection on Swan's reminiscences. We also included Doig's fine novel about the early 19th century Northwest Coast, *Sea Runners*. Classic ethnographies include Drucker's for the Nootka (Nuu–chah–nulth), Boas' many works, Suttles' for the Salish, and de Laguna's and Oberg's for the Tlingit. Roy Carlson's edited book *Indian Art Traditions of the Northwest Coast*, provides ready access to much of the literature and thought on Northwest Coast Art before 1983. The archaeology papers are somewhat out of date, but the others are not. Knut Fladmark's 1986 book, *British Columbia Prehistory*, is intended for a public audience and an excellent introduction both to archaeology and to the prehistory of the province. Matson and Coupland's 1995 book, *The Prehistory of the Northwest Coast* offers the reader a different approach to the coast's prehistory than that taken here.

The journals of Lewis and Clark, the Cook and Vancouver expeditions are also extremely interesting. Jewitt's account of his captivity by Maquinna in the first decade of the 1800s (at the same time Lewis and Clark were on the Oregon Coast) repays reading, as does Sproat's reminiscences of his life on the West Coast of Vancouver Island in the mid-19th century.

The reader interested in Northwest ethnography should start with *The Handbook of North American Indians, Vol. 7, The Northwest Coast*, edited by Wayne Suttles and published by the Smithsonian Institution. The book, as are all the books in this series, is aimed at the educated lay-reader. It contains articles on the ethnography each of the tribal groups recognized by along the Northwest Coast, as well as articles on the coast's archaeology and other topics (linguistics, physical anthropology). The ethnographic articles describe what is known of the lifeways of Northwest Coast peoples in the late 18th and 19th centuries and have quite complete bibliographies. The archaeology papers, on the other hand, are generally obsolete, though they also have excellent bibliographies and provide the reader with basic information. For the coast's environment, *The Rainforests of Home*, edited by Schoonmaker, von Hagen, and Wolf, is an excellent starting point, with papers describing both the history of the coastal environment as well as its current condition.

Acheson, S.R., 1991, *In the Wake of the ya'Åats' xaatg·ay ['Iron People']: A study of Changing Settlement Strategies among the Kunghit Haida*. Ph.D. Dissertation. Oxford University.

Ackerman, R.E., 1968, The Archaeology of the Glacier Bay Region, southeastern Alaska. *Laboratory of Archaeology Report of investigation* 44. Washington State Univeversity, Pullman.

Ackerman, R.E., 1970, Archaeoethnology, Ethnoarchaeology, and the Problems of Past Cultural Patterning. In *Studies in Anthropology 7: Ethnohistory in Southwestern Alaska and the Southern Yukon*, M Lantis ed., pp. 11–48. The University Press of Kentucky, Lexington.

Ackerman, R.E. (ed.), 1996, Bluefish Caves. In *American Beginnings: The Prehistory and Paleoecology of Beringia*. F. H. West, ed. pp. 511–513, Chicago: University of Chicago Press.

Ackerman, R.E., D.T. Hamilton, and R. Stuckenrath, 1985, Archaeology of Hecata Island, a survey of 16 timber harvest units in the Tongass National Forest. *Center for Northwest Anthropology Project Report* 3. Washington State Universtiy, Pullman.

Ackerman, R.E., K.C. Reid, J.D. Gallison, and M.E. Roe, 1985, Archaeology of Heceta Island: A Survey of 16 Timber Harvest Units in the Tongass National Forest, Southeastern Alaska. Pullman: *Washington State University. Center for Northwest Anthropology. Project Reports* 3.

Adams, J. W., 1973, *The Gitksan Potlatch, Population Flux, Resource Ownership and Reciprocity*, Toronto: Holt, Rinehart, and Winston of Canada

*Aikens, C.M. and T. Higuchi, 1982, *Prehistory of Japan*. Academic Press, New York

Aikens, C.M., K.M. Ames, and D Sanger, 1986, Affluent collectors at the edges of Eurasia and North America: some comparisons and observations on the evolution of society among north –temperate coastal hunter –gatherers. In Prehistoric hunter –gatherers in Japan; new research methods, T. Akazawa, and CM Aikens, eds., pp 3 –26. *Bulletin 27, The University Museum, University. of Tokyo*.

Alabeck, P. and J. Pojar, 1997, Vegetation from Ridgetop to Seashore. In *The Rainforests of Home: Profile of a North American Bioregion*, PK Schoonmaker, B von Hagen and EC Wolf eds., pp 69 –88. Island Press, Washington DC.

Alaska Department of Parks—Office of History and Archaeology, 1989, *Archaeological Mitigation of the Thorne River Site (CRG-177), Prince of Wales Island, Alaska, Forest Highway No. 42 (DT-FH70-86-A-00003)*. Anchorage: Office of History and Archaeology, Report 15.

Aldenderfer, M., 1993, Ritual, Hierarchy, and Change in Forager Societies, *Journal of Anthropological Archaeology* 12:1 –40

Allaire, L., 1979, The cultural sequence at Gitaus: a case of prehistoric acculturation. In Skeena River Prehistory, G.F. MacDonald, and R.I. Inglis eds., pp. 18 –52. *National Museum of Canada, Mercury Series Paper* 89

Allaire L., and G.F. MacDonald, 1971, Mapping and excavations at the Fortress of the Kitselas Canyon, B.C. *Canadian Archaeological Association Bulletin* 3, pp.48 –55.

Allaire, L., G.F. MacDonald, and R.I. Inglis, 1979, Gitlaxdzawk – Ethnohistory and Archaeology. In Skeena River Prehistory, G.F. MacDonald, and R.I. Inglis, eds., pp. 53 –166. *Archaeological Survey of Canada Mercury Series No. 89*. Ottawa.

Ames K.M., 1981, The Evolution of Social Ranking on the Northwest Coast of North America, *American Antiquity* 46:789 –805.

Ames K.M., 1985, Hierarchies, Stress and Logistical Strategies among Hunter – Gatherers in Northwestern North America. In *Prehistoric hunter gatherers, the emergence of cultural complexity*, T.D. Price, and J. Brown, eds., pp. 155 –80. New York: Academic Press.

Ames K.M., 1988, Early Holocene forager mobility strategies on the southern Columbia Plateau. In Early human occupation in Western North America. J.A. Willig, C.M. Aikens, and J. Fagan eds., pp. 325 –60, *Nevada State Museum Papers.* 21. Carson City: Nevada.

Ames, K.M.,. 1989 Art and Regional Interaction among Affluent Foragers on the North Pacific Rim. In *Development of Hunting –Gathering –Fishing Maritime Societies on the Pacific*, A. Blukis Onat ed..Washington State University Press, Pullman.

Ames, K.M., 1991a, Sedentism, a Temporal Shift or a Transitional Change in Hunter –Gatherer Mobility Strategies." In *Between Bands and States: Sedentism, Subsistence, and Interaction in Small Scale Societies*, Susan Gregg, ed. pp 108–133. Southern Illinois University Press, Carbondale.

*Ames K.M., 1991b, The Archaeology of the *Longue DurÈe*: Temporal and Spatial Scale in the Evolution of Social Complexity on the Southern Northwest Coast, *Antiquity* 65:935 –945.

*Ames, K.M. 1994, The Northwest Coast: Complex Hunter-Gatherers, Ecology, and Social Evolution. *Annual Reviews of Anthropology* 23:209-229.

Ames, K.M.,. 1996a, Life in the Big House: Household Labor and Dwelling Size on the Northwest Coast. In "People Who Lived in Big Houses: Archaeological Perspectives on Large Domestic Structures", G. Coupland and E.B. Banning eds., pp. 131 – 150. *Monographs in World Prehistory No. 27, Prehistory Press*, Madison.

Ames, K.M., 1996b, Chiefly Power and Household Production on the Northwest Coast. In *Foundations of Inequality*, T.D. Price

and G.M. Feinman eds., pp. 155 – 187. Plenum Press, New York.

Ames K.M., 1998a, *The North Coast Prehistory Project excavations in Prince Rupert Harbour, British Columbia: The Artifacts.* National Museum of Canada, in press

Ames K.M., 1998b, Economic Prehistory of the north British Columbia Coast. *Arctic Anthropology* 35(1):.

Ames, K.M., D.F. Raetz, S.C. Hamilton and C. McAfee, 1992, Household Archaeology of a Southern Northwest Coast Plank House, *Journal Field Archaeology* 19:275 –90

Ames K.M., C. M. Smith, W.L. Cornett, S.C. Hamilton, and E.A. Sobel, 1998, Archaeological Investigations (1991–1996) at 45CL11 (Cathlapotle), Clark County Washington: A Preliminary Report. *Wapato Valley Archaeological Project Report Number 7*. Portland State University, Portland, Or.

Ames K.M., D.E. Dumond, G.R. Galm and R. Minor, 1998, The Archaeology of the Southern Columbia Plateau. In *Handbook of North American Indians, Vol. 12, The Plateau*. D. Walker ed. Smithsonian Institution, Washington DC.

Archer D.J.M., 1984, *Prince Rupert Harbour Project Heritage Site Evaluation and Impact Assessment*. Report on file, National Museum ofMan, Ottawa, Ontario.

Archer D.J.M., 1992, *Results of the Prince Rupert Radiocarbon DatingProject*. Paper on file, British Columbia Heritage Trust, Victoria.

Archer D.J.M., 1996, *New Evidence on the Development of Ranked Society in the Prince Rupert Area*. Paper presented to the 29th Annual Meetings of the Canadian Archaeological Society, Halifax.

Archer D.J.M., and K. Bernick, 1990, *Perishable artifacts from the Musqueam Northeast Site*. Report on file, Archaeology Branch, Victoria, BC.

Arndt K.L., R.H. Sackett, and J.A. Ketz, 1987, *A Cultural Resource Overview of the Tongass National Forest, Alaska, Part 1: Overview*. GDM Inc. Report on file, Tongass National Forest, Juneau, Alaska.

Arnold J.E., 1996, The Archaeology of Complex Hunter –Gatherers. *Journal of Archaeological Method and Theory* 3(2): 77–125.

Atwater, B.F., 1987, Evidence of Great Holocene Earthquakes along the outer coast of Washington State. *Science* 236:942-944.

Atwater, B.F., 1992, A Tsunami about 1000 years ago in Puget Sound, Washington. *Science* 258:1614–1616.

Atwater, B.F., A. R. Nelson, J.J. Clague, G.A. Carver, D.K. Yamaguchi, P.T. Bobrowsky, J. Bourgeois, M.E. Darienzo, W.C. Grant, E. Hemphill-Haley, H.M. Kelsey, G.C. Jacoby, S.P. Nishenko, S.P. Palmer, C.D. Peterson, and M.A. Reinhart, 1995, Summery of Coastal Geologic Evidence for past Great Earthquakes at the Cascadia Subduction Zone. *Earthquake Spectra* 2: 1-8.

Barbeau M., and W. Beynon, 1987, Tsimshian Narratives 2: Trade and Warfare. GF MacDonald and J.J. Cove eds. *Canadian Museum of Civilization. Mercury Series Directorate Paper* 3, Ottawa.

Barnett H.G., 1944, Underground Houses on the British Columbia Coast. *American Antiquity* 9:265 –70

Barnowsky, C.W., P.M. Anderson, and P.J. Bartlein, 1987, The Northwestern U.S. during Deglaciation: Vegetational History and Paleoclimatic Implications. In *North America and*

Adjacent Oceans During the Last Deglaciation,W.F. Ruddiman, and H.E. Wright Jr. eds. pp. 289 –322. Boulder: Geological Society of America.

Beattie, O.B., 1981. *An Analysis of Prehistoric Human Skeletal Material from the Gulf of Georgia Region of British Columbia*. Ph.D. Dissertation, Simon Fraser University. Burnaby, BC.

Bedwell S., 1973. *Fort Rock Basin: Prehistory and Environment*. University of Oregon Press, Eugene.

Bender B., 1978, Gatherer –hunterer to Farmer: a Social Perspective. *World Archaeology*, 10:204 –222.

Bernick, K., 1983, A Site Catchement Analysis of the Little Qualicum River Site, DiSc 1: A Wet Site on the East Coast of Vancouver Island, BC. *Archaeological Survey Of Canada Mercury Series. 118*. Ottawa.

Bernick, K., 1989, *Water Hazard (DgRs 30) Artifact Recovery Project Report Permit 1988 –55*. Report on file,the Archaeology and Outdoor Recreation Branch, Province of British Columbia.

Bernick, K., 1998, Stylistic Charactistics of Basketry from Coast Salish Area Wet Sites. In *Hidden Dimensions: The Cultural Significance of Wetland Archaeology*, K. Bernick ed., pp. 139 –156. University of British Columbia Press, Vancouver. B.C.

K. Bernick (ed.), 1998, *Hidden Dimensions: The Cultural Significance of Wetland Archaeology*. University of British Columbia Press, Vancouver. B.C.

Berreman G.D. (ed.). 1981, *Social Inequality: Comparative and Developmental Approaches*. Academic Press, New York.

Betz V.M., 1991, Sampling, Sample Size, and Artifact Assemblage Size and Richness in Oregon Coast Archaeological Sites. In *Prehistory of theOregon Coast: The Effects of Excavation Strategies and Assemblage Size on Archaeological Inquiry*, by R. L. Lyman, pp. 50 –63. Orlando: Academic Press

Binford LR 1988. Willow smoke and dogs' tails: Hunter-gatherer settlement systems and archaeological site formation. *American Antiquity* 45:4 –20.

*Binford, L.R., 1983. *In pursuit of the past*. New York/London: Thames and Hudson

Birket-Smith, K., and F. de Laguna, 1938, *The Eyak Indians of the Copper River Delta, Alaska*. Copenhagen: Levin and Munksgaard.

Blackman, M.B., 1990, Haida: Traditional Culture. In *Handbook of North American Indians, Vol. 7: Northwest Coast*, W. Suttles, ed. pp. 240-260. Smithsonian Insitution. Washington DC.

Blaise, B., J.J. Clague, and R.W. Mathewes, 1990, Time of Maximum Late Wisconsin Glaciation, West Coast of Canada. *Quaternary Research* 34: 282 –295.

Blake, M., G. Coupland and B. Thom, 1994, *Burial Mound Excavations at the Scowlitz site, British Columbia*. Manuscript in possession of the authors.

Boas, F. 1916 *Tsimshian Ethnography*. Thirty –first Annual Report, U.S. Bureau of American Ethnology, 1909 –1910. Smithsonian Institution, Washington DC

Boas, F. 1921, Ethnology of the Kwakiutl (Based on data collected by George Hunt). 2 pts. In *35th Annual Report of the Bureau of American Ethnology for the years 1913–1914*, pp 43–1481. Washington DC.

Boas, F. 1927, Primitive Art. Instituttet for Sammenlignende Kulturforskning, H. Aschehoug, Oslo.

Borden C.C., 1968, Prehistory of the Lower Mainland. In "Lower Fraser Valley: Evolution of a Cultural Landscape," A.H.

Siemens, ed., pp. 9–26. *University of British Columbia Georgraphical Series 9*. Vancouver.

Borden C.C., 1970, Culture History of the Fraser–Delta Region: An Outline. BC Studies 6–7: 95–112.

Borden C.C., 1975 Origins and Development of Early Northwest Coast Culture to about 3000 B.C. *Archaeological Survey Of Canada Mercury Series* 45.

Borden C.C., 1979, Peopling and Early Cultures of the Pacific Northwest. *Science* 203:963 –71.

Borden C.C., 1983, Prehistoric art in the lower Fraser region. In *Indian Art Traditions of the Northwest Coast*. R.L. Carlson, ed, pp. 131 –65. Burnaby BC: Simon Fraser University Press.

Bowers P.M., and R. C. Betts, 1995, *Late Holocene Microblades on the Northern Northwest Coast: Preliminary Report on an Intertidal Site at Port Houghton, Alaska*. Paper Prepared for the 22nd Annual Meeting of the Alaska Anthropological Association, Anchorage, March 23-25.

Boyd, R., and P.J. Richerson, 1985, *Culture and the evolutionary process*. University of Chicago Press, Chicago.

Boyd, R.T., 1985, *The introduction of infectious diseases among the Indians of the Pacific Northwest, 1774 –1874*. Ph.D. Dissertation, University of Washington, Seattle.

Boyd, R.T., 1986, Strategies of Indian burning in the Willamette Valley. *Canadian Journal of Anthropology* 5 (1):65 –86.

Boyd, R.T., 1990, Demographic History: 1774-1874. In *Handbook of North American Indians, Vol. 7: Northwest Coast*, W. Suttles ed., pp. 135-148. Smithsonian Insitution, Washington DC. *American Ethnologist*: 14:309 –26

Boyd, R. T., and Y.P. Hajda, 1987, Seasonal population movement along the lower Columbia River: the social and ecological context. *American Ethnologist* 14:309–326.

Brauner, D.R., 1985, *Early Human Occupation in the Uplands of the southern Plateau: Archaeological Excavations at the Pilcher Creek site, Union County, Oregon*. Report on File, Department of Anthropology, Oregon State University, Corvallis.

Brauner, D.R., R.L. Lyman, H. Gard, S. Matz and R. McClelland 1990 *Archaeological Data Recovery at Hatiuhpah, 45WT134, Whitman County, Washington*. Department of Anthropology, Oregon State University, Corvallis.

Brown, R. 1873-1876 *The Races of Mankind: Being a Popular Description of the Characteristics, Manners and Customs of the Principal Varieties of the Human Family*. 4 vols. Cassell, Petter, and Galpin, London.

Brown, S.C., 1998, *Native Visions: Evolution in Northwest Coast Art from the Eighteenth through the Twentieth Century*. University of Washington Press, Seattle, WA.

Bucknam, R.C., E Hemphill-Haley, E.B. Leopold, 1992, Abrupt Uplift within the past 1700 years at Southern Puget Sound, Washington. *Science* 258:1611-1613.

Burley, D.V., 1980, Marpole: anthropological reconstructions of a prehistoric culture type. *Department of Archaeology Publication* 8. Burnaby BC: Simon Fraser University.

Burley, D.V., 1989, SenewÈlets: Culture History of the Nanaimo Coast Salish and the Falso Narrows Midden. *Royal British Columbia Museum Memior. 2*, Victoria BC

Burley, D.V, and C. Knusel. 1989 Burial Patterns Archaeological Interpretation: Problems The Recognition of Ranked Society in the Coast Salish Region. In *Development of Hunting –Gathering –Fishing Maritime Societies on the Pacific*, A. Blukis Onat ed.

Pullman, Wash. State University. Press. In press

Butler, B.R., 1957 *Archaeological Investigations on the Washington Shore of The Dalles Reservoir, 1955–1957.* Report on File, US National Park Service.

Butler, B.R., 1960 *The Physical Stratigraphy of Wakemap Mound.* Unpublished MA theses, University of Washington, Seattle.

Butler, B.R., 1961 The Old Cordilleran Culture in the Pacific Northwest. *Occasional Papers of the Idaho State University Museum 5.* Pocatello.

Butler, V.L., 1987, Distinguishing Natural from Cultural Salmonid Remains in the Pacific Northwest of North America. in "Natural Formation Processes and the Archaeological Record," DT Nash, and MD Petraglia eds. pp 131 –47. *BAR International Series* 352.

Butler, V.L., 1993, Natural vs. Cultural Salmonid Remains: Origin of the Dalles Roadcut Bones, Columbia River, Oregon. *Journal of Archaeological Science* 20:1 –24.

Butler, V.L., and J.C. Chatters, 1994, The Role of Bone Density in Structuring Prehistoric Salmon Bone Assemblages, *Journal of Archaeological Science* 21:413–424..

Byram, S. and J. Erlandson, 1996, *Fishing Technologies at a Coquille River Wet Site: The 1994 –94 Osprey Site Project.* University of Oregon Department of Anthropology and State Museum of Anthropology Coastal Prehistory Project. Eugene.

Caldwell, J.R., 1964, Interaction Spheres in Prehistory. In Hopewellian Studies, JR Caldwell and R.L., Hall, eds., pp 134–143. *Illinois State Museum Scientific Papers No. 12.*

Caldwell, W.W., 1956, *The Archaeology of Wakemap.* Unpublished Ph.D. dissertation, University of Washington, Seattle.

Calvert, S.G., 1970, *A Cultural Analysis of Faunal Remains from three Archaeological Sites in Hesquiat Harbour, B.C.* Unpublished Ph.D. dissertation, University of British Columbia, Vancouver.

Campbell, S.K., 1989, *Postcolumbian Culture History in the Northern Columbia Plateau: A.D. 1500 –1900.* Ph.D. Dissertation, University of Washington, Seattle.

Cannon, A., 1991, *The Economic Prehistory of Namu.* Burnaby BC: Archaeology Press, Simon Fraser University, Burnaby, B.C.

Carl, G.C., W.A. Clemens, and C.C. Lindsey, 1967, The Fresh –water Fishes of British Columbia. *British Columbia Provincial Museum Handbook No. 5,* Victoria.

Carlson, C., 1979, The Early Component at Bear Cove. *Canadian Journal of Archaeology* 3:177 –94.

*Carlson, R.L., 1983, Prehistory of the Northwest Coast. In *Indian Art Traditions of the Northwest Coast,* R.L., Carlson,, ed, pp. 13 –32.Simon Fraser University Press, Burnaby BC.

Carlson, R.L., 1987, *Cultural and ethnic continuity on the Pacific Coast of British Columbia.* Presented at 17th Congress of the Pacific Science Association, Seoul, Korea.

Carlson, R.L., 1990a, History of Research. In *Handbook of North American Indians, Vol. 7, The Northwest Coast,* W. Suttles, ed. pp. 107 – 115. Smithsonian Institution Press, Washington DC.

Carlson, R.L., 1990b, Cultural Antecedents. In *Handbook of North American Indians, Vol. 7, The Northwest Coast,* W. Suttles, ed, pp. 60 – 69. Smithsonian Institution Press, Washington DC.

*Carlson, R.L., 1991, The Northwest Coast before A.D. 1600. In, *Proceedings of the Great Ocean Conferences, Volume One The North Pacific to 1600,* pp. 109 –37. Oregon Historical Society, Portland.

Carlson, R.L., 1992, *Paleo –Shamanism on the Northwest Coast.*

Presented at the 45th Annual Northwest Anthropological Conference, Burnaby B.C.

Carlson, R.L., 1994, Trade and Exchange in Prehistoric British Columbia. *In Prehistoric Exchange Systems in North America,* T.G. Baugh and J.E. Ericson, eds., pp 307–361, Plenum Press, New York.

Carlson, R.L., 1996a, Early Namu. In *Early Human Occupation in British Columbia,* R.L., Carlson and L. Dalla Bona eds, pp. 83 – 102. University of British Columbia Press, Vancouver.

Carlson, R.L., 1996b, Introduction to Early Human Occupation in British Columbia. In *Early Human Occupation in British Columbia,* R.L., Carlson and L Dalla Bona eds, pp. 4 – 10. University of British Columbia Press, Vancouver.

Carlson, R.L., 1997, *Early Maritime Adaptations on the Northwest Coast.* Paper presented to 163rd Annual Meeting, American Association for the Advancement of Science. Seattle.

Carlson, R.L., and P.M. Hobler, 1993, The Pender Island Excavations and the Development of Coast Salish Culture. *BC Studies* 99:25 –52.

Carniero, R.L., 1970, A Theory of the Origin of the State. *Science* 169:733 –38.

Chang, K.C., 1992, The Circumpacific Substratum of Ancient Chinese Civilization. In *Pacific Northeast Asia in Prehistory: Hunter– fishers– gatherers, Farmers, and Sociopolitical Elites,* C.M. Aikens and S.N. Rhee eds., pp 217–222. Washington State University Press, Pullman.

Chartkoff, J.L. and K.K. Chartkoff, 1984, *The Archaeology of California.* Stanford Universty Press, Stanford.

Chatters, J.C., 1981, *Archaeology of the Shabadid site, 45KL1151, King County, Washington.* Office of Public Archaeology, University of Washington, Seattle.

Chatters, J.C., 1986, The Wells Resevoir Archaeological Project. *Central Washington Archaeological Survery, Archaeological Report 86-6,* Central Washington University, Ellensburg.

Chatters, J.C., 1988, *Tualdad Altu, a 4th century village on the Black River, King County, Washington.* First City Equities, Seattle.

Chatters, J.C., 1989a, Resource Intensification and Sedentism on the Southern Plateau. *Archaeology in Washington* 1: 1 –20

Chatters, J.C., 1989b, The Antiquity of Economic Differentiation within Households in the Puget Sound Region, Northwest Coast. In *Households and Communities.* S. MacEachern, et al., eds. pp. 168 –178. Archaeological Association, University of Calgary, Calgary AL.

Chisholm, B.S., and D.E. Nelson, 1983, An Early Human Skeleton from South Central British Columbia: Dietary Inference from Carbon Isotope Evidence. *Canadian Journal of Archaeology.* 7: 85 –87

Chisholm, B.S., D.E. Nelson and H.P. Scharcz, 1982, Stable Carbon Isotope Ratios as a Measure of Marine vs. Terristrial Protein in Ancient Diets. *Science* 216:1131 –32

Chisholm, B.S., D.E. Nelson and H.P. Scharcz, 1983, Marine and Terristrial Protein in Prehistoric Diets on the British Columbia Coast. *Current Anthropology* 24:396 –98

Clague, J.J., 1984 Quaternary Geology and Geomorphology, Smithers –Terrace–Prince Rupert Area, British Columbia. *Geological Survey of Canada Memoir 413,* Ottawa

Clague, J.J. 1989 Introduction (Quaternary stratigraphy and history, Cordillerna ice sheet). In *Quaternary Geology of Canada and Greenland,* RJ Fulton, ed. Geological Survery of Canada,

Ottawa.

Clague, J.J., J.R. Harper, R.J. Hebda, and D.E. Howes, 1982, Late Quaternary sea levels and crustal movements, coastal British Columbia. *Canadian Journal of Earth Sciences* 19:597 –618.

Clark, G. 1987, *Archaeological testing of the Coffman Cove site, southeastern Alaska*. Paper presented to the 32nd Annual Northwest Anthropological Conference, Eugene.

Cleland, C.E., 1976, The focal –diffuse model: an evolutionary perspective on the cultural adaptations of the eastern United States. *Midcontinental Journal of Archaeology.* 1:59 –76

Cobb, C.R., 1993, Archaeological Approaches to the Political Economy of Nonstratified Societies. *Archaeological Method and Theory*, 5: 43 –100.

*Codere, H., 1950, *Fighting With Property: A Study of Kwakiutl Potlatching and Warfare 1792-1930*. University of Washington Press, Seattle.

*Codere, H., (ed.), 1966, *Kwakiutl Ethnography: Franz Boas*. University of Chicago Press, Chicago.

Cohen, M.N., 1981, Pacific Coast Foragers: Affluent or Overcrowded? In "Affluent Foragers: Pacific Coast East and West." *Senri Ethnological Studies* 9, S. Koyama, and D.H. Thomas, eds., pp. 275 –95. National Museum of Ethnology, Osaka

Cohen, M.N., 1985, Prehistoric Hunter –Gatherers: The Meaning of Complexity. In *Prehistoric Hunter –Gatherers: The Emergence of Cultural Complexity*, T.D. Price and J.A. Brown, eds., pp. 99 –122. Academic Press, Orlando.

*Cohen, M.N, 1989, *Health and the Rise of Civilization*. Yale University Press, New Haven.

*Cole, D., 1985, *Captured Heritage, The Scramble for Northwest Coast Artifacts*. University of Washington Press, Seattle.

*Cole, D., and I. Chaikin 1992, *An Iron Hand upon the People : The Law against the Potlatch on the Northwest Coast*. Douglas and McIntyre, Vancouver BC

Colinvaux, P. A., 1986, Plain Thinking on Bering Land Bridge Vegetation and Mammoth Populations. *Quarterly Review of Archaeology* 7$^{(1)}$:8-9.

Connolly, T.J., 1992, Human Responses to Change in Coastal Geomorphology and Fauna on the Southern Northwest Coast Archaeological investigations at Seaside, Oregon. *University of Oregon Anthropology Papers* 45, Eugene.

Connolly, T. J., 1995, Archaeological Evidence for a former bay at Seaside, Oregon. *Quaternary Research* 43, 362-369.

Connolly, T.J., 1998, *Newberry Crater: A 10,000 Year Record of Human Occupation and Environmental Change in the Basin–Plateau Borderlands*.University of Utah Press, Salt Lake City.

Cope, C., 1991, Gazelle hunting strategies in the Southern Levant. In *The Natufian Culture in the Levant* O. Bar –Yosef and F.R. Valla, eds.,pp. 341 –358. International Monographs in Prehistory, International Series 1, Ann Arbor MI.

Cosmides, L., and J. Tooby, 1987, From evolution to behavior: evolutionary psychology as the missing link. In *The latest on the best: essays on evolution and optimality*, J. Dupre. ed. pp 277 –306. The MIT Press, Cambridge Ma.

Coupland, G., 1985a, Household Variability and Status Differentiation at Kitselas Canyon, *Canadian Journal of Archaeology* 9:39 –56

Coupland, G., 1985b, Restricted access, resource control and the evolution of status inequality among hunter –gatherers. In *Status, Structure and Stratification: Current Archaeological Reconstructions*, M. Thompson et al., eds., pp. 245 –52. Archaeological Association of the University of Calgary, Calgary, AL

Coupland, G., 1988a, Prehistoric Culture Change at Kitselas Canyon. *Archaeogical Survey of Canada Mercury Series* 138. Ottawa.

Coupland, G., 1988b, Prehistoric Economic and Social Change in the Tsimshian Area, *Research in Economic Anthropology*, supplement 3: 211 –45.

Coupland, G., 1991, The Point Grey Site: A Marpole Spring Village Component. *Canadian Journal of Archaeology.* 15:73 –96

Coupland, G., 1996a, The Early Prehistoric Occupation of Kitselas Canyon. In *Early Human Occupation in British Columbia*, R.L. Carlson and L. Dalla Bona ,eds., pp. 159 – 166. University of British ColumbiaPress, Vancouver.

Coupland, G., 1996b, The Evolution of Multi-Family Households on the Northwest Coast of North America. In "People Who Lived in Big Houses: Archaeological Perspectives on Large Domestic Structures", G. Coupland and E.B. Banning eds., pp. 121 –130. *Monographs in World Prehistory No. 27*. Prehistory Press, Madison.

Coupland, G., and E.B. Banning, 1996, "People Who Live in Big Houses: Archaeological Perspectives on Large Domestic Structures." *Monographs in World Prehistory No. 27*. Prehistory Press, Madison, WA.

Coupland, G., G. Bissel and S. King, 1993, Prehistoric Subsistence and Seasonality at Prince Rupert Harbour: Evidence from the McNichol Creek Site. *Canadian Journal of Archaeology* 17: 59 –73.

Coues, E. (ed.), 1897, *New Light on the Early History of the Greater Northwest: The Manuscript Journals of Alexander Henry, Fur Trader of the Northwest Company, and of David Thompson... 1799-1814*. 3 vols. Francis P. Harper, New York. (Reprinted: Ross and Haines, Minneapolis, 1965).

Coutre, A. 1975 Indian Copper Artifacts from Prince Rupert. *Physical Metallurgical Laboratories Report MRP/ PMRL –75 –3(IR) Canada Centre for Mineral and Energy technology, Energy and Mines Resources Canada*, Ottawa. Archaeological Survey of Canada Archives Ms. No. 1079.

Cowan, I.M., and C.J. Guiguet, 1965, The Mammals of British Columbia. *British Columbia Provincial Museum Handbook No. 11*. Victoria.

Cressman, L.S., D.L., Cole, W.A. Davis, T.M. Newman and D.J. Scheans, 1960, Cultural Sequences at The Dalles, Oregon: A Contribution to Pacific Northwest Prehistory. *Transactions of the American Philosophical Society, New Series* 50(10).

Croes, D.R., (ed.), 1976, The Excavation of Water –Saturated Archaeological Sites (Wet Sites) on the Northwest Coast of North America, *Archaeological Survey Of Canada Mercury Series* 50

Croes, D.R., 1988, The Significance of the 3,000 BP Hoko River Waterlogged Fishing Camp in Our Overall Understanding of Southern Northwest Coast Cultural Evolution. In *Wet Site Archaeology*, B. Purdy ed., pp. 131 –52.Telford Press, Caldwell N.J

Croes, D.R., 1989, Prehistoric Ethnicity on the Northwest Coast of North America: an Evaluation of Style in Basketry and Lithics.

Journal of Anthropological Archaeology 8:101 –30

Croes, D.R., 1991, Exploring Prehistoric Subsistence Change on the Northwest Coast, In "Long –Term Subsistence Change in Prehistoric North America," DR Croes, et al. eds., pp. 337 –66. *Research in Economic Anthropology*, supplement 6.

Croes, D.R., 1992, An Evolving Revolution in Wet Site research on the Northwest Coast of North America.In *The Wetland Revolution in Prehistory*,. B. Coles, ed., pp. 99 –111. Prehistoric Society: London.

Croes, D.R., 1995. *The Hoko River Archaeological Complex: the Wet/Dry Site (45CA213), 3,000- 1,700 B.P.* Washington State University Press, Pullman.

Croes, D.R., and S. Hackenberger, 1988, Hoko River archaeological complex: modeling prehistoric Northwest Coast economic evolution. *Research in Economic Anthropology*, supplement 3: 19 –86

*Curtis, E.S. 1907-1930, *The North American Indian: Being a Series of Volumes Picturing and Describing the Indians of the United States, the Dominion of Canada, and Alaska.* F.W. Hodge, ed. 20 volumes. Plimpton Press, Norwood, Mass. (reprinted Johnson Reprint, New York, 1970).

Cybulksi, J.S. 1975, Skeletal variation in British Columbia coastal populations: a descriptive and comparative assessment of cranial morphology. *National Museum of Canada Mercury series, Archaeological Survey of Canada Paper No. 30.* Ottawa.

Cybulski, J.S., 1979, *Conventional and Unconvential Burial Postions at Prince Rupert Harbour, British Columbia.* Archaeological Survey of Canada Archive Manuscript No. 1486.

Cybulski, J.S., 1991, Observations on Dental Labret Wear at Crescent Beach, Pender Canal, and other Northwest Coast Prehistoric Sites. Appendix to: *1989 and 1990 Crescent Beach Excavations, Final Report: The Origins of the Northwest Coast Ethnographic Patterns: The Place of the Locarno Beach Phase*, R.G. Matson, et al.. Report on file, Archaeology Branch, Victoria

Cybulski, J.S., 1993, *A Greenville Burial Ground: Human Remains in BritishColumbia Coast Prehistory.* Archaeological Survey of Canada, Canadian Museum of Civilization, Ottawa.

Cybulski, J.S., 1994, Culture Change, Demographic History, and Health and Disease on the Northwest Coast. In, *In the Wake of Contact: Biological Responses to Conquest.* R.G. Miller and C.S. Larsen, eds., pp. 75 –85. Wiley –Liss, New York.

Cybulski, J.S., D.E. Howes, J.A. Haggerty, and M. Eldridge, 1981, An Early Human Skeleton from South –Central British Columbia: Dating and Bioarchaeological Inference. *Canadian Journal of Archaeology* 5:49 –60

Darienze, M.E., and C.D. Peterson, 1995, Magnitude and Frequency of Subduction-Zone earthquakes along the Northern Oregon Coast in the past 3,000 years. *Oregon Geology* 57(1): 3-12.

Daugherty, R.D., 1956, Archaeology of the Lind Coulee Site, Washington. *Proceedings of the American Philosophical Society* 100(3): 223 –278.

Daugherty R.D., J.J. Flenniken and J.M. Welch, 1987a, A Data Recovery Study of Layser Cave (45-LE-223) in Lewis County, Washington. *Studies in Cultural Resource Management No. 7.* U.S. Forest Service, Portland, Or.

Daugherty RD, J.J. Flenniken, and J.M. Welch, 1987b, A Data Recovery Study of Judd Peak Rockshelters (45-LE-222) in Lewis County, Washington. *Studies in Cultural Resource Management No. 8.* U.S. Forest Service, Portland, Or.

Davidson, G., 1901, Explanation of an Indian Map of the Rivers, Lakes, Trails and Mountains from the Chilkaht to the Yukon Drawn by the Chilkaht Chief Kohklux in 1869. *Mazama* 2(2):75-82.

Davis, S.D., (ed.), 1989a, The Hidden Falls Site, Baranoff Island, Alaska. Aurora: *Alaska Anthropological Association Monograph Series.*

Davis, S.D., 1989b, Cultural Component I. In "The Hidden Falls Site, Baranoff Island, Alaska", SD Davis ed. Aurora: *Alaska Anthropological Association Monograph Series*, pp.. 159 – 198.

Davis, S.D., 1990, Prehistory of Southeast Alaska. In *Handbook of North American Indians, Vol. 7, The Northwest Coast*, W. Suttles, ed, pp. 197 –202. Smithsonian Institution Press, Washington, DC.

de Laguna, F., 1953, Some Problems in the Relationship between Tlingit Archaeology and Ethnology. *Memoirs of the Society for American Archaeology 3.*

de Laguna, F., 1960, The Story of a Tlingit Community: A Problem in the Relationship between Archaeological, Ethnological, and Historical Methods. *Bureau of American Ethnology Bulletin No. 172.* U.S. Government Printing Office, Washington, D.C.

*de Laguna, F., 1972, Under Mount St. Elias: The History and Culture of the Yakutat Tlingit. *Smithsonian Contributions to Anthropology Vol. 7* (in three parts). U.S. Government Printing Office, Washington D.C.

de Laguna, F., 1983 ,Aboriginal Tlingit Political Organization, in: *The Development of Political Organization in Native North America*,E. Tooker ed.,pp. 71 –85. The American Ethnological Society, Washington D.C.

de Laguna, F., 1990, Tlingit. In *Handbook of North American Indians, Vol. 7: Northwest Coast*, W. Suttles, ed.,pp. 203-228. Washington D.C.: Smithsonian Institution.

de Laguna, F., F.A. Riddel, D.F. McGeein, K.S. Lane, J.A. Freed, and C. Osborne, 1964, Archaeology of the Yakutat Bay Area, Alaska. *Bureau of American Ethnology Bulletin No. 192.* U.S. Government Printing Office, Washington, D.C.

Desgloges, J.R., and J.M. Ryder, 1990, Neoglacial History of the Coast Mountains near Bella Coola, British Columbia. *Canadian Journal of Earth Sciences* 27(2): 281 –290.

Dewhirst, J., 1980, The indigenous archaeology of Yuquot, a Nootkan outside village. "The Yuquot project, Volume ¾," *History and Archaeology No. 39*, Parks, Canada, Ottawa.

Dikov, N.N., 1977, *Arkeologicheskie Pamiatniki Kamchatki, Chukotki, i Verkhnio Kolyme.* Mockva: Nauka.

Dikov, N.N., 1979, *Drevnie Kul'tury Severo-Vostochnoj Azii.* Mockva: Nauka.

Dikov, N., 1994, The Paleolithic of Kamchatka and Chukotka and the problem of the peopling of America. In *Anthropology of the North Pacific Rim*, W.W. Fitzhugh and V. Chaussonet eds. pp 87 –96. Smithsonian Institution, Washington.

Dikov, N., 1996, The Ushki Site, Kamchatka Peninsula. In *American Beginnings: The Prehistory and Paleoecology of Beringia*, F.H. West ed., pp 244 –250. The University of Chicago Press, Chicago.

* Dobyns, H.E., 1983, *Their Number Become Thinned, Native American Population Dynamics in eastern North America.*

University. Tennessee Press, Nashville.

*Doig, I., 1982, *Winter Brothers: A Season at the Edge of American*. Harcourt Brace, New York.

*Doig, I., 1991 *The Seas Runners*. Penguin, USA (reprint.)

Donald, L., 1983, Was Nuu –chah –nulth –aht (Nootka) society based on slave labor? In "The Development of Political Organization in Native North America," E Tooker ed., pp. 108 –119. *Proceedings of the American Ethnological Society*.

Donald, L., 1984, Slave Trade on the Northwest Coast of North America. *Research in Economic Anthropology* 6:121-158.

Donald, L., 1985, On the Possibility of Social Class in Societies Based on Extractive Subsistence. In, *Status, structure and stratification current archaeological reconstructions*, M Thompson, et al. eds., pp. 237 – 243. Archaeological Association of the University of Calgary, Calgary.

*Donald, L., 1997, *Aboriginal Slavery on the Northwest Coast of North America*. University of California Press, Berkeley.

Donald, L., and D.H. Mitchell, 1975, Some correlates of local group rank among the Southern Kwakiutl. *Ethnology* 14(3): 325 –346.

Donald, L., and D.H. Mitchell, 1994, Nature and Culture on the Northwest Coast of North America: The Case of the Wakashan Salmon Resource. In *Key Issues in Hunter–Gatherer Research*, E.S. Burch, Jr., and L.J. Ellanna eds., pp65–95. Berg, Oxford.

Dumond, D.E. and R.L., Bland, 1995, Holocene Prehistory in the Northernmost North Pacific. *Journal of World Archaeology* 9(4): 401–445.

Driver, J.C., 1993, Zooarchaeology in British Columbia. *BC Studies* 99:77–104.

Drucker, P., 1943, Archaeological survey on the northern Northwest Coast. *Bureau of American Ethnology Bulletin 133*: pp. 17 –132. Smithsonian Institutions, Washington DC.

*Drucker, P., 1951, The Northern and Central Nootkan Tribes, *Bureau of American Ethnology Bulletin 144*, Smithsonian Institution, Washington DC

Duff, W.,1956, Prehistoric Stone Sculpture of the Fraser River and Gulf of Georgia. *Anthropology in British Columbia* 5:15–51.

Duff, W., 1964, The Indian History of British Columbia:Vol.1; The Impact of the White Man. *Anthropology in British Columbia Memoirs 5*. Victoria.

Dunnell, R.C., and S.K. Campbell, 1977, History of Aboriginal Occupation of Hamilton Island, Washington. *University of Washington Reports in Archaeology 4*. Seattle.

Durham, W.H., 1991, *Coevolution: genes, culture and human diversity*. Stanford University Press, Palo Alto.

Eakin, D.H., 1987, *Final Report of Salvage Investigations at the Split Rock Ranch Site (48FR1484), Highway Project SCPF-020-2(19), Fremont County, Wyoming*. Report on File, Wyoming Highway Department.

Easton, N.A., 1985, *The Underwater Archaeology of Straits Salish Reef-netting*, MA Thesis, University of Victoria, Victoria BC

Edwards, P.C., 1989a, Revising the broad spectrum revolution: and its role in the origins of Southwest Asian food production. *Antiquity* 63:225 –46.

Edwards, P.C., 1989b, Problems of Recognizing Early Sedentism: The Natufian Example. *Journal of Mediterranean Archaeology* 2/1:5–48.

Eels, M., 1985, *The Indians of Puget Sound, The Notebooks of Myron Eels*, G.B. Castile, ed. University of Washington Press, Seattle.

Eldridge, M., and S. Acheson, 1992. The Antiquity of Fish Weirs on the Southern Coast: A Respons to Moss, Erlandson and Stuckenrath. *Canadian Journal of Archaeology* 16: 112 –116.

Emmons, G.T., 1991, *The Tlingit Indians*. F de Laguna. ed. University of Washington Press: Seattle.

Engelbrecht, W.E., and C.K. Seyfert, 1994, Paleoindian watercraft: evidence and implications. *North American Archaeologist* 15(3): 221 –234.

Erlandson, J.M., 1989, Faunal Analysis of Invertebrate Assemblage. In "The Hidden Falls Site, Baranoff Island, Alaska" S.D. Davis,ed, pp. 131 – 158. Aurora: *Alaska Anthropological Association Monograph Series*.

Erlandson, J.M., 1994, *Early hunter-gatherers of the California coast*. Plenum Press, New York.

*Fagan, B.M., and H.D.G. Maschner, 1991 The Emergence of Cultural Complexity on the West Coast of North America, *Antiquity* 65:974 –76

Feinman, G.M., 1996, The Emergence of Inequality: A Focus on Strategies and Processes. In *Foundations of Social Inequality*, T.D. Price and G.M. Feinman eds., pp 255–280. Plenum Press, New York.

Fedje, D., A.P. Mackie; J.B. McSporran; and B. Wilson 1996 : Early Period Archaeology in Gwaii Haanas: Results of the 1993 Field Program. In *Early Human Occupation in British Columbia*, R.L., Carlson and L Dalla Bona eds., pp. 133–150. University of British Columbia Press, Vancouver.

Fedje, D.W.; A.R. Mason, and J.B. McSporran, 1996, Early Holocene Archaeology and Paleoecology at the Arrow Creek site in Gwaii Haanas. *Arctic Anthropology*.

Ferguson, R.B., 1984, A reconsideration of the causes of Northwest coast warfare. In *Warfare, culture and environment,*. R.B. Ferguson,ed. pp., 267 –328. Academic Press, New York Press

*Fitzhugh, W.W., 1988, Comparative Art of the North Pacific Rim. In *Crossroads of Continents: Cultures of Siberia and Alaska*. W.W. Fitzhugh and A. Crowell, eds., pp 294 –313. Smithsonian Institution Press, Washington, DC.

Fladmark, K.R., 1973, The Richardson Ranch Site: a 19th century Haida house. In *Historical archaeology in northwestern North America*. R.M. Getty and K.R. Fladmark eds., pp. 53 –95. Archaeological Association, University of Calgary, Calgary, AL.

Fladmark K.R., 1975, A Paleoecological Model for Northwest Coast prehistory. *Archaeological Survey of Canada Paper, Mercury Series, No. 43*. Ottawa.

Fladmark, K.R., 1979, Routes: Alternative Migration Corridors for Early Man in North America. *American Antiquity* 44: 55 –69

Fladmark, K.R., 1982, An Introduction to the Prehistory of British Columbia. *Canadian Journal of Archaeology* 3:131 –144.

Fladmark, K.R., 1983, Times and Places: Environmental Correlates of Mid-to Late Wisconsin Human Population Expansion in North America. In R.. Shutler, ed. pp. 13-41. *Early Man in the New World*. Beverly Hills, CA: Sage Publications.

Fladmark, K.R., 1985, Glass and Ice, The Archaeology of Mt. Edziza. *Department of Archaeology, Simon Fraser University Publication* 14, Burnaby BC.

Fladmark, K.R., 1986, Lawn Point and Kasta: Microblade Sites on the Queen Charlotte Islands, British Columbia. *Canadian Journal of Archaeology* 10:39-58.

*Fladmark, K.R., 1988, *British Columbia Prehistory*. Archaeological Survey of Canada, National Museums of Canada, Ottawa.

*Fladmark, K.R.,1989, The Native Culture History of the Queen Charlotte Islands. In G.G.E. Scudder and N. Gessler, eds., *The Outer Shores*, pp. 199-221, Proceedings of the Queen Charlotte Islands First International Symposium, University of British Columbia, August 1984. Second Beach, Skidegate: Queen Charlotte Islands Museum Press.

Fladmark, K.R., D.E. Nelson, T.A. Brown, J.S. Vogel, and J.R. Southon 1987, AMS Dating of Two Wooden Artifacts from the Northwest Coast. *Canadian Journal of Archaeology* 11:1 –12.

Fladmark, K.R., K.M. Ames, and P.D. Sutherland, 1990, Prehistory of the North Coast of British Columbia. In *Handbook of North American Indians, Volume 7, Northwest Coast*, W Suttles ed., pp. 229 – 239. Smithsonian Institution, Washington, D.C.

Flannery K.V., 1969, Origins and Ecological Effects of Early Domestication in Iran and the Near East. In *The Domestication and Exploitation of Plants and Animals*, P.J .Ucko and G.W. Dimbleby eds., pp. 73–100. Duckworth, London.

Flannery K.V., 1972, The Origins of the Village as a Settlement Type in Mesoamerica and the Near East: A Comparative Study. In *Man, Settlement and Urbanism*, P.J. Ucko, R. Tringham and G.W. Dimbleby eds., pp. 23 –54. Schenkman Publishing Company, Cambridge, Mass..

Flenniken, J.J., 1981. Replicative Systems Analysis: A Model Applied to the Vein Quartz Artifacts from the Hoko River Site. *Washington State University, Laboratory of Anthropology Reports No. 59*. Pullman.

Folan, W.J., 1972 *The Community, Settlement and Subsistence Pattern of the Nootka Sound Area: A Diachronic Model*. Ph.D. Dissertation. Southern Illinois Univesity, Carbondale.

Ford P.J., 1989, Archaeological and Ethnographic Correlates of Seasonality: Problems and Solutions on the Northwest Coast, *Canadian Journal of Archaeology* 13:133 –50.

Franchere, G., 1967, *Adventures in Astoria, 1810-1814*. H.C. Franchere ed. and trans. University of Oklahoma Press, Norman.

Fricke, T.E. 1986 *Himalayan Households: Tamang Demography and Domestic Process*. UMI Research Press, University Microfilms Inc., University of Michigan, Ann Arbor.

Fried, M., 1967, *The Evolution of Political Society*. Random House, New York.

Galm, J.R., 1994, Prehistoric Trade and Exchange in the Interior Plateau of Northwestern North America. In . *In Prehistoric Exchange Systems in North America*, T.G. Baugh and J.E. Ericson, eds.,pp 275–306., Plenum Press, New York.

Gallant, T.W., 1991, *Risk and Survival in Ancient Greece: Reconstructiong the Rural Domestic Economy*. Standford University Press, Stanford.

*Garfield, V.,*Tsimshian Clan and Society*. University of Washington Publications in Anthropology 7(3):169 –340.

Gaston, K. and J.V. Jermann, 1975, Salvage Excavations at Old Man House (45-KP-2), Kitsap County, Washington. *University of Washington Office of Public Archaeology, Institute For Environmental Studies Reconnaissance Reports 4*. Seattle.

*Gibson J.R., 1992, *Otter Skins, Boston Ships, and China Goods : The Maritime Fur Trade of the Northwest Coast, 1785 –1841*.

University of Washington Press, Seattle.

Goebel, T., W.R. Powers and N. Bigelow, 1991, The Nenana Complex of Alaska and Clovis Origins. In *Clovis: Origins and Adaptations*. R. Bonnichsen and K.L. Turnmire, eds. pp. 41–79. Center for the Study of the First Americans, Corvallis, OR.

Goetcheus V.G., D.M, Hopkins, M.E. Edwards, and D.H. Mann, 1994, Window on the Bering Land Bridge: A 17,000-Year-old Paleosurface on the Seward Peninsula, Alaska. *Current Research in the Pleistocene*. 11:131-132.

Golovnin, P.N., 1983, *Civil and Savage Encounters*. B. Dmytryshyn, and E.A.P. Crownhart-Vaughan, trans.The Press of the Oregon Historical Society, Portland.

Gottsfeld, A.S., R.W., Mathewes, and L.M. Johnson–Gottsfeld, 1991 Holocene Debris Flows and Environmental History, Hazelton Area, British Columbia. *Canadian Journal of Earth Sciences* 28(10):1583 –1593.

Green, T.J., 1993, Aboriginal Residential Structures in southern Idaho. *Journal of California and Great Basin Archaeology* 15(1):58–72.

Gruhn, R., 1961, The Archaeology of Wilson Butte Cave, Southcentral Idaho. *Occasional Papers of the Idaho State College Museum, No. 6*. Pocatello.

*Guthrie, R.D., 1990, *Frozen Fauna of the Mammoth Steppe*. Chicago: University of Chicago Press.

Haas, J., 1982. *The Evolution of the Prehistoric State*. New York: Columbia University. Press

Haggarty, J.C., 1982 *The Archaeology of Hesquiat Harbour: The Archaeological Utility of an Ethnographically Defined Social Unit*. Ph.D. Dissertation. Washington State University, Pullman

Haggerty, J.C., and R.I. Inglis, 1984, *Coastal site survey: theoretical implications of a new methodology*. Presented to 17th Annual Meeting, Canadian Archaeological Association, Victoria, BC.

Hajda, Y., 1984 *Regional Social Organization in the Greater Lower Columbia, 1792 –1830*. Ph.D. dissertation, University of Washington, Seattle.

Halpin, M. and M. Seguin, 1990 Tsimshian Peoples: Southern Tsimshian, Coast Tsimshian, Nisga, and Gitksan. In *Handbook of North American Indians, Volume 7, Northwest Coast*, W. Suttles ed., pp. 267 –284. Smithsonian Institution, Washington, D.C.

Ham, L.C., 1983, *Seasonality, Shell Midden Layers, and Coast Salish Subsistence Activities at the Crescent Beach Site, DgRr 1*. Unpublished Ph.D. dissertation, University of British Columbia, Vancouver.

Ham, L.C., 1990, The Cohoe Creek site: A Late Moresby Tradition Shell Midden. *Canadian Journal of Archaeology* 14: 199 –221

Ham, L.C., A. Yip, L. Kullar, and D. Cannon, 1986, *A Charles Culture Fishing Village*. Report on file, Heritage Conservation Branch, Victoria.

Hansen, HP. 1967, Chronology of Postglacial Pollen in the Pacific Northwest (USA). *Review of Palaeobotany and Palynology 3*: 103 –5

Hanson, D.K., 1991, *Late Prehistoric Subsistence in the Strait of Georgia Region of the Northwest Coast*. PhD. Thesis, Simon Fraser University. Burnaby BC

Harlan, J.R., 1967, A Wild Wheat Harvest in Turkey. *Archaeology*, 20:197 –201.

Harrell L., and S. McKern, 1986, The Maxon Ranch Site: Archaic and Late Prehistoric Habitation in Southwest Wyoming. *Cultural Resource Management Report No 18*. Western Wyoming College, Rock Springs.

Hassan, F., 1982, *Demographic archaeology*. Academic Press, New York.

Hayden, B., 1981, Research and Development in the Stone Age: Technological Transitions among Hunter –Gatherers. *Current Anthropology* 22:519 –548.

Hayden, B., 1990, Nimrods, Piscators, Pluckers, and Planters: the Emergence of Food production, *Journal of Anthropological Archaeology* 9(1):31 –69.

Hayden B., (ed.),. 1992a, *A Complex Culture of the British Columbia Plateau: Traditional Stl'-tl'imx Resource Use.* Vancouver: University. British Columbia Press

Hayden, B., 1992b, Conclusions: Ecology and Complex Hunter –Gatherers, In *A Complex Culture of the British Columbia Plateau: Traditional Stl'-tl'imx Resource Use.* B. Hayden, ed, pp 525–563. University of British Columbia, Vancouver.

Hayden, B., 1996, Pathways to Power: Principles for creating socioeconomic inequalities. In *Foundations of Social Inequality*, T.D. Price and G.M. Feinman eds., pp 15–85. Plenum Press, New York.

Hayden, B., and A. Cannon, 1982, The corporate group as an archaeological unit. *Journal of Anthropological Archaeology* 1(1):132 –158.

Hayden B., J.M.Ryder, 1991, Prehistoric Cultural Collapse in the Lillooet Area. *Am. Antiq.* 56:50 –65.

Hayden, B., and R. Schulting, 1997, The Plateau Interaction Sphere and Late Prehistoric Cultural Complexity. *American Antiquity* 62(1):51–85.

Hayden, B., G.A. Reinhardt, D. Holmberg and D. Crellin 1996 Space Per Capita and the Optimal Size of Housepits. In "People Who Lived in Big Houses: Archaeological Perspectives on Large Domestic Structures," G. Coupland and E.B. Banning eds., pp 151–163. *Monographs in World Prehistory No 28*, Prehistoric Press, Madison, WI.

Hebda, R., and R. Mathewes, 1984, *Postglacial history of cedar and evolution of Northwest Coast native cultures.* Paper presented to the 35th annual Northwest Anthropological Conference, Simon Fraser University, Burnaby.

Hebda, R., and C. Whitlock, 1997, *The Rainforests of Home, Profile of a North American Bioregion*, ed. P.K. Schoonmaker, B. von Hagen and E.C. Wolf, eds., pp. 227 – 254. Island Press, Washington D.C.

Hendon, J.A., 1996, Archaeological approaches to the Organization of Domestic Labor: Household Practices and Domestic Relations. *Annual Review of Anthropology* 25:45–61.

Henry, D.O., 1985, Preagricultural Sedentism: The Natufian Example. In *Prehistoric Hunter –Gatherers: The Emergence of Cultural Complexity*, T.D. Price and J.A. Brown eds., pp. 365 –384. Academic Press, Orlando.

Henry, D.O., 1989, *From Foraging to Agriculture, the Levant at the End of the Ice Age*. University of Pennsylvania Press, Philadelphia.

Henry, D.O. 1991. Foraging, Sedentism, and Adaptive Vigor in the Natufian: Rethinking the Linkages. In *Perspectives on the Past, Theoretical Biases in Mediterranean Hunter –Gatherer Research*. G.A. Clark.ed. pp. 353-370. University of Pennsylvania press, Philadelphia.

Hester, .J., and S. Nelson (eds.) 1978. Studies in Bella Bella Prehistory. *Department of Archaeology Publication 5*. Simon Fraser University, Burnaby BC

Heusser, C.J., 1960, Late –Pleistocene Environments of North Pacific North America. *American Geographical Society Monographs No. 35*.

Heusser, C.J., 1985, Quaternary Pollen Records from the Pacific Northwest Coast: Aleutians to the Oregon –California Boundary. In *Pollen Records of Late –Quaternary North American Sediments*, V.M. Bryant and R.G.. Hollow eds., pp.. 141 –165. Association of Stratigraphic Palynologists Foundation, Dallas, Tx..

Heusser, C.J., and L.E. Heusser, 1981, Palynological and paleotemperature analysis of the Whidbey Formation, Puget lowland, Washington. *Canadian Journal of Earth Sciences* 18:136 –149.

Heusser, C.J., L.E. Huesser, and S.S. Streeter,. 1980, Quaternary Temperatures and Precipitation for the North –west Coast of North America. *Nature* 286:702 –4

Hewes, G.W., 1947, *Aboriginal Use of Fishery Resources in Northwestern North America*. PhD Thesis, University. Calif. Berkeley.

Hill-Tout, C. 1930, Prehistoric Burial Mounds of British Columbia. *Museum and Art Notes*, V(4): 120–126

Hilton, S.F., 1990, Haihais, Bella Bella, and Oowekeeno. In *Handbook of North American Indians, Vol. 7: Northwest Coast*. W. Suttles, vol. ed. pp. 312-322. Washington D.C.: Smithsonian Institution.

Hobler, P.M., 1978, The Relationship of Archaeological Sites to Sea Levels on Moresby Island, Queen Charlotte Islands. *Canadian Journal of Archaeology* 2:1-13.

Hobler, P.M., 1990, Prehistory of the Central Coast of British Columbia, *in Handbook of North American Indians, Vol. 7, The Northwest Coast*.W. Suttles ed., pp. 298 –305. Smithsonian Institution, Washington, DC.

Hoffecker J.F., W.R. Powers and T. Goebel, 1993, The Colonization of Beringia and the Peopling of the New World. *Science*. 259:46-53.

*Holm, B., 1965, Northwest coast Indian art: an analysis of form. *Monograph No. 1*, Thomas Burke Memorial Museum. University of Washington Press, Seattle.

Holm, B., 1990, Art. In *Handbook of North American Indians, Vol.7, The Northwest Coast*, W. Suttles ed. pp. 602–632. Smithsonian Institute, Washington.

Holm, M., 1990, *Prehistoric Northwest Coast Art: A Stylistic Analysis of the Archaeological Record*. Unpublished Master's thesis, University of British Columbia, Vancouver.

Holmberg, H.J., 1985, *Holmberg's Ethnographic Sketches*, originally published 1855-63, English translation by F. Jaensch, M. Falk ed., The Rasmuson Library Historical Translation Series, vol. 1. Fairbanks: The University of Alaska Press.

Holmes, C.E., 1996, Broken Mammoth. In *American Beginnings: The Prehistory and Paleoecology of Beringia*. F.H. West, ed. pp. 312-318. Chicago: University of Chicago Press.

Holmes, C.E., R. Vanderhoek., and T.E .Dilley, 1996, Swan Point. In *American Beginnings: The Prehistory and Paleoecology of Beringia*. F.H. West, ed. pp. 319-323. Chicago, University of Chicago Press.

Hopkins, D.M. (ed.), 1967, *The Bering Land Bridge*. Stanford,

Stanford University Press.

Hopkins, D.M., 1996, Introduction: The Concept of Beringia. In *American Beginnings: The Prehistory and Paleoecology of Beringia*. F.H. West, ed., pp. Xvii-xxi. Chicago, University of Chicago Press.

Hopkins, D.M., J.V. Mathews, Jr., C.E. Schweger, and S.B. Young, 1982, *Paleoecology of Beringia*. New York, Academic Press.

Huelsbeck, D.R., 1983, *Mammals and Fish in the Subsistence Economy of Ozette*. Unpublished Ph.D. dissertation, Washington State University, Pullman.

Huelsbeck, D.R., 1988, The Surplus Economy of the Northwest Coast. *Research in Economic Anthropology, supplement 3*, 149 –177.

Huelsbeck, D.R., 1989, Food Consumption, Resource Exploitation and Relationships with and between Households at Ozette. In *Households and communities*, ed. S. MacEachern, D.J.W. Archer, and R.D. Garvin, pp. 157 –66. Archaeological Association,. University of Calgary, Calgary Ala

Hultn, E., 1937, *Outline of the History of Arctic and Boreal Biota During the Quaternary Period*. Stockholm, Borforlag Aktiebolaget Thule.

Hutchinson, I., 1992, Holocene Sea Level Change in the Pacific Northwest: A Catalogue of Radiocarbon Dates and an Atlas of Regional Sea level Curves. *Institute of Quaternary Research, Simon Fraser University, Discussion Paper*, 1 Burnaby BC

Hutchinson I., and A. D. McMillan, 1997, Archaeological Evidence for village abandonment associated with Late Holocene Earthquakes at the Northern Cascadia Subduction Zone. *Quaternary Research* 48: 79-87.

Inglis, R., 1976, 'Wet' Site Distribution – The Northern Case GbTo 33 – The Lachane Site. In. *The Excavation of Water –Saturated Archaeological Sites (Wet Sites) on the Northwest Coast of North America*, D.R., Croes ed. *National Museums of Canada Archaeological Survey of Canada Mercury Series Paper No. 50*. Ottawa,.

Ingold, T., 1987, *The Appropriation of Nature*. University of Iowa Press, Iowa City.

*Imamura, K., 1996, *Prehistoric Japan: New Perspectives on Insular East Asia*. University of Hawai'i Press, Honolulu.

Jermann J.V., D.L. Lewarch, and S.K. Campbell, 1975, Salvage Excavations at the Kersting Site (45CL21), A Preliminary Report. *Reports in Highway Archaeol.* 2, Office of Public Archaeology, Institute for Environmental Studies, University of Washington.

Jewitt, J.R., 1807, *A Journal Kept at Nootka Sound, by John R. Jewitt. One the the Surviving Crew of the Ship Boston, of Boston; John Salter, Commander Who Was Massacred on 22d of March, 1803. Interspersed with Some Account of the Natives, Their Manners and Customs*. Printed by the author, Boston.

*Jewitt, J.R., 1967, *A Narrative of the Adventures and Sufferings of John R. Jewitt; only Survivor of the Crew of the Ship Boston [1815])*. Ye Galleon Press (reprint), Fairfield Wa.

*Jonaitas, A., 1986, *Art of the Northern Tlingit*. University of Washington Press, Seattle.

*Jonaitas, A., 1993, Traders of Tradition: Haida Art from Argillite Masters to Robert Davidson. In *Robert Davidson, Eagle of the Dawn*. Vancouver Art Gallery, Vancouver.

Jonaitas, A., 1995, Introduction: The Development of Franz Boas' Theories on Primitive Art. In *A Wealth of Thought: Franz Boas on Native American Art*, A Jonaitas ed., pp 3–37. University of Washington Press, Seattle.

Jopling, C.F., 1989, The Coppers of the Northwest Coast Indians: Their Origin, Development and Possible Antecedents. *Transactions of the American Philosophical Society*, Vol. 79, Part 1, Pp. 1 –164.

Jorgensen, J.G., 1980, *Western Indians: Comparative Environments, Languages and Cultures of 172 Western American Indian Tribes*. W.H. Freeman and Co. San Francisco.

Kamenskii Fr. A., 1906, *Tlingit Indians of Alaska*. Translated and Supplemented by S Kan, The Rasmuson Library Historical Translation Series, Volume II, M.W. Falk ed. The University of AlaskaPress, Fairbanks.

Keddie, G.R., 1981. The Use and Distribution of Labrets on the North Pacific Rim. *Syesis* 14:60 –80.

Kelly, R.L., 1991, Sedentism, Sociopolitical Inequality, and Resource Fluctuations, In Gregg. pp.135 –60

Kelly, R.L., 1992, Mobility/Sedentism: Concepts, Archaeological measures, and Effects. *Annual Review of Anthropology*, 21: 43 –66.

Kelly, R.L., 1995, *The Foraging Spectrum: Diversity on Hunter-Gatherer Lifeways*. Smithsonian Institution Press, Washington DC.

Kennedy, D.I.D., and R.T. Bouchard, 1990, Bella Coola. In *Handbook of North American Indians, Vol. 7: Northwest Coast*. W. Suttles, vol. ed. pp. 323-339. Washington D.C.: Smithsonian Press.

Kew, M., 1992, Salmon Availability, Technology, and Cultural Adaptation in the Fraser River Watershed. In *A Complex Culture of the British Columbia Plateau: Traditional Stl'-tl'imx Resource Use*, B. Hayden, ed, pp 177–221. University of British Columbia, Vancouver.

Khlebnikov, K.T., 1973, *Baranov, Chief Manager of the Russian Colonies in America*. Translated from the Russian edition (St. Petersburg, 1835) by C. Bearne. The Limestone Press, Ontario.Press.

Kosse, K., 1990, Group Size and Societal Complexity: Thresholds in the Long –Term Memory. *Journal of Anthropological Archaeology* 9(3): 275 –303.

Koyama, S. and D.H. Thomas (eds), 1981, Affluent Foragers, Pacific Coasts East and West. *National Museum of Ethnology Senri Ethnological Series No. 9*. Osaka.

*Krause, A., 1970, *The Tlingit Indians*. University of Washington Press, Seattle.

*Kroeber, A.L., 1939, Cultural and Natural Areas of North America. *University of California Publications in American Archaeology and Ethnology 38*. Berkeley.

Kunz, M.L., and R.E. Reanier, 1996, Mesa Site, Iteriak Creek. In *American Beginnings: The Prehistory and Paleoecology of Beringia*. F.H. West, ed. pp. 497-504, University of Chicago Press: Chicago.

LeClair, R., 1976, Investigations at the Mauer site near Agassiz. In "Current research reports", *Department of Archaeology, Simon Fraser University Publication number 3*, R.L., Carlson ed., pp.33 –42.

Lambert, P.M., 1993, Health in prehistoric populations of the Santa Barbara Channel. *American Antiquity* 58:509 –521.

Lee, R.B,, and I. DeVore, 1968, Problems in the Study of Hunter and Gatherers. In *Man the Hunter*, ed. RB Lee, I DeVore, pp. 3

–12. Chicago: Aldine

Lee, R.B., and I. DeVore, 1968, *Man the Hunter*. Aldine, Chicago.

Legros, D. 1985, Wealth, Poverty and Slavery among the 19th –Century Tutchone Athabaskans. *Res. Econ. Anthrop.* 7:37 –64

Leonhardy, F.C. and D.G. Rice ,1970, A Proposed Culture Typology for the Lower Snake River Region, Southeastern Washington. *Northwest Anthropological Research Notes* 4(1):1–29.

Lightfoot, K.G., 1993, Long –term Developments in Complex Hunter –Gatherer Societies: Recent Perspectives from the Pacific Coast of North America. *Journal of Archaeological Research* 1:167 –200

Lightfoot, R.R., 1989, Cultural Component II. In The Hidden Falls Site, Baranoff Island, Alaska, edited by S.D. Davis. Aurora: *Alaska Anthropological Association Monograph Series*, Pp. 199 – 268.

Lowrey, N.S., 1994, *An Ethnoarchaeological Inquiry into the Interactive Relationship Between Northwest Coast Projectile Point and Armor Variants*. Unpublished manuscript on file at the University of Wisconsin, Madison.

Luternauer, J.L., J.J. Clague, K.W. Conway, J.V. Barrie, B. Blaise, and R.W. Mathewes,1989, Late Pleistocene terrestrial deposits on the continental shelf of western Canada: Evidence for rapid sea –level change at the end of the last glaciation. *Geology* 17: 357 –360.

Lyman, R.L., 1989, Seal and sea lion hunting: a zooarchaeological study from the southern Northwest Coast of North America. *Journal of Anthropological Archaeology* 8: 68-99

Lyman R.L., 1991, *Prehistory of the Oregon Coast: The Effects of Excavation Strategies and Assemblage Size on Archaeological Inquiry*. Academic Press, Orlando.

MacDonald, G.F. 1969 Preliminary culture sequence from the Coast Tsimshian area, British Columbia. *Northwest Anthropological Research Notes* 3(2): 240 –254.

MacDonald, G.F. 1983 Prehistoric art of the northern Northwest Coast. *In Indian art traditions of the Northwest Coast*, R.L. Carlson ed. Simon Fraser University Press, Burnaby. Pp. 99 –120.

MacDonald, G.F., 1984, The Epic of Nekt: the Archaeology of Metaphor. In *The Tsimshian: Images of the Past Views of the Present*, M. Seguin ed, pp.65 –81. University of British Columbia Press, Vancouver.

MacDonald,G.F., 1989 *Kitwanga Fort Report*. Canadian Museum of Civilization, Quebec.

MacDonald, G.F., and J.J., Cove (eds.), 1987 : Tsimshian Narratives (in two volumes). *Canadian Museum of Civilization, Mercury Series Directorate Paper No. 3. Ottawa*

MacDonald, G.F. and R.I. Inglis, 1981, An overview of the North Coast prehistory project (1966 –1980). *BC Studies* 48: 37 –63.

*MacDonald, G.F., G. Coupland and D. Archer, 1987, The Coast Tsimshian, ca 1750. In *Historical Atlas of Canada, Volume I, From the Beginning to 1800*, R.C. Harris and G.J. Mathews, eds. University of Toronto press, Toronto.

Magne, M.P.R.. 1996. Comparative analysis of Microblade Cores from Haida Gwaii. *In Early Human Occupation in British Columbia*, R.L. Carlson and L. Dalla Bona eds. pg. 151 – 158. University of British Columbia Press, Vancouver.

Mallery G., 1886, Pictographs of the North American Indians: A Preliminary Paper. pp. 3-256 in *4th Annual Report of the Bureau of American Ethnology for the Years 1882-1883*. Smithsonian Institution, Washington DC.

Mann D.H., and D.M. Peteet, 1994, Extent and timing of the last glacial maximum in southwestern Alaska. *Quaternary Research*, 42:136-148.

Marshall, Y., 1989, The House in Northwest Coast, Nuu –Chal –Nulth, Society: The Material Structure of Political Action. In *Households and Communities*, ed. S MacEachern, David DJW Archer, RD. Garvin, pp. 15 –21. University. Calgary Archaeol. Assoc., Calgary.

Marshall, Y., 1993, *A Political History of the Nuu –chah –nulth People: A Case Study of the Mowachaht and Muchalaht Tribes*. Unpublished Ph.D. dissertation, Simon Fraser University, Burnaby.

Maschner, H.D.G., 1991, The Emergence of Cultural Complexity on the northern Northwest coast, *Antiquity*,65(6): 924 –934.

Maschner, H.D.G., 1992, *The Origins of Hunter –Gatherer Sedentism and Political Complexity: A Case Study from the Northern Northwest Coast*. Unpublished Ph.D. disssertation, University of California at Santa Barbara.

Maschner, H.D.G., 1996. "American Beginnings" and the Archaeology of Beringia: A Comment on Variability. Review Article of American Beginnings, Frederick Hadleigh West, ed. *Antiquity* pp. 723–728.

Maschner, H.D.G., 1996. The Politics of Settlement Choice on the Prehistoric Northwest Coast. In *Anthropology, Space, and Geographic Information Systems*, M. Aldenderfer and H. Maschner eds. pp. 175-178. Oxford University Press, New York.

Maschner, H.D.G., 1997. Settlement and Subsistence in the Later Prehistory of Tebenkof Bay, Kuiu Island. *Arctic Archaeology* 18: pp. 74–99.

Maschner, H.D.G., 1997. The Evolution of Northwest Coast Warfare. In *Troubled Times: Violence and Warfare in the Past*. D. Martin and D. Frayer, eds. Pp 267–302. Gordon and Breach, New York.

Maschner, H.D.G., and J. Stein, 1995, Multivariate Approaches to Site Location on the Northwest Coast. *Antiquity* 69: pp 61–73.

Maschner, H.D.G., J.W, Jordan, B, Hoffman, and T. Dochat, 1997, *The Archaeology of the Lower Alaska Peninsula*. Paper No. 4 of the Laboratory of Arctic and North Pacific Archaeology. 1997.

Mason, A.R., 1994, *The Hatzic Rock Site: A Charles Phase Settlement*. Unpublished MA thesis. The University of British Columbia,Vancouver.

Matson, R.G., 1976, The Glenrose Cannery Site. *Canadian National Museum, Archaeological Survey of Canada Paper, Mercury Series No. 52*, Ottawa.

Matson, R.G., 1983, Intensification and the Development of Cultural Complexity: The Northwest versus the Northeast Coast. In "The Evolution of Maritime Cultures on the Northeast and Northwest Coasts of America". R. J. Nash, ed. pp 124 – 148. *Department of Archaeology Publication No. 11*, Simon Fraser University.

Matson, R.G., 1985, The relationship between sedentism and status inequalities among hunter –gatherers. In *Status, Structure and Stratification: Current Archaeological Reconstructions*, M. Thompson, M.T. Garcia and F.J. Kense eds., pp. 245 –252. Archaeological Association of the University of Calgary, Calgary.

Matson, R.G., 1989, The Locarno Beach Phase and the Origins of the Northwest Coast Ethnographic Pattern. In *Development of Hunting –Gathering –Fishing Maritime Societies on the Pacific*, ed. A. Blukis Onat. Pullman: Washington State University Press. In press.

Matson, R.G., 1992, The Evolution of Northwest Coast Subsistence. In Long –Term Subsistence Change in Prehistoric North America, D.E. Croes, R.A. Hawkins, and B.L. Isaac, eds.. *Research in Economic Anthropology*, Supplement 6. Pp. 367 –430

Matson, R.G., and G. Coupland, 1995, *The Prehistory of the Northwest Coast*. Academic Press, Orlando.

Matson, R.G., D. Ludowicz, and W. Boyd, 1980, *Excavations at Beach Grove in 1980*. Report on File, Heritage Conservation Branch, Victoria, BC.

Matson, R.G., H. Pratt, and L. Rankin, 1991, *1989 and 1990 Crescent Beach Excavations, Final Report: The Origins of the Northwest Coast Ethnographic Pattern: the Place of the Locarno beach Phase*. Report on File, Archaeology Branch, Victoria.

Mauger, J.E., 1978, Shed Roof Houses at the Ozette Archaeological Site: A Protohistoric Architectural System. *Project Report* 73 Washington Archaeological Research Center, Washington State University, Pullman.

McCartney ,A.P., and D.W. Veltre, 1966 , Anangula Core and Blade Site. In *American Beginnings: The Prehistory and Paleoecology of Beringia*, F.H. West ed., pp 443–450. University of Chicago Press, Chicago

*McGhee, R., 1996, *Ancient people of the Arctic*. Universityof British Columbia Press, Vancouver.

McGhee, R., 1984, Contact between Native North Americans and the Medieval Norse: A review of the evidence. *American Antiquity* 49:4–26.

McGuire, R.H., 1983, Breaking down cultural complexity: inequality and heterogeneity. *Advances in Achaeological Method and Theory* 6:91 –142.

McKern, S., 1987, The Crooks Site: Salvage Excavation of an Archaic Housepit Site. *Cultural Resources Management Report No. 36*. Western Wyoming College, Rock Springs.

*McKee, B. 1972. *Cascadia: The Geologic Evolution of the Pacific Northwest*. McGraw –Hill Book Co., New York.

McMillan, A.D., 1979 Archaeological Evidence for Aboriginal Tuna Fishing on Western Vancouver Island. *Syesis* 12:117–119.

McMillan, A.D., 1996. *Since Kwatyat lived on Earth: An examination of Nuu –Chal –Nulth Culture History*. Unpublished Ph.D. dissertation, Simon Fraser University, Burnaby, British Columbia.

McMillan, A.D., and D.E. Nelson, 1989, Visual punning and the whales tail: AMS dating of a Marpole –age art object. *Can. Journal Archaeol.* 13:212 –18

McMillan, A.D., and D.E. St. Claire, 1982, *Alberni Prehistory: Archaeological and Ethnographic Investigations on Western Vancouver Island*, Theytus Books, Penticton B.C.

Newberry J. and C. Harrison, 1986, The Swift Creek Site. *Cultural Resource Management Report No. 19*. Western Wyoming College, Rock Springs.

Minor, R., 1983, *Aboriginal Settlement and Subsistence at the Mouth of the Columbia River*. Unpublished Ph.D. dissertation, University of Oregon, Eugene.

Minor, R., 1984, An Early Complex at the Mouth of the Columbia River. *Northwest Anthropological Research Notes* 18(2):1–22.

Minor, R., 1991, Yaquina Head: A Middle Archaic Settlement on the North-Central Oregon Coast. *Cultural Resource Series No. 6*. Oregon State Office, Bureau of Land Management, US Department of the Interior, Portland.

Minor, R., and W.C. Grant, 1996, Earthquake-induced Subsidence and Burial of Late Holocene Archaeological Sites, Northern Oregon Coast. *American Antiquity*, 61:772-781.

Minor, R., K.A. Toepel, and S.D. Beckham, 1989, An Overview of Investigations at 45SA11: Archaeology in the Columbia River Gorge (Revised Edition, 1989). *Heritage Research Associates Report No. 83*. Eugene, Or.

Minto, J., 1900, The Number and Condition of the Native Race in Oregon When First Seen by the White Man. *Oregon Historical Quarterly* 1(3):296-315.

Mitchell. D., 1971, Archaeology of the Gulf of Georgia Area, A Natural Region and its Culture Types, *Syesis* 4, suppl. 1. Victoria, BC

Mitchell, D., 1984, Predatory Warfare, Social Status and the north Pacific Slave Trade. *Ethnology* 23(1):39 –48.

Mitchell, D., 1985, A Demographic Profile of Northwest Coast Slavery.In *Status, Structure and Stratification: Current Archaeological Reconstructions*, M. Thompson, M.T. Garcia and F.J. Kense,eds., pp. 227–236. Archaeological Association of the University of Calgary, Calgary..

Mitchell, D., 1988, Changing Patterns of Resources Use in the Prehistory of Queen Charlotte Strait, British Columbia. In Prehistoric Economies of the Northwest Coast, *Research in Economic Anthropology*, suppl. 3, pp. 245 –92.

Mitchell, D., 1990, Prehistory of the Coasts of Southern British Columbia and Northern Washington, In *Handbook of North American Indians, Vol. 7, The Northwest Coast*. W Suttles ed. pp 340 –358. Smithsonian Institution, Washington DC.

Mitchell, D., and L. Donald, 1985, Some Economic Aspects of Tlingit, Haida and Tsimshian Slavery. *Research in Economic Anthropology* 7:19 –35.

Mitchell, D and L. Donald, 1988, Archaeology and the Study of Northwest Coast Economies. *Prehistoric Economies of the Northwest Coast, Supplement No. 3, Research in Economic Anthropology*, pp 293–351. JAI Press, Inc, Greenwich, Conn.

Mithen, S., 1990, *Thoughtful foragers: a study of prehistoric decision making*. Cambridge University Press, Cambridge UK

*Mithen, S., 1996, *The prehistory of the mind: the cognitive origins of art, religion and science*. Thames and Hudson, London.

Mobley, C.M., 1984, *An Archaeological Survey of 15 Timber Harvest Units at Naukati Bay on Prince of Wales Island, Tongass National Forest, Alaska*. Report on file, U.S. Forest Service, Ketchikan, Alaska.

Mochanov, Iu.A., 1977, *Drevnejshie Etapy Zaseleniia Chelovekom Severo- Vostochnoj Azii*. Novosibisk, Nauka.

Mochanov, Y., and S.A. Fedoseeva, 1996, Ust-Timpton (Strata Vb-X).In *American Beginnings: The Prehistory and Paleoecology of Beringia*, F.H. West ed., pp 199–205. University of Chicago Press, Chicago

Mochanov, Iu. A., S.A. Fedoseeva, and A.N. Alekseev, 1983, *Arkheoloicheskie Pamiayniki Iakutii: Basseiny Aldana I Olokmi*. Novosibirsk, Nauka.

Monks, G.G., 1987, Prey as Bait: the Deep Bay Example. *Canadian Journal of Archaeology* 11: 119 –42

Moseley, M., 1975,*The Maritime Foundations of Andean*

Civilization. Cummings, Menlo Park.

Moss, M.L., 1989, *Archaeology and Cultural Ecology of the Prehistoric Angoon Tlingit*. Unpublished Ph.D. Dissertation, University of California, Santa Barbara.

Moss, M.L., 1993, Shellfish, Gender and Status on the Northwest Coast: Reconciling Archeological, Ethnographic, and Ethnohistoric Records of the Tlingit. *American Anthropologist*. 95:631–52

Moss, M.L., and J.M. Erlandson, 1992, Forts, Refuge Rocks, and Defensive Sites: The Antiquity of Warfare along the North Pacific Coast of North America. *Arctic Anthropology*. 29:73–90

Moss, M.L., J.M. Erlandson, and R, Stuckenrath, 1990, Wood Stake Fish Weirs and Salmon Fishing on the Northwest Coast: Evidence from Southeast Alaska, *Canadian Journal of Archaeology* 14:143–158.

Moss, M.L., J.M. Erlandson, R.S. Byram, and R. Hughes, 1996, The Irish Creek Site: Evidence for a Mid–Holocene Microblade Component on the Northern Northwest Coast. *Canadian Journal of Archaeology* 20:75–92.

Møllenhus, K.R., 1975, Use of Slate in the Circumpolar Region. In *Prehistoric Maritime Adaptations of the Circumpolar Zone*, W. Fitzhugh ed., pp 57–74. Mouton Publishers, The Hague.

*Moulton G.E. (ed.), 1990, *The Journals of the Lewis and Clark Expedition Vol. 6, November 2, 1805–March 22, 1806*. University of Nebraska Press, Lincoln.

Murray, J., 1981, Prehistoric Skeletons from Blue Jackets Creek (FlUa 4), Queen Charlotte Islands, British Columbia. In "Contributions to Physical Anthropology, 1979–1980", J.S. Cybulski ed., pp. 127–68. *Archaeological Survey of Canada Mercury Series Paper No. 106*

Netting, R.M., 1982, Some Home Truths about Household Size and Wealth. *American Behavioral Scientist* 25:641–662.

Newman, T.M., 1959, *Tillamook Prehistory and its relationship to the Northwest Coast Culture Area*. Unpublished Ph.D. dissertation, University or Oregon. Eugene.

Newman, T.M., 1966, Cascadia Cave. *Occasional Papers of the Idaho State University Museum 18*. Pocatello.

*Niblack, A.P., 1970, *Coast Indians of Southern Alaska and Northern British Columbia*. Johnson Reprint Corporation, New York. Originally published 1888, Report of the National Museum, Washington, D.C.

Norton, H.H., 1985, *Women and Resources on the Northwest Coast: Documentation from the Eighteenth and Nineteenth Centuries*. PhD Thesis,University. Wash., Seattle.

*Oberg, K., 1973, *The Social Economy of the Tlingit Indians*. University of Washington Press, Seattle.

O'Connell, J.F., 1975, The Prehistory of Surprise Valley. *Ballena Press Anthropological Papers No. 4.*

O'Leary, B.L., 1985, *Salmon and Storage: Southern Tutchone Use of an "Abundant Resource*. Unpublished Ph.D. dissertation. University of New Mexico, Alburquerque.

Olszewski, D.I., 1991, Social Complexity in the Natufian? Assessing the Relationship of Ideas and Data. In *Perspectives on the Past, Theoretical Biases in Mediterranean Hunter–Gatherer Research*. G.A. Clark ed. University of Pennsylvania press, Philadelphia. Pp. 322–340.

Okada, H.A., A. Okada, K. Yakima, W. Olson, M. Sugita, N. Shionosaki, S. Okino, K. Yoshida, and H. Kaneka, 1992, *Heceta Island, Southeastern Alaska: Anthropological Survey in 1989 and*

1990. Department of Behavioral Science, Hokkaido University, Sapporo, Japan.

Panowski, E.J.T., 1985, *Analyzing hunter-gatherers: population pressure, subsistence, social organization, Northwest Coast societies, and slavery*. Unpublished Ph.D. Dissertation. University of New Mexico.

Pavesic, M.G., 1985 Cache Blades and Turkey Tails: Piecing Together the Western Idaho Archaic Burial Complex. In *Stone Tool Analysis: Essays in Honor of Don E. Crabtree*, M.G. Plew, J.C. Woods, and M.G. Pavesic, eds., pp. 55–90. University of New Mexico Press, Albuquerque.

Pearson, G.W. and M. Stuiver, 1986, High precision calibration of the radiocarbon time scale, 500–2500 BC. *Radiocarbon* 28:839–862.

Peterson, M.S., 1978, *Prehistoric Mobile Sculpture of the Lower Columbia River Valley: A Preliminary Study in a Southern Northwest Coast CultureSubarea*, MA Thesis, Portland State University. Portland

Pettigrew, R.M., 1990, Prehistory of the Lower Columbia and Willamette Valley, *in Handbook of North American Indians, Volume 7, The Northwest Coast*, W Suttles, ed., pp. 518–29. Smithsonian Institution, Washington DC.

Piddocke, S., 1965, The Potlatch System of the Southern Kwakiutl: A New Perspective. *Southwestern Journal of Anthropology* 21:244–264.

*Pojar, J., and A. MacKinnon, 1994, *Plants of Coastal British Columbia*. Lone Pine Press, Vancouver.

Powell, J.V., 1990, Quileute. In *Handbook of North American Indians, Vol. 7: Northwest Coast*. W. Suttles, vol. ed., pp. 431-437, Smithsonian Institution, Washington D.C.

Powers, W.R., and J.F. Hoffecker, 1989, Late Pleistocene Settlement in the Nenana Valley, Central Alaska. *American Antiquity* 54(2):263-287.

Price, T.D. and J.A. Brown (eds), 1985, *Prehistoric hunter –gatherers: the emergence of cultural complexity*. Academic Press, Orlando.

Price, T.D. and J.A. Brown, 1985, Aspects of Hunter-Gatherer Complexity. In *Prehistoric Hunter-Gatherers: The Emergence of Cultural Complexity*, T.D. Price and J.A. Brown eds. Pp. 3–20. Academic Press, Orlando.

Price, T. Douglas 1985 : Affluent Foragers of Mesolithic Scandinavia. In *Prehistoric Hunter–Gatherers: The Emergence of Cultural Complexity*, T.D. Price and .J.A. Brown eds. Academic Press, Orlando. Pp. 341–364.

*Quimby, G.I. Jr., 1985, Japanese Wrecks, Iron Tools, and Prehistoric Indians of the Northwest Coast. *Arctic Anthropology* 22(2):247–255.

Rabich –Campbell, C., 1984, *Results of Test Excavations at Sarkar Cove, Southern Southeastern Alaska*. Paper presented to the 11th Annual Meeting of the Alaska Anthropological Association, Fairbanks.

Rafferty, J.E., 1985, The archaeological record of sedentariness: recognition, development and implications. In *Advances in archaeological method and theory, Volume 8*. Pp. 113–156.

Ramenofsky, A., 1987, *Vectors of Death, the Archaeology of European Contact*. University. New Mexico Press, Albuquerque.

Raymond, J.S., 1981, The Maritime Foundations of Civilization: A Reconsideration of the Evidence. *American Antiquity* 46(4): 806–821.

Redmond, K., and G. Taylor, 1997, Climate of the Coastal Temperate Rainforest. *In The Rainforests of Home, Profile of a North American Bioregion*, P.K. Schoonmaker, B. von Hagen, and E.C. Wolf, eds, pp 25 –42. Island Press, Washington DC.

Renfrew, C,. 1986, Introduction: Peer Polity Interaction and Socio-political Change. In *Peer Polity Interaction and Socio-Political Change*, C Renfrew and JF Cherry eds., pp.1–18. Cambridge University Press, Cambridge.

Renouf, M.A.P., 1991, Sedentary Hunter–Gatherers: A Case for Northern Coasts, In *Between Bands and States: Sedentism, Subsistence, and Interaction in Small Scale Societies,* S. Gregg ed, pp 89–10. Southern Illinois University Press, Carbondale.

Rice, H.S., 1985, *Native American Buildings and Attendant Structures on the Southern Plateau.* Archaeological and Historical Services, Eastern Washington State University, Cheney.

*Richards, T.H., and M.K. Rousseau, 1987, Late Prehistoric Cultural Horizons on the Canadian Plateau. *Department of Archaeology, Simon Fraser University, Publication No. 16.* Burnaby.

Richardson, A. 1981, The Control of Productive Resources on the Northwest Coast of North America. In *Resource Managers: North American and Australian Hunter–Gatherers*, N Williams and ES Hunn eds., pp. 93–112. AAAS Selected Symosium No. 67.

Ricks, M.F., 1995, *A Survey and Analysis of Prehistoric Rock Art in the Warner Valley Region, Lake County*, Oregon. Ph.D. dissertation, Portland State University, Portland.

Rohner, R.P., and E.C. Rohner, 1969, *The Ethnography of Franz Boas*. University of Chicago Press, Chicago

Roll, T.E., 1974, *The Archaeology of Minard: A Case Study of a Late Prehistoric Northwest Coast Procurement System.* Unpublished Ph.D. dissertation, Washington State University, Pullman

Ross, R.E., 1990,. Prehistory of the Oregon Coast, in *Handbook of North American Indians, Volume 7, The Northwest Coast*, W. Suttles ed., pp. 554 –59. Smithsonian Institution, Washington DC.

Rostlund, E., 1952, *Freshwater Fish and Fishing in Native North America*. University of California Press, Berkeley.

Rowley –Conway, P., and M. Zvelebil, 1989, Saving it for later: storage by prehistoric hunter –gatherers in Europe. In *Bad year economics, cultural responses to risk and uncertainty,* P.P. Halstead, and J. O'Shea, eds, pp. 40 –56. Cambridge University Press, Cambridge.

Ruyle, E. 1973, Slavery, Surplus and Stratification on the Northwest Coast: The Ethnoenergetics of an Incipient Stratification System. *Current Anthropology* 14: 603 –31

Sahlins, M., 1972, *Stone Age Economics*. Aldine, Chicago.

Saleeby, B. 1983, *Prehistoric Settlement Patterns in the Portland Basin on the Lower Columbia River: Ethnohistoric, Archaeological and Biogeographic Perspectives.* Unpublished Ph.D. dissertation, University of Oregon, Eugene.

Salmon, D.K., 1997, Oceanography of the Eastern North Pacific. In *The Rainforests of Home: Profile of a North American Bioregion,* PK Schoonmaker, B von Hagen and EC Wolf, eds., pp 7 –24. Island Press, Washington DC.

Samuels, SR 1983 *Spatial patterns and cultural processes in three Northwest Coast longhouse floor middens from Ozette.* Unpublished Ph.D. dissertation, Washington State University, Pullman.

Samuels, S.R. (ed.), 1991, House Structure and Floor Midden, *Ozette Archaeological Project Research Reports, Volume I. Washington State University Reports of Investigation 63.* National Park Service Northwest Regional Office. Washington State University, Pullman.

Samuels, S.R. (ed.), 1993 The Archaeology of Chester Morse Lake: Long–Term Human Utilization of the Foothills in the Washington Cascade Range. *Project Report Number 21*, Center for Northwest Anthropology, Department of Anthropology, Washington State University, Pullman.

Sasaki, K. 1981, Keynote Address. In "Affluent Foragers", edited by S Koyama and DH Thomas. *Senri Ethnological Studies No. 9*, National Museum of Ethnology, Osaka. Pp.13 –18.

Seaburg, W.R., and J. Miller, 1990, Tillamook In *Handbook of North American Indians, Vol. 7: Northwest Coast*, W. Suttles, ed., pp. 560-567. Smithsonian Institution, Washington DC.

Schaepe, D.M., 1998, *Recycling Archaeology: Analysis of Material from the 1973 Excavation of an Ancient House at the Maurer Site.* Unpublished M.A. Thesis, Simon Fraser University, Burnaby, B.C.

Schalk. R.F., 1977, The Structure of an Anadromous Fish Resource. In *For theory Building in Archaeology*, Lewis R. Binford, ed. Academic Press, Orlando. Pp. 207 –249.

Schalk, R.F., 1981, Land use and organizational complexity among foragers of northwestern North America. In "Affluent foragers: Pacific coasts East and West," S Koyama and DH Thomas eds. *Senri Ethnological Studies No. 9*, National Museum of Ethnology, Osaka. Pp. 53 –76.

*Schalk, R.F., 1987, Estimating Salmon and Steelhead Usage in the Columbia Basin before 1850: The Anthropological Perspective. *The Northwest Environmental Journal* 2(2):1 –29.

Schulting, R.J. 1995, *Mortuary Variability and Status Differentiation on the Columbia –Fraser Plateau.* Archaeology Press, Simon Fraser University, Burnaby.

*Schoonmaker, P.K., B. von Hagen, and E.C. Wolf, (eds.), 1997, *The Rainforests of Home: Profile of a North American Bioregion.* Island Press, Washington DC

Scouler, J. 1905, Dr. John Scouler's Journal of a Voyage to N.W. America [1824]. FG Young,ed. *Oregon Historical Quarterly.* 6(1)(:54-75, (2):159-205, (3):276-287.

Service, E.R., 1962, *Primitive Social Organization: An Evolutionary Perspective.* 2nd ed., 1971. Random House, New York.

Severs, P., 1973, A View of Island Prehistory: Archaeological Onvestigations at Blue Jackets Creek 1972 –73. *The Charlottes, A Journalof the Queen Charlotte Islands* 3: 2 –12.

Severs, P., 1974, Recent Archaeological Research at Blue Jackets Creek, F1Ua 4, The Queen Charlotte Islands. *The Midden* 6(2): 22 –24.

Shimkin, E.M., 1968, The Upper Paleolithic in North-Central Eurasia: Evidence and Problems. In *Views of the Past: Essays in Old World Prehistory and Paleoanthroplogy*, L.G. Freeman ed., pp 193–315. Mouton Publishers, The Hague.

Shipek, F.C., 1989, An Example of Intensive Plant Husbandry: the Kumeyaay of southern California. In *Foraging and Farming: The Evolution of Plant Exploitation*, D.R. Harris, and G.C. Hillman eds., pp. 159–167. Unwin Hyman, London.

Sillen, A. and J.A. Lee–Thorpe, 1991, Dietary Change in the Late Natufian. In "The Natufian Culture in the Levant," O. Bar–Yosef and F.R. Valla eds, pp 399–411. *International*

Monographs in Archaeology Archaeological Series No.1, Ann Arbor.

Silverstein, M., 1990, Chinookans of the Lower Columbia. In *Handbook of North American Indians, Vol. 7: Northwest Coast*, W. Suttles, ed., pp. 533-546. Washington D.C.: Smithsonian Institution.

Simonsen, B.O., 1973, Archaeological Investigations in the Hecate Strait –Milbank Sound Area of British Columbia. *National Museum of Man, Archaeological Survey of Canada Papers Mercury Series No. 13*, Ottawa.

Smith, C.M., 1996, *Social stratification within a protohistoric plankhouse of the Pacific Northwest coast : use-wear and spatial distribution analysis of chipped lithic artifacts*. Unpublished MA thesis, Portland State University, Portland.

Smith, E.A., and B. Winterhalder (eds), 1992 *Evolutionary ecology and human behavior*. Aldine de Gruyter, New York.

Smith, H.I., 1909, Archaeological remains on the coast of northern British Columbia and southern Alaska. *American Anthropologist* 11(1): 595 –600.

Smith, H.I., 1927, Kitchen middens of the Pacific Coast of Canada. *National Museum of Canada Bulletin 56*: 42 –6. Ottawa

Smith, J.L .and M. McCallum, 1993, *Cultural Resource Survey and Test Excavations for the Starfish Timber Sale, Anita Bay, Etolin Island, Alaska. Project 93-02-01-A*. USDA Forest Service, Tongass National Forest, Stikine Area, Wrangell Ranger Disrict.

Smith, M.E., 1987, Household Possessions and Wealth in Agrarian States: Implications for Archaeology. *Journal of Anthropological Archaeology* 6: 297 –335.

Soffer, O., 1989, Storage, Sedentism and the Eurasian Palaeolithic Record. *Antiquity* 64:719 –732.

Spier, L., and E. Sapir, 1930, Wishram Ethnography. *University of Washington Publications in Anthropology*. 3(3): 151–300. Seattle.

Spencer, C.S., 1993, Human Agency, Biased Transmission, and the Cultural Evolution of the Chiefly Authority, *Journal of Anthropological Archaeology* 12:41 –70

*Sproat, G.M., 1868, *Scenes of Savage Life*. Smith, Elder. London.

Stanford, M., and T. Thibault, 1980 *Archaeological Investigation at Traders Island (49 SIT 120) and Catherine Island, Alaska*. Ms. on file, Chatham Area Office, USDA Forest Servie, Sitka, Alaska.

Stewart, F.L., and K. Stewart, 1996, The Boardwalk and Grassy Bay Sites: Patterns of Seasonality and Subsistence on the Northern Northwest Coast, B.C. *Canadian Journal of Archaeology* 20: 39 –60.

Stewart, H., 1977. *Indian Fishing: Early Methods on the Northwest Coast*. University of Washington Press, Seattle.

*Stewart, H., 1981, *Artifacts of the Northwest Coast Indians*. Hancock House Publishers, North Vancouver.

Stiefel, S.K,. 1985, *The Subsistence Economy of the Locarno Beach Culture (3300 – 2400 B.P.)*. Unpublidhed MA Thesis. University of British Columbia, Vancouver.

Strong, D.W., W.E. Schenk and J.H. Steward, 1930, Archaeology of The Dalles–Deschutes Region. *University of California Publications in American Archaeology and Ethnology* 29⁽¹⁾:1–154.

Stryd, A.H., 1983, Prehistoric Mobile Art from the mid–Fraser and Thompson River areas. In *Indian Art Traditions of the Northwest Coast*, R.L., Carlson ed., pp 167–181. Archaeology Press, Simon Fraser University, Burnaby.

Stuiver, M., and G.W. Pearson, 1986, High Precision Calibration of the Radiocarbon Time Scale, AD 1950 –500 BC. *Radiocarbon* 28(2B): 805 –838

Stuiver, M. and P.J. Reimer, 1986, A Computer Program for Radiocarbon Age Calibration. *Radiocarbon* 28:1022 –1030

Stuiver M., and P.J. Reimer, 1993, Extended 14C database and revised CALIB radiocarbon calibration program. *Radiocarbon*, 35, 215-230.

*Suttles, W., 1951, *Economic Life of the Coast Salish of Haro and Rosario Straits*. Unpublished Ph.D. dissertation, University of Washington, Seattle.

Suttles, W., 1962, Variation in Habitat and Culture on the Northwest Coast. *Proceedings of the 34th International Congress of Americanists*, Vienna. Pp.522 –536.

Suttles, W.,. 1968. Coping with Abundance:Subsistence on the Northwest Coast. In *Man the Hunter*, ed. RB Lee, and I DeVore, pp. 56 –68. Aldine, Chicago.

Suttles, W. 1983. Productivity and its constraints: a Coast Salish case. In *Indian art traditions of the Northwest Coast*, R.L., Carlson,ed. pp. 67 –88. Simon Fraser University Press, Burnaby.

Suttles, W., 1990a. History of Research: Early Sources. In *Handbook of North American Indians, Volume 7, Northwest Coast*, W Suttles ed. pp.70 – 72. Smithsonian Institution, Washington, D.C.

Suttles, W., 1990b Introduction. In . In *Handbook of North American Indians, Volume 7, Northwest Coast*. W Suttles, ed. pp 1 – 15. Smithsonian Institution, Washington D.C.

*Suttles, W., (ed.) 1990 *Handbook of North American Indians, Volume 7, Northwest Coast*. Smithsonian Institution, Washington, D.C.

Suttles, W., and A. Jonaitas, 1990, History of Research in Ethnography. In *Handbook of North American Indians, Volume 7, Northwest Coast*. W. Suttles, ed. pp 73 – 88. Smithsonian Institution Press, Washington D.C.

Suttles, W., and B. Lane, 1990, Southern Coast Salish In *Handbook of North American Indians, Vol. 7: Northwest Coast*, W. Suttles, ed., pp. 485-502 Smithsonian Institution Press, Washington D.C..

Swadesh, M., 1948, Motivations in Nootka Warfare. *Southwestern Journal of Anthropology* 4:76-93.

*Swan, J., 1857, *The Northwest Coast; Or, Three Years Residence in Washington Territory*. Harper, New York (reprinted in 1972 University of Washington Press, Seattle.

Swan, J., 1870, The Indians of Cape Flattery; at the Entrance to the Strait of Juan de Fuca, Washington Territory. *Smithsonian Contributions to Knowledge* 16 (8):1 – 106. Smithsionian Institution, Washington D.C.

Swanton, J.R., 1905, Contributions to the Ethnology of the Haida.*Publications of the Jesup North Pacific Expedition 5: Memoirs of the American Museum of Natural History* 8(1):1-300. New York.

Swanton, J.R., 1970, *The Social Conditions, Beliefs, and Linguistic Relationship of the Tlingit Indians*. Johnson Reprint Corporation, New York.

Taylor, H.C. Jr., and W. Duff ,1956, A Post-contact Southward Movement of the Kwakiutl.*Washington State College Research Studies* 24(1):55-66. Pullman.

Teit, J.A., 1928, The Middle Columbia Salish. *Publications in*

Anthropology 2(4):83–128. University of Seattle, WA.

Testart, A. 1982, The Significance of Food Storage among hunter –gatherers: residence patterns, population densities, and social inequities.*Current Anthropology* 23:523 –537

Thom, B.. 1992, An Investigation of Interassemblage Variability within the Gulf of Georgia Phase, *Canadian Journal Archaeology* 16: 24 –31

Thwaites, R.G. (ed.), 1904-1905, *Original Journals of the Lewis and Clark Expedition, 1804-1806*, 8 vols. Dodd, Mead, New York.

Thompson, G. 1978, Prehistoric Settlement Changes in the Southern Northwest Coast, A Functional Approach. *University of Washington, Department of Anthropology, Reports in Archaeology Number 5*.

Thoms, AV., 1989, *The northern roots of hunter –gatherer intensification: camas and the Pacific Northwest.* Unpublished PhD dissertation, Washington State University, Pullman.

Tihkmenev, P.A., 1979, *A History of the Russian America Company, Volume 2,Documents.* D. Krenov trans., R Pierce and A Donnelly (eds.). Limestone Press, Kingston, Ontario

Torrence R 1983 Time budgeting in prehistory. In *Hunter-Gatherer Economy in Prehistory*, G Bailey ed. Pp. 11 –22. Cambridge University Press, Cambridge.

Torrence, R. 1989., Retooling: towards a behavioral theory of stone tools. In *Time, Energy and Stone Tools*, R Torrence ed. University of Cambridge Press, Cambridge. Pp. 57 –66.

Turner, N., *1991*, Burning mountain sides for better crops: Aboriginal landscape burning in British Columbia. In *Archaeology in Montana*, special issue 3(2).

Turner, N., 1996, Traditional Ecological Knowledge. In *The Rainforests of Home, Profile of a North American Bioregion*, PK Schoonmaker, B. von Hagen and EC Wolf eds, pp. 275 –298. Island Press, Washington DC.

Vastokas, J.M., 1966, *Architecture of the Northwest Coast Indians.* Unpublished Ph.D. dissertation. Columbia University, NewYork.

Vayda, A.P., 1961, A Re-examination of Northwest Coast Economic Systems. *Transactions of the New York Academy of Sciences*, ser. 2. Vol. 23 (7):618–624.

Veniaminov, I .1984, "Notes on the Islands of the Unalaska District [1840]." L Black and RH Goeghegan, trans., R.A. Pierce, ed. *Alaska History* 27. The Limestone Press, Kingston, Ont.

Warner, B.G., J.J. Clague, and R.W. Mathewes, 1982. Ice –free Conditions on the Queen Charlotte Islands, British Columbia, at the height of late Wisconsin glaciation. *Science* 218:675 –77

Wasson, P.K., 1994, *The Archaeology of Rank.* Cambridge University Press, Cambridge.

Watanabe, H., 1992, The Northern Pacific Maritime Culture Zone: A Viewpoint on Hunter-Gatherer Mobility and Sedentism. In *Pacific Northeast Asia in Prehistory*, C.M. Aikens and S.N. Rhee, eds., pp 105–112. Washington State University Press, Pullman.

Weinberg, D., 1973 Models of Southern Kwakiutl Social Organization. In *Cultural Ecology, Readings on the Canadian Indians and Eskimo*, B.A. Cox ed., pp 227–253. McClelland and Stewart, Toronto.

Wessen, G., 1982, *Shell Middens as Cultural Deposits: a Case Study from Ozette.* Unpublished Ph.D. dissertation, Washington State University, Pullman.

Wessen, G., 1988, The use of Shellfish Resources on the Northwest Coast: the View from Ozette, in Issacs. etc. pp 179–210

Wessen, G., 1990, Prehistory of the Ocean Coast of Washington, In *Handbook of North American Indians, Vol. 7, The Northwest Coast.* W. Suttles ed. pp. 412 –421. Smithsonian Institution, Washinton DC.

West F.H., 1996, Preamble: The Study of Beringia. In *American Beginnings: The Prehistory and Paleoecology of Beringia.* F. H. West, ed. pp.1–10, Chicago, University of Chicago Press.

West FH 1981 *The Archaeology of Beringia.* New York, Columbia University Press.

Wingert, P.S., 1951, *Prehistoric Stone Scultures of the Pacific Northwest.* Portland Art Museum, Portland, Or.

Whitlock, C. 1992, Vegetational and Climatic History of the Pacific Northwest during the last 20,000 Years: Implications for UnderstandingPresent –day Biodiversity. *Northwest Environ. Journal* 8:5–28

Wilk, R.R., 1991, *Household Ecology: Economic Change and Domestic Life among the Kekchi Maya in Belize.*University of Arizona Press, Tucson.

Wilk, R.R., and W.L. Rathje, 1982, Household Archaeology. *American Behavioral Scientist* (25)6:631 – 640.

Wilson, I.R., 1992, *Excavations at the Baker Site, EdQx 43, Permit 91-107.* Report on File, Simon Fraser University, Burnaby, BC.

*Wilson, P.J., 1988, *The domestication of the human species.* New Haven: Yale University Press.

Wike, J.A., 1958, Social Stratification Among the Nootka. *Ethnohistory* 5:219–241.

Winterhalter, B., 1980, Environmental Analysis in Human Evolution and Adaptation Research. *Human Ecology* 8: 135 –70

Wissler, C. 1917, *The American Indian: An Introduction to the Anthropology of the New World.* Douglas C. McMurtrie, New York.

*Wolf, E., 1982, *Europe and the people without history.* University of California Press, Berkeley.

Woodburn, J., 1980, Hunter –Gatherers Today and Reconstructing the Past. In *Soviet and Western Anthropology*, E Gellner ed, Columbia University Press, New York. Pp. 94 –118.

Wooley, C.B. 1984, *Isla de la Empalizada: Defensive Sites and Early Culture Change in Southeast Alaska.* Fairbanks: Paper presented at the 13th Annual Meeting of the Alaska Anthropological Association.

Wooley, C.B., and J.C. Haggarty, 1989, Tlingit –Tsimshian interaction in the Southern Alexander Archipelago. Presented 17th Annual Meeting, Alaska Anthropological Association, Anchorage, Alaska.

Wright, G.A., 1985, Social Differentiation in the Early Natufian. In *Social Archaeology*, edited by CL. Redman et al, pp. 201 –4. New York: Academic Press

Yen, D.E. 1989. The Domestication of the Environment. In *Foraging and Farming, the Evolution of Plant Exploitation*, DR Harris and GC Hillman eds.,pp. 55 –78. Unwin Hyman, London.

Yesner, D.R., 1980, Maritime Hunter-Gatherers: Ecology and Prehistory. *Current Anthropology* 21:727-750.

Yesner, D.R., 1987, Life in the Garden of Eden: Causes and Consequences of the Adoption of Marine Diets by Human Societies. In *Food and Evolution*, M. Harris and E. Ross eds., pp 285–310. Temple University Press, Philadelphia.

Index